Charles I and the Popish Plot

CAROLINE M. HIBBARD

Charles I and the Popish Plot

The University of North Carolina Press   Chapel Hill

To My Mother
and Father

Library of Congress Cataloging in Publication Data

Hibbard, Caroline M., 1942–
    Charles I and the Popish Plot.

    Bibliography: p.
    Includes index.
    1. Great Britain—Politics and government—
1642–1649. 2. Charles I, King of England, 1600–
1649. 3. Great Britain—History—Civil War,
1642–1649. 4. Catholics—Great Britain—Political
activity. 5. Great Britain—Court and courtiers.
I. Title.
DA395.H46   941.06′2   81-23075
ISBN 0-8078-1520-9   AACR2

Contents

Preface

I wish to thank the Research Board of the University of Illinois for financial assistance in the preparation of this book. The Andrew W. Mellon foundation generously provided a grant for several weeks of research in the Vatican Film Library at St. Louis University. The citations to the Barberini Latini manuscripts in my notes refer to microfilm copies that were consulted there or purchased through the Vatican Film Library. I wish to thank the Earl Fitzwilliam, Lord Downshire, and the Duke of Northumberland for permission to consult manuscripts deposited by them in public repositories.

The staffs of the British Museum, the Public Record Office, the Bodleian Library, the Kent and Berkshire record offices, the Bristol Archives Office, Sheffield Central Library, and the John Rylands Library all offered assistance that made my research much easier, as did the staffs of the Beinecke and Sterling Libraries at Yale University and the library of the University of Illinois. I should like to record particular debts to Elisabeth Poyser of the Westminster Cathedral Archives, Father Lowrie Daly of the Vatican Film Library, Father Francis Edwards at the Jesuit archives in London, and Dom Philip Jebb of Downside Abbey, for helping me to make profitable use of the collections in their care. Father Justin McCarthy, O.F.M., kindly provided copies of material from the English Franciscan archives. I am grateful to Penry Williams for information from the Ellesmere manuscripts in the Huntington Library, which I was unable to visit.

Professor Wallace MacCaffrey and Professor Conrad Russell read the typescript of this work and made invaluable suggestions. A number of other colleagues and friends read parts of the draft and gave me helpful advice; I should like particularly to thank Anthony Fletcher, Gillian Lewis, Father Albert Loomie, and David Lunn. Marcella Grendler spent many hours helping me to turn the first draft of this book into a clearer and more coherent narrative; I am deeply grateful to her for taking on this task despite the many other demands on her time.

My research into early Stuart Catholicism began when I was a doctoral student at Yale University, and I owe thanks to Professor J. H. Hexter, who supervised my thesis, for his continuing help and encouragement. He set high standards of clarity in presentation for all his students, both by precept and by example; and I suspect that influence has contributed whatever grace there is to this narrative. Where it plods (and where it errs) the fault is entirely my own.

A number of people have provided practical assistance of various kinds without which this book would never have been completed. I should like to thank Linda Bryceland, Marianne Burkhard, Ann Franklin, Vincent Hammond, Helen Hundley, Robert Miller, and Hannelore Petrucci for their cheerful support of my efforts.

Note on Spelling and Dates

The spelling, capitalization, and punctuation of quotations have been modernized, but titles of books and pamphlets have been left in their original form. Dates in the text and notes are old style but the year is taken as starting on 1 January. Where the dates of documents in the notes are new style, they have been so noted. Translations from French and Italian are my own.

Charles I and the Popish Plot

1. Popish Plotting in Perspective

Seventeenth-century accounts of the English civil war and its background agree almost unanimously that Catholic activities and fears of "popish plotting" were a leading cause of the distrust between Charles I and his opponents. The pamphleteering before the outbreak of war was hysterically anti-Catholic; anti-Catholic riots and agitation occurred sporadically in London and the provinces. The House of Commons debates of 1640–42 and the documents that they produced returned almost obsessively to the notion of a Catholic conspiracy against English liberties and religion.

Yet the popish plot explanation of the war has been completely ignored by modern historians, when not ridiculed and disparaged. Until quite recently, there has not even been an attempt to explore the popish plot explanation as a phenomenon in its own right, part of a long and powerful tradition of English political ideology, or as a valuable entrée to the psychological world of Protestants, expressive of tensions and anxieties generated by Calvinist doctrine and nurtured by contemporary political conditions.[1] Now, short studies by Carol Wiener and Robin Clifton have dealt with antipopery as a form of political psychopathology, Wiener finding indications in its vocabulary of feelings of insecurity and inferiority, Clifton portraying anti-Catholic agitation as a form of reflex reaction to political crisis, only remotely related to actual Catholic activity.[2]

The traditions of English Catholic historiography have done little to clarify the origins of political antipopery. Most twentieth-century studies of English Catholicism have neglected its international context. Even Gordon Albion, whose *Charles I and the Court of Rome* is the most extended and broadly documented account of Anglo-Roman contacts during this period, seems oblivious to the Thirty Years War and its impact on English public opinion. Reduced to a purely English context, Catholicism seems scarcely menacing, rather on the defensive.

Many Catholic historians, for understandable motives, have virtually ignored the international connections of English Catholics, and the activities of the zealous minority that compounded the troubles of the Catholic community. The apologetic tradition from which English Catholic studies emerged emphasized the disabilities of the Catholics rather than the agility with which they managed to evade the legal penalties of recusancy.[3] The last few decades, during which the history of English Catholicism has acquired academic respectability, coincided with the efflorescence of county studies—a genre that has been fruitfully adopted by historians of Catholicism, but does not lend itself to answering the questions raised by the plot tradition. Recent quantitative analyses of Catholics in the counties have shown that even in the shires where they were most numerous, they were only a minority presence, apparently incapable of posing a military threat to Protestant supremacy. A recent attempt to quantify Catholic participation in the civil war concludes that the great majority of Catholics in every county studied remained neutral in the civil war.[4] These findings suggest little statistical basis for the anxieties expressed in the plot theory.

The possibility that English Catholicism posed any real threat to Protestant England has been discounted not only on the grounds that the English Catholics were numerically weak, but also because they are (correctly) perceived as for the most part politically quiescent by the early seventeenth century. The relatively high Catholic "profile" at the court of Charles I—the percentage of courtiers who were Catholic, and the political activism of some of these—is regarded as a politically insignificant anomaly. The anachronistic political model of "majority rule" implicit in this interpretation is one, I suspect, that few of its proponents would consciously espouse. They are only secondarily concerned with national politics, they are vividly aware that Catholics were and remained a minority in England, and they desire to rescue the "average Catholic" from centuries of Protestant misunderstanding and polemic.

The subject of this work is not the "average Catholic," whoever that might be, but court Catholicism, and particularly the role of political antipopery in the 1637–42 crisis. This study is meant to complement, not contradict, the current valuable work on English Catholics in the counties. I have argued elsewhere that antipopery as a political-religious phenomenon ought to be approached from an international and London perspective, rather than on a county, grassroots basis.[5] London and the court not only dominated the political, legal, and economic life of the British Isles, but weighed heavily in the educational, social, and religious life of the country. London was the center of the communications network; most news, if it did not originate in London, passed through the metropolis on its way back to the counties. The presence of the court near London lent further significance to news emanating from the capital. Events in London occurred, as it were, under the eye of the prince; when his displeasure was not made clear, his approbation might reasonably be inferred. The strength and visibility of London and court Catholicism should not, therefore, be written off as anomalous and thus insignificant. The court Catholics of the 1630s were an unrepresentative minority within the Catholic community, but they had disproportionate influence on the politics of 1637–42 through the favor they enjoyed at court and the reaction this provoked among Protestants.

A court perspective does much to explain the vehemence and power of parliamentary antipopery rhetoric in 1640–42. When they met at Westminster, M.P.s were influenced by the mood of the city, by what they observed there, and by the latest news and rumors of the court. What the M.P.s who gathered for two successive parliaments in 1640 heard and saw around them may help to explain how John Pym was able to dominate the Commons with his popish plot ideology, although few of its members shared what has recently been called his immunity from "the countervailing pressure of good neighbourhood."[6] Reluctant as they were to proceed harshly against their recusant neighbors in the counties—not until the late summer of 1641 would the Commons move to disarm local Catholics—many members came to share Pym's anxiety about court Catholicism.

Given the prominence of the popish plot theme in parliamentary rhetoric and the amount of scholarly attention that has been devoted to the Long Parliament, it is surprising that non-Catholic historians, unimpeded by confessional loyalties, have not examined the matter more closely. One reason for this may be unfamiliarity with Catholic history and with Catholic sources, which has made it difficult to connect parliamentary rhetoric with actual Catholic activities. More important, I suspect, has been the wholesale rejection of the popish plot explanations of the civil war so congenial to seventeenth-century writers. There are a number of reasons for this. The extreme language in which these explanations are often couched discredits them, the conspiracy theory they embody is distasteful to modern historians, and the religious prejudice, even fanaticism, among the leaders of parliament that they seem to reveal embarrasses the admirers of the parliamentary leadership. Preoccupation with constitutional issues framed in secular terms dominated late nineteenth- and early twentieth-century treatment of the seventeenth-century crisis. This perspective obscured issues that were, or seemed, peripheral to long-term constitutional development, and even directed attention away from those portions (often quite lengthy) of important political documents that dealt with these issues. More recently, detailed work has been undertaken on the social and economic conditions of the early Stuart period, and the national perspective has been supplemented by a local perspective on the economic and political background to the war, although not by an international one. There has been a reluctance to explore similarities between the conditions of English political life and those of continental powers such as France. The court politics of early seventeenth-century France, replete with intradynastic coups, assassinations, court conspiracies, and attendant shifts in religious and foreign policy, has not seemed as relevant to English experience as it did to worried Englishmen at the time. Moreover, with some notable exceptions, recent historians have tended to neglect both the foreign policy of the early Stuart governments and the broader questions of England's political and religious relations with the rest of Europe. Yet the international ramifications of the alleged popish conspiracy of Charles I's reign are crucial to any appreciation of the fears it aroused.

S. R. Gardiner's account of the Catholic factor in Caroline politics is characteristically meticulous and well documented; it also embodies telltale ambiguities of attitude and weaknesses of analysis. If these did not necessarily shape the perceptions of subsequent historians, they have certainly found a frequent echo. A closer look at Gardiner's treatment of the subject will provide a framework for critique of the modern writers, and a background for the alternative approach that I have adopted. Gardiner's discussion of 1630s Catholicism culminates in 1637, in dramatic and highly effective juxtaposition to the trial of Prynne, Burton, and Bastwick. His allusions to Catholicism and the papal agents in the succeeding five years are scattered, frequently in lengthy footnotes, and rest on the periphery of his main story. Gardiner thus leaves the impression, perhaps intentionally, that religious tensions had reached their peak by 1637 and that they resulted from Archbishop Laud's misunderstood and unpopular religious policies.[7]

This notion that agitation about popery was little more than distress over, and misunderstanding of, the Laudian program has had a surprisingly long life. William Prynne's prominence in that version of the story may be a reason for this, for Prynne has only lately been rescued from the lunatic fringe to which, for centuries, historians had assigned him. Prynne's attempt to smear Laud by identifying him as the head of a Catholic party at the English court convinced few of his contemporaries and fewer later historians. But such a party—or at least a clique, some of whose members were trying to turn it into a party—did exist. As some of his seventeenth-century defenders pointed out, Laud attempted in vain to control its activities, and it was a cruel injustice that he came to be identified as its inspiration.

In back of this identification was the Puritan conviction that Laud and the Arminian party in the Church of England, if not actually crypto-Catholic, were well down the slippery slope to Rome. This view was hotly and sincerely contested by many of the accused, including, of course,

Laud himself. That it ought retrospectively to be labeled a "misinterpretation" is less clear. Recent study of the Arminian doctrinal revolution and the reactions it provoked in dedicated Calvinists such as John Pym suggest that the equation between Arminianism and Catholicism was made with utter conviction.[8] Differences between the two were recognized, but regarded as subordinate to the central matter of doctrinal convergence. For a significant number of members of the Church of England in the 1620s and 1630s, Calvinist doctrine was the defining feature of their communion. To them, the indifference toward the Catholic threat evinced by some Arminians seemed perplexing and dangerous, a sign that the English church was half-reformed, a "church of Laodicea."[9] They were aghast at the attitudes expressed by men such as the Restoration historian, Sir George Radcliffe, who, in commenting upon the accusation that Laud had intended a gradual reconciliation with Rome, said he could not condemn such a policy, if it had been pursued, because the Roman church was "a member of the true Catholic church of Christ notwithstanding all new opinions or abuses crept in."[10] In assessing reactions to court Catholicism, it is worth remembering that for some English Protestants, the court Catholic activities confirmed a suspicion they already held, namely, that Arminianism was close to popery and thus would foster the growth of popery.

Another feature of Gardiner's treatment that has parallels in later work is his uneasiness over the religious fanaticism that seems to be embodied in the plot tradition, coupled with a dismissive attitude toward the Catholic religion. This ambiguous attitude is found in other historians who view the parliamentary opposition as constitutionally or politically progressive. If Gardiner is uneasy about the language of seventeenth-century antipopery, it is partly because of his conviction that all the embarrassingly illiberal-sounding fuss was unnecessary. His own contempt for Catholicism as a religion and as a potential political force emerges clearly from what he says of the court conversions of the 1630s:

> The danger from Rome was less serious than it seemed. The bait held out by the papal clergy appealed to the lower and more selfish side of human nature. Fantastic speculators like Sir Kenelm Digby, witty intriguers like Walter Montagu, brought no real strength to the cause which they espoused; whilst the gay court ladies, whose life had hitherto been passed in a round of amusement, were personally better by submitting to a sterner discipline than any which they had hitherto known. The arguments by which they had been moved appealed to motives too low to exercise any attractive force over the real leaders of the age, or to be otherwise than repulsive to the

sense of honour which was the common property of English
gentlemen.[11]

Gardiner's treatment of John Pym and of parliamentary investigations
into Catholicism is uncharacteristically awkward. He makes a lengthy
attempt to assess the sincerity of Pym's belief in popish plots, apparently
anxious both to discredit the idea of a plot and to exonerate Pym from
the charge of cynically exploiting an obvious fiction. He derides the
notion that "Laud and Strafford had been conspiring with Con and
Rossetti to lay England at the feet of the Pope" as "entirely in contradiction with the facts," but admits that intriguers at the queen's court "had
made her apartments at Whitehall the centre from which radiated the
wildest schemes for setting at defiance the resolute will of the English
people." Gardiner distinguishes the queen's circle from the "real" government of the king, a government represented by Strafford and Laud,
who were innocent of complicity with Rome's "insensate projects." Pym
and his associates, ignorant of this distinction, misunderstood "everything that related to the political designs of the king's ministers . . . [and]
everything that related to the ecclesiastical designs of the same men."[12]
Gardiner is obliged by his careful reading of the Roman transcripts to
recognize that by the end of 1640 the king was personally involved in
negotiations for a papal loan and in other features of the popish plot. But
he would prefer to see these schemes as responses to parliamentary agitation: "No doubt if [the opposition leaders] had been more tolerant, there
would have been no plot. Evil begets evil, and the hard measures which
they were dealing out to the Catholics led to this invitation to a foreign
priest and a foreign king to intervene in the affairs of England."[13] But as
we shall see, these invitations well antedated the convocation of the Long
Parliament.

The above passages illustrate Gardiner's sense of an established English
Protestant and parliamentary tradition that already protected the country
from any real possibility of Catholic subversion and had already set her
on a unique path of constitutional development. England is seen as a
world politically distant from the continent. Unlike the Spain of Philip
IV, the court of the Cardinal Infante at Brussels, or the France of Richelieu, the England of Charles I could not, in Gardiner's eyes, have been
controlled by court faction or shaped by royal dynasticism. The schemes
for alliance with the pope or with foreign princes or with Irish Catholics
were foredoomed to failure because they flew in the face of English
tradition. He therefore found it scarcely credible, to say nothing of honorable, that the king should have attempted such alliances. Neither
Charles nor his opponents shared Gardiner's certainties.

Although few modern historians would pronounce so confidently as did Gardiner about whom the king was listening to, Strafford and Laud have continued to dominate the picture, as they did in Gardiner's account. Gardiner exaggerates the prominence of Strafford and Laud in policy making through the decade of the 1630s, as did, indeed, the leaders of the Long Parliament, for whom these two figures (birds in the hand, when others had escaped to the French bush) had both symbolic and immediate political significance. Until other councillors such as Windebank and Northumberland have received more attention, it will be difficult to draw a revised and more accurate picture of central politics during the personal rule than the one bequeathed to us by the parliamentary rhetoric and show trials of the 1640s. Meanwhile, caution and a keen eye for those constant shifts in the channels of influence at court, shifts that so distressed the king's advisors, would seem to be in order.

Gardiner makes an artificial distinction between councillors and "mere courtiers" such as Digby, Montagu, or Endymion Porter, allowing little influence to the latter in formation of policy. This is a mistake that the M.P.s of 1640–42 did not make, as their attempts to purge the royal household reveal. Privy councillors like Northumberland complained that important business was transacted without conciliar consultation, and recent work on Windebank's career suggests that that was true.[14] Historians need to look more closely at the king's associates, without regard to their official position.

Finally, Gardiner distinguishes carefully between the queen's court and that of the king. This is undoubtedly a distortion of perspective; of the few things we can say with certainty about the character of Charles I, that he doted on his wife is one of the most important. Court reports make it clear that they were very frequently together; this, indeed, was the source of the papal agent's access to and influence on the king, with whom he could have no official relations. Gardiner says of Henrietta Maria that "nothing in her birth or education had taught her to comprehend the greatness of the cause which she was opposing";[15] but it would seem that this blindness was shared by Charles I, despite his birth and education. A contrast between kingly gravity and queenly frivolity does not advance understanding of the actual functioning of the court.

In concentrating on the court, this study of popery and antipopery in the 1630s adopts a perspective not unlike that of John Miller in his study of *Popery and Politics in England 1660–1688*. Miller himself is skeptical about the antipopery of 1640–42, arguing that Pym "tried to excite deliberately what had been initially a spontaneous response to a highly tense political situation" until the charge of popery or cryptopopery against the king's party became a "purely propaganda assertion."[16] According to Miller's description, "as the radicals came closer to attacking the king directly, . . . they intensified the antipopish element in their propaganda, accusing the court of plotting to bring in popery and absolutism." This was also the pattern in the 1670s, and for that period Miller believes it made sense; popery scares that focused on the court and the royal family were based on a justifiable anxiety about the future of Protestantism and of representative government.[17]

One of the main arguments of this work is that the political and religious themes of the late 1630s were closer to those of the 1670s than is generally recognized. In the 1630s, as in the 1670s, the Catholics were a minority, most powerful at court and in London, and for the most part politically quiescent. None of this prevented the political hysteria of the popish plot of 1678–81, nor the grave political crisis caused by the accession of a Catholic ruler in 1685. For the 1630s as for the 1670s, anxiety about court Catholicism and a possible Catholic succession, in the context of resurgent European Catholicism, was acute; in neither case was it unfounded. The more closely the king's critics looked at the royal family in the 1630s, the more popery they found. And the connection they drew between Catholicism and tyranny was no mere propaganda ploy. It rested on deeply rooted assumptions about the nature of government and the relations between church and state, on their interpretation of the king's secular policies in the light of his religious policies, and on their understanding of current European politics.

The definition of the "court" in the early Stuart period has been a much debated matter. My working definition for this study has been a flexible one, in which office plays less role than access to the king and queen. The court is thus a place, although a movable and even divisible place—the surroundings of the king and queen. At the same time it is a group of persons—those who were habitually or frequently in attendance on the royal family and who were thus in a position to advise and influence them, or to obtain favors from them.[18] The Florentine agent, Salvetti, referred to "the palace" from time to time, and this term is a useful reminder of what the court was when the royal family was in London, that is, during most of the time covered by this study. Periods of campaign, such as the Bishops' Wars in 1639 and 1640, and periods when parliament was in session obviously require some modification of this working definition, but do not destroy its utility. The court thus included (at least until the convocation of the Long Parliament) stalwart Puritans such as Sir John Coke and Georg Rudolph Weckherlin, as well as professed or crypto-Catholics such as Endymion Porter and Sir Toby Mathew. It included no local officials of any hue.

An argument could be made that figures such as Strafford in Ireland or the English ambassadors abroad ought properly to be included in the court. But there is abundant evidence that their geographical distance from the king made them feel isolated and anxious, and they made incessant efforts to act through their friends at court. They are, it is true, borderline cases; but the eagerness with which they sought permission to return to London when their vital interests seemed threatened is suggestive.

Those who attended on the royal family included members of their households, including their chaplains; privy councillors both in their official function and as courtiers; secretaries of state, often operating outside the official channels of the privy council; and those figures who enjoyed access to the royal family without official position. This last group ranged from Scottish peers to missionary priests. It included a considerable number of Catholics of various nationalities.

There were also a number of foreigners who were unofficially a part of the court. If the court was the summit of the domestic political and social pyramid, it was also the arena in which foreign agents jockeyed for alliance and position on behalf of their governments. This cosmopolitan character of the court was important; foreigners at court, preoccupied with the drift of English foreign policy, often described court factions in terms of their foreign sympathies, for example, as the "French party" or the "Spaniards." This was an oversimplification; the court was divided on domestic as well as foreign policy, and factions were shifting and overlapping. But it reminds us that the British political crisis of 1637–42 developed within an international context. When the Long Parliament convened in November 1640, the king's ministers as well as their parliamentary critics were entangled with one or another group of foreign agents operating in London—French, Spanish, papal, imperial, Dutch, Bohemian, exile Spanish, or exile French. This was a crucial period of the Thirty Years War, during which the tide turned against the Habsburgs and the threat to the survival of Protestantism in western Europe began to subside. It was also a period of the war in which the role, or at least the potential role, of England seemed more than ever significant. The course of the war, especially after the entry of France in 1635, made control of the Channel an increasingly vital concern for both the Habsburgs and the Franco-Dutch alliance. These parties, and others as well, also looked to the British Isles as a field for recruiting the ever more urgently needed mercenaries to replenish depleted and exhausted armies.

London and the court were thus alive with foreign agents and foreign visitors, some very eminent indeed, like the aristocratic refugees who were losers in the domestic power struggles of Richelieu's France and the Spanish Netherlands. The exiles plotted in London with their countries' enemies, hoping to overthrow their rivals at home or at least bargain their way back into position. Foreign agents who were in particular favor at court, or distinguished foreign visitors such as Marie de Medici or the duchess of Chevreuse, might be more frequently with the king, and find their advice more readily accepted, than most of his official advisors.

This foreign element at court provides the most striking reminder of how casual the formulation of policy could be. Important decisions could be and were taken by the king in consultation with unofficial advisors who belonged to his "household" in the broadest sense of that term. Even when matters were brought formally before the privy council, they might be presented as already decided, not for consultation. Foreign policy was as likely to be shaped in secret deliberation with Secretary Windebank, in the queen's bedchamber, or in the queen mother's residence, as in the privy council. The members of the council were themselves in frequent attendance on the king as courtiers—seeking his favor, building their own patronage systems, advising him privately, and waiting for his decisions on questions affecting their personal interests as well as the common weal. It was the king on whom all policy ultimately depended, whether by his active intervention or his passive acquiescence. So the eyes of the political nation were often focused on the king—in this case, a remote, reticent, even secretive, man who perplexed his closest advisors as much as his distant critics.

In portraying court politics and personalities, I have drawn not only on English sources but also on the reports of foreign agents at the English court. These reports need to be used cautiously; they contain material that is often difficult to corroborate and are biased toward interpreting court politics in an international context that sometimes misleads. The ambassadorial letters, full of rumors heard on the Rialto, are often more useful in distinguishing political attitudes than in ascertaining the facts of royal policy making. The reports are usually maddeningly vague about the identity either of their informants or of the members of the court factions they describe. References to the "French party," the "friends of Spain," the "Bohemian party," the "Catholic party," the "parliamentarians," the "Protestants," and the "Puritans" need to be fleshed out by careful comparison of a number of sources; in many cases, the groupings are overlapping or transient. Certain individuals with consistent sympathies can, however, be identified.

The criticism that the foreign agents were ill informed on domestic politics has some merit. However, when they repeat the gossip of London and the court, they reflect the political perceptions of their sources: on the one hand the "palace," on the other the critical rumors about the palace that were likely to get out into the country. When the Catholic ambassadors refer in what seem to be sloppy ways to the "Catholic,"

"Puritan," and "Protestant" parties, we need not accept their labels as accurate; but we may find in them valuable clues, for example, about the queen's attitudes towards the religious basis of political maneuvering. If it is true that the foreign agents were wont to accuse anti-Catholics ("Puritans") of subversion so as to discredit their anti-Catholicism, we should remember that Laud, too, was quick to see sedition behind every criticism of his regime.[19] Similarly, the over-polarized view of English politics presented by the Venetian and Florentine agents particularly, and also by the papal agents in the 1630s, may have helped to create polarization. These men were not only interpreters of English politics for their own governments; they often took it upon themselves to press interpretations and advice upon the king.

With all their faults, these reports are indispensable for the light they shed, albeit indirectly, on the development of the king's ideas, a subject upon which there is very little other information. The letters of the agent George Con, whose intimacy with the king is confirmed by numerous contemporary accounts, are particularly instructive, including as they do lengthy accounts of his conversations with Charles I. While the king's privy councillors were writing dolefully to their friends in 1638 that they had no idea how the king expected to handle the Scottish crisis, the papal agent was reporting on the likelihood that his proposals to the king would be accepted.

Quite clearly, this study does not provide a complete account of faction at the court of Charles I. Much of it had roots in local politics and financial struggles that are outside the purview of this study; much of it remained immune from ideological interpretation. I have concentrated on the Catholics and their critics and on foreign policy trends as they interacted with court power groupings. I have tried to assess these aspects of court life and policy as they related, or seemed to relate, to issues of high policy such as the handling of the Scottish crisis and the relations between the king and the parliaments of 1640–42. Religion and foreign policy were not the only issues shaping politics in this period. They were, however, issues that profoundly affected Englishmen's understanding of the nature and intentions of the king's government in many areas of policy. Contemporaries thought them of sufficient importance to enshrine them prominently in the major constitutional documents of the Long Parliament.

This is a study of change—the development of profound distrust between the king of England and those who would be prepared in 1642 to take arms against him—and as such, it requires a narrative treatment. Only by documenting the king's persistence in what would prove to be politically suicidal policies, and by tracing the gathering cloud of suspicion and rumor that accompanied this, could the breakdown of English government in these years be explained without giving a misleading impression of inevitability to the events of 1642 and after. But narrative has its drawbacks and dangers. One is that the reader will find himself lost in a myriad of unfamiliar names and detail. I have attempted to meet this problem by providing summary introductions and conclusions to each chapter.

A more serious difficulty in narrative history is the submersion of important concepts in the narrative of events. It may be useful here to indicate a few of these motifs that have emerged from my research, or been corroborated by it. No particular originality is claimed for them; concepts explored by other scholars, either in a general way or with reference to other periods of time, have proven extraordinarily useful. I trust that I have made these debts clear in my citations to the text.

Two intellectual constructs of the seventeenth century are of particular significance in understanding the reaction to court Catholicism; they were central to Pym's thinking and became dominant motifs of the Long Parliament. One was the connection between subversion of religion and subversion of government. By an association of ideas that had appeared in the rhetoric of the parliaments of the 1620s and would become obsessive in the Long Parliament, threats to English religion evoked fears for English liberties, and vice versa. Arminianism thus made monopolies look like harbingers of absolutism; ship money aroused worries about purity of religion.[20] In this inextricably tangled knot of worries, court Catholicism was an important strand.

The second notion was that of "subversion by division," a charge that had been used in the parliaments of the 1620s and was emphasized in the allegations against Strafford and Laud in 1640–42.[21] Dividing the king from his people, dissolving the unity of the commonwealth by inflaming the mind of one party against the other, could be done in the religious or the secular sphere. Because of the association of ideas described above, charges of "subversion by division" in one area often spilled over into the other. Thus those who were thought to have counseled the king against holding parliaments were likely also to be suspected of advising him that his loyal Protestant subjects were subversive "Puritans."

"Subversion by division" was a dangerous charge to bring against members of government because it could so easily be seized by them and used against their critics.[22] When they "went public," for example, by printing pamphlets—the printing of the Grand Remonstrance is the starkest example here—they could plausibly be charged with inflaming the minds of the people against the king. In the period under discussion, the king was, in fact, the first to bring the charge of "subversion by division," when he accused the Scottish Covenanters of collaborating unwittingly (if not deliberately) with the Catholics in a design to divide and weaken England that could only profit foreign Catholic powers. There were precedents for such charges against religious dissidents. In a parliamentary speech of 1588, Lord Keeper Puckering had argued that despite Puritan claims to be at war with the Jesuits, they in effect "do both join and concur with the Jesuits" in sowing discord at a time of threatened invasion.[23] James I had said that "Jesuits are nothing but Puritan-papists"; it was a good line, and his son seems actually to have believed it. Charles I frequently complained that the Jesuits and Puritans were equally troublesome and seditious, for both challenged the royal supremacy.[24]

Antiepiscopal movements such as the Covenanters were particularly vulnerable to this line of propaganda that branded them as Jesuits in disguise, because of the well-known antipathy between Jesuits and bishops. Catholic anti-Jesuit writers associated Jesuits and Puritans as a polemical device. One of them, the controversialist William Watson, commented that "of all the sects and religions the Jesuit and Puritan come nearest, and are fittest to be coupled like cats and dogs together . . . for their schismatical humor."[25] The association of Puritans (or, after the Restoration, of nonconformists) with Jesuits became a staple of royalist polemic and historiography. Abraham Cowley, in his satire *The Puritan and the Papist* (1643), began:

> So two rude waves, by storms together thrown,
> Roar at each other, fight, and then grow one.[26]

He went on to argue that Jesuit disloyalty was no worse than Puritan.

Behind this rhetorical union of opposites lay assumptions shared by all parties about the motives and methods of Catholics, or at least of those with disloyal intentions. By sowing dissension between one part of the English church and another, or between the king and parliament, or between England and Scotland, the Catholics could divide the king's subjects and weaken royal authority. This would pave the way for a popish coup d'etat in which a foreign invasion would be supported by a native fifth column. Disunity within the church or state was regarded as unnatural, even un-Christian, and its persistence indicated that the devil was at work. By a progression of ideas natural to many Protestants, discord would thus be blamed on those prime agents of the devil, the papacy and the Jesuits.[27] Thus, behind every political crisis, Catholic conspiracy might be suspected, the more so because the Jesuit order was identified with support for theories of resistance[28] and because its followers were widely believed responsible for the assassination of several

European monarchs as well as for the Gunpowder Plot. In England in the 1630s, Jesuit writings kept alive the fears of Catholic designs on the monarch, as did the actions of a few fanatics such as the man put in the Tower early in 1637 for saying he would go to Rome, but would first kill the king so as to be better received by the pope.[29]

In a purely English context, given the developments of the 1630s, the charge of Catholic "subversion by division" was clearly easier to aim at courtiers and ministers than at their critics. Most criticism had in any case been silenced by government censorship. The court was swarming with Catholics, and some of the king's chief ministers were justly suspected of Catholic sympathies. It was not, after all, so farfetched to wonder whether it was because of these figures that the king was brought to treat orthodox Calvinists as "Puritans," make war on the Scots in defense of the bishops, and to "fall out of love with parliaments."

This account begins with the arrival of the agent George Con at the English court in late 1636 and concludes with the departure of Queen Henrietta Maria from England in early 1642. The terminal date has more than symbolic significance. A major argument of this work is that the identification of the Royalists as a "popish force" was neither a groundless parliamentarian propaganda ploy nor an argument developed in the heat of war. The king did rely on a "popish" strategy, and it was one that well antedated the war, originating in his plans to cope with the Scottish crisis of 1637–40. By the time the Catholic queen left England, the most politically dangerous features of the king's policy were already mature; this is one reason why her departure did so little to alleviate political tensions.

The latter part of 1636 provides an appropriate starting point for several reasons. The death of Lord Treasurer Portland in the previous year had removed the king's chief minister in secular affairs and initiated a period of domestic political reshuffling. The entry of France into direct and open participation in the European conflict in the spring of 1635 had similarly shaken the international scene and begun a series of realignments that were still underway when Con arrived. So George Con arrived at a time of uncertainty and tentative reappraisals in both domestic and foreign affairs, and was able to influence both.

The two-year visit of Con's predecessor Gregorio Panzani had prompted speculation (some hopeful, some horrified) about possibilities of reunion between the Church of England and the papacy. Panzani had done little to discourage Catholic or Anglican reunionists; and his conciliatory attitude had given to English Catholics and court Arminians alike a misleading impression, as it proved, of Rome's willingness to compromise. Con was much less sanguine and took a harder line both on the crucial issue of the 1606 oath of allegiance and on doctrinal issues at stake between the two churches. At the same time, he was more influential than Panzani at the English court and intervened effectively in politics. His Scottish background and contacts gave sinister significance to his presence in London as the Scottish crisis developed. His combination of success and intransigence, following upon the excitement and publicity generated by Panzani's "soft-line" approach, heightened public awareness of the Roman agency and Protestant anxiety about it. Con also took a different approach at the court, adopting a far more sympathetic attitude to the Spanish agents. For all these reasons, Con became a symbol for British Protestants of the Catholic influences at court that they feared.

The second and third chapters of this study describe court factions and court Catholicism in the mid-1630s, notably George Con's entry into this world and his attempt to build a court Catholic party among English and Scottish courtiers, of which he and the queen would be the leaders. George Con by no means controlled the activities of all court Catholics, but his attempts to dominate the group were not lost on English Protestants, who readily believed in its unity and nefarious influence. The fourth chapter examines the foreign policy fluctuations of the period between Con's arrival and the buildup of the Scottish crisis, with particular attention to the role of the court Catholics. During this period England moved from a neutral but effectively pro-Spanish policy to a near alliance with France, but by the end of 1638 had retreated again into cooperation with Spain.

The fifth and sixth chapters describe the development of the king's response to the Scottish crisis in 1638–39 and the way in which the court Catholics attempted to use the situation to bring the king into dependence on a domestic Catholic party supported by foreign Catholic powers. Chapter seven covers a complex and important period between Strafford's arrival at court in the latter part of 1639 and the opening of the Long Parliament a year later. The unwillingness of the king and his ministers to detach themselves during this period from a pro-Spanish and pro-Catholic orientation alienated some important and relatively moderate political leaders (or potential leaders), thus damaging the chances for compromise on the eve of the Long Parliament.

The eighth and ninth chapters explore both the continued Catholic activity at court in 1640–42 and the political response of the Long Parliament to court Catholicism. In the session of 1640–41, the leaders of parliament brought their accusations of Catholic plotting chiefly against the crown's leading ministers, toppling most of them. From the discovery of the army plot in spring 1641 onwards, there were ever more direct attacks on the intimate advisors of the royal family, and the Ten

Propositions in June 1641 contained specific proposals relating to the royal household. The outbreak of the Irish Rebellion in October 1641 seemed to corroborate these mounting anxieties. The concluding chapter evaluates the policy of the king in the years 1637–42 in broad outline and indicates the role of both his policy and the interpretation of it that the popish plot embodied in providing a justification for his opponents to resist his use of force with their own.

2. The English Court in 1636

he court of Charles I in 1636 seemed to be a haven of peace and prosperity. Clarendon remembered it thus:

> This kingdom, and all his majesty's dominions . . . enjoyed the greatest calm, and the fullest measure of felicity, that any people in any age, for so long time together, have been blessed with; to the wonder and envy of all the parts of Christendom. . . .

The happiness of the times I mentioned was enviously set off by this, that every other kingdom, every other province were engaged, some entangled, and some almost destroyed by the rage and fury of arms . . . whilst the kingdoms we now lament were alone looked upon as the garden of the world.[1]

Nor was he the only Englishman to contrast the state of England with the miseries of a Europe rent by the Thirty Years War. But both within and outside the court this unity was more apparent than real. If there were few hints of the millennial storm that would break when the Long Parliament met in 1640, it needed no very astute observation to see that both the religious and the foreign policies of Charles I were widely unpopular.

In 1636 there was still a possibility to calm these discontents without a major political crisis; then and later, the king might have admitted to his council, and listened to, figures who were potential political powers, but who would lose hope in the court between 1635 and 1640. The death of Lord Treasurer Portland in March 1635 had removed the king's chief minister and initiated a period of maneuvering and realignment in both domestic and foreign affairs. His successor William Juxon, bishop of London, appointed in March 1636, did not exercise the general control over policy, particularly foreign policy, that Portland had wielded. At the center of government in 1636, there was no new strong man; and in competition for office during 1635–36, the influence of Queen Henrietta Maria had been for the first time felt at the very summit of politics.[2] Her strategic potential, now recognized, would not henceforth be ignored.

The Issues

In domestic affairs, the issues of finance and religion continued to be the most controversial, apart from the related question that dominated political speculation in the 1630s—whether and when the king would call a parliament. The financial devices that enabled the king to govern without parliament until the Scottish wars of 1639–40 are too familiar to need rehearsal here. As the attacks on them in the Long Parliament showed, they were unpopular in themselves and because they were a means of dispensing with parliament. The most important source of nonparliamentary income, moreover, was the customs; and the increasing customs revenue in both England and Ireland was a fruit of English neutrality in the Thirty Years War, supplemented by income derived from favors to Spain that went beyond mere neutrality.[3] This connection between royal prosperity and foreign policy provided additional cause for grievance to those who did not approve of ship money, or nonparliamentary government, or papist Spain.

It is tempting, if perhaps idle, to wonder how long the king could have maintained financial independence from parliament had the Scottish crisis not intervened. The needs of government were real; the debates of the 1620s had shown that many M.P.s and presumably many of the gentry class they represented had little realistic comprehension of these needs. A constitutional crisis could surely not have been indefinitely postponed.[4] The changing of the guard in the mid-1630s signaled no radical shift in financial policy. Although Archbishop Laud had been a stern critic of the former lord treasurer, and had the satisfaction of seeing his own client Juxon installed in Portland's place, no radical restructuring of crown finances was undertaken, only a few changes rung on the old system.[5] Broader plans for settling the king's finances on a sounder basis, while remedying many grievances, were being developed by the future leaders of the Long Parliament, men who were outside the court, although they took advice from friends in senior levels of administration.[6] When the possibility of war with Spain was seriously raised in the winter of 1636–37, its financial implications were clear to most; it would at the same time threaten the customs revenue and greatly increase the likelihood of a parliament.

A seeming unity about the years of personal rule has obscured the period of excitement in 1636 and 1637 when the possibility of war, and of a parliament, seemed very real. Already in late 1635, the jockeying for position after Portland's death had caused a flurry of anticipation and gossip. Wentworth returned from Ireland, ambitious for the treasurer's position and likely, many said, to get it. Given his confidence in 1640 that he could manage a parliament for the king, would Wentworth not have advised parliamentary courses if he had become chief minister four years earlier? The agitation for war with the Habsburgs that erupted in the winter of 1636–37 revived speculation about the calling of parliament. Later, as the Scottish crisis deepened and the king began military preparations, this too suggested to the politically aware that a parliament might be in the offing. When the king's decision to convoke a parliament was finally announced at the end of 1639, it occasioned surprise only because observers who had watched one expectant year pass after another had almost concluded that no crisis was great enough to overcome the king's reluctance.

Those within and outside the court circle who wanted the king to call parliament were animated by particular issues, as well as by a general sense that parliaments were an established part of English politics and must be given the chance to air grievances and consider legislation. They did not form a single party but a pressure group representing a variety of interests: alliance with France or war with Spain, the promotion of themselves at court and in the council that might follow upon a successful "management" of parliament for the king (i.e., grant of supply), the dismantling of the Laudian regime in the church.

Of those at court who opposed the calling of parliament, many feared they would become the object of parliamentary attack, and none more sharply than William Laud. The archbishop of Canterbury dominated all aspects of church policy, with the significant exception of the treatment of Roman Catholics. Virtually from his succession, it had been clear that the king was an Arminian in theology, rejecting the Calvinist doctrine of predestination that had been the unofficial orthodoxy of the Church of England since Elizabeth's day. The king's dependence on William Laud as an ecclesiastical advisor was already evident in the late 1620s and was confirmed by his appointment of Laud to the primacy of Canterbury in 1633. The Arminian theology, aggressive clericalism, and ceremonial emphasis of the Laudian regime were imposed upon the localities, where they were regarded as alien to the traditions of the English church.[7] His policies made Laud vulnerable to accusations of cryptopopery, and the severity of his attack on (newly redefined) nonconformity helped to broaden the very opposition that he feared.[8] The archbishop had an unfortunate aptitude for seeing rebels and subversives under every bush. The show trials he conducted of critics like Leighton and Prynne convinced their sympathizers that he was an evil man, quite possibly guilty not only of maintaining a "church of Laodicea" but even of collaborating with the Romish anti-Christ.

Aware of the unpopularity of his church policy, Laud was apparently in fear for his very life as early as 1633. His conviction that any parliament would attempt, at the least, to deprive him of office, was not unreasonable.[9] Reform of the church by parliament—turning it away from the Arminian current and back toward intimacy with the continental churches—had already been foreshadowed in the 1620s, and there had been violent rhetorical attacks on the Arminians. In 1628, the parliamentary leader John Pym had suggested that parliaments had the right to legislate for the church. The years of Laudian dominance would only have increased the number of M.P.s prepared to resort to that expedient. It seems likely, too, that Laud's belief in the inherently subversive aims of "Puritans" (with whom he lumped so many old-style English Calvinists) influenced the king. The equation between Calvinism and subversion had hitherto been a Catholic polemical device; it would become a feature of Royalist historiography.[10]

The one aspect of religious policy that Laud was unable to dominate in the 1630s was the treatment of Roman Catholics, and the futility of his efforts in this sphere left him dangerously vulnerable to the rhetoric that linked Arminianism with Catholicism. Francis Rous's speech in the 1629 session of parliament had pictured Arminianism as the precursor of "Romish tyranny and Spanish monarchy," and had forcefully enunciated the theme of a design to alter both religion and government: "I desire that we may look into the very belly and bowels of this Trojan horse to see if there be not men in it, ready to open the gates, to Romish tyranny and Spanish monarchy; for an Arminian is the spawn of a papist. . . . And if there come the warmth of favor upon him, you shall see him turn into one of those frogs, that arise out of the bottomless pit."[11] The warmth of favor did indeed come, not only to Arminians but to English Catholics in the 1630s; to men of Rous's mind, the English court by the late 1630s must have seemed to be positively jumping with the frogs of hell.

The king was personally responsible for the immunities enjoyed by Catholics. Without his tolerance and willingness to limit Laud's anti-Catholic activities, his queen, courtiers, and officials could have done little. The king's affection for the queen influenced his policy, as did his indifference to the theological distinctions that weighed so heavily with many Calvinists. Although interested in questions of church government, the king evinced little concern for fine points of doctrine and some impatience with those who erected theological barriers between churches. He once remarked that each would be saved according to his own beliefs, "so as he be an honest pious man," and was reported to believe that "so long as a man believed in Christ, he could save his soul whatever religion he was born, baptised and bred."[12]

Charles I disliked anything that smacked of insularity; and his trip to

Spain when Prince of Wales (to which he often referred in later years) had helped to form his deliberately cultivated cosmopolitanism.[13] He was the first monarch since Henry VIII to leave the shores of Britain and was greatly impressed by the culture that he observed on the continent. He imported into his court an Italianate art and architecture that found ephemeral manifestation in the masques of Inigo Jones, but left a more permanent record in Jones's building projects and in the Van Dyck and Rubens portraits of the court. Several of his courtiers were equally enthusiastic consumers and patrons of the new art: Arundel, Endymion Porter, and Pembroke. Sensitivity to opinion abroad helped to shape the king's attitudes toward Catholics. Charles believed that a policy of persecution in England would breed reprisals overseas. Even more important, English pretensions vis-à-vis other European courts directed the king, like his father, to search for dynastic alliance with Catholic rather than Protestant powers. The courts with which the king aspired to equality, those of France, Spain, and the Empire, were all Catholic.[14]

The king's tolerance for Catholicism had limits, not only the profit motive so frequently alleged, but his own sense of the royal dignity. The royal supremacy was a facet of his authority, and he demanded loyalty from his courtiers. He was therefore offended by newsworthy conversions to Catholicism, such as that of the courtier Wat Montagu. Nonconformity of any kind was a slight to his prestige; and Charles, like his father before him, was wont to compare the more zealous Catholics with Puritans. The analogy was incomprehensible to many of his Protestant subjects.

Contemporaries frequently supposed that the king's tolerance for Catholicism around him meant that he was personally sympathetic to it and possibly susceptible to conversion.[15] As Trevor-Roper long ago pointed out, this view is tenable; what later historians saw as his uncompromising Anglicanism was maintained in the face of Protestant, not Catholic, threats and inducements.[16] Moreover, the Stuart line had been chiefly a Catholic one. James VI had been baptized a Catholic, cultivated a Catholic party at the Scottish court in the 1580s, and negotiated with the pope. His wife, Anne of Denmark, was a Catholic convert; and James himself was fond of saying, as Charles did, that he was a Catholic if not a Roman Catholic. The D'Aubigny-Lennox branch of the Stuarts, of which James, duke of Lennox, was head in the 1630s, was entirely Catholic save for Lennox and two brothers, whose conformity looks very much like royal "church popery."[17]

Foreigners noted that the king listened to sermons praising the sacrament of confession and deploring the break with Rome, that he tolerated foreign ecclesiastics around the court, and that he welcomed attempts to show the "Catholic" character of the English church.[18] Much of what was being said abroad came back to England indirectly, to unnerve anxious Protestants.[19] Comment in England was restrained by fear of punishment; for the king reacted fiercely to criticism of his or the queen's religious practice. One man was fined heavily in Star Chamber and condemned to be whipped and to have his ears cropped, for having said that the king was a Catholic in his heart.[20]

Such insinuations were both illegal and dangerous to the king. The 1534 Treason Act had made it treason to "slanderously and maliciously publish . . . that the king . . . should be heretic, schismatic, tyrant, infidel," and the 1571 Second Treason Act of Elizabeth had reiterated the offence of "writing, printing, preaching, speech, express words or sayings . . . [that] Queen Elizabeth is an heretic, schismatic, tyrant, infidel."[21] The treason legislation reflected widely held assumptions about heresy and rebellion. Some believed that there was a right to resist actively a heretic prince; but even those who did not share this belief agreed that a ruler regarded by his subjects as a heretic ran the risk of encountering resistance on those grounds. The association of the king with Catholicism opened a dangerous avenue toward rebellion and justification of rebellion.

The activities of the court Catholics in the period 1635–40 played a very significant role in the development of distrust between the king and his subjects. Popish plot theories were nothing new; they were always at hand and had appeared in the rhetoric of the parliaments of the 1620s. But the dominance achieved by this explanation of politics in 1640–42, and the severity of the measures that it was used to justify, were something new. They would be hard to explain without the developments described in this study. The court Catholic party was not, after all, an inevitable outgrowth of the Arminianism of the 1620s and 1630s; it was a separate phenomenon, a willed disaster, for which in the final analysis the responsibility lay with the king.

The issues of foreign policy that confronted the government revolved around the central question of what role England could or should play in the Thirty Years War; and for many Englishmen these questions were highly charged with religious significance. In confronting its foreign policy choices, the government had better weapons and more options in 1635–40 than has usually been assumed, and more than it was prepared to utilize. Its failure to seize any opportunities was politically dangerous, for it provoked widespread skepticism about the commitment of the king to the Protestant cause and suspicion about the possible influence of court Catholics on English foreign policy. The foreign relations of England in the 1630s deserve far more extensive treatment than can be accorded them here. They must not, however, be neglected, for neither court Catholicism nor the reaction to it can be understood outside the context of the diplomacy of the 1630s. Furthermore, the king's reaction to the Scottish crisis of 1637–40 seems to have been highly colored by his preoccupation with foreign affairs.

After the military debacles of the 1620s, England had settled down to a neutrality that profited both Spain and England. The English government derived an increasing profit from customs revenues on trade with both sides. Mercenaries from the British Isles fought on all sides of the conflict; and, as each combatant became increasingly short of manpower, the English government profited from granting permissions to levy men in Ireland, Wales, Scotland, and England. Agents from France, Sweden, and Spain were active in this recruitment, which gave them a reason to cultivate parties of their friends at court even when they could not draw England directly into the European conflict. In addition to men, Spain needed protection for its ships carrying troops, money, and arms through the English Channel to Flanders. For a good price, Charles I allowed Spanish ships to unload silver at Plymouth and take it overland to London where it was shipped to Spanish Flanders.[22] These concessions did not satisfy the Spanish, who were inclined to think that the English should offer more in exchange for the profit they derived; and successive Spanish agents in London reported home on English coldness as regularly as the English accused the Spanish of arrogance. But the privileges enjoyed by Spain were of real and increasing importance to its campaigns in the Low Countries.

This comfortable arrangement was distressing to those who wanted England to intervene in Europe on the Protestant side, either in alliance with the unlikely but essential Protestant ally, the France of Cardinal Richelieu, or in some parallel Protestant league. The family of the king's sister Elizabeth provided a focus for Protestant loyalty and gave life to the ideological conviction that England must join the battle against the Romish anti-Christ. Elizabeth, now a widow in exile in The Hague, was known as the "Queen of Bohemia" or the "Winter Queen," in memory of her husband's brief reign in Prague. Around the elector Palatine there had clustered millennial expectations and prophecies in which Frederick V figured as a potential world leader who would destroy anti-Christ, restore peace, and introduce an age of world reform.[23] Millenarian hopes, implicit in the mainstream as well as on the extreme fringe of English Protestantism, had been heightened and focused by the drama of the Thirty Years War, which many Englishmen regarded as the final struggle between the forces of good and evil. The elector's eldest son, Charles Lewis, had inherited some of the loyalties that his father had aroused; he now claimed the electoral title and the Palatine lands that had been torn from his defeated family and bestowed on Maximilian of Bavaria. Anxious to exploit the new phase of diplomatic activity initiated by France's entry into the war, Elizabeth sent the eighteen-year-old prince and his younger brother Rupert to the English court in the autumn of 1635.[24] They were popular in England, and their presence at court reawakened sympathy and hope for their cause.

Of the numerous English and Scottish supporters of Elizabeth and her family, some—her brother Charles I among them—were motivated entirely by dynastic loyalty. Many others saw the religious implications of the European conflict as paramount and the cause of the Palatinate as symbolic of beleaguered Protestantism throughout the continent. Adulation of Elizabeth and hatred of Spain formed a simple pattern with a wide popular appeal. To all who viewed foreign policy from this perspective, the unwillingness or inability of Charles I to intervene on behalf of his nephew and the "Protestant international" detracted from his image as a godly prince. From time to time there were even grumblings that the elector's family, the reversionary interest to the English throne, would provide more suitable rulers for England than Charles I and his heirs.[25]

But how could England intervene effectively to restore the Palatine family to their lands and dignities? The attempts on land and sea in the 1620s had been a woeful series of disasters. An expeditionary force into Germany on the scale required for the reconquest of the Palatinate was something that parliaments had not been prepared to subsidize in the past; there was little reason to suppose that a new parliament would be any more willing, or indeed able, to match rhetorical zeal with ready money. Any effort to help the prince was complicated by the fact that three powers controlled what he claimed was his inheritance. The Upper Palatinate, centering on Amberg and bordering Bohemia and Bavaria, had been granted by the emperor to Maximilian of Bavaria, who had assisted in its conquest in the 1620s. The Lower (or Rhenish) Palatinate, around Heidelberg and Mannheim, lay along a vital Spanish communication route between Italy and the Netherlands: a Spanish army under Spinola had swept through it in 1620, parts of it had subsequently been occupied by Sweden and France, and in the mid-1630s it was a desolate countryside prey to the shifting troops of Spain, the Empire, and Bernard of Saxe-Weimar. It had been technically a Swedish protectorate since the Treaty of Heilbronn of 1633, which permitted its government in exile to return from The Hague to Heidelberg, with Louis Philip, count of Pfalz-Zimmern (and brother of Frederick), as administrator. But it could not in actuality be returned to Charles Lewis without the consent of Spain, the emperor, and France, which now cast a shadow over the Rhine, as Sweden had done before the battle of Nördlingen. Finally, restoration of the electoral dignity, also transferred by the emperor to Maximilian of Bavaria, must be negotiated with both those parties.

It is impossible to say what might have happened in Germany if Charles I had followed a more interventionist policy, or if Charles Lewis had been a more decisive leader than he proved to be. But several observations can be made. The first regards the complicated position of France, long a covert participant in the conflict and in open hostilities with Spain and Austria since 1635. France wished to detach Bavaria from the imperial camp; right up to the Peace of Westphalia, this flirtation with Bavaria led France to support Maximilian's claims to the electoral dignity and Palatine lands. But France also had an interest in maintaining a chain of friendly princes along the Rhine between Habsburg and French territory. English negotiators with France argued that France had a political interest in the restoration of the Palatine, whereas England had only sentiment and consanguinity. As the experience of Hesse-Cassel was to show, there was something to this argument, and there would have been more had the young prince Palatine been a general of real initiative and talent.[26] Had he been more energetic, had there been stronger military support from England, had Charles I been able to overcome his deep distrust of Richelieu, which, to be sure, was shared at every other European court, the conflicting French interests in the Rhenish Palatinate and in Bavaria might have been differently balanced.

The Palatine cause was certainly not a lost one in the 1630s. Elizabeth's residence at The Hague, where she was surrounded by swarms of German and Bohemian refugees, symbolized her primary reliance upon the United Provinces; the stadtholder family of Orange-Nassau was closely allied to the Palatine Wittelsbachs and had welcomed and assisted them both in triumph and in misfortune.[27] Sweden had been an ally before the death of Gustavus Adolphus, and it would be at Swedish insistence and as a result of Swedish victories in the Empire that Charles Lewis would later be restored to part of his patrimony in the Treaty of Westphalia. What he then received—the Rhenish Palatinate and a compromise on the electoral dignity, at the expense of losing the Upper Palatinate completely to Bavaria—he might well have received much earlier. For both the emperor and Charles I had been prepared to negotiate on such terms. Elizabeth's intransigence had prevented any such negotiations, although these might have provided an interim restoration for the prince and a basis for further gains.

In this complex and shifting situation, the argument for continued English neutrality had obvious appeal. The failures of the 1620s had been humiliating, expensive, and politically dangerous. In case of war with Spain, the profits of neutrality would be lost (both customs revenue and income derived from special favors offered to the Habsburgs) and it might well be necessary to summon a parliament. Moreover, the potential threat of a France unified under Richelieu was beginning to be recognized by some observers,[28] although most of the English court and government continued to rate very highly the wealth and power of Spain.[29] There was real concern about Dunkirk and other Flemish ports; this was a consistent motif in English foreign policy. Rather than risk the Flemish ports passing into the hands of France or the United Provinces (as the Franco-Dutch treaty of 1635 envisaged), the government had at one point been prepared to negotiate for an Anglo-Spanish attack on, and subsequent partition of, the Dutch provinces. A weakened Spanish Flanders might seem a distinctly attractive alternative to French hegemony across the Channel.[30]

Considerations of diplomatic and financial prudence, however, had to be weighed against the domestic unpopularity of the king's pro-Spanish neutrality. It could be argued, moreover, that the progress of the war had created a new set of conditions on the continent that demanded a rethinking of English policy and options. The utility, even the possibility, of a British land expeditionary force had been limited by the death of Gustavus Adolphus and the retreat of the Swedes down the Rhine. But this did not make it useless for Charles Lewis to attempt, as he was repeatedly to do, to put himself in the field. As a combatant, his claims and their constitutional foundation would have to be considered in any peace negotiation, but as a noncombatant, he could much more easily be ignored. And in 1635, no one realized that peace was more than a decade away; to the contrary, peace negotiations were constantly, if clandestinely, under way between France and Spain from 1635 onward, and rumors of impending settlement filled contemporary newsletters. Papal initiative to begin a peace conference led to the sending of a legate to Cologne in 1636.[31] So Charles Lewis's attempts to get control of the armies of Hesse-Cassel, and later those of Saxe-Weimar, with English subsidies made political and diplomatic sense.

At the same time, the possibility of exerting real and effective pressure on the Habsburgs by sea, rather than by land, had been opened up by the reverses the Habsburgs suffered in the 1630s. These had the effect of greatly increasing the value of English naval power in the English Channel. The successes of Sweden in Germany in the early 1630s had forced the emperor to turn to Spain to help recover his losses, while the entry of France into the war in 1635 caused Spain to tighten its alliance with Austria. The German Habsburgs, Spain, and the government at Brussels were increasingly interdependent. Moreover, the French occupation of Savoy, Alsace, and Lorraine cut off Spanish land routes from Italy through Germany into Flanders. At the end of 1638, Bernard of Weimar's capture of the Rhine fortress of Breisach would tighten even further this stranglehold on land communication. The Habsburg victories of 1634–36 thus masked a serious vulnerability; thrown back on the sea route controlled by England, the Habsburgs depended on English friendship to supply both Flanders and Germany.[32]

The English government had recognized these advantages. The ship money fleet was developed partly as a foreign policy weapon with several uses; not only would it protect the English coast from North African pirates and force the Dutch to pay for the right to fish in "English" waters, but it would also enable the English to make good their claim that they could protect the Flemish ports and the communications between Spain and Flanders. Alternatively, it might be used to cut this Habsburg lifeline. It thus provided an alternative to outright alliance with France, of which Charles was always wary. By threatening to withdraw the special privileges enjoyed by Spain, to transfer them to France, or even to grant privateering licences to anti-Spanish entrepreneurs to operate both in the West Indies and on the European coast, the king could put pressure on Spain, and through Spain, on the emperor and Bavaria. By the late 1630s, it may not have been the case, as Gardiner claimed, that the ship money fleet was "not powerful enough to enable [Charles] to regain the Palatinate."[33]

If the English withdrew Spanish privileges and began a deliberate harassment of Spanish shipping (especially if this stopped short of war), English revenue would be cut, but such actions would not necessarily require calling a parliament. It is true, nevertheless, that men such as Warwick who supported the privateering proposals were not men who could be trusted to moderate their activities so as to stop short of an Anglo-Spanish war. They wanted such a war for a variety of motives, and they wanted the parliament that war would necessitate. Giving rein to such entrepreneurs would be a calculated risk.

Whether pressure exerted on Spain could be conveyed into central Europe so as to influence the prince Palatine's fortunes there must remain a moot question. Emperor Ferdinand II was a devout Catholic, who followed a policy of no compromise with Protestants until the mid-1630s.[34] In 1635 Maximilian of Bavaria married the emperor's daughter, thus bringing at least a temporary end to Bavaria's flirtation with France and the Protestant league. Through a treaty with Saxony, the emperor ended the internecine squabbles among the German princes; and when this treaty was solemnized in the Peace of Prague, Maximilian was confirmed in possession of the Upper Palatinate and the electoral dignity.[35] Elizabeth of Bohemia's family seemed more than ever isolated. Could Ferdinand contemplate a reversal of the policy of concessions to Maximilian, pushing the Bavarian ruler back into the arms of France from which he had so recently wooed him? Richelieu, at least, appears to have thought that sufficient pressure from Spain could accomplish this; one reason he gave for wariness about an Anglo-French alliance was that England could not be depended upon, as Spain could so easily satisfy the claims on the Palatinate if she chose to do so.[36]

Whether indeed the circumstances of the war had so changed to England's advantage; whether this advantage could have been effectively exploited without resort to actual war with Spain; whether Spanish influence with Austria could have been exerted to provide the Palatine family with an earlier and perhaps better settlement than was achieved at Westphalia—these possibilities were never really tested. What is clear is that such a policy required a more skillful and more resolute direction than Charles I and his nephew proved able to provide. When the opportunity fell into the king's hands in 1639 as the Spanish fleet lay at his mercy in the Downs, he failed to exploit his advantage effectively. Although the significance given to this episode in popular mythology and parliamentary rhetoric embodied much that was exaggerated and ill informed, it was not inappropriate. It provided a symbolic point of reference for what was perceived as the faint-hearted and wrong-headed direction of English foreign policy in the late 1630s, and lent credibility to the charge that the court had become "Spaniolized." Had Charles I been prepared not only to threaten, but also to act on his threats, and had his nephew been capable of bold initiatives, the English role in the Thirty Years War might have been quite different from what it was. That it was so ineffectual was attributed by many English Protestants to the subversive influence of elements around the court that were seen as friendly to Catholics as well as to Spain. This was an over-simplification, but it was not entirely wrong.

The Factions

Foreign observers described English political factions according to categories of religion and foreign policy. In certain contexts, they referred to "Puritans," "Protestants," and Catholics.[37] In others they mentioned the "French party," the "Spanish party" (or simply, the "dons"), and the "friends" of the Dutch or of the Palatine family. Although there was a lot of wishful thinking or fear reflected in these categorizations, they reflected central preoccupations of the court itself and were not mere distortions manufactured by ignorant foreigners. There was, however, a considerable and subtle range of individual permutations with respect to these two issues; only in a few cases could simple connections be drawn between religious outlook and foreign policy orientation. Foreign policy positions were, moreover, apt to fluctuate, because the foreign policy of the government was neither as consistent nor as well-defined at any one time as was the Laudian religious program in the 1630s.

The divisions between the "ins" and the "outs" cut across the differences on these two issues and can most easily be defined in terms of financial program, although finances had, of course, implications for domestic and foreign policy. Those in power in court had developed their ways of keeping the king and themselves in funds during the 1630s. Public hostility to their programs made them fearful of parliament or of any policy (such as overt war with Spain) that would necessitate a parliament. Those out of office who aspired to be in office needed (and had developed) an alternative financial program for the king that had parliamentary supply as its centerpiece.

One end of the spectrum of the foreign policy and financial program was occupied by Protestant zealots who favored war with Spain, in alliance only with Protestant powers. These men were sufficiently hostile or indifferent to the Laudian regime to welcome the chance a parliament would bring for further reform of the church. These figures were mainly outside the court. Within the court, they were represented by certain friends of the Palatine family, notably Sir Thomas Roe and Georg Rudolph Weckherlin. Roe was Elizabeth of Bohemia's most outspoken ally, but he had been passed over several years earlier for the secretaryship of state and remained outside the inner circle of the court.[38] Roe agreed with Elizabeth that France was not a reliable ally; whenever it served their interests, Roe believed, the French would sacrifice the Protestants of Europe. It was to Sweden and a northern Protestant alliance that England should look for long-term support.[39] Roe's friend Georg Rudolph Weckherlin was translator, general factotum, and assistant in foreign affairs to Secretary of State Sir John Coke. Weckherlin was a stalwart adherent to the Protestant cause international and to Protestant unity.[40] Roe and Weckherlin were part of a group of Englishmen who supported political and religious alliance among the Protestant states and sponsored the ecumenical endeavors of John Dury. Dury trudged about the continent in the 1630s negotiating with Lutherans and Calvinists for a common Protestant platform and unity against the Habsburgs. The task of Protestant union seemed urgent; to Dury and his associates, the time was ripe for a purification of religion and a restructuring of society. Reform of the English church, unity with European Protestants, militant opposition to the Habsburgs, and active assistance to the Palatine house—these were but different facets of the struggle between Israel and the popish anti-Christ.[41] For all these tasks, calling an English parliament would be necessary.

A somewhat more flexible position was maintained by those who favored war with Spain and the convocation of parliament, but who, despite their Protestant convictions, were willing to consider an alliance with France. After the crushing of the Huguenots at La Rochelle in 1629, France must have appeared an ambiguous ally; but in 1635–36, the fate of European Protestantism seemed to hang in the balance and no assistance should be scorned.[42] This group included noncourtier entrepreneurs who hankered after an enriching sea war with Spain on the Elizabethan model, such as Robert Rich, earl of Warwick, a stalwart sponsor of Puritans and privateers alike.[43] Other members of the Providence Island Company—John Pym, John Hampden, Lord Brooke, Viscount Saye and Sele—espoused a militant Puritanism that combined hostility to Spain with colonial ambitions for England. The earl of Bedford was also a "friend" of France, in the sense of regarding a pro-French posture as more consonant with England's interest than friendship with Spain. Henry Rich, earl of Holland, was a courtier and favorite of the queen, who had been associated with her and with French interests since his participation in the marriage negotiations in the 1620s. He provided a court link for his brother Warwick and other noncourtier proponents of a French alliance. In the early and middle 1630s, as Malcolm Smuts has shown, the French ambassador was encouraging both courtiers like Holland and country peers such as Bedford and Warwick who were hostile to the Laudian church regime. These members of the French party hoped for high office, and they would welcome the parliament that wholesale participation in the European war would necessitate. It would open the avenue to church reform and would serve to strengthen their own position at court. The "parliamentarians" would make themselves useful if not indispensable to the king through their management of parliament and success in negotiating subsidies. They claimed in 1635–36 (and appear to have been still convinced in 1640–41) that they could help the king to the money he needed.[44] The very groups that had been most obstructive during the parliaments of the late 1620s favored an anti-Habsburg policy and were well disposed to the French party. Through her friends at the English court, Elizabeth of Bohemia cultivated this group, which had always supported the interests of her husband and her son.[45]

Another set of points on the spectrum was provided by a group of courtiers that had established contacts with France. Their utility, and thus influence, would rise if England were to enter a French alliance. This

group evinced less hostility to the Laudian regime and less overt commitment to the convocation of parliament than the groups earlier mentioned.
It was Protestant and anti-Spanish, but not as zealous; its members
possessed, or had reasonable hope of, high position and responsibility.
They occupied a moderate, relatively unideological position. Their movement away from sympathy with the king at the end of the 1630s was
significant and was motivated less by idealistic attachment to any religious or parliamentary cause than by reaction against the tenor and
policies of the court. This group was in part a Percy family connection.[46]
Lucy Percy, countess of Carlisle, was the queen's most intimate English
friend. Her brother Henry Percy was another favorite of the queen; another brother, Algernon Percy, earl of Northumberland, was a promising
young nobleman who could expect rapid advancement. Northumberland's father-in-law, William Cecil, earl of Salisbury, also belonged to the
group. A final and pivotal figure was Robert Sydney, earl of Leicester,
married to yet another Percy sister. In the spring of 1636, Leicester was
sent as extraordinary ambassador to Paris, where he would prove to be a
consistent proponent of wider commitments to France. Sir John Coke,
the senior secretary of state, probably ought to be included at this point
in the spectrum; he and his assistant Weckherlin provided a staunchly
Protestant and anti-Habsburg wing of the secretariat.[47] The members of
the French party who were privy councillors in 1642 (Holland, Leicester, Northumberland, and Pembroke) would all join the parliamentary
camp.

The next groups on the spectrum were ideologically much more varied
than the former. They included Protestants and Catholics, the religiously
zealous and the indifferent; they were united only in their support of a
pro-Spanish neutrality and in the fact that they would be suspect to, or
actually attacked by, the leaders of the Long Parliament.[48] The closest
to the Percy family connection, both personally and ideologically, was
Thomas Viscount Wentworth, the future earl of Strafford. He stood
alone because his pro-Spanish orientation was not accompanied by a
firm opposition to calling parliament; a parliamentary leader in the
1620s, he would believe as late as 1640 that an English parliament could
be successfully managed for the king. His commitment to neutrality
stemmed most obviously from his situation as governor of Ireland. His
position there and his favor with the king rested on the financial independence that the Irish customs revenues had brought him. In the mid-
1630s, however, Wentworth was on excellent terms with Sir John Coke
and carried on a constant friendly correspondence with various members
of the Percy family group; like them, he represented a relatively moderate
centrist position.

Other members of the government, also pro-Spanish in the neutralist sense, were more resolutely set against calling a parliament. They did not need parliament to give them a voice in government; indeed, a parliament might threaten their own positions. Laud was little interested in foreign policy, but he was aware of the unpopularity of his church program and feared the almost certain parliamentary attack on it. Chancellor of the Exchequer Francis Cottington had experience in Spain and working relationships with its governors. Moreover, like Lord Treasurer Portland before him, whom he had succeeded as the government's chief "businessman," he feared war as unsettling and financially ruinous. Long suspected as a crypto-Catholic, Cottington nevertheless does not seem to have intervened to protect endangered Catholics. But as master of the Court of Wards, he discontinued the policy of using wardship to wean Catholic heirs from their religion by placing them with Protestants.[49]

Another figure suspected in the 1630s to be a crypto-Catholic was Sir Francis Windebank, junior secretary of state and a former protégé of Archbishop Laud who had moved into Cottington's orbit. Windebank was used by the king for secret negotiations with Spain that bypassed both his senior colleague Sir John Coke and the rest of the privy council. Windebank and his nephew Robert Reade provided a hispanophile and pro-Catholic wing of the secretariat that was often in tension with the Protestants Coke and Weckherlin. Windebank kept up a correspondence with Catholic agents in Rome, he was a leading conduit for negotiations between successive papal agents and the king, and it was to him that the king, the queen, or important courtiers turned to execute their acts of clemency to Catholic priests and laymen.[50]

Involved less directly than these royal officers with the formation of policy were two powerful and wealthy courtier family connections, the Howards and the Villierses, both of which were more Catholic than Protestant in orientation and were considered, probably because of their coolness to France, friends of Spain at court.[51] Bitter rivals during the lifetime of Buckingham, they had settled down in the 1630s to enjoyment of the lavish grants and benefits that the king showered on them. The ladies of both families were intimate with the queen and conspicuous at her court.

The head of the Howard connection was Thomas, earl of Arundel, prospective heir to the Norfolk title. Descendant of two markedly Catholic lines, he had conformed to the Church of England in 1616, but was widely regarded as a crypto-Catholic and identified by foreign ambassadors as potential head of a Catholic party.[52] He had been a strong proponent of the Spanish marriage project in the early 1620s. Attached, as was the king, to the cultural world of Mediterranean Catholicism, Arundel had visited Rome in 1614 when it was still legally out of bounds for

English travelers. In subsequent years he used a network of contacts in Italy to build his formidable collection of Renaissance and classical art. Although his chief office was the largely ceremonial one of earl marshal, Arundel may have had more influence on the king than is usually assumed. He was on several committees of the privy council and was almost continually one of the "junta" for foreign affairs.

Aletheia, countess of Arundel, was coheiress to the Shrewsbury fortune; she did not make even the nominal deviation from her Catholic upbringing that her husband had conceded. She encouraged Catholic marriages for her sons, with the ultimate result that the main branch of the Howard family returned firmly to the Catholic fold after the Restoration and provided English Catholics with their first cardinal in one hundred years.[53] The other branches of the family had not remained firm in their faith, save for the family of Arundel's uncle, Lord William Howard ("Belted Will"), who was not a courtier at all, but lived at his great house of Naworth in Cumberland.[54]

The Villiers family had much less influence on policy after Buckingham's death, but lost neither their place at court nor the enormous fortune that the king guarded for the duke's young son. From the early 1620s the family had shown a marked preference for Catholicism, which provided some substance for the parliamentary charges of "maintaining popery" that were brought against the duke at the end of the decade. The conversion of the duke's mother in 1622 was a very public one; it was the occasion for a disputation between Laud and the Jesuit John Percy (alias Fisher). Laud's published account of the *Conference with Fisher* was said to have dissuaded the duke himself from following his mother over to Rome. Cosin's book of Anglican devotions, drawn up for the use of Protestant court ladies in the late 1620s, was another tribute to the faltering Anglicanism of the Villiers family; it was composed for Susan Villiers, countess of Denbigh, who wavered for years between Rome and Canterbury. The duke's remaining sister, Elizabeth Boteler, and two of his surviving brothers converted during the 1630s.[55]

The duke's widow, Katherine, duchess of Buckingham, had been raised a Catholic in the Manners family and nominally conformed at the time of her marriage. Within a year of the duke's assassination, she publicly recanted Protestantism at the church of St. Martin's-in-the-Fields and purged her household of Protestant servants. In 1635 she married the Irish Catholic Randall McDonnell, earl of Antrim. The new countess of Antrim, her sister-in-law the countess of Denbigh, and Lady Denbigh's daughter Mary (another waverer) remained in honored positions at the queen's court in the 1630s, and the Villiers-Feilding connection made advantageous marriages. Like the Howard connection, the Villiers family was predominantly pro-Spanish in its sympathies.[56]

To Wentworth, Cottington, Windebank, the Howards, and the Villiers, the slogans of the Protestant zealots were distasteful and irrelevant. Their support for the Palatine family would always be cautious, founded on personal loyalty and old-fashioned chivalry rather than zeal for the maintenance of international Protestantism. If the restoration of the Palatine could be procured by negotiation with Spain, the emperor, or Bavaria, it was worth pursuing. It was not worth pursuing to the brink of war.

At the opposite end of the political spectrum from the Protestant zealots was a small group, mostly without official position, whose importance increased between 1636 and 1642. It consisted of native and foreign Catholics who, for one reason or another, were persuaded that England should enter an active alliance with Spain and who urged this point of view on the king with increasing vigor. Among them were the courtiers Wat Montagu and Sir Toby Mathew, both converts to Catholicism; the secular priest George Gage and his brother Colonel Sir Henry Gage; the courtier Endymion Porter, whose reception into the Catholic church was prevented only by his fear of losing office; the group of eminent anti-Richelieu exiles visiting the English court (of whom the duchess of Chevreuse was the most active); and the Spanish, imperial, and papal agents. These individuals portrayed an alliance with Spain as an alternative source of income to the convocation of parliament; and they objected to a parliament in any case because they feared it would adopt anti-Catholic measures.

Conclusion

Between 1635 and 1640, the king's options in domestic and foreign policy were first to widen and then to narrow as the Scottish crisis initiated by the new prayer book became an English crisis and forced the government increasingly on the defensive. In the period of maneuvering and realignment that followed Portland's death, the possibility of a parliament and of effective action against the Habsburgs was first opened and then closed. England swung away from a pro-Spanish orientation to a near alliance with France; then, by the beginning of 1638, it shifted back to a neutrality that was pro-Spanish in effect. The "Spanish party" regained its footing and coalesced with a specifically Catholic party, which was shaped and directed by the papal agents.

The effect of these developments on Protestant opinion both inside and outside the court proved devastating. Catholics and foreigners were perceived to be influencing both the domestic and the foreign policy of the court, shaping the king's response to the Scottish crisis, conspiring against a parliament, and damaging the interests of the prince Palatine. By the middle of 1640, even the moderates of the "French party" centered around the Percy connection had lost faith in the king and his advisors and were looking to a parliament to redress the balance that they could not maintain within the court and council.

When parliament finally met in 1640, its leaders explained the disappointments of the preceding decade and a half in terms of popish plotting and subversion. Exaggerated and sometimes comical as their allegations were, there was some basis for them in the activities of the king and the court in 1636–40. Before 1636, there were Catholics at court, there was an Arminian church regime that could with a certain Calvinistic logic be termed "popish," there was indecision and futility in foreign policy. From 1636 onwards, there was a papal agent actively working to form a Catholic party at court, thwarting the efforts of the archbishop of Canterbury to enforce the anti-Catholic laws, and counseling the king in foreign and domestic policy. The fearful predictions of the 1620s seemed to have been fulfilled.

3. Court Catholicism and the Role of George Con

he period 1636–39 during which George Con served as papal agent at the court of Henrietta Maria coincided with the rise and decline of the French alliance project and with the development of the Scottish prayer-book crisis. There is no evidence that Con influenced the development of foreign policy, but to those who feared and exaggerated the power of Spain at court, his friendship with Spanish diplomats and his dealings with the exiled Marie de Medici and other anti-Richelieu partisans put him in the enemy camp and triggered their obsessive concern about the relation between Spanish and Catholic ambitions.

There was more justification for associating Con with the Scottish crisis, not with its origins, as the shriller Covenant propaganda insisted, but with the king's response to the challenge of Scottish resistance. That George Con was a Scot was from one point of view a mere coincidence; it had nothing to do with the program for church uniformity that the king and Archbishop Laud were pursuing. But the role of Scottish Catholics in initiating the Anglo-Roman agency and the presence of Con at court when the new prayer book was introduced looked anything but coincidental to the more fearful Scottish spirits. Con's influence on Scottish policy as the crisis developed lent some credibility to allegations of a link between Rome and the prayer book that might otherwise have been dismissed as fantastic by cooler heads.

Fears about Con's nefarious influence on policy were heightened by his successful interference on behalf of individual English Catholics, by his attempts to make a Catholic party out of the unstructured court Catholic milieu he entered, and by the contrast between his attitudes and those of his predecessor Gregorio Panzani. During his residence in England from 1634 to 1636, Panzani did little to discourage speculation (some hopeful, some horrified) about possibilities of reunion between the Church of England and Rome. He was unrealistically optimistic about Rome's willingness to compromise; Con was less sanguine. Panzani was ecumenical in spirit and tolerated a bit of vagueness about doctrine; Con took a more orthodox line on doctrine and a less flexible stance on the crucial issue of the 1606 oath of allegiance. The combination of Con's success at court and his intransigence following upon the excitement and publicity generated by Panzani's visit, sharpened public awareness of the Roman agency and Protestant anxiety about it.

This chapter discusses the world of court and London Catholicism that Con entered, his role within it, his attempt to organize a party among the court Catholics, and his activities on behalf of British Catholics. Some attention is given to his stand on issues that divided the Catholic community because his failure to resolve those disputes, as well as his partly inadvertent identification with one side of the struggles, left him vulnerable to attack from within the Catholic community. There is some evidence that disgruntled Catholics contributed to the tide of rumor and suspicion about Con, adding what purported to be inside information identifying him as that most feared variety of Catholic—the "Jesuited, Spaniolized" one. Con was certainly the most important of the three papal agents in shaping Protestant response to court activities. Although his successor Rossetti, who served from 1639 to mid-1641, was involved in the most dangerous aspects of the "popish plotting"—plans to use the Irish army and papal loans to quiet English discontent—it was Con who had laid the foundations for this. His success at court made him a symbol of Catholic influence that even outlasted his death; Con's activities, not Rossetti's, were dragged up before the Long Parliament for investigation.

The Queen and the Court Catholics

Henrietta Maria provided the first royal focus for Roman Catholicism at court since the death of Mary Tudor. Her predecessor, Anne of Denmark, had converted privately to Catholicism, but Anne lived in retirement from court after 1609 and never exercised much influence on her husband. Henrietta's religion, by contrast, was a matter of state. The religious liberties accorded her in the marriage treaty could not be abrogated without risking an international incident.

The baptism and education of the royal children was a compromise between the stipulations of the marriage treaty and the king's wishes.[1] The marriage contract had specified that the children would be baptised Catholic and raised in their mother's faith until the age of thirteen. The king insisted on Anglican baptisms for the two older boys, but Henrietta's influence remained powerful in the children's religious education. The infant Charles, Prince of Wales, was entrusted to the care of the Catholic countess of Roxborough; when popular complaint forced her removal, she was replaced by Mary, countess of Dorset, although the Sackville family were unlikely to exercise a beneficent Protestant influence on the prince.[2] In the mid-1630s, the queen began to take Prince Charles to mass with her. When the king put a stop to this, the queen turned her attention to the little princesses. The Northamptonshire cleric who was arrested in 1633 for praying publicly that "the prince be not brought up in popery, whereof there is great cause to fear," had reason for his distress.[3]

The circle surrounding the royal family included many Catholics and Catholic sympathizers. The queen's Catholic chancellor, Thomas Savage, died in 1635 but Lady Savage continued to be an intimate of the queen and her daughter's Catholic marriage caused a mild sensation in 1637.[4] Endymion Porter, crypto-Catholic groom of the bedchamber, was one of many who glutted themselves on royal grants of patents and monopolies. Sir John Winter, a proclaimed Catholic, was another monopolist and familiar figure around the court. Sir Kenelm Digby's name was a reminder of the Gunpowder Plotters, of whom his father had been one. At one time a conformist, Digby reverted to the family religion by the mid-1630s. His lengthy periods of residence abroad made him a symbol, like Sir Toby Mathew, convert son of an archbishop of York, of the cosmopolitan, deracinated Catholic courtier of the early Stuart period.[5] Another such figure was Wat Montagu, younger son of the earl of Manchester and a perennial favorite of the queen. He created a scandal in 1635 by his conversion and subsequent flight to the continent, followed by an attempt to justify his actions in a lengthy letter to his indignant father, which Wat apparently circulated among his acquaintances.[6]

The young Edward Somerset, Lord Herbert of Raglan, represented the enormously wealthy Catholic family headed by his father, the fifth earl of Worcester. Lord Herbert spent most of the late 1630s at Worcester House in the Strand, which was a center for London Catholics. The family, which was highly regarded by the king and intimate with the earl and countess of Arundel, had married into the Catholic aristocracy. The Somersets were great supporters of the Jesuits in England, and Raglan Castle was the center of the Jesuit mission in south Wales.[7]

The Catholicism of London and the court was cosmopolitan, quite unlike the gentry Catholicism of the countryside. The only Catholic chapels that had official sanction were those of the Catholic ambassadors and the queen. These enjoyed immunities that made them useful for evangelism in the London area. Already in the reign of James I, when negotiations for a Spanish marriage entered a serious phase and the restrictions on English Catholics were temporarily lightened, the Spanish ambassador Gondomar had attracted thousands of English Catholics to his chapel.[8] The occasional raids the king allowed the London authorities to make were ineffectual sops to outraged Protestant opinion. After 1625 there was a continuing tacit toleration of the ambassadors' illegal practice of

The Role of George Con   41

supporting English as well as foreign priests in their chapels and admitting the king's subjects to services.[9] Preaching, catechizing, and the hearings of confessions could be carried out in English. This aggressive proselytizing of the English by English-speaking priests based in foreign embassies on English soil prompted xenophobic reactions quite different from the alarums that occasionally disturbed the tacit toleration of the countryside.[10]

London was the center not only of court Catholicism but also of the Catholic missionary effort in England, which had much expanded since the reign of Elizabeth. Since 1633 the secular priests had been guided by a dean and chapter. The dean and the chapter secretary—in the late 1630s this was George Gage, protected by his appointment as cupbearer to the queen—usually resided in London.[11] The Jesuits, whose mission had expanded more rapidly than any other branch of the clergy in the early seventeenth century, were governed by a provincial. In 1636 this was Henry More, who moved between the London and Essex residences of his noble patrons, the Petre family; there were several dozen Jesuits in the London mission.[12] The Benedictines, divided among themselves by controversy, had a prefect who went under the name of William Price. Price was a habitué of the court, as were several other Benedictine missionaries. The Franciscans, although much less numerous than the preceding groups, were rapidly expanding their work in England.[13] Both of their provincials during the 1630s lived in London; the second of them, Christopher Davenport, lodged with the queen's Capuchin priests at Somerset House. The vigor of the Franciscan mission and the welcome the Franciscans enjoyed at court may have owed something to Giles Chaissy, O.F.M., a noted French preacher and controversialist against the Huguenots, who had come to England with the queen as one of her chaplains.[14] Most of the very few British Dominicans, Minims, and Carmelites engaged in missionary work were in the London area.[15]

Centering the missionary organization on London was perhaps inevitable, given the need for constant communications with Rome and with the English Catholic institutions on the continent. But according to one estimate, the number of priests located in London exceeded the actual needs of the lay Catholics of the area.[16] This concentration was partly due to the lure exercised by the wealthy potential patrons in the metropolis; policy might dictate attaching oneself to the wealthy and powerful, and so might self-indulgence. London also offered a very practical advantage, the protection offered by sympathetic courtiers and privy councillors. With the assistance of Secretary of State Windebank, a regular technique had been developed for assisting captured priests. Those arrested in London would be released after providing surety, while those arrested in the counties were transferred under Windebank's personal warrant to London prisons, where they were similarly delivered on bond after a few days.[17]

As a result of mitigations of official policy, Catholics in the capital, and to some extent those in the country as well, enjoyed considerable freedom and security. Contemporary observers, both hopeful Catholics and horrified Protestants, were agreed on this point.[18] Foreign observers looking at the English court in the mid-1630s often expressed the opinion that if the king should convert to Catholicism, the country would follow, invoking England's religious history in the sixteenth century in support of this view. John Stoye has remarked that the number of English visitors to Spain who converted or at least conformed to Catholicism during the seventeenth century "may well have fortified a conviction that heresy in England was not immoveable."[19] The case of Henry IV of France suggested that religious conviction, if indeed heretics could be said to have such a thing, could yield to political necessity. It was an example that would not be forgotten by Pope Urban VIII, who had been nuncio in Paris during Henry's reign, nor by Henry's daughter Henrietta Maria, who had been sent as a bride to England with letters from the pope reminding her of the example of Bertha, the Frankish princess who had helped bring Christianity to Anglo-Saxon England.[20]

Englishmen, more aware of the strength of English Protestantism, were far less likely to adopt this *politique* view about the prospects of Catholicism in England. But they were also apprehensive about the royal family's present religiously divided status and what that boded for the future. Until the birth of Prince Charles in 1630, the family of Elizabeth of Bohemia was the "reversionary interest," the potential heirs to the throne. Even in the 1630s, there were occasional expressions of preference for the prince Palatine over the Prince of Wales or over the king himself, a situation that presaged that of the 1670s.[21]

The Scottish Catholic Initiative

As a small minority within Scotland, without the presence of a protective court, the Catholics often had to appeal to foreign ambassadors at the English court for aid. They also hoped for help from Rome, but this would require a new and more amicable relationship between the courts of Rome and England. It had been Scottish Catholic courtiers in the reign of James I who had most actively pressed for the reestablishment of diplomatic relations between the two courts and who had sustained hopes in Rome of the king's conversion.[22] This was also the case in the reign of Charles I.

Partly because Scotland itself was becoming increasingly uncomfortable territory for Catholics, even noble ones, the Scots represented a considerable group among the court Catholics of the 1630s. The earls of Douglas, Nithsdale, Semple, and Abercorn were all Catholic, as were the elder marquis of Huntley (d. 1636) and the earl of Argyll (d. 1638).[23] With the active assistance of the queen's Scottish confessor, Father Robert Philip of Sanquhar, the Scottish court Catholics initiated a diplomatic rapprochement with Rome in the early 1630s. Two Scottish courtiers were sent to urge Urban VIII to exploit the advantages presented by the sympathetic attitude of the court and to ask him also to name a British cardinal. The Scots had long cherished this project of a British cardinal, who would provide both leadership and protection for Catholics in the British Isles.[24]

The queen supported the mission to Rome, and her accompanying letters named George Con, a Scot in Barberini's entourage, as her candidate for the biretta. The queen's motives (so far as we can reconstruct them) were mixed. A nominated cardinal would add to her prestige among the princesses of Europe. As the 1630s progressed, moreover, she developed an increasingly genuine concern for the English Catholics and a desire to play the role of protectress for them.[25]

Charles did not just tacitly tolerate this "mutual agency," as it was called;[26] he encouraged it. Apart from his interest in acquiring art treasures from Rome, which has probably been overemphasized as a motive for the agency, the king had other concerns relating both to the English Catholic community and to the Palatine house.[27] He wanted Rome's approval for English Catholics to take the 1606 oath of allegiance (a long disputed matter) and he would have liked to persuade the pope to withdraw the Jesuits, whose public opposition to that oath angered him deeply. The king also instructed the agent in Rome to urge the pope to intervene on behalf of the young prince Palatine in the peace conference that Urban himself was trying to organize in Cologne. The pope's refusal to associate himself with any peace conference that recognized representatives of heretic princes (i.e., Protestants) was a matter of record; Charles may well have seen in the cardinalate negotiation a way of getting around this problem. A British cardinal whose elevation he and the queen had sponsored would be uniquely suitable for representing the Palatine's interests at the impending conference.

The papal court was well aware of this aspect of the king's interest and little inclined to respond to it, although a pretense of response was made by sending the Capuchin father, Alexander of Hales, to the emperor in Vienna, ostensibly on behalf of the Palatine prince.[28] More puzzling were the enthusiastic representations of the Scottish agent, Sir Robert Douglas, about the possibilities of church reunion and the conversion of the king.

Other reports from England in the early 1630s had referred to the king's sympathy for Catholicism and the queen's growing influence on him. The pope's advisors on British affairs, Cardinals di Bagno and Bentivoglio, were skeptical about these claims, but felt they could not be wholly ignored.[29] Francis Ingoli, the secretary of the Congregation for the Propagation of the Faith (Propaganda Fide), spoke on the side of the optimists, especially noting the report by Father Leonard of Paris, provincial of the French Capuchins, on the good disposition of William Laud toward Catholicism and on Laud's influence with the king.[30] The true character of Laud's opinions and the meaning of the Laudian program were always misunderstood in Rome, as well as by Rome's optimistic informants in England. This misunderstanding caused a (presumably) unauthorized offer of a cardinal's cap to be made in 1633 to Laud as an inducement to his conversion.[31]

The political interests of the papacy on the Italian peninsula made the possibility of another Catholic power on the western seaboard of Europe very appealing. Anxious to avert the threat of Habsburg hegemony in Italy, Urban had been forced to shut his eyes to France's complicity with Protestant princes in the continental war, which reduced the pope's authority as peacemaker among the Catholic powers.[32] A re-Catholicized England would restore to Urban VIII much freedom to maneuver.

In any case, there was a real need for a reliable witness to investigate the state of British Catholicism and to report on the divisions that had torn the community apart in the late 1620s and early 1630s. Would the appointment of a new Catholic bishop to supervise the missionary priests, for example, be acceptable to the English crown? Finally, Rome hoped, as did the king, that a compromise might be reached over the oath of allegiance in order to relieve Catholics from the disabilities they suffered for refusing it, to say nothing of removing the scandal created by the numerous Catholics who accepted it despite papal prohibition.

The decision was therefore made to exchange agents between the papal court and that of the queen, and Sir Robert Douglas was sent home in 1634 with assurances (albeit vague as to time and person) that a British cardinal would be named. He was shortly followed by the first Roman agent to the queen's court, the Oratorian priest Gregorio Panzani. Panzani's sojourn in England, from December of 1634 to December of 1636, was a source of encouragement to the queen and to court Catholics; it was a source of alarm not only to Laud and to English Protestants but to Panzani's own superiors in Rome. They came to regard him as dangerously ready to compromise with the Church of England and to exceed his commission by entering into ambitious negotiations about reunion of the churches.[33]

During Panzani's visit to England the queen's rivalry with Archbishop Laud became an important feature of the court scene. The queen was encouraged by her spiritual advisors to regard the condition of English Catholics as a reflection on her dignity and to work on their behalf; she, like others, initially misunderstood Laud's position and was surprised when he did not collaborate in the 1633 overtures to Rome. At the same time, his role in the successive christening squabbles as her children were born—he baptized the Prince of Wales in 1630, although he was not yet archbishop, and later James, duke of York, in 1633—created some personal rancor between them.[34] Sensitive to any rival for the king's affections since Buckingham's ascendancy, the queen quickened her efforts for Catholics to demonstrate that her influence exceeded Laud's. She and her circle never entirely abandoned hopes of winning him, but she came to rely on political inducements rather than his religious sympathy. She alternated between wooing and wounding him, and regarded every reprieved Catholic as a victory for herself and a defeat for Laud.[35]

For his part, Laud was deeply embarrassed by the warmer relations with Rome. The diplomatic overtures of 1633 immediately followed his elevation to the primacy, and those who already suspected him of "popish" leanings naturally connected the two events. A man who alleged that the new archbishop was under house arrest for treasonable dealings with the pope found himself under arrest instead and brought up for trial.[36] Early in 1634, the Franciscan convert Christopher Davenport—usually known to contemporaries under his name in religion, Franciscus à Sancta Clara—a chaplain of the queen and friend of Windebank, published *Deus, Natura, Gratia*, a book that became the talk of London. Dedicated to the king, who was much pleased with it, the work embodied a commentary on the Thirty-nine Articles and a treatise on justification; it purported to demonstrate that at almost every point Anglican beliefs could be reconciled with Roman doctrine.[37]

This was followed by the visit to England in 1634 and 1635 of the Benedictine Leander Jones, a convert who had been Laud's friend at St. John's College, Oxford. A rumor circulated through England that Laud had invited Jones, intending to discuss with him theology and possible Anglo-Roman reconciliation. This rumor and the related suggestion that Leander was some sort of official Roman envoy to the Church of England were almost certainly wrong;[38] but it remains entirely possible that Jones met with Laud during his stay in England. Leander's reports to Rome on the English church, which seem to have circulated in England, encouraged the impression that he was involved in high-level negotiations that went far beyond the questions of Benedictine missionary organization with which he was empowered to deal. Leander minimized the differences between the Church of England and the Roman church, portrayed the English bishops as ripe for conversion and the king as willing to cooperate in this, and suggested that chances were very good for a religious coup d'etat whereby Catholicism would again become the state religion. Helpless to end the negotiations with Rome of which he disapproved, Laud had to endure rumors that he had initiated them.[39]

The Mission of George Con

Notwithstanding the concern felt in both Roman and English church circles that these enthusiasts were exploring possibilities that orthodox churchmen could not support, the mutual agency was not abandoned. Wat Montagu, sent to Rome early in 1636 with a letter of introduction and entreaty from Queen Henrietta, campaigned vigorously for continuation of the agency and promotion of George Con. Panzani's mission had not been entirely fruitless. He had brought most of the missionary groups to a "concord" among themselves, he had made valuable contacts with the royal ministers, and his exploratory talks with them gave Rome some hope of lifting the onerous 1606 oath of allegiance.

Thus, in the summer of 1636, Sir William Hamilton, brother to the earl of Abercorn, was sent to Rome, while George Con was dispatched to England. Con was to replace Panzani and to provide, it was hoped, a more balanced view of the situation of the English Catholics and the intentions of the English government. George Con came from a Catholic family in the Aberdeen area and had been educated in Catholic establishments abroad. Secretary first to Cardinal Montalto, then to the pope's nephew, Cardinal Francesco Barberini, he had come to be regarded by the late 1620s as an expert on British Catholic affairs and a special patron in Rome of British Catholics.[40] By all accounts suave and charming, he nonetheless had the relatively intransigent outlook of the religious exile. Unlike many of his friends among the Scottish Catholic clergy, he had no missionary experience; he had never confronted heresy on its own ground and knew little of the daily compromise with an unfriendly environment that was the experience of most British Catholics, both lay and clergy. Con's own temperament, his exile mentality, his ambitions, and his duty would all nudge him into a posture of apparent alliance with the two forces, one secular and one religious—to wit, Spain and the Jesuit order—that English Protestants had come to regard as most threatening.

Con's ambitions dictated a strict orthodoxy, a visible and primary loyalty to the interests of the papacy, and an impartiality in his relations with all branches of the clergy and the representatives of Catholic powers in England. As the pope's delegate and as a man aspiring to be raised to the cardinalate, Con could not afford to let continue the antagonism that had developed between Panzani and the Spanish agents in England.

Con's approach had not been welcomed by Spanish agents in England. When he heard of Con's coming, via France where Con stopped to confer with Richelieu, the Spanish ambassador announced publicly that the agent was coming to receive the English king into the church of Rome, a deliberate invention that was intended to mar Con's reception.[41] Spain had been uncomfortable with the new agency for several reasons. First of all, it tended to diminish Spain's influence over the Catholic community.[42] Moreover, it was a project promoted by the French government; Con's appointment had been recommended by Mazarin, who was already identified with French interests. The Scottish Catholics, although not exclusively French in orientation, had traditional ties with France, and a number of prominent Scottish Catholics were in exile there. If an English bishop were appointed (and Panzani had favored this plan), he would come from the ranks of the secular clergy, whose links were primarily with France. Spain had thus been watching the development of the agency very warily.

Bad relations with Spain would do Con no good with the Curia, which had been perceptibly cooling toward France since 1635. French war finance entailed pressures on the income of the French clergy that created quarrels between Paris and Rome. Bolognetti, the nuncio in Paris, was slighted by Richelieu and Louis XIII, who had been urging Mazarin's appointment to that position. The French ambassador in Rome, the maréchal d'Estrées, became persona non grata with the Holy See.[43] There continued to be an important French party in the Curia, but Con's chances for promotion might be diminished were he to be identified as a "French" candidate.[44] Urban VIII's advancing age also had to be considered; he was seriously ill in the late 1630s and his successor might well be inimical to France and the friends of France. For all these reasons, Con moved quickly to establish friendly relations with the Spanish representatives in England.[45]

Motives of both policy and principle also guided Con to a friendly relation with the English Jesuits, who had got along poorly with his predecessor Panzani. They were protected in England by the Spanish embassy and had powerful supporters in the Curia.[46] Moreover, there was a real community of outlook between Con and the Jesuits, who welcomed his arrival in England. Although they might differ on controversial matters affecting the English Catholic community, both Con and the Jesuits were proud to be champions of Rome and orthodoxy against any concessions that might compromise, or even seem to compromise, papal authority. This similarity of approach caused Con to be more closely identified with the Jesuit position on matters such as the oath of allegiance and the organization of the mission than the facts warranted.

The image of Con as a friend of Spain and of the Jesuits could not be other than damaging in the eyes of the Protestant public. He became an object of suspicion for some segments of the Catholic community as well, because he took positions, or sometimes was forced into positions, on issues that had long bitterly divided the community. This provided ammunition for the apostate English priests, who contributed significantly to the exposés of "popish plotting" that appeared in the crisis years between 1638 and 1642.

Con did not merely try to walk the tightrope between the contending international powers and quarreling religious factions at the English court. He also took positive steps on behalf of English Catholicism and his own promotion.[47] He attempted to act as a peacemaker within the community, arbitrating its private quarrels in the interests of a united Catholic front. He intervened energetically to rescue individual Catholics from the dilemmas created by the recusancy laws, and he encouraged the queen to widen her own protective net. He began to create at the English court a *dévot* party that would protect Catholics, exemplify by its own loyalty to the king's interests (especially in contrast to the Puritans) the superior virtues of Catholicism as a bulwark for monarchy, and ultimately lobby for freedom of Catholic practice.

Finally, Con continued Panzani's exploration of possible reunion between the English church and Rome. Although he did not share Panzani's optimism on the subject, he had advantages that his predecessor had lacked: a knowledge of English and a developing relationship with the king. Con could hardly have failed to realize that the conversion of the king himself was the one achievement that would virtually guarantee him the biretta.

Con and the Royal Family

Within a few months of his arrival at the English court, George Con had established himself as a successful courtier with a wide acquaintance and a particular intimacy with the royal family. In contrast to his predecessor, whose ignorance of English restricted his contacts, Con came to be lionized, if not always loved, by both Catholics and Protestants at the court.

The basis for this success was his relationship with the king. He had been presented to Charles I publicly on his arrival, and from the start the king treated Con as though he had been accredited to his court as well as to the queen's. The king and the agent saw each other almost daily; Con was in constant attendance on the queen as one of her spiritual advisors, and this gave him the chance to encounter the king informally without special appointments. Soon a genuine intimacy grew between them, or at least as much intimacy as Charles permitted with any courtier of the 1630s.[48] It was certainly more than any foreign agent had enjoyed since the Spanish ambassador Gondomar had basked in the favor of James I and created such vivid, albeit mistaken, impressions of Spanish domination of that court.

Charles was intrigued by the possibility of papal support for the prince Palatine at the Cologne peace conference. Because of this, and also because Con professed a discreet neutrality between the superpowers, the king discussed foreign affairs freely with the agent. He also sparred gently with Con on religious issues. Over private dinners, the king and queen, Father Robert Philip, and Con bantered about the relative advantages and disadvantages of reunion with Rome.[49]

Con reported back to Rome that the king's beliefs were close to Catholic; he was certainly averse to "Calvinism."[50] This appears to represent the king's own view of his position. Charles was seriously, although not urgently, interested in church reunion and willing to discuss it at some length. He aspired to a Gallican type of settlement for England that would restore the prestige of the English church in the eyes of Catholic Europe without depriving it of independence. But Charles made clear to Con the limits of any possible compromise with Rome; he was not prepared to abandon communion in both kinds, the vernacular liturgy, or the right of clergymen (except possibly bishops) to marry.[51]

Con realized, as Panzani had not, that Rome would not accept these conditions, and he waited instead for an opportunity to persuade the king to yield. Meanwhile he negotiated with Charles about the oath of allegiance and other Catholic business and waited hopefully for his elevation to the purple. Early in 1637, the queen's representative in Rome, Sir William Hamilton, wrote that her wishes would be met by September at the latest, and the French and Spanish ambassadors at the Holy See corroborated this. In London, the Catholic ambassadors began to give Con the precedence usually accorded to a cardinal; and English courtiers inquired about the proper form of address.[52]

But September and the rest of 1637 passed without the promotion. Rome delayed and temporized, repeating the old arguments used with Douglas. The English king, quite apart from being a heretic, had not merited special consideration from Rome. He had violated the marriage treaty, ill-treated Catholics, and permitted violent attacks on the papacy in the English press. Some "signal grace" must be offered to the English

Catholics to show Con's power and Charles I's good intentions. In reply, Con emphasized the need for a visible symbol of Roman authority in England, one that could draw the Catholics into unity and obedience, while offering hesitant converts (especially bishops) an example of the rewards Rome could provide. The promotion would gratify the queen and reassure the king, perhaps hasten his conversion. At court Con redoubled his efforts to demonstrate his own influence.[53]

Con's ambition and the king's partiality to him did not pass unnoticed. Con reported grumbling at court over the amount of time the king spent with him. When Charles held up the installation of the Knights of the Garter so as to escort Con around his picture gallery, Arundel warned Con that the so-called Puritan councillors resented this. A man Con identified as a "Brownist" complained about the court that the presence of a papal envoy was intolerable, that Con was an enemy of the state, and that those who associated with him were disloyal subjects. One of the queen's Protestant ladies repeated to Con the murmurings she heard; the king was endangering the purity of English religion, Con was harming the Protestant cause, and the king committed sacrilege each time he took Con by the hand. It was said that one of the agent's letters had been intercepted, in which he asserted that the king would be Catholic within two years. Con was identified as a priest; it was rumored that he heard the king's confession. Con's early polemical works, in which he had called Queen Elizabeth a bastard and the oath of allegiance "impious," were brought to the king's attention, but Charles showed no interest. The two men continued in a long discussion of religion and state matters, "to the great distaste of the Puritan observers," as Con gleefully reported.[54]

Many Catholics began to agree with these worried Protestants that major religious change seemed imminent. When, at the end of 1637, the departing Venetian ambassador Correr reported comprehensively to his government on the state of England, he lingered over the religious issue. Pointing out that the state religion had changed four times by royal fiat in the sixteenth century with relatively little popular opposition, he described the numerous conversions to Catholicism during the previous year and the "notable concessions" the king seemed willing to make in the cause of reunion. Panzani's mission had aimed, Correr said, at profound changes in government and religion, and he concluded that the mutual agency gave the English Protestants "good cause for suspicion, and the world (good cause) for expectation." He noted how alarmed the Protestant lords were by Con's warm reception. Correr's successor, Giustiniani, expressed similar views; the real aim of the pope in this diplomatic exchange, he said, was the conversion of the king, and there were signs that this might actually occur.[55]

The king paid little heed to the forebodings of his subjects and did not restrain Con's activities on behalf of Catholics. The agent encouraged the queen's efforts to draw her children, particularly the Prince of Wales, into sympathy with her religion. Con made overtures to the prince's tutor, Dr. Brian Duppa, who he thought might be converted. On the occasion of his appointment in 1634, Duppa had preached before the king, describing the breach with Rome as "unfortunate" and advising the king to consider reunion.[56] When the Prince of Wales acquired his own governor and household in 1638, Con cultivated the earl of Newcastle, who he reported was unsympathetic to Puritans.[57]

The Palatine princes absorbed a good deal of Con's attention during their visit to the English court. Con attempted to persuade them that only by converting could they ensure the restoration of their father's lands and titles to their house. His effort was seconded by the earl of Arundel, who had always had a chivalrous attachment to the family of Elizabeth of Bohemia. With the complicity of Arundel, his countess, and the queen, Con befriended Charles Lewis and Rupert, explaining that their conversion would remove the only pretext the emperor had for excluding them and might persuade the pope to pronounce in their favor. Reviving a proposal that had been made earlier by Urban VIII, Con and Arundel suggested that Charles Lewis might go to live in Italy or at the imperial court, where presumably he would be gradually drawn into the Catholic camp.[58] The prince was polite but unenthusiastic; although he seemed to share his uncle's anti-Puritan bias, he had also imbibed his mother's dedicated anti-Catholicism.

Rupert, more excited at the possibility of a trip to Rome, proved more susceptible to Con's suggestions; and Con found him, at second glance, altogether more promising than his brother—"in spirit and nobility very much superior," "a young man of infinite ability for his age." The projects of conversion ended for the time being with the prince's departure in June 1637. Elizabeth of Bohemia was aghast at the influence the court Catholic milieu had had on Rupert, exclaiming that had he stayed four more days in England he would have converted.[59]

The Court Catholic Party

Con aimed to form a *dévot* party at the English court that would advance English Catholicism. In trying to create it, he transformed the queen's circle, formerly ambivalent in its religious and foreign policy orientation, into a more self-consciously Catholic group hostile to French interests. Already in 1637, Laud was writing unhappily to Strafford, "I conceive it most true that the party of the queen grows very strong. And, I fear some consequences of it very much."[60]

Both Catholic clergy and courtiers were enlisted in Con's effort. In the first year of his agency, he was assisted by James DuPerron, bishop of Angoulême, the queen's almoner and head of her ecclesiastical establishment. The choice of DuPerron for this high position had been symbolically important, for his uncle, the great Cardinal Jacques Davy DuPerron, had been instrumental in arranging Henry IV's reception into the Catholic church. But the nephew was a man of lesser talents; Con came to hold a low opinion of him, in part perhaps because DuPerron harbored his own ambitions for the cardinal's cap.[61]

Father Robert Philip, the queen's Scottish confessor, provided the most reliable assistance to all three papal agents. He had been an initiator of the agency, had introduced a number of Scottish Catholics into the queen's household, and was an intermediary with Sir William Hamilton, her agent at Rome. He had been the chief confidant of Gregorio Panzani, an Oratorian like himself. Most important, the queen was wholly devoted to Philip and had resisted French efforts to replace him with one of her Capuchins.[62]

Among the lay courtiers, Wat Montagu was of prime importance. This son of the earl of Manchester and brother of Lord Mandeville (the future parliamentarian peer) had been forced into exile by his conversion to Catholicism in 1635. At the Roman court in 1636, he had strenuously advocated Con's appointment as papal agent and his elevation to the purple. Early in 1637, Con negotiated Montagu's return to England, with the queen, the duchess of Buckingham, and the earl of Holland all helping to smooth the way. Arriving in England in April, Montagu moved into Con's residence and, despite an initially cold welcome from his father and the king, was shortly received again at court. Always a favorite with the queen, Montagu was a valuable ally for Con in the early months of the agency. But he, like DuPerron, was a potential rival whose relations with Con had cooled by 1639. He had made a good impression on Cardinal Barberini and maintained an independent correspondence with him, frequently relaying the queen's requests.[63]

Montagu drew into the court Catholic group his friend Sir Kenelm Digby, son of the Gunpowder Plotter Sir Everard Digby (as Protestant pamphleteers were to reiterate endlessly in succeeding years). Like Montagu, Digby was a convert to Catholicism who had retired to France in 1635; like Montagu, he returned to England in the spring of 1637. Con would never be wholly comfortable with Digby, describing him as indiscreet and dangerously speculative in his approach to religion. The king, moreover, was not Digby's friend. During two years abroad, Digby had become a busy proselytizer for his new faith, converting several English expatriates and writing controversial pieces. The English ambassador in Paris had reported disapprovingly on this activity: "Sir Kenelm Digby is busy in seducing the king's subjects in these parts from the church of England." Digby's indiscretion appeared again in late 1637, while he was on a diplomatic mission for the queen in France. In Paris he published a pamphlet setting forth Charles I's supposedly pro-Catholic views, much to the king's displeasure. Only with difficulty could Con calm the king's irritation. When he returned to England in 1638, Digby continued his literary defense of Catholicism, attempting in a series of letters on the subject of religious authority to bring his cousin George Digby, the future earl of Bristol, into the Catholic church. These letters were widely circulated in manuscript form and later published.[64]

An even more ambiguous associate for Con was Sir Toby Mathew, son of the Protestant archbishop of York. Mathew had left the Church of England for the Church of Rome more than thirty years before. He had spent most of his life outside England and was regarded as very pro-Spanish. He too returned to England by the end of 1636. Mathew had achieved an almost legendary notoriety as the prototype of the "Jesuited, Spaniolized" court Catholic, and his name was likely to be brought into any rumor or scare about Catholic activities.[65] Not only was Mathew identified with the Jesuit point of view, he was rumored to be one of their number. Older and different in his experiences from Digby and Montagu, he was never very close to the queen. However, he enjoyed good relations with many prominent courtiers, being a client of both the Howard and the Villiers families.

Mathew was useful to Con, and for a time he acted as a go-between with Wentworth in Ireland, but their relations remained fairly cool. Con thought Mathew opposed his bid for the cardinal's cap and sometimes attempted to discredit him in his reports to Rome. But Con could scarcely ignore Mathew; the man was too well connected.[66] As time would show, the two men came to be associated in the public mind as symbols of court Catholicism.

More helpful to Con in his day-to-day interventions on behalf of Catholics was Secretary of State Windebank, who had also been an intimate of Panzani. Con derived a good deal of information about conciliar activities and politics from Windebank, either directly or through the countess of Arundel, and the secretary continued to play an essential role in arranging reprieves for Catholics and thwarting the agents of the church courts. A man with a large family and few resources, he had taken patronage where he could find it. Initially a protégé of Laud, to whom he owed his appointment, he had been under the wing of Cottington, Laud's rival, since 1635. In the late 1630s, Con had favors to offer Windebank that Cottington could not match, such as the famed Barberini hospitality for Windebank's sons, who were studying and traveling on the continent in preparation for government service. Windebank had never been a favorite of the queen, who regarded him as too overtly pro-Spanish in his sympathies; and she had once tried to remove him from office. But within six months of his arrival at court, Con had effected a rapprochement between the two, recognizing how vital their partnership was for the routine defense of English Catholics.[67]

Useful as Windebank could be, he was a difficult figure to deal with. Con thought him unnecessarily fearful of taking risks for Catholics, unless backed to the hilt by the king and queen, and lacking in judgment and conviction. Windebank was one of those pliable men who, guided perhaps by the desire or need to please, expected too much from both parties to any negotiation. Like Philip and DuPerron, he was an enthusiastic reunionist. Even after Con's arrival at court, he often took his cue from the unorthodox reunionists with whom Con was at odds. Windebank's assessment of English politics was as unrealistically optimistic as Panzani's view of Rome's capacity for compromise; together they had created false hopes and misunderstanding. Con felt it necessary to dispel the sanguine latitudinarianism that Panzani had communicated to Windebank. When Windebank said that he was Anglican but that his religion was essentially the same as that of Rome, Con quickly contradicted him. As much as possible, Con avoided using Windebank as an intermediary on the oath negotiation, and moved into an independent relation with the king.[68]

Within the group of court Catholics, we have seen how two family alliances enjoyed particular favor: the Howards and the Villierses. Con's personal charm, his connections with Rome, and his official standing made him a focus of new activity and intrigue for these two connections, and they became more clearly identified with Catholic interests. His chief patrons were the earl and countess of Arundel. He developed a friendship with Arundel early in his mission; the two men dined and wined together, Arundel relating his diplomatic adventures and confiding to Con details of current negotiations. Arundel was also keen to arrange art purchases in Rome and used Con frequently for this purpose. The countess of Arundel, Con's greatest friend and admirer among the court ladies, was, he said, "Catholic in all but profession." She frequently entertained Con and other Catholics, including priests, which she claimed she would never have dared do before his arrival. By late 1638, she was arranging for Con to say mass at the various Howard residences, probably without her husband's knowledge. At court it was rumored that Con had reconciled the countess to the Church of Rome.[69]

Con established equally friendly relations with the duchess of Bucking-ham and her circle. He was frequently in her company during 1637 and cajoled her into a stricter religious observance. For example, he ensured that she did not attend her own daughter's Protestant marriage to the duke of Lennox. Until she moved to Ireland late in 1638 with her second husband, the earl of Antrim, the duchess occasionally carried messages between Con and Archbishop Laud.[70]

A new wave of conversions within the Villiers-Feilding connection began with Olive Porter, Buckingham's niece. In the spring of 1637, Olive had her father, Lord Boteler, received into the Catholic church on his deathbed, quarreling with her Protestant sister, Lady Newport, in the process. During the summer her brother-in-law, Captain Tom Porter, was also received into the church on his deathbed.[71] Next, Olive made a de-termined attempt on the conscience of her cousin Mary Feilding, mar-chioness of Hamilton. Then came the conversion of her sister, Lady Newport, which created a genuine sensation. Newport, whom Con de-scribed with some exaggeration as "one of the chief Puritans," was out-raged; the queen had to ask the king to intervene to moderate Newport's harsh treatment of his convert wife. Mrs. Porter, who by now was main-taining a Jesuit chaplain in her house, was quite undaunted by the fuss. In February of 1638 she experienced an allegedly miraculous escape from death in childbed, which she attributed to her Catholic devotions and relics, winning over a few more souls to her faith. These successes were related by one of Wentworth's London correspondents: " 'Tis true, notwithstanding all the care and vigilancy the king and prelates take for suppressing of popery, yet it much increaseth about London. . . . Our great women fall away every day."[72]

Endymion Porter himself did not lapse from communion with the Church of England, but this was a matter of policy rather than prefer-ence. His long and close association with Spain—he had been for a while a page in the house of Olivares and had conformed to Catholicism while there—left him sympathetic to Rome. For a time, he discussed with Con the possibility of a secret conversion that would not preclude his obliga-tory attendance at the royal chapel as a groom of the king's bedchamber, but the Curia would not hear of this. Nonetheless, Porter's three sons were brought up Catholic, and their friendship with the Palatine princes in 1637 worried Protestant observers.[73]

The significance of Porter's Catholic leanings, as of all this burgeoning court Catholicism, lay on the borderline where symbolism hardened into political reality. Porter's influence on the larger issues of policy may not have been great, but he was unquestionably one of the men whom the king delighted to honor. He was a dispenser of patronage for Charles I as he had been for his former master Buckingham.[74] Given Endymion Porter's position at court, his family's religious activities helped to define what was acceptable, even pleasing, to the king. When Porter silenced a French Huguenot for daring to criticize the papal agent or was praised by the king for dressing down another critic, these incidents were noted by the court as a sign of which way the wind blew.[75]

The increased prestige of the papal agent was marked by his acceptance by the court at large. He became a general favorite, entertained by Protestant lords such as Holland, Northumberland, Hamilton, Goring, and Pembroke. William Juxon, lord treasurer, bishop of London, and Laud's associate, gave a dinner party for Con that caused much talk in London.[76] The papal agent had, in effect, the free run of the court and city.

Catholic Activism

In retrospect, Con's interventions and the flurry of court Catholic excitement that his mission evoked can be seen as the rather minor triumphs that they were. But contemporaries already made anxious by the Laudian program were naturally puzzled and misled by the king's failure to restrain active proselytizing, court conversions, and interference with ecclesiastical discipline. The most notorious incidents involved the Catholic chapels in London.

The queen herself had chapel rights wherever she resided. She maintained a permanent chapel at St. James's Palace, where more than a dozen French Capuchins, under the leadership of Father Jean Marie Trélon, were settled.[77] The choice of Capuchins as the queen's chaplains was an obvious one; Richelieu's chief advisor, the "grey eminence" Père Joseph, was a member of the order. The choice was obvious in another way that could scarcely have reassured knowledgeable Protestants; the Capuchins were a preaching and proselytizing order that had been aggressively pro-Ligue in the French wars of religion. Those sent to England undertook to learn English; and some preached, catechized, and held disputations in that language. All paraded openly through the streets of London in their exotic habits. In December 1636 they opened the new chapel in Somerset House that Inigo Jones had specially designed for the queen, where the reserved sacrament was displayed at the high altar, surrounded by gold plate, huge angel figures, and hundreds of candles.[78] In the spring of 1637 the Spanish ambassador, who had been living in the countryside (partly out of pique at Charles I's negotiations with France), found a London house that would permit him a large chapel.[79]

In these chapels services were celebrated with some publicity and numbers of English gathered there. The queen held a special Christmas mass at Somerset House in 1637, at which she ordered Lady Newport and other recent converts to appear in public as Catholics for the first time. In Holy Week 1638 Mrs. Porter and the duchess of Buckingham were confirmed at Somerset House by Bishop DuPerron, the queen acting as godmother for both.[80] Con opened his own chapel where the Barberini arms were displayed; and he reported happily in November 1637 that as many as nine masses were being said there on feast days. This "pope's chapel," as it was called, became the venue for fashionable Catholic weddings and ceremonies such as a papal requiem for the queen's brother-in-law, the duke of Savoy.[81] At the same time, the London chapels of the Catholic nobility flourished and were made more grandiose; at Worcester House in the Strand there was an impressive display of the Holy Sepulchre during the 1638 Easter season.[82]

It was the Spanish ambassador Oñate whose indiscretions finally provided a focus for public resentment, provoking a minor riot on Maundy Thursday of 1638. Con had complained before that his incautious and ostentatious behavior threatened the liberties enjoyed by London Catholics. When Oñate paraded through the streets with clergy and English Catholics, crucifixes in hands and torches carried aloft, from mass at the queen's chapel to Con's house and then to the ambassador's Queen Street residence, protests were loud and the king finally issued a warning.[83]

Not all Protestants were horrified at the chapels and services; some were curious, others even attracted. The open preaching of Catholic doctrine was a novelty, and the chapels provided settings for a ceremonial more elaborate than that of the Church of England. The earl of Bath, escorted to Easter Mass in 1638 by George Con, wondered aloud why Protestants were deprived of what he called the aesthetic "consolations" offered by Rome.[84] Other English Protestants were attracted by the religious art and liturgy of the Counter-Reformation, and by Catholic devotional literature. During the early seventeenth century, the products of Catholic presses circulated fairly freely in England. Although Puritans reacted to the chapels and books by an even more violent recoil from the "whore of Babylon" and all her works, the Laudian party attempted to provide for this religious perspective within the Church of England. One impulse for Laud's ceremonial reforms was the attempt to reconcile Catholics, or potential Catholics, to the English church. In the court environment where Laud chiefly moved, this task may well have seemed more urgent, as well as more congenial, than the task of accommodating Puritans.[85]

Con's successes, so much more visible than the stresses within the Catholic community, extended beyond the court circle. He attempted to protect Catholics from the burdens of legal disabilities, in particular the harassment and illegal extortions of the pursuivants. These agents of the church courts, many of them apostate Catholics who profited from inside information, were generally held in low regard. Investigations of their activities in 1635 and 1636 by commissions of royal judges had uncovered abuses and corruption, but led to little reform. With the assistance of the queen, Arundel, and Windebank, Con had the inquiry reopened in late 1637, and the issue was referred to Windebank and Manchester. Their hearings in mid-1638 accepted evidence even from professed Catholic priests. It was impossible to eliminate the pursuivants, as Con would have liked, but he remained vigilant in curbing their activities.[86]

The family life of Catholics could be disrupted by the government practice of using prerogative rights over wardship and marriage to encourage conformity to Anglicanism. Con successfully intervened in two wardship cases in 1637 to protect Catholic wards from attempts to transfer them to Protestant households. One involved the earl of Pembroke, whose eldest son had died just after a youthful marriage, apparently leaving the earl fearful that he would have no surviving son. In that case, his heir would be a young Catholic relative, and he wanted the boy raised Protestant so that the earldom would not pass to a Catholic. After a bitter public struggle, the queen and Con frustrated the plan. In retaliation, Pembroke and Laud sponsored a proposal in the privy council "to take away the eldest sons of all who were popishly affected, and breed them up in the religion established." To Con's relief and the regret of Protestant observers, this project, which had been suggested many times since Elizabeth's accession, also came to naught.[87]

Marriage also presented Catholics with many difficulties, because resort to a priest was illegal and Catholic authorities refused to recognize or condone Anglican ceremonies. Mixed marriages caused additional complications. Several times during his agency, Con intervened with the queen's assistance to facilitate Catholic marriages.[88] Beyond the court and beyond the aristocracy, Con endeavored to assist the poor recusants of England. They often could not afford the legal fees associated with compounding for recusancy, and thus suffered disadvantages that composition might relieve. Con devised a scheme whereby the poor would be permitted to join in group compositions, thus sharing the legal expenses, although this seems never to have been put into effect.[89]

Nor did the agent or the queen hesitate to reach across the Irish Sea on behalf of the Catholics there.[90] Since his arrival in Ireland, Viscount Wentworth had pursued a complex policy vis-à-vis the Catholic majority there. Although it contrasted with the zealous anti-Catholic policy of the New English administration that had preceded him (thus providing the New English with another motive to resent him), his policy was by no means pro-Catholic. Wentworth's authoritarian temperament, his desire to profit from the Catholics as from other Irish groups, and his animus against various individual Catholics alienated the Catholics of Ireland from him and his regime. Their discontent found expression through their friends at the English court.[91]

Con wrote to Wentworth in the winter of 1636–37, using Toby Mathew as an intermediary. In reply to Con's account of Irish grievances, Wentworth said that "my master's councils moved not to their [Catholic] disquiet in matter of religion." He counterattacked by claiming that the Irish were ungrateful and disloyal. Wentworth, in fact, was quite worried about the implications of Irish discontent in the winter of 1636–37 because of the possibility of war with Spain. Any hostilities with Spain endangered English control of Ireland owing to the traditional ties between Irish Catholics and Spain. The descendants of the noble Irish rebels of the 1590s were mercenary soldiers in the employ of Spain, as were many of their compatriots; and they had never abandoned hope of regaining what they regarded as their patrimony. Although he had supported Spanish recruitment in Ireland more enthusiastically than earlier deputies—for one thing, it rid Ireland of potential troublemakers—Wentworth was careful to keep track of this floating population of expatriates under foreign control through his correspondence with the English ambassadors in Spain and Brussels.[92]

Early in 1637 Wentworth heard disturbing stories about the Irish in Flanders communicating seditiously with friends in Ulster.[93] Should England break with Spain, these Irish mercenaries might be encouraged by their employers to cause trouble in Ireland. Wentworth's second letter to Con, in May 1637, was therefore emphatic in warning of the dangers of the Irish exiles and the hollowness of their claims: "[They] wander abroad, most of them criminous, all lewdly affected people, that forth of an unjust, yet habitual hatred to the English government, delight to have it believed, and themselves pitied, as persecuted forth of their country, and ravished of their means for their religion only, stirring and inciting all they can to blood and rebellion, and keeping themselves in countenance, by taking upon themselves to be grand seigniors."[94] Wentworth followed this with a warning to the king that

> the Irish abroad do nothing in the world more publicly and
> constantly, than incite the pope and king of Spain to undertake the
> restoring of them again to their country and free exercise of their
> religion, and divers propositions I understand they have made to
> that purpose; they likewise do hold by means of the pope's clergy
> continual intelligence here with those of the mere [Gaelic] Irish, and

believe themselves to be so strong in men as they desire nothing of Spain but to furnish them with arms for 12,000 men, all the rest they will be able to do for themselves. . . .

The knowledge of thus much was the principal occasion that drew me to write to Mr. Con, that so their mouths in present might be stopped, or at least a deafer ear given abroad to their clamours.[95]

This discouraged neither Con nor Henrietta Maria from continuing to intervene in Irish Catholic affairs. She interceded for the Catholic Maurice Lord Roche and for the young convert and Jesuit priest Francis Slingsby.[96] At Con's urging, she attempted to persuade Wentworth to permit the reopening of Ireland's oldest and most revered pilgrimage site, St. Patrick's Purgatory.[97]

Con and the Archbishop

Con's rising star did not go unremarked or unresisted by Archbishop Laud, who had enjoyed an almost unchallenged control over religious policy before Con's arrival. Con's social conquest of the court put Laud on the defensive. Con drew members of the Villiers family from their adherence to the Church of England that Laud had labored so long to preserve; and the archbishop's complaints in the privy council against this proselytizing were of little avail. Con encouraged the queen to involve herself in ecclesiastical appointments and to work for the promotion of bishops she believed sympathetic to Rome. This exercise of patronage over English ecclesiastics was no secret at court and could only contribute to the impression that the Laudian church was on the path to Rome. The Venetian ambassador commented that Con was "trying to insinuate into the minds of the leading men of the church here the belief and observance of the Catholic institutions."[98]

A final humiliating feature of Con's mission, from Laud's point of view, was that he symbolized a rival hierarchy threatening to the cherished belief in the apostolic succession of the English clergy. Firmly resolved against the readmission of any Catholic bishop to England, Laud was even more horrified at the possibility that Con would be created a cardinal. The break with Rome had left the English hierarchy intact, save for this highest dignity. Should it be conferred on Con, the archbishop would find himself ecclesiastically outranked at the English court.[99]

Initial relations between the archbishop and the papal agent had been tentative rather than acrimonious. At first Con seems to have shared the Roman view that Laud was a potential convert. Playing a carrot-and-stick game with the primate, Con tried to communicate with him through intermediaries, while at the same time encouraging the queen to challenge him. Con's depiction of the queen as struggling with Laud for the souls of the English was a dramatic idea that she seems to have found appealing. Although she complained to Con of the traditional attachment of the English Catholics to Spain, saying they "wouldn't care for paradise if the Spanish hadn't procured it for them," the queen did not slacken her attempts to make herself the center of English Catholicism.[100]

Neither Con nor Laud would feel comfortable in an open struggle for power; each recognized that the other enjoyed much influence with the king. So they negotiated. The meaning, extent, and content of these negotiations remain shrouded in mystery; even Laud's archenemy William Prynne was unable to present firm evidence when he helped draw up the case for treason against Laud in 1643. But if Con's reports to Rome are to be believed, some contacts between the two were sustained, despite Laud's politic reluctance to agree to a meeting.[101] One intermediary was William Howard; the chief go-between was the duchess of Buckingham, an old favorite of Laud despite her defection from the Church of England. Con reported that after his success at court in 1637 Laud tried to appease him by compliments passed through the duchess and Wat Montagu. But by the time the duchess left for Ireland in 1638, Laud had passed from appeasement to sustained opposition, partly as a result of the developing crisis in Scotland and the accusations made against him by the Scots.[102]

The struggle between the archbishop and the agent came to a head at the end of 1637, as a result of the court conversions. Attempting to stem the tide, Laud complained to the privy council of being hampered by letters of royal grace and protection to recusants. He took measures against Catholic pilgrimages in Wales, and he hastily sponsored a public burning of François de Sale's *Introduction to the Devout Life*, recently licensed in an expurgated de-Romanized version by one of his own chaplains. In the wake of Lady Newport's conversion, Laud began to prepare a second edition of his *Conference with Fisher*, which had proved a successful antidote to court popery in the 1620s. According to one report, he even asked the king outright to send Con away, but lost to the queen's entreaties.[103]

Laud then sponsored a proclamation against Catholic proselytizing and the attendance of English Catholics at the London chapels.[104] He was not alone in thinking that these chapels were much to blame for the increase of popery, and he was supported in the attack by Sir John Coke and several other councillors. But his determination was again matched by that of the queen, who made the issue a test of wills. Con's description of "the audacity of Laud, the danger to religion, and to herself" sent her running to the king, who assured her that her chapel would not be affected. This was not enough. Con, Philip, and Montagu, with the assistance of Windebank and Cottington, tried to defer if not defeat the proclamation. As several council meetings passed in debate with no decision, publicity mounted and the proclamation came to be viewed as a test of strength between Con and Laud.[105]

In the end, neither side won. Laud went as far as he dared, capitalizing on the king's anger over Lady Newport's conversion, calling in pursuivants to testify about recusant activities, and describing the rumors about his own alleged negotiations with Rome and the possibility of his and the king's conversion. Ignoring the last-minute pleas of Con and the queen, the king finally agreed to publish the proclamation, saying that "I want to show that I am of that religion that I profess." But the proclamation issued on 20 December 1637 was less precise than Laud wished, and the king promised further exemptions to anyone named by the queen. Soon, at Con's urging, Charles ordered Windebank to ensure that the poorer Catholics did not become the chief victims of it. As Con reported in satisfaction and its sponsors recognized in consternation, the proclamation was a gesture, not a real threat.[106]

A second struggle between Laud and Con was not long delayed. When the queen's secretary, Sir Robert Aiton, died in March 1638, speculation about his successor first revolved around likely Protestants such as Sir William Boswell and Henry Jermyn. But Con and the queen persuaded the king to permit her a Catholic secretary, a departure from the policy followed since the 1620s of excluding professed Catholics from public office[107] and a step toward Con's objective of a *dévot* party at court and, if possible, in office.

Of the Catholic candidates, Con favored Wat Montagu, as did the queen. He regarded Windebank's son as unqualified and knew Sir Kenelm Digby was unacceptable to the king. The candidate who most worried him, however, was Sir William Howard. Howard belonged to the reunionist group of court Catholics, who approved and took seriously the ideas of Leander Jones and Christopher Davenport. Like others of this camp, Howard was anxious to reach a compromise on the oath of allegiance, although willing to take it if none could be reached.[108] This English Gallican was favored by the king and by Laud, but not by Con and not, of course, by the Roman authorities. As the Howards were Con's patrons, it was a delicate matter, but Con prevailed. At the end of April, the appointment was announced of "a man never thought of," Sir John Winter. Nephew of the earl of Worcester and related to one of the Gunpowder Plotters, Winter was closely associated with the Jesuits, like the rest of his family. If the appointment of a Catholic was unpopular with Protestant courtiers, the appointment of one with such a back-ground was doubly so.[109]

Laud was not yet prepared to give up. His biographer has suggested that Laud had been supplanted by Con by the end of 1637 as the most important religious influence at the court of Charles I. Laud was by then aware, as the king seemed not to be, of the political dangers of this situation. As the crisis between the king and the Scottish Covenanters became more acute, Laud's attacks on court Catholicism grew more vigorous, for he was desperate to clear himself from the accusations of Catholic sympathies flung at him by the Covenanters. Some observers recognized that Laud was no more a friend of the Catholics than he was of the Puritans and that he actually aimed to neutralize both parties, but the popular view was different.[110] Laud's critics gave him no credit for his almost single-handed attempts to stem the tide of the papal agent's influence. They noted that Con's successes in 1637 were matched by defeats for the Puritans at the hands of Laud; they saw Con, seated in the countess of Arundel's box, at the trial of the famous Puritan triumvirate, Burton, Bastwick, and Prynne.[111]

If there was a circumstantial basis for Puritan suspicions of the arch-bishop, it arose from Laud's attempts to divide the Catholics by playing on their internal dissensions and befriending selected individuals. He made common cause with the juring Catholics (those who accepted the oath of allegiance); for instance, he supported Sir William Howard as candidate for secretary to the queen. He encouraged them, as he did the king, to regard Con as an agent of the Jesuits. He discouraged the king from continuing negotiations on the oath with Con, reminding him that Rome had never condemned the Gunpowder Plot. He pictured the opposition to the oath as a product of Jesuit pressure and Con as a tool of the order.[112]

Laud also cultivated those members of the Benedictine order who opposed the oath but were enemies of the Jesuits, suspicious of Con, and antipathetical to his ambitions. One of these was the Benedictine superior William Price;[113] before Con's arrival, Price had had considerable influence over Windebank, some of which he lost to Con in 1637. Attempting to thwart Con's bid for the biretta, Price presented to Windebank a memorandum on the nomination of a British cardinal. He argued that the choice of a candidate was in the king's hands and that Charles should nominate his own cousin, Ludovick Stuart d'Aubigny. Price and Laud drew closer together, and one Catholic described the Benedictine as "a great politician, and very familiar, private and secret with the archbishop of Canterbury."[114]

Playing on the king's annoyance at the delay in Con's promotion, which seemed a slight to his and the queen's dignity, Laud speculated aloud whether Con were "ambassador, agent, or spy" and tried to persuade Charles that the agent's elevation depended on his opposing the king on every matter of importance. By the end of 1638 Laud had convinced the king to withdraw from active support of Con's promotion. Windebank wrote Sir William Hamilton on the king's orders that Charles "expect[ed] no courtesy thence" in the matter.[115]

Dissent within the Catholic Community

While Con's success at court won disapproving attention from Protestants, his failure to resolve the internal disputes of the Catholic community created animosity within his own camp. His attempts to discipline errant missionaries, his role as bearer of sometimes unwelcome news from Rome, and his defense of the Jesuits (whose Catholic enemies could be as bitter as their Protestant critics) were all well-meant efforts to bring unity and order to a fragmented, disorganized situation by exerting his authority as papal emissary. These efforts, however, only sharpened old tensions among English Catholics and made him a focus for grievances. Discontented Catholics, as they had on previous occasions, made common cause with anti-Catholic zealots, lending authenticity to tales of popish conspiracy.

The community had long been disturbed by complex internal struggles within the church international and by the special difficulties faced by Catholicism in Protestant countries, where it had to operate as a mission rather than an established church.[116] These quarrels were most serious among the priests, especially those in the London area, and in the upper echelons of missionary organization. The secular clergy, disorganized since the end of the sixteenth century, resented the rapid expansion of missionary endeavors by the regulars in the early seventeenth century. They especially resented, and they were not alone in this, the success of the Jesuits. These clerical rivalries and the issues around which they focused had some effect too on the laity, whose support was enlisted in complaints and countercomplaints to Rome.

Rivals of the Jesuits within the Catholic community could and did align themselves with English Protestant writers, and even with the English government, in portraying the Jesuits as uniquely subversive and politically active. Here they could draw on a long international tradition of anti-Jesuit polemic that exploited the writings of such Jesuits as Bellarmine and Mariana on the legitimacy of resistance to monarchs. The Gunpowder Plot of 1605, as a result of which the Jesuit Henry Garnet was executed, and the assassination of Henry IV of France in 1610 were held up as examples of supposed Jesuit aims and methods. In the violent controversy over missionary organization that racked the English mission at the turn of the century, the Appellant (or anti-Jesuit) party among the secular clergy had blasted the Jesuits and their supporters as treasonous conspirators in a number of pamphlets printed under English government sponsorship.[117] William Watson, a secular polemicist, had objected to the appointment in 1601 of an allegedly pro-Jesuit "archpriest" to head the seculars in the following terms: "All Catholics must hereafter depend upon Blackwell [the archpriest] and he upon Garnet and Garnet upon Persons [Robert Persons, S.J.] and Persons upon the Devil, who is the author of all rebellions, treasons, murders, disobedience, and all such designments as this wicked Jesuit hath hitherto designed against her Majesty [Elizabeth], her safety, her crown and her life."[118]

This rancor never completely died, and it was sustained in later decades by the two central controversies within the Catholic community, the oath of allegiance and the question of whether there should be a Catholic bishop. In each case the Jesuits became identified with an intransigence that was widely unpopular, although in reality they were not unique in the positions they adopted. Their opposition to the oath, by which Catholics were required to abjure as "heretical" and "impious" the doctrine of papal deposition of princes, irritated the considerable segment of the community that saw little harm in the oath if it would ease their burdens and permit them to live quietly with their Protestant neighbors. Needless to say, the Jesuits' position on the oath was taken as corroborating their supposed support of tyrannicide. The Jesuits' equally forceful (and in this case, successful) campaign against the reestablishment of the hierarchy in England had fewer reverberations outside the Catholic community, but confirmed the hotheads among the secular clergy in their hatred of the rival order.[119]

Both of these issues were kept alive in the 1630s not only by polemical writings but also by the king's interest in them. Charles I resented Jesuit opposition to the oath and hoped to use the mutual agency to get the Jesuits withdrawn from England. This was also Panzani's ambition; he had been unable to draw the Jesuits into the agreement among the missionary groups that he had devised (the "instrument of concord") and thought them arrogant in their independence.[120]

Unlike Panzani, Con came to be identified with the Jesuits because of his friendship with and defense of individuals and because of the positions he took on the issues of the oath and the episcopacy.[121] The Jesuits did not circulate much in the royal courts; the king was unfriendly and the queen did not offer them patronage. But they had powerful patrons in the London area, and several prominent Jesuits were active there. The controversialist John Percy (alias Fisher), who had converted the countess of Buckingham and many others and had participated in a noted debate with Laud in the 1620s, was captured by a pursuivant and brought before the privy council in 1635. He was condemned to exile, but was subsequently bailed and lived in London under Villiers patronage.[122] Worcester House in the Strand harbored several Jesuits; altogether there were nearly forty on the London mission. They wrote approvingly to Rome of Con on his arrival, and the general replied: "as to Mgr. Con's prudence and equity, and his marked kindness towards us, it agrees with what I have always thought of him that his qualities give every promise of eminence; and as these hopes become realized, my gratification is great in proportion."[123]

Con's sympathies were tested soon after his arrival. Father Henry Morse, S.J., was arrested while working with plague victims in London and was brought before the privy council; thrown into Newgate Gaol, he was presented for trial in April 1637.[124] The queen, Father Philip, and George Con all pleaded his case with the king, and Charles was reluctant to let the man be executed for his priestly character alone. With the assistance of Windebank and the queen, Con got Morse freed in June.[125]

Con's good relations with the Jesuits seem to have drawn them somewhat more into court society. When the former Jesuit provincial Blount died in May 1638, numerous priests of the London area attended his funeral in the queen's chapel. His successor, Henry More, could be seen at Lady Arundel's soirées, where he was once heard speculating rather rashly about the king's real religious beliefs.[126]

Con's relations with the secular clergy, on the other hand, became increasingly awkward. The leaders of the seculars looked at the mutual agency chiefly from the perspective of the opportunity that it would provide to negotiate the episcopal question and the confirmation of their chapter. Panzani, who had been instructed by Rome to investigate the opinions of the Catholic laity and English government on this subject, had been sympathetic to the seculars. His court informants had encouraged him to hope that the king would permit a Catholic bishop if Rome compromised on the oath of allegiance. All this, together with Panzani's friendship with the queen's influential confessor, had left the seculars in a hopeful mood. When Panzani's return to Rome was not followed by an episcopal appointment or an official confirmation of their chapter, the seculars were very disappointed.[127]

Members of the secular chapter then turned to sound out Con's views on these matters. They would have paid court to him in any case, given his anticipated preferment. George Leybourne was one of the queen's chaplains, an intimate of Panzani, and a familiar figure around the court; he reported optimistically on his early conversations with Con.[128] For his part, Con soon realized that a more effective supervision of the mission was required; he recommended the appointment of a vicar apostolic and the confirmation of the secular chapter.[129] Despite Con's repeated urgings and Rome's repeated promises to confirm the chapter, no action was taken until the spring of 1638, when Con was instructed to submit a list of candidates for a new bishop. This did not suit the agent, who reiterated his advice that Anthony Champney, whom he regarded as a capable and moderate person, should be confirmed in his de facto office of dean of the chapter.[130]

The delays made the seculars suspicious and impatient, and they decided on an independent initiative. Late in 1638 they sent George Leybourne as their agent to Rome to replace Peter Fitton (*vere* Biddulph). Leybourne was joined there by Henry Holden, an English professor at the Sorbonne who had long been a controversialist for the seculars. Leybourne carried a letter from the queen and, apparently unbeknownst to Con, was prepared to push strenuously for a bishop. Another seemingly endless round of curial deliberations in the winter of 1638–39 was complicated by conflicting reports on the state of affairs in England—Con urging a dean but arguing against a bishop, Leybourne assuring the cardinals that the king was ready to accept a bishop.[131]

By this time the seculars were deeply distrustful of Con, and reverberations of the issue were felt in the London Catholic community.[132] Discontented seculars began to whisper that Con's lady friends, at the instigation of their Jesuit confessors, had persuaded the agent to block confirmation of their chapter. When Leybourne and Holden returned empty-handed from Rome in 1639, they were hostile to Con. Predictably, the Benedictines had done what they could to muddy the waters.[133]

Having proposed a compromise that Rome rejected, Con found himself defending a purely negative position, opposition to the bishop. His defense of the seculars and their needs had won nothing for them or for him; he found himself depicted as the stumbling block to an appointment that he actually favored. The seculars came to identify him with what they regarded as Jesuit opposition to their interests, the more so since he championed one of their chief literary opponents, Edward Knott, S.J.[134]

Knott, the young vice-provincial of the English Jesuits, was one of the most promising and most controversial men in his order. He had made a broad theoretical attack on the powers of the episcopacy in the early 1630s and had subsequently engaged in anti-Protestant polemics across a wide range of issues.[135] He was effective enough to have prompted Laud to decide on a counterattack, and William Chillingworth had been preparing the work that appeared in 1637 as *The Religion of Protestants*. Even before it was out, Knott had produced a reply, *A Direction to be Observed by N.N.* (1636), in which he asserted that the Laudian party, by appealing to patristic authorities, had set the course of the English church toward Rome. As this was the charge that the Puritans were making on ceremonial grounds, Laud was outraged. Reiterating one of the king's favorite themes, the similarities between the Jesuits and Puritans, he demanded Knott's expulsion from the country.[136]

At this point, when Laud and others were agitating for Knott's punishment, Con intervened. At first he agreed with the Jesuit superiors that Knott should be removed from the scene; but he soon acquired a high opinion of Knott's abilities and wanted to keep him in England as a literary warrior for Catholicism. With the collaboration of Sir Toby Mathew, Father Philip, and the Jesuit provincial, he arranged this through the queen.[137] Knott remained in England and became increasingly influential in his order, despite reiterated complaints about him from Protestants; in 1639 he would be named provincial for England.[138]

Con's handling of negotiations over the oath of allegiance was equally damaging to his reputation among the Protestants. It also aroused distrust among some of his coreligionists. He was unable to find a formula acceptable both to Rome and to the king. Concerned as always for the prestige of the English monarchy, Charles I felt that his own position was little different from that of the French king. The doctrine of papal deposition of princes had been condemned by the Sorbonne; if Rome tacitly tolerated this situation in France, why should they refuse to do the same for England? Not only was refusal an indignity, but it might also have a sinister significance, as though the pope were reserving the option to support an armed rebellion in England or a Catholic crusade against the country. Many English Catholics approved the oath in principle; and many took it even in the present form, despite papal condemnation. The king inferred that this was a matter on which Rome could bend if it so chose.[139]

The government had therefore attempted to discredit opponents of the oath and destroy their support among English Catholics. In 1634 the Benedictine Thomas Preston, one of the government's oldest and most prolific "Clinker" propagandists on this issue, published a summary of his arguments in favor of the oath under the pseudonym of William Howard, in a book dedicated to Howard's relative and patron, the earl of Arundel. Preston's book was almost immediately answered by the Jesuit Edward Courtenay (*vere* Leeds) in a work defending, in the most uncompromising terms, the doctrine that popes could excommunicate and depose princes.[140]

The Courtenay case became a cause célèbre as Preston and his allies contrived to draw ever more compromising statements from the imprisoned Jesuit. Charles I's instructions to the agent going to Rome in 1636 included the specific request that Rome condemn Courtenay's book. The Benedictine Leander Jones, always conciliatory in his attitudes toward the English government, wrote a refutation of Courtenay's essay. In letters to Rome, Jones urged the pope to withdraw the condemnation of the oath, but his efforts won him nothing but a severe reprimand from Rome.[141]

Panzani had attempted to deal with the Courtenay case and find a compromise on the oath, but had met with very limited success.[142] The issue landed in Con's lap almost as soon as he arrived in England. Encountering Sir William Howard—who, although not the author of the book that passed under his name, shared the views it expressed—he immediately quarreled with him. Howard was convinced that Jesuits at the imperial court had sabotaged recent English negotiations in Vienna.[143] He was disposed to see Jesuits behind any of Con's moves of which he did not approve. He hovered about suspiciously as Con negotiated with the king.

Despite Rome's reluctance to negotiate seriously about the oath, the king's preoccupation with it made the subject impossible for Con to avoid. He tried to work out a compromise formula and a method of offering a new oath without parliamentary sanction.[144] Previously suggested compromise formulas, none of which had been accepted by Rome, had eliminated the most objectionable features (from the Catholic point of view) of the 1606 wording. The language had been generalized so as to appear less specifically antipapal. By dint of hard bargaining, Con persuaded the king to make one important change, and in January of 1637 he triumphantly sent off the new formula, which was approved by representatives of the Jesuits and secular priests. But what was applauded by the court Catholics was not welcomed at Rome; the formula was utterly rejected and negotiations on the subject lapsed by mid-1637.[145]

This failure was daunting for Con, and it put him in a difficult position. Since Rome refused compromise, Con shifted his efforts to reversing the tendency among English Catholics to accept the oath as pro forma evidence of loyalty to the sovereign. As in the case of the episcopacy, his unsuccessful advocacy of a compromise left him supporting a negative proposition—opposition to the oath. Windebank was piqued at what he saw as Con's stubbornness, compared with the encouragement and flexibility he had found in Panzani and Jones. Laud was convinced, and said as much to the king, that Con spoke only for himself and the Jesuits on this issue, not for the pope.[146]

In court and Catholic circles the stories that had circulated before

Con's arrival about his complete devotion to Rome and to the Jesuits began to revive. By the end of 1638 segments of the Catholic community, the juring Catholics in particular, felt disappointed and betrayed by the agent.[147] Sir William Howard, rebuffed by Con and frustrated in his ambition to become a leader of the court Catholic party, struck out on his own. In collaboration with Laud, he organized a petition among the juring Catholic laymen, complaining of priests (mainly Jesuits and other regulars) who refused absolution to jurors. The petition asked the king to punish or exile the nonjurors and to take the jurors under his protection. It was discussed in the privy council and transmitted to Sir William Hamilton in Rome, with instructions to start his own negotiation over the oath with curial officials.[148] Howard, and others like him who were disappointed in Con or suspicious of him, contributed through their discontented murmuring to the rumors that congealed into the conspiracy theory of 1640–41.

One disgruntled priest made a particularly striking contribution to the plot exposés of that period; this was the Scottish Minim John Browne.[149] Browne's story encapsulates many of the troubles of the English mission priests. He was an aged and distinguished scholar whose chief ambition for many years had been to found a Scottish Minim college in Flanders. By the late 1630s he had gathered over £2,000 for this purpose, but in the process he had got into scrapes with English authorities and with his fellow Catholics. Roman authorities had made several efforts to send him and his fellow Minim John Francis Maitland back to France; in addition to his allegedly fraudulent financial dealings, Browne was suspected of heterodox views.[150]

Con was instructed to send Browne out of London, but found this difficult. The Minim produced doctors' certificates attesting that he was too sick to travel; they were signed by a Benedictine friend with powers as apostolic notary. Moreover, Browne was firmly entrenched in London Catholic circles, preaching at the French ambassador's chapel and even at the papal chapel, where Con had admitted him in ignorance of his irregular ecclesiastical status. Instructed to warn Catholics away from Browne, Con replied that it would cause a scandal, for Browne was popular and had been in London many years. In fact, neither Con nor his successor Rossetti was able to dislodge the Minim.[151]

This unedifying episode says much about the difficulties of supervising the English mission, where Catholic priests were by definition outlaws and the temporal authorities offered obstacles rather than assistance to ecclesiastical authority. The Browne case had a strange sequel, for in 1641 Browne made a lengthy and detailed exposé of "popish plotting" at the court to a committee of the House of Commons.[152] By then Con was not only long gone from England, but dead as well; he nonetheless figured prominently in Browne's story, pursued even after death by the resentment of those with whom he had grappled as agent in England in 1636–39.

Conclusion

From a religious and ecclesiastical point of view, neither Con's agency nor the work of his successor was very successful. The numerous conversions of the 1630s can be seen in retrospect as one of a series of waves that would draw Englishmen into the Church of Rome without effecting the conversion of England. The temporary relief afforded to Catholics by the efforts of the papal agents and the queen was more than offset by the backlash of anti-Catholic sentiment that began to take effect in 1640. In the long run, it would prove to be not government compromise but Catholic compromise in the form of "church popery" that would ensure the persistence of English Catholicism into a more tolerant age.

The political reverberations of the mutual agency, however, would prove to be of great significance, not so much for English Catholicism as for the Stuart monarchy. Con's prominence at the court, his interventions on behalf of English Catholics, and the efflorescence of court Catholicism during the whole period of the agency (especially from the beginning of 1637) provided one segment of the picture that frightened English Protestants. In addition, the court Catholics seemed to be steering English foreign policy back into paths congruent with those of Spain in the late 1630s. Although this perception was something of an optical illusion, there was reality behind the suspicion that court Catholics were helping to shape the king's reaction to the Scottish crisis of 1637–40. The fears and suspicions aroused by all these activities—real and imaginary, known and suspected—prepared the ground for the Scottish allegations that popish agents provocateurs were working to divide and then conquer the two Protestant kingdoms. Court Catholicism became associated with papal meddling, Spanish intrigue, and repressive domestic policies, and the king with all of these.

4. The Catholic Party and English Foreign Policy

on's arrival in England in 1636 coincided with a period of diplomatic excitement when it seemed that England might drop its neutrality in European affairs and enter an alliance against the Habsburgs for the sake of the young prince Palatine. This prospect dimmed over the years of Con's agency, and the court became identified once again with the prevalence of Spanish interests. During the same period, the court Catholic party began to include increasing numbers of friends of Spain, and the queen's circle, under Con's influence, became more distinctively Catholic in orientation.[1]

These developments, although largely independent of each other, had serious implications for the way the court was perceived in the context of domestic politics. Given the alignment of factions at the English court, to be pro-Spanish was to be antiparliament. In the late 1620s the Spanish party had been identified as an antiparliamentary interest and the French party as "parliamentary." As the possibility of active alliance with France receded in the later 1630s, so did the likelihood that parliament would be called. Likewise, the more Catholic the court, the less likely it was to welcome a parliament, whether or not the court was also sympathetic to Spain. A parliamentary attack on the Laudian church, had it occurred in 1637 or 1638, might not have been accompanied by such hysterical anti-Catholic rhetoric as was unleashed in 1640–42. But few doubted that Catholics would suffer from the calling of a parliament or from a war that necessitated calling parliament.

Meanwhile the young prince Palatine, around whom a mist of millennial Protestant expectations clung and who also embodied a concrete political tradition of resistance to Habsburg absolutism, suffered one defeat after another as his uncle passively looked on. It was easy for Protestant observers to attribute the unpopular direction of English foreign policy to Catholic influence, and they were not entirely wrong.

New Initiatives: 1635–1636

France's entry into the war initiated a new phase of diplomatic activity at the English court, as it did throughout Europe. Each of the combatants sustained discussions with the English government, attempting to neutralize England if it could not be drawn into alliance. And each party used its discussions with England as diplomatic leverage with others.

Eager to profit from the opportunities for bargaining that the new alignments offered him, Charles I sent out a series of new agents. By negotiating with all sides simultaneously, he hoped to extract a firm commitment to restoration of the Palatinate from one of them. As a new French ambassador extraordinary, Henri de Seneterre, arrived in London, Lord Scudamore crossed to Paris. There he proposed a solution that would cost England nothing: in exchange for the restoration of the prince Palatine, France should offer Lorraine back to its duke.[2] London and Madrid also exchanged new ambassadors,[3] and the Dutch sent Joachimi to England to try to construct an Anglo-Franco-Dutch league. John Taylor, a Catholic diplomat with experience in Madrid and Brussels, was sent on an exploratory mission to the imperial court.[4]

It was from Vienna that the first encouraging sounds came, although they were to prove very misleading. In the spring of 1636, Ferdinand II had some reason to fear that England would be provoked into belligerence. The Peace of Prague had outraged English opinion, and the emperor was planning further moves that would give offense. A meeting of the electoral college at Ratisbon later in the year, from which the prince Palatine would be excluded, was intended to designate Ferdinand's son as "king of the Romans," thus settling on him the succession to the imperial title. To divert English attention from these preparations, the imperial ministers beguiled the gullible Taylor with assurances of Habsburg friendship, reviving an earlier project of marriage between the prince Palatine and one of the emperor's daughters. For the first time in years, an imperial agent, Clement Radolt, was sent to the English court.[5]

Alternately disturbed and intrigued by reports from Vienna, Charles I dispatched the earl of Arundel as ambassador extraordinary in April 1636. The mission proved an expensive failure.[6] Arundel discovered the purpose of the Ratisbon conclave and found that Taylor had made generous and quite unauthorized offers of English aid to the emperor against France and Holland. He returned to England at the end of 1636, exasperated and humiliated, and threw himself into an uncharacteristic promotion of alliance with France. The rebuff to England was a gamble for the Habsburgs, one that proved successful but looked dangerous in the short term.[7]

Even before Arundel's return, Anglo-French relations had been warming up. Charles I had sent the earl of Leicester as ambassador extraordinary to join Scudamore in France in May 1636. Leicester offered the French the privileges that Spain enjoyed from England: levies of men, protection of the French coast, and an end to transport of enemy men and money. Leicester was personally eager for an Anglo-French alliance and urged greater commitments from England. The French were in a mood to talk of alliance, for they were panicked by the imperialist invasion in the summer of 1636, which had swept in close to Paris itself. At the beginning of 1637, the French ministers seemed ready to take the first step of accepting an "auxiliary" treaty incorporating English offers of mercenaries and naval aid.[8] Charles I wrote heatedly to Wentworth in Ireland of the insults from Vienna that were pushing him to the brink of war.[9]

The Failure of the War Party: 1637

The French party at court that clustered around the Percy connection took heart at these developments, as did Puritan peers such as Bedford and Warwick.[10] A French alliance would draw them into the center of events, whereas hostilities with Spain, however delicately launched, would revive the possibility of a parliament that had been in the air since Portland's death. In January 1637 Warwick and other peers confronted the king to urge war on Spain and the calling of parliament, promising, according to one report, that parliament "would readily consent to supply him with all he might desire."[11]

Charles Lewis was overjoyed at the transformation of the court mood and wrote happily to his mother that the king had promised money, arms, and permission to levy volunteers, together with the support of the English fleet.[12] One plan widely discussed at court was that the prince should be lent ships to be manned in part by volunteers under his command. This would create the appearance of autonomy, a ploy necessary to avoid (if possible) an official break between England and Spain and the loss of trade and revenue it would entail.[13]

Even Salvetti, who was inclined to be skeptical about any break with Spain, admitted in March that what he called the "French" and "Puritan" factions, with the queen's support, "have almost all the government in their hands."[14] Those who favored a Protestant over a French alliance also received encouragement in early 1637. Sir Thomas Roe, distrustful as ever of the French, heard from Sweden that the Swedes were determined to continue the anti-Habsburg struggle. At Roe's prompting, the king made verbal offers to Sweden of levies of "men, and the assistance of his fleet, besides other particular helps to their armies in Germany."[15]

But the rush to war slowed to a stroll by the late spring of 1637, then ground to a halt. Almost as soon as Charles I had approved the Anglo-French treaty in February and sent it back to Paris, the French began to hedge, complaining that England had fixed no date for entry into the war and raising side issues about fishing rights in English waters.[16] Charles Lewis issued a manifesto in justification of his cause and tried to keep his spirits up; but, although he went away in June with a gift of money from his uncle, it was clear that he would receive no further aid that summer.[17] The Anglo-French treaty was referred to Hamburg, where France and Sweden were renegotiating their own alliance, and English agents were sent there.[18] Seneterre left England in July—"disgusted," as Salvetti remarked—effectively concluding this phase of Anglo-French negotiations.[19]

The cause of the breakdown is unclear. Gardiner and others following him concluded that Charles never meant to act and that Richelieu never expected him to.[20] But most reports from the English court in the winter of 1636–37 emphasized the mood of expectation and agitation that reigned there.[21] It is probable that France retreated as fast as England, perhaps for domestic reasons.[22] In any case, by the summer of 1637 it was clear that the English government was falling back on the familiar pattern of negotiation with the Habsburgs.

One reason for English hesitation was surely the king's fear of fatally weakening the Spanish Netherlands. The treaties between France and Holland provided for the conquest and division of this area, as he knew. In the 1637 campaign the Dutch, urged on by Richelieu, did try unsuccessfully to capture Dunkirk.[23] Charles, like his successors, was determined not to let Dunkirk fall into French control.[24]

The king's reluctance to call a parliament undoubtedly contributed to the mutual Anglo-French retreat, but perhaps more indirectly than is usually assumed. It is likely that risking loss of the profits of neutrality and taking on military expenses would have forced Charles I to call parliament for supply. But the king seems to have envisaged a primarily naval strategy that might be financed without recourse to parliament.[25] Moreover, as his response to the Scottish crisis would later show, the king could be oblivious to financial implications when sufficiently committed to a course of action.[26] What may have weighed more heavily with him, however, was the shift in the balance of power at court that an alliance with France would bring, namely, the ascendance of the friends of France, who were also friends of Puritans. And for various reasons these figures would press for a parliament.[27] As the influence of Portland, Cottington, and Wentworth was buttressed by their nonparliamentary money-raising abilities, so the route of parliamentary supply appealed to their rivals. This meant a threat to Laud that the king would not entertain.[28] Lacking the zeal for the Protestant international that animated many of his subjects, the king saw only self-interest, not conviction, behind the maneuvers of the war party. Salvetti reported this in May 1637, saying that those who wanted a war did all they could "to force His Majesty to take them into his service by means of a parliament. But as this scheme is very well understood by His Majesty, there is no sign that they will be obliged."[29]

Whatever the reasons for the retreat, the French explanation of it is important, because it contributed to popular perceptions of the court in the late 1630s and seems to have been accepted by the leaders of the Long Parliament. The French asserted that the Spanish party had captured the English government and would "divert" the king from honoring any treaty with France. In terms of official influence on policy, this interpretation seems to refer chiefly to the continued importance of Cottington and Windebank; the French could regard neither as friendly to their interests, and their efforts to buy off Cottington had failed.[30]

It is certainly true that agents for Habsburg interests were at work in England in the spring of 1637, trying to profit from the delay in the Anglo-French treaty. The Spanish ambassador extraordinary Oñate, whose father was blamed for the failure of Arundel's Vienna mission, remained persona non grata with king and queen.[31] But John Erskine, earl of Buchan, a free-lance diplomat, served as go-between for negotiations in April. Buchan told Con that Spain was offering the English the city of Dunkirk "on deposit" until Dutch coastal towns were captured.[32] This negotiation collapsed, each side having pitched its demands too high, but not before suggestions had been made of marriages between the English and Spanish royal families, proposals that would be explored in the future. Oñate had dismissed English objections that the government could not afford to go to war as Spain's ally; if England entered the conflict against the Dutch, he said, the king could have a parliament "after his own fashioning," for Philip IV would send "an army of Spanish infantry to frighten them and make them act according to the will of this king."[33]

The abbot Scaglia, another long-time proponent of Anglo-Habsburg friendship, arrived in England in July 1637 on his way from Brussels to Madrid. He was an inveterate intriguer against Richelieu, described as "very welcome and acceptable to this king and government."[34] Scaglia nudged the king to resume talks with the emperor, as did the still-optimistic Taylor in Vienna.[35] From Brussels, center of the migratory colony of anti-Richelieu nobles, came other feelers to England.[36] In July an agent sent from Brussels proposed that England enter a conspiracy against Richelieu that involved the queen of France herself, discontented members of the upper nobility, and Marie de Medici's circle in Brussels.[37] Charles I listened to the plan but shrugged off the invitation to participate. The agent, Monsigot, came to England again in September, pressing the interests of the queen mother and (it was rumored) negotiating for Austria.[38]

These negotiations culminated in a "diversion" of the sort that Richelieu had gloomily predicted. The anti-Richelieu design was exposed, with the result that one of its leaders—Marie de Rohan, duchess of Chevreuse—had to flee France. Richelieu described the whole affair as an effort to prevent the Anglo-French alliance. This was less far-fetched than it might sound, for Marie de Chevreuse had twice before entangled English courtiers and officials in complicated machinations against Richelieu, and both times she had been assisted by Wat Montagu.[39] Whether Montagu had a part in the 1637 conspiracy is not clear, but he had lingered in France over the winter of 1636–37 and may well have renewed old acquaintances. After he returned to England in April 1637, Montagu no longer posed as the friend of the French government that he had played in 1635.[40] Meanwhile, the duchess of Chevreuse had made a romantic escape across the Pyrenees to Spain, and six months later she proceeded to England, where she had long been expected.[41]

Because the Scottish prayer-book crisis developed in the summer of 1637, as Anglo-French relations deteriorated, there has long been speculation whether Richelieu was fomenting trouble in Scotland as early as 1637 or 1638. Until the late summer of 1637, Spain had as much motive, although less opportunity, to encourage distractions at home that might cripple the English abroad.[42] The only evidence of French involvement before 1639 in the British domestic crisis comes from some 1637 letters between Richelieu and one of his diplomatic agents, the comte d'Estrades, the authenticity of which has been questioned.[43] But Richelieu had agents in Scotland trying to arrange troop levies there, and it is altogether probable that they were instructed to find out the political lay of the land. Active encouragement to the Scots would not have been inconsistent with Richelieu's mode of operations, but on the other hand (as Gardiner long ago pointed out) the Scots did not need this external stimulus. As French diplomatic correspondence reveals, the political crisis in Scotland actually frustrated French attempts to draw out the large numbers of mercenaries for which they hoped.

Whether Richelieu was meddling in Scotland may have been less important politically than Charles I's conviction that he was. In the summer of 1637 rumors of French involvement were already circulating at the English court among both foreign observers and English merchants and courtiers. At least one contemporary connected the Scottish troubles with French intentions on Dunkirk that summer.[44] Scudamore and Leicester were repeatedly questioned on the subject by the secretaries of state. The anti-Richelieu faction of French exiles that descended on London in the late 1630s made every effort to sharpen the king's already acute suspicions of Richelieu. Their influence may help explain why Charles clung so tenaciously to his view that the Scottish crisis was a political rebellion disguised in religious garb.

The Fortunes of the Prince Palatine

The conduct of foreign affairs thus disappointed the French party and all the supporters of the prince Palatine in and outside the English court, and this continued to be the case right through 1640. Disappointment was even more keen because of the prince Palatine's presence at the court during much of this time. His maturity and active interest in pursuing his claims, coupled with the Franco-Swedish successes on the Rhine in the late 1630s, reinvigorated both England and foreign supporters of the Protestant international. The electoral family, the Palatinate, and the fate of Bohemia were for them deeply and symbolically important in the struggle for survival of European Protestantism.[45] As the hope for immediate action in conjunction with France and Sweden dwindled in 1637, Charles Lewis pondered alternatives. The death of the Protestant landgrave Wilhelm of Hesse-Cassel opened the possibility of the prince acquiring the Hessian army if financial support could be found, for the Hessian general Melander was sympathetic to the prince and his cause and willing to serve under his command.

Elizabeth of Bohemia wrote urgently to England for the necessary funds, explaining that "all the chiefs are ready to have him, so that he will give them good conditions and show them how they may subsist."[46] The effort to get this army—"10,000 foot and 4 of horse, all good men"—would drag on for eighteen months, frustrated by the failure of funding from England until early in 1639 when France succeeded in the takeover bid long planned by Richelieu.[47]

This period of maneuvering casts light on the young prince's character. As Dame Veronica Wedgwood has observed of his behavior in 1641, the prince "lacked the courage of his ambitions."[48] A young man in his predicament needed "intelligence, unscrupulousness and resolution," and Charles Lewis proved lacking. Even before the landgrave of Hesse died, the French ambassador in England had advised the prince not to wait in London but to join the Hessian service with whatever men and money he could scrape together; he remarked that the prince had not the courage to act on this advice. At the end of 1637, Sir Thomas Roe revealed his impatience more discreetly. He had urged the prince to "do somewhat to be seen in Germany"; by bold action, he might force his uncle's hand. "The prince," he wrote to Elizabeth, "ought to put that to hazard which wisdom cannot always warrant."[49] When Charles Lewis finally did decide to hazard, the results were poor. Wishing to impress the convening Hamburg conference early in 1638, he found a Westphalian rendezvous, gathered English volunteers, raised German troops, and prevailed on his uncle to provide £20,000 for this venture.[50] But the rendezvous was captured by imperialist troops in May 1638.

The prince's supporters did not yet give up hope. Perhaps he would yet prove himself a second Gustavus Adolphus; perhaps the king of England would finally provide him with substantial support. Bernard of Saxe-Weimar's successes against the Habsburgs on the Rhine were encouraging.[51] Charles Lewis continued his levies in England and on the continent, assisted by his councillor Colonel Sir Thomas Ferentz, by Lord Craven, constant benefactor of the Palatine family, and by a Scottish general lent him by the Swedes. There was considerable popular excitement in England and Scotland in the summer of 1638 about the prince's activities; Scottish enthusiasm was running particularly high, and a rumor circulated in the Netherlands to the effect that the Scots, dissatisfied with Charles I, wanted to put the prince Palatine on their throne.[52] A Scottish commander offered the prince eight companies of horse and dragoons and 1,200 soldiers from Scotland. In London there were numerous volunteers for the prince's service.[53] In October Charles Lewis launched his campaign, but it ended in disaster. His army, marching toward the Palatinate, was utterly defeated by Hatzfeld's imperial forces on the river Weser, and Prince Rupert was taken captive.

These discouraging events occurred against a backdrop of continued fruitless negotiations by England. In May 1638 Sir Thomas Roe was sent to Hamburg to treat with the French and Swedes. Neither he nor Elizabeth were as sanguine about the king's commitment to the cause as they had been a year before. Observers sympathetic to Spain were openly skeptical of the mission; Salvetti described Roe as "a man who says a great deal and accomplishes little, and has no gifts except to be a Puritan and an enemy of the house of Austria."[54] Roe had little faith in France and could not offer the Swedes the English subsidies they wanted. In his letters and reports to London, Roe expressed his lasting distrust of France. By all means, let England join France and Sweden in their slow negotiations with the emperor at Lübeck; but once in that treaty, Charles I could form a "league apart" with Denmark, Sweden, the German princes, and the United Provinces in defense of their liberties and Protestant religion. The rest of reformed Europe would surely support this confederation, "which will balance both Spain and France, and all the subtlety of Rome and Italy."[55] Believing that France could not be trusted, Roe thought the long-range security of England as well as the interests of the Palatine family could best be served by a northern European Protestant alliance headed by England.[56]

This notion of a Protestant league was dear to the hearts of the Calvinist international that had developed in the 1620s, of which Roe was a part. Its general staff was provided by Palatine and Bohemian exiles, and its symbol had been Frederick, the prince elector Palatine.[57] The millenarian expectations that surrounded his figure had not been wholly destroyed by his death in 1633. The ultimate restoration of the young prince Palatine was still an important part of the Protestant international program. Meanwhile, attention was attracted by the Transylvanian prince George Rakoczi I (1630–48), whose intervention on the Habsburgs' eastern borders might help free the Protestants from the ambiguities of dependence on Catholic France.[58] These Protestant émigrés, many of them clustered about Elizabeth's court at The Hague, had developed a polemical and millenarian interpretation of the Thirty Years War. According to this, European Protestantism had been threatened since the Council of Trent by a papist conspiracy led by Jesuits in league with Spain.[59] The constitutional corollary to the papist conspiracy was the attempt by the house of Austria to achieve an absolute monarchy in Germany, with the destruction of Bohemian constitutional liberties and estates being held up as a portent for the future.[60]

Sir Thomas Roe and Georg Rudolph Weckherlin, who were the champions of the Palatine family closest to court circles, shared the fiercely anti-Habsburg bias of this group. Roe was very probably the author of an account of the Habsburg destruction of Bohemian liberties and Protestantism published in the 1620s under the title *Bohemiae Regnum Electivum*.[61] His correspondence in the late 1630s (particularly with Weckherlin, to whom he wrote most frankly) shows a continuing preoccupation with Habsburg policy in central Europe. Early in 1639 he sent Weckherlin a printed account of Bohemian news, suggesting that it be circulated in England; later that year he remarked in connection with events in Germany, "thus our religion is on every side, and in every place, assaulted, the public infringed, and there is no refuge." He favored subsidies to Rakoczi and to Bernard of Saxe-Weimar.[62]

In the later 1630s Weckherlin was involved in most of the foreign negotiations of the government, partly because of his linguistic skills and partly because of the increasing age and disability of his superior, Sir John Coke.[63] Weckherlin corresponded tirelessly with his friends in the household of Elizabeth of Bohemia and at the Paris embassy. He was particularly close to Ludwig Camerarius, a chief minister of Elizabeth and a leading propagandist for the Protestant international.[64] In Weck-herlin's diary and in correspondence with friends such as John Dury and Theodore Haak in the late 1630s, his violently anti-Catholic sentiments emerge clearly.[65]

The intersection of the Protestant international—in the persons of Samuel Hartlib, John Dury, and Jan Amos Comenius—with the Long Parliament during 1640–41 was mapped long ago by Hugh Trevor-Roper.[66] But the activities and ideas of these men had been known and supported in England at an earlier date. The Scot John Dury, an ecumenicist and client of Roe, spent the 1630s trying to bring about ecclesiastical unity among the Protestants of northern Europe in preparation for a political anti-Habsburg league.[67] Dury's writings on church union emphasized the subversive character of Jesuit politics and propaganda. He portrayed their cunning attempts to divide and conquer the Protestant world as secret agents in a master plan directed by the pope.[68] Dury's efforts were supported by a number of future leaders of Parliament, including a selection of leading Puritans such as Essex, Brooke, Mandeville, and Pym.[69] His projects were familiar to country Puritans like John Yonge, who reported in 1636 on Dury's work in Sweden and Germany, as well as on the recent creation of an alleged Jesuit army in Europe, formed of the "most barbarous and vilest miscreants that ever have been upon the stage."[70]

Samuel Hartlib, like Dury and Comenius, is best known for his positive ecumenical and educational vision. He had great faith in the *renovatio mundi*, when society would be transformed, Christians united, and learning renewed. But Hartlib, a refugee from the Habsburg takeover of Polish Prussia, also shared with these men a black political view of the Thirty Years War and the assumption that Babylon, in the form of Rome and the Habsburgs, would be overthrown in the *renovatio mundi*. A popularizer of utopian works and a communications center for English, German, and Transylvanian reformers, Hartlib sent out a regular newsletter in 1638–40 to subscribers who included a number of future leaders of the Long Parliament.[71]

The Bohemian refugee philosopher, Jan Amos Comenius, had associations with England that predated 1641; he too had marked anti-Habsburg political views that have attracted relatively little attention but are likely to have interested contemporary Englishmen at least as much as his utopian schemes. In 1636, when there was talk of a parliament being called, there had also been talk of Comenius visiting England, and copies of his works were circulated at the time.[72] His friend and agent in England, the Palatine refugee Theodore Haak, was a fervent supporter of the prince Palatine, as were Comenius himself, Dury, and Hartlib.[73]

Comenius had urged Prince Frederick to continue his struggles in the 1620s and in 1632 wrote a *Historia Persecutione Ecclesiae Bohemicai*, which was designed as a supplement to Foxe's *Book of Martyrs*. The *Historia* applied to the Bohemian situation the apocalyptic tradition in which Rome was portrayed as Babylon and the Jesuits as special agents of anti-Christ.[74]

A distant link between England and Transylvania was provided by Hartlib and two German Calvinist émigrés, John Henry Alsted and John Henry Bisterfeld. Both had attended the synod of Dort, studied in Holland, and formed ties with Dutch reformed leaders. In 1629 Alsted, who was a teacher of Comenius, moved to Transylvania to take a post in theology there at the invitation of Prince Gabriel.[75] Bisterfeld, educated in Holland and England, followed his friend and entered the diplomatic service of Prince George Rakoczi in the 1630s.[76] Rakoczi's reported views of English affairs certainly suggest that his news of England came through Puritan filters, because he is said to have attributed the elevation of Laud to Jesuit strategy and to have expected England to go to war with Spain "should the Puritans be victorious."[77]

Hungarian students went to London to study, where they were welcomed by Hartlib. One of them returned to his home in 1638 with a copy of a chiliastic work by the English Puritan John Stoughton, *Felicitas Ultimi Saeculi*, and a letter from Stoughton to Rakoczi. Stoughton's work alluded frequently to the lion symbolism associated with the Palatine house and praised the activities of Dury and Comenius as heralding the start of a new world era.[78]

On a wider front, too, there were intellectual contacts between English Puritan writers and their European counterparts. The real flowering of English millenarian publication would come after the beginning of the Long Parliament, but there was already an element in the thinking of English reformers that could respond to the European tradition and interpret English politics within the millenarian context.[79] John Napier's *Plaine Discovery of the whole Revelation of St. John* had identified 1639 as the year when a new trumpet would sound to usher in the final warfare between good and evil. John Brightman, whose works would be reissued in popular form in 1641, had depicted the Church of England as Laodicean but capable of renewal and of playing the role of elect nation in leading the *renovatio mundi*. In his 1628 publications Alexander Leighton had painted an even sharper picture of the foreign and domestic dangers facing England, whose church was falling into a Laodicean slumber and whose mission as leader of European Protestantism was being neglected. England should beware lest pope, emperor, and Jesuits triumph in their long-held plans of conquest.[80] The *Clavis Apocalyptica* of

Joseph Mede was influenced by the millenarian ideas of Alsted and reflected deep concern over the war in Europe; Mede's works also would appear in English translation in the early 1640s, but even before that he had helped to make millenarian ideas respectable among English scholars.[81] In the 1620s and 1630s, Henry Burton repeatedly appealed to images of Laodicea (or, as in *Israel's Fast* of 1628, of Achan hiding the Babylonish garment and bringing down God's wrath) to condemn the torpor of the Church of England, which failed to heed the warnings provided by the Thirty Years War; only by vigilance could England escape the Jesuitical plot of world dominion.

This international coterie tried to keep alive in England throughout the 1630s the conviction that the fates of English Protestantism and continental Protestantism were mutually dependent. For them and the Englishmen to whom their ideas appealed, the failure of Charles I to support more vigorously the interests of the prince Palatine suggested the work of anti-Protestant agents at the court. One of the articles of impeachment later presented against Laud by the Long Parliament would be the charge that he had attempted to "cause a division" between the English church and other reformed churches, thus advancing the cause of popery. Laud's indifference to Dury's work and the king's tepid concern for his nephew's fate provided part of the background for this accusation. The suspicion had developed that Spanish-Jesuit-Habsburg intrigue had frustrated the hopes entertained for the Palatine family.

There were a number of men in the court who were sympathetic to the Palatine cause and were also in a position to observe the diplomatic evolution of 1635–38: Roe, Weckherlin, Coke, Leicester, and Northumberland, among others.[82] Before the Long Parliament convened, their interpretation of events would be assisted by information provided by the French ambassadors, who had every reason to nourish English suspicion of Spain. In fact, the court had been invaded by the friends of Spain in 1637–39, and the court Catholics, now a more "Spaniolized" group than in the earlier years of the reign, had played a role in nudging England back to its traditional role of aiding and abetting the Habsburgs.

The "Spaniolization" of the Court Catholic Party

The presence of an active and successful papal agent at the English court in the late 1630s and the influx of foreign friends of Spain, both occurring at a time when Spain's interests drew her to seek closer cooperation from England and when the English king's interests tempted him to ask favors from Spain, created a picture that was compelling and frightening to many Englishmen. But each of these various parties had its own interests, and their priorities were quite different. George Con was attempting to advance British Catholicism and realize his own ambitions; for these purposes, Spain's support could be useful but might also prove ambiguous. Most of the foreign friends of Spain who descended on the English court were more intent on dislodging Richelieu than on permanently benefiting Spain; their interest in British Catholicism was peripheral and political. The governments of Madrid and Brussels did not always see eye-to-eye with each other, or with Vienna, and they found the French exiles' scheming of quite limited utility. Of far more urgency and importance was perpetuating, and if possible expanding, the protection and support services offered by England. Total political domination of England, if it could be cheaply achieved, might be the best insurance; the proposed loan of soldiers to Charles I to enable him to control his own subjects seems to have been conceived in this spirit. That Spain's few friends at the English court itself were almost all Catholic was natural, but the interests of British Catholicism took a decidedly second place in Spanish calculations to the importance of conserving the friendship of Charles I. That even fewer of these English Catholics would have regarded Spanish political domination with equanimity is not surprising; the outlook of a colonial power is seldom understood by its overseas admirers until too late. To conclude this survey of actors and motives, Charles I was not pursuing the interests of either Spain or Catholicism, but of himself; if, in this pursuit, he took help wherever it seemed available, this only proved that he was a European monarch of his day.

As it was in the interest of each of these parties (or so it seemed to each, for different reasons) to conceal their actual divergence of interests and present an appearance of closer cooperation than they in fact enjoyed, it is not surprising that Catholic and Spanish influences on policy were drawn larger than life, that their degree of solidarity was exaggerated, and that the control of England could be seen as the central focus of their ambition. Whether or not George Con violated the professions of neutrality between the Catholic powers that he maintained in his reports to Rome, he did become identified both at court and in the country with Spanish interests. His letters confirm that he had frequent lengthy conferences with the Spanish agents, although we are left in the dark as to the subject of their talks, and that these became a source of embarrassment for him, which he had to excuse to the queen. There were uncomplimentary mutterings about London that he was only an "agent of Spain."[83] Little as we know of any interventions he made or advice he gave the king on foreign affairs, Con does seem to have been kept well informed on the subject. Not only did the king and earl of Arundel enjoy discussions on such subjects with a man of his cosmopolitan experience, but additional information came through the countess of Arundel, who made a point of cultivating Windebank as a source.[84] Foreign agents at the court who thought Con's intimacy with the king might make him useful courted him, so he gathered tidbits also from French, imperial, and Venetian envoys.

At the same time, the phalanx of Catholics and crypto-Catholics around the court, whom Con was trying to mold into a party, turned away from the French-oriented group of the early and middle 1630s and acquired a far more Spanish hue. The reappearance of Sir Toby Mathew at court and the rapprochement between Windebank and the queen both contributed to this effect, as did the shift in Montagu's orientation. Montagu had always had contacts with the anti-Richelieu forces as well as with the French government; now the former regained ascendancy.[85] It was during 1638 that Montagu began to harbor his own ambitions for the cardinalate; and this may have suggested to him, as to Con, the wisdom of avoiding identification with a single national interest.

The arrival of distinguished French exiles, opponents of Richelieu and therefore intriguers with Spain, also accentuated the Spanish aspect of the English court in 1638–39. The duchess of Chevreuse arrived in May 1638 to visit the queen, with whom she had long been friendly. She accompanied the new Spanish agent, Alonso de Cárdenas, who had instructions to assist her efforts to gain troop levies for the house of Lorraine.[86] Related to or allied with almost every noble opponent of Richelieu, Marie de Rohan—Huguenot by birth, Guise by marriage, both Anglophile and Hispanophile in sympathy—represented both a social phenomenon and a policy. Plot and conspiracy, coup and countercoup, succeeded one another in the France of Richelieu and Mazarin. Often dismissed as reactionary, self-interested, and concerned solely with personalities, these noble revolts in fact represented a real alternative policy for France in the 1630s, namely, opposition to the war with Spain and to its domestic consequences.[87] Marie de Chevreuse, like other French exiles who found refuge at the court of Charles I, represented this party and this policy. By their active advancement of Spanish interests with the English government, they contributed to thwarting the ambitions of the French party and the "parliamentarians."[88] At the same time, they epitomized the world of aristocratic faction and conspiracy that (in its pro-Spanish manifestations at least) so frightened the English Protestant public.

The duchess arrived from Spain, where she had fled after the collapse of her intrigue with Anne of Austria the summer before. In Spain she had been offered a warm welcome, a pension, and political conversation with

Olivares. She brought to England gifts for the royal family from that of Spain and renewed offers of marriage between the royal houses. The queen loaned her £4,000 to set up her household in London, and Charles I provided her with a pension of 200 guineas a week.[89] She formed a working association with the Spanish resident, Cárdenas, and became effectively a second representative of Spain in England.[90] The pace of negotiations, carried on concurrently in Brussels, London, and Madrid, quickened.[91]

Six months earlier the Spanish ambassador in England had proposed that serious Anglo-Spanish negotiations be transferred to Brussels where (so he claimed) the Cardinal Infante had full powers to treat. From Brussels, the princess Phalzburg[92] had long been urging that Charles I use her as an intermediary to negotiate the exchange of the Palatinate for the restitution of the house of Lorraine, to which she belonged. This treaty at Brussels was under way by the summer of 1638 and did nothing to help Sir Thomas Roe in his Hamburg negotiations. Rumors of the Brussels talks spread by the autumn of 1638, much to the discomfiture of Elizabeth of Bohemia. Cárdenas wrote about them from London to his counterpart at the imperial court, where the English agent John Taylor clumsily allowed the news to become public and found himself called home in disgrace.[93] But the damage had been done.

The French were naturally alarmed at these developments. In March 1638, attempting to placate Henrietta Maria, Richelieu had finally granted her request for the release of her favorite, the chevalier de Jars, who had been imprisoned for conspiring against Richelieu in the early 1630s.[94] But this long-delayed gesture had no positive effect. Madame de Chevreuse had resumed her intimacy with Henrietta Maria and with the powerful countess of Carlisle;[95] she was offered special privileges at court, while the French ambassador found himself out of favor. He insisted that his wife be granted the privileges enjoyed by the duchess in the queen's court—the *tabouret*, the right to sit in the queen's presence. Refused this, he made sure that Leicester's wife in Paris was deprived of equivalent honors.[96] Relations between France and England thus became more strained than they had been for over two years. The French ambassador in England and the English ambassador in France both retired disgruntled from the courts to which they were accredited, and negotiations between the two powers came to an end.

Madame de Chevreuse had quickly gathered about her in London a group of French émigrés with similar views. Through her renewed friendship with Wat Montagu and her cultivation of the queen's confessor, Father Philip, she helped to draw both of these courtiers firmly out of the French orbit.[97] Henceforth, the French government would be consistently hostile to both these men. Richelieu made fruitless efforts in 1638 and 1639 to lure the duchess back to France, or at least away from England.[98]

Madame de Chevreuse drew into her circle not only Montagu but also Con, who hoped to use her to further the Catholicization of the court. He was pleased, while the king was annoyed, that she took the Princess Mary to mass. Ultimately, he was to find her more troublesome than useful; but the identification between the papal agent and the most flamboyant of the Spanish party had already been made.[99] Under Marie de Chevreuse's influence, and perhaps that of Montagu as well, the queen invited her mother, Marie de Medici, to visit England.[100] The queen mother, as she was aptly called (for she was the mother not only of the queen of England and the king of France, but also of the queen of Spain and of the princess of Savoy), had languished abroad since her final unsuccessful power struggle with Richelieu in 1631.

Marie de Medici's descent on England in mid-October 1638, trailing dozens of impecunious courtiers of various nationalities in her wake, was not unexpected. Indeed, it had long been dreaded.[101] The king, who had not wanted her to come, was softened by his wife's entreaties and by his customary concern for the proprieties; unable to stop her on the other side of the Channel, he allotted her £100 a day for her household and allowed his wife to spend £3,000 in redecorating St. James's Palace for her mother's use. Even Laud, whose attachment to the Palatine family was feeble and formal, contrasted her reception with the exiguous support being offered the prince Palatine. He wrote to Roe, "I pray God her coming do not spend the King more than . . . would content the Swedes."[102] Marie de Medici's entry into London was greeted with a magnificent display of fireworks, and by terrible storms and floods that unsympathetic Londoners dubbed "queen mother's weather." Worse omens accompanied her, too, for news of the prince Palatine's disastrous defeat reached England just as the queen mother arrived.[103]

Richelieu was unhappy about the queen mother's move to England and had warned Charles against receiving her.[104] In Flanders her incessant intriguing had been dangerous, but there she was also discredited by living on the bounty of France's enemies. In England she would be better placed to embarrass the French government into permitting her return to France, the last thing Richelieu wanted.

The queen mother constituted an uncompromising Catholic presence at the English court, taking one of the Palatine princesses to mass with her[105] and opening her own chapel in St. James's Palace that was served by her Jesuit confessor and as well provided as that of the queen.[106] This highly visible Catholicism accorded with the *dévot* politics that the queen mother had supported in France and answered her current objectives.

After twenty-three years of childless marriage between Louis XIII and Anne of Austria, the birth of a Dauphin in France had opened the possibility of a regency. Convinced that her son had not long to live, Marie de Medici was ambitious to regain power at his death, when it might be hoped that Richelieu would fall. As she waited, she maneuvered to put herself in the best possible light. A *dévot* image was a useful weapon to use against Richelieu's Protestant alliances. The pope might be induced, moreover, to support her readmission to France; in any case, her courtiers (especially those from Tuscany) needed favors from the papal court.[107]

It was therefore not surprising that the queen mother made herself agreeable to George Con. He initially had little good to say about her or her entourage, but seems to have been gradually won over by her extreme respect, her outward piety, and by instructions from Rome to treat her well.[108] Marie further associated Con and the queen's court with a Mediterranean version of Catholicism. From the beginning, the English had viewed her arrival with a trepidation that was grounded in fears for foreign policy and religion. She was seen as too Spanish as well as too expensive; and it was murmured that her coming would facilitate major religious changes. Since Richelieu stood firm against her entreaties to return to France, even when supported by those of Henrietta Maria (who sent Henry Jermyn on a special mission to Paris for her mother), both queens maintained an anti-Richelieu stance.[109] The presence of other prominent opponents of Richelieu at the English court during this period, La Vieuville and La Vallette, added to the significance of the group and made London a center for intrigue against France.[110]

Conclusion

The summer and autumn of 1638 thus marked a turning point in the atmosphere of the court and in outside perceptions of it, as well as in the progress of the continental war. For several years after the deaths of Gustavus Adolphus and Prince Frederick, English pamphleteering on the European conflict had waned, but the prince Palatine's visit to England and Arundel's mission to Vienna coincided with and probably stimulated a revival of publishing on the war. The relatively straightforward *Swedish Intelligencer* was joined in 1636–38 by more sensational pieces emphasizing the horrors of the war in Germany. By 1638 these pieces began to develop the theme that England should take warning from the German example, repent, and nurture piety, lest God's punishment fall on her as well.[111] But neither at home nor abroad could it seem to the zealous Protestant that England was playing the role of Protestant champion or

Protestant model. She had failed to aid the prince Palatine, whose fortunes would subsequently worsen despite a few nods in his direction from the English government.[112] With the arrival of Marie de Chevreuse, followed by the queen mother and other exiles, the court shifted to a more Spanish orientation as negotiations with Spain were renewed and relations with France worsened. Meanwhile, Con's increasing influence had accentuated the Catholic character of the court at the same time that the king was adopting, partly on Con's advice, a series of Catholic party strategies to cope with the gathering Scottish crisis.

In 1638 only a small number of zealots outside the court voiced generalized fears of popish conspiracy that connected the various elements described above. The paucity of politically interesting correspondence from the Puritan Providence Island group (possibly due to the destruction of documents during government raids in 1639 and 1640) forces us to infer their reactions from their subsequent comments and from ambassadorial reports that are often vague and impossible to corroborate. Gentry correspondence before the latter part of 1639 is, for the most part, very restrained in political comment. Whether this is due to destruction of material, prudence of expression, a sense that political initiative was the business of the king and greater nobility, or simply a lack of anxiety about the court is difficult to say. Even in 1640–42 it proved difficult for many of the gentry to accept the radical critique of the court that a popish conspiracy theory represented.

Among those in a position to follow foreign policy within the court, we may suspect a developing uneasiness on the part of men like Coke and Weckherlin, who were animated by antipopery and anti-Habsburg fervor. Friends of France like Leicester and Northumberland, whose hopes for advancement would be revived and then dashed with Wentworth's accession to power in late 1639, were not yet speaking of conspiracy, but with the development of the Scottish crisis they would begin to do so. Their more radical allies, who came to accept the popish conspiracy explanation of the personal rule and the radical critique of the court that it implied, would rewrite the history of the years 1637–40 retrospectively, in the series of parliamentary documents that signpost the road to civil war.

5. The Catholics and the Scottish Crisis

he crisis that ended the personal rule developed in Scotland as a result of the king's attempt to impose a new version of the prayer book on the Scottish church, a prayer book closer in content to that of the Church of England. The Scots, who were accustomed to a service more shorn of "remnants of popery" than the English church liturgy, immediately protested that the new prayer book was little better than a popish Mass. Nobles and clergy began to organize a campaign of protest and resistance that came to a head in February 1638 with the adoption of a national "Covenant" or oath for the protection and further reformation of the Scottish church.

The Scottish protesters early began a vigorous campaign of propaganda, issuing declarations and explanations of their actions, many of which were directed to rallying English support for their cause.[1] In their publications, they depicted the dispute as a central episode in the holy war between Catholicism and the reformed religion. Over the several years before the meeting of the Long Parliament in November 1640, this propaganda persuaded a widening segment of the English public that the policies of the 1630s, especially those from 1637 to 1640, reflected the workings of a Catholic conspiracy that aimed at the conquest and re-Catholicization of the British Isles.[2] The theme of crusading antipopery in the Scottish response to the new prayer book is sometimes dismissed as either paranoid or transparently hypocritical. But if one considers Con's attitude toward the crisis, his attempts to influence the king's Scottish policy, and the way Charles I actually responded to the situation, the Covenanters' suspicions about Catholic influences on royal policy look more reasonable.

As the political crisis in Scotland developed from the middle of 1637, Con perceived the opportunity for which he had been waiting. He would draw the king—and the "Puritans" of England and Scotland would force him—into dependence on a Catholic party in England, Scotland, and Ireland, a party that might possibly be reinforced by foreign Catholic aid.[3] In exchange for this support, the king (even if unwilling to follow the example of Henry IV of France and himself convert to Catholicism) would have to grant a measure of religious toleration to his Catholic subjects. Charles I never granted the concessions for which Con hoped, but he proved willing enough to turn to his Catholic subjects for help; in so doing, he strengthened suspicions that would ultimately prove fatal to him.

It is difficult to reconstruct the king's response to the Scottish troubles in the crucial first year when he unwisely committed himself to a policy of forceful repression of the Scots.[4] Apparently inattentive in the early months to his councillors' warnings that law and order were seriously threatened, he failed to sanction or make provision for the use of force. At the same time, he maintained a characteristically authoritarian tone in his pronouncements and refused any alteration or compromise in his policy. His later statements suggest that he saw a relatively small number of conspirators in back of the northern troubles, and the prominence of Lord Balmerino in the events of 1637 may have confirmed his view; four years earlier, Balmerino had been tried for treason for protests against royal policy.

From an early point, the king was persuaded that French intrigue was an element in the Scottish turmoil,[5] and he persisted in this belief despite the absence of any information to support it. If indeed the king's view of the Scottish protesters was modeled to any degree on what he knew of the character and activities of the French exiles then congregating at his court, his response becomes more comprehensible—dismissal of the alleged issues of principle involved, resort to threats of force, some efforts at bribery of individuals, and dependence on support from any quarter where it was available, without ideological tests.

Scottish Catholicism and the "Holy War"

The Scottish preoccupation with popish plotting was certainly not based on the numerical strength of Scottish Catholicism, the weakness of which could be, and has been, cited by those who would dismiss Scottish fears.[6] Numerically the Catholics were probably less than one percent of the Scottish population. As in England, the survival of Catholicism depended on the support of the aristocracy, but the fate of Catholicism in Scotland suggests that the assistance of the crown was also crucial. With the court far off in London and the Scottish privy council unwilling to intervene, the relentless anti-Catholic propaganda of the kirk, which was both more powerful and more rabidly anti-Catholic than the official Church of England, went virtually unchecked. The kirk was willing and able to excommunicate peers of the realm, banish lairds, confiscate estates, and generally make life intolerable even for aristocratic Catholics.

Neither the papacy nor the European Catholic powers (save for occasional gestures by France) provided much assistance. During the Spanish and French marriage negotiations of the 1620s, the ambassadors of those powers had intervened occasionally, but the relief provided was short-lived. Rome knew little and cared less about Scotland, and had left both the government and the finances of the Scottish church in utter confusion. As in England, these conditions had worked to the relative advantage of the Jesuit mission that reentered the country in 1617.[7] But no group of Catholic clergy enjoyed much influence or security in Scotland; even the Jesuits complained constantly of poverty. There were never more than twenty missionary priests in Scotland at any one time before 1640; there were sometimes as few as five. They clustered in the lowlands and in Aberdeen where a few noble patrons supported them. In the highlands, much of which remained semipagan and untended by either Protestant or Catholic pastors, Catholicism languished more from the absence of clergy than from actual persecution.

The strongholds of the Catholic peers were islands in a sea of Calvinism; many aristocrats were exiles in northern England, in London, or on the continent. In the 1630s the lowland Catholic magnate families were Douglas, Maxwell of Nithsdale, Hamilton of Abercorn, Seton of Winton, and Semple.[8] Insofar as any of these figures was influential outside a restricted territorial and familial circle, it was because of court contacts. The landed power of the Douglas family was not great; and, perhaps because of its Catholicism, it had few clients or political adherents. The earl of Abercorn, head of the junior branch of the Hamilton clan, was a relative of Sir William Hamilton, the queen's agent at Rome. Deeply in debt, Abercorn had, like Douglas, lost touch with Scotland during long absences abroad.[9] The Setons of Winton, who were a courtier family, had great wealth but little influence in the countryside.[10] The Semples of the western lowlands had a traditional association with Spain and with the Jesuit order.[11] Only the Maxwells of Nithsdale, strengthened by the junior Herries branch of their clan, by hordes of Catholic dependents, and by possession of the great fortress of Carlaverock on Solway Firth, had a firm territorial base.[12]

At court, however, Scottish Catholics were a highly visible group, prominent out of all proportion to their weakness in the country. Catholic nobles were attracted to the court by the same lures of pensions and perquisites that drew other Scottish aristocrats. They were also pushed there by the aggressive interference of the kirk in their affairs. Douglas, Nithsdale, and Abercorn had played a major role in the diplomatic initiative to Rome. Surrounded by lesser Catholic satellites like Roxborough, Ruthven, and Crawford, and acting in conjunction with Protestant lords, these courtiers would play a loyalist role in the Scottish crisis and a royalist one in the subsequent civil war. English propaganda, even more than Scottish, would associate this courtier group, with its relatively high profile, with the origins of the Scottish troubles.[13] A number of Scottish priests also moved in court circles and around London. Father Robert Philip, the queen's confessor, was the most important figure. Others included William Thomson, O.F.M., one of the queen's chaplains; the Minims Maitland and Browne; and William Pendryck, a Carmelite whose brother Robert was secretary to Hamilton in Rome.

The Covenanters' propaganda seized upon the role played by these Scottish Catholics in the crisis of 1637–40, but the Scottish obsession with Catholic conspiracy was of long standing. Indeed, the apocalyptic vision of the early Covenanters and the strong Covenant tradition on which they drew (both of which had antipopery as an almost automatic corollary) have been so convincingly presented by Professor Sidney Burrell[14] as to risk deflecting our attention from the actual activities of Scottish Catholics during these years. Convinced that their church was the purest in Europe, Scottish Calvinists regarded English practice as corrupt. John Knox had proclaimed that "we (all praise to God alone) have nothing within our churches that ever flowed from that Man of Sin." The Covenant of 1638 belonged to a self-consciously anti-Catholic tradition; it was modeled on the Negative Confession of 1581 that had been directed against the influence of the court Catholic lords on the young James VI.[15]

Court Catholicism had aroused Scottish alarm early in the 1630s. The king's Scottish coronation in 1633, the occasion for his first visit to that kingdom, coincided with measures for church reorganization that were labeled "popish" by some. Protest against these ecclesiastical changes led to a treason case against Lord Balmerino; his condemnation hardened resentment and suspicions in Scotland about the Laudian regime.[16]

That the Covenanters branded the new prayer book as "popish" therefore surprised no one except the king. As early as 1637 he had been advised of the genuine fears in Scotland that he would change the religion of his kingdoms. From general allegations of popishness in the prayer book, the Covenanters moved to specific accusations that it had been composed in part by Catholics. Lamenting the warm welcome Con had received in England, they murmured that the agent had brought the prayer book with him from Rome. The king responded by declarations and proclamations to the effect that he remained firmly committed to the Protestant faith; these failed to convince the Scots.[17]

The holy-war aspect of the movement impressed observers and suggested that the crisis would be difficult to resolve. Traquair, the treasurer of Scotland, reported to London that it would be as easy to introduce the Catholic missal in Scotland as the new service book.[18] Scottish Catholics regarded the Covenanting movement as anti-Catholic in its essence. Reports from Jesuits in Scotland emphasized the "madness and hatred of the Puritans against the Catholics [that] grow fiercer every day, and many whole families of Catholics have been compelled to seek a refuge in England." In fact, the reaction against the prayer book provoked a new phase of persecution for Scottish Catholics that would last through the 1640s.[19]

The Role of George Con

Con, too, regarded the Covenanting movement as an anti-Catholic crusade. During the early part of his mission, he had not paid much attention to Scottish affairs; but as the king began to take the northern furor seriously in the autumn of 1637, Con also began to recognize the potential of this crisis.[20] From then on he tried to influence the king's policy toward Scotland, endeavoring both to shape the king's general attitude to the troubles and to suggest specific tactics. Con's eagerness to be involved and his outspokenness left an impression that was only heightened by the king's refusal to discuss the Scottish crisis in the privy council before July 1638. For many months, as the king continued his consultations with Con, the councillors complained that they were left uninformed and unconsulted.[21]

Even before the signing of the Covenant in February 1638, Con had adopted the approach that he would henceforth press upon the king at every opportunity.[22] Urged by the earl of Stirling to persuade the king of the wisdom of a policy of appeasement, Con took exactly the opposite line. He portrayed the Scottish troubles as but one incident in the international Calvinist conspiracy, subversive to both temporal and spiritual authority. At the same time, he cast doubt on the sincerity of the Covenanters' professed religious sentiments. Privately he must have remembered the orthodox polemical point that heretics, by definition, could not be sincere, for the pride at the root of their heresy perverted all their values. Aloud he argued that this rebellion was the product of greed and ambition cloaked by religion.

Con hoped to use the crisis to the advantage of the Catholics, as did Barberini, who showered him with advice ranging from the dangerous to the merely ridiculous. Con therefore lost no opportunity to contrast Catholic loyalty with the treachery of the Covenanters and their supposed well-wishers, the English Puritans. Urging the king to reward Catholic loyalty by relieving Catholic disabilities, Con implied that Rome might provide concrete assistance in return. He repeatedly put the Scottish crisis into an international context, harping on the possibility of foreign intervention in Scotland, something that already worried Charles I. He first accused the Protestant Dutch and Swedes, then fed the king's fears that France was fishing in muddy waters and awaiting an opportunity, should the king become engaged in the north, to swoop down upon the unprotected southern coast of England. The pope's authority, Con assured the king, might restrain the Catholic powers from any intervention and might even secure foreign military assistance against the Scots.

In addition to protection, Con hoped to extract power for the Catholics from the Scottish crisis. This emerges vividly from his letters to Rome, in which he emphasized the opportunity for the advancement of Catholicism in the British Isles and urged that his own promotion be no longer delayed. With strong leadership, the Catholics of Britain would be able to take a less defensive posture; united they could offer invaluable support to the king, who would come to depend on them. In his conversations with the king, Con made positive proposals for military and political use of Catholic groups in the Scottish crisis. By June 1638 he reported that the king seemed ready to rearm the Catholics, who had been legally forbidden to bear arms since the reign of Elizabeth.

During the next twelve months, Con and the court Catholic party were involved in several schemes for Catholic military or financial aid to the king. Con did not mastermind all these schemes, but he did support them, and his attitude from the beginning of the crisis encouraged them. In the First Bishops' War of 1639, three Catholic groups—Scottish, Irish, and English—would play a role. Each of these projects was launched with royal support by the early summer of 1638, before Charles had consulted his own privy council about the Scottish crisis and before he had drawn up plans for a general English military expedition. Thus, at the moment when the English political nation first became aware of the gravity of the northern crisis, it looked very much as though the king were forming a Catholic party, as Con had suggested, to oppose the Scottish Protestants.

This was also the way it looked to the Scots, who learned of these projects from the marquis of Hamilton, who was sent to negotiate with them on the king's behalf. Con was already well acquainted with Hamilton, who was the king's emissary to Scotland from the beginning of serious negotiations in May 1638 until their collapse in early 1639. A courtier Scot and a close relative of the king, Hamilton had married into the Villiers connection and patronized his Catholic as well as his Protestant relations.[23] He told Con that if the king were Catholic, he would serve him just as willingly.[24] He was thus far removed socially and mentally from figures like the younger Argyll, who were country Scottish and zealously Protestant.

During 1638 Con cultivated Hamilton, hoping, with his support, to convince the king to grant liberty of conscience to Scottish Catholics. Unsuccessful in that, he nonetheless won Hamilton to his own point of view on the Scottish crisis and received regular reports during Hamilton's two missions to the northern kingdom in 1638. Hamilton decided at an early date that a show (or more) of force would be needed to bring the Covenanters into line.[25] During his first trip north in the summer of 1638, Hamilton warned the Covenanters (presumably on the king's instructions) that if they did not accept the king's offers, they would be "threatened with an Irish army on the West, [and] by all the power three marquesses in Scotland and the popish party can make with the help of the north of England." Subsequently he warned them of "the readiness of the King's army to set upon [the Covenanters] with 10,000 land soldiers well-trained" and the "readiness of a Spanish army in West Flanders to be employed where the king would direct."[26]

These were allusions to plans to use Catholic forces from Ireland, Scotland, England, and the continent to restore the king's authority in Scotland, plans that were being nurtured by Con and the court Catholic party during the summer and autumn of 1638 and would be either adopted or attempted by the king in the spring of 1639. These projects, and the related efforts to raise funds for the king from the English Catholics and from the pope, are worth closer examination, for they provide the circumstantial background and stimulus for Long Parliament investigations into Catholic plotting.

Scottish and Irish Forces

The Scottish plan involved all the great lowland Catholic families—Douglas, Maxwell of Nithsdale, Hamilton of Abercorn, Herries, Seton of Winton, and Semple—reinforced by Huntley and the northern clans.[27] The scheme seems to have begun at court with Robert Maxwell, tenth earl of Nithsdale, who remained its strongest supporter. By April 1638 Con had persuaded the queen that Nithsdale must be used in any military action that developed in Scotland. As Hamilton negotiated in the north, Nithsdale circulated a letter for subscription among the Scottish Catholics at court, professing their fidelity to the king. At the same time, the Catholic nobles within Scotland were making preparations, whether as part of the project or in fear at the temper of the Covenanting movement is difficult to say. Baillie reported in April that "Douglas, Abercorn, Semple are openly arming among us; readily after their example other noblemen will provide presently their houses with musquet, picks, powder and lead."[28]

But the situation for Catholics within Scotland was rapidly worsening. They were more and more identified with royal policy. Baillie reported that a number of lords, mainly Catholic (he mentioned Abercorn, Winton, Herries, and Huntley), were expected to appear armed at Edinburgh to "encourage" other Scots to accommodation when Hamilton arrived there. Some, such as Abercorn, were forced to flee to England, and pressure was brought to bear upon Douglas and others who remained to sign the Covenant. In exchange they were apparently offered private assurances of religious toleration. Refusing this, Douglas wrote the king for a new grant of protection for his family; but such a document no longer meant anything in Scotland, and Douglas too soon found himself in London.[29]

In consultation with the Catholic nobles exiled in London, Con planned a military strategy. He persuaded the king that Nithsdale should be permitted to arm and play an active role in the upcoming military action. He nurtured the friendship between Douglas and Nithsdale, natural leaders of the Scottish Catholic party. The three men were constantly in conference during the autumn of 1638, and at Con's urging the king decided to send both Douglas and Nithsdale back to Scotland to rally their followers to sign the "king's covenant" that Hamilton had (so far unsuccessfully) proclaimed. In November they left for the north. Wentworth, hearing of the project, approved it; he thought that with Carlaverock and Dunbarton secured, the western lowlands might be held for the king.[30]

In Ireland, much to Wentworth's dismay, similarly ambitious plans were being laid. Behind the "army in the west" to which Baillie had referred, the moving spirit was Randal, second earl of Antrim, chief of the fervently Catholic McDonnell-MacDonald clan. Married to Buckingham's widow, Antrim enjoyed the favor of both king and queen. He had come to court in mid-1637 just as the Scottish crisis was developing. He presented his plan at the beginning of 1638; he was to take an army of his Ulster clansmen, of whom he claimed he could raise 10,000, across to Scotland, where he would rally his kinsmen in the western islands and highlands for the king. It was a self-serving plan, intended to expel the Campbell clan (whose chief, the new earl of Argyll, was a leading Covenanter) from disputed land in Kintyre. But it also took on definite religious overtones from the contrast between the crusading Catholicism of Antrim and the Covenanter convictions of Archibald, eighth earl of Ar-

gyll. The flamboyance of Antrim and the daring of his plan at first startled
Con, who did not immediately respond to the proposal.[31]

Hamilton, however, was won over to the project, pressed it upon the
king, and used it to threaten the Scots. The effect was to push the young
Archibald Campbell into the arms of the Covenanters just as he was
about to succeed his father as earl of Argyll.[32] He rapidly became their
acknowledged lay leader. Throughout the summer and autumn of 1638,
Wentworth corresponded with the young nobleman, who warned him
that the MacDonalds in western Scotland were communicating with their
kin in Ulster and also those overseas in Spanish service. Chided by the
deputy for his failure to support the king against the Covenanters, Campbell replied that favor to popery was incompatible with loyalty to the
king; the Covenanters, he maintained, were defending true religion. Convinced by the king's support for Antrim's project that he was to be
robbed of his birthright in favor of a papist, Campbell was lost to the
king's cause by the time he succeeded to his father's title. He began to
arm his men and fortify his territory.[33]

Wentworth opposed Antrim's project from the start, but to no avail;
not only Hamilton but Archbishop Laud had prevailed on the king to
give Antrim his blessing. Antrim's assurance that his invasion force would
cost the king nothing must have assisted his cause. In September 1638
Antrim and his duchess embarked for Ireland to get operations under
way. Wentworth, however, did not abandon his resistance to the scheme.
He pointed out that Antrim was the grandson of Hugh O'Neill, great earl
of Tyrone, who had kept Ireland in turmoil throughout the 1590s; that
his relations were mercenary soldiers in the employ of Spain; that he
probably intended to call in those relatives in Flanders for his expedition.
The Irish regiments in Flanders also contained Scottish MacDonalds,
who were reported as saying that they had been "sent for by their friends
who say they shall presently have need of them." Arms provided to
Antrim's men might be used against the Dublin government if the "contagion of rebellion" spread from Scotland to Ireland. This was no fantasy
on Wentworth's part; Sir Arthur Hopton was reporting to him from
Spain that Tyrone and Tyrconnell were urged by friends in Scotland to
create a diversion under cover of Antrim's expedition. Even if Antrim
were loyal, Wentworth believed him to be motivated mainly by self-
interest and doubted his ability to raise the men and arms he needed
without financial assistance from the crown. These objections, raised in a
series of letters from Wentworth to London in late 1638, were overridden
by the king, who ordered his deputy to arm Antrim's men and to assist
him in any way required.[34]

The King's "Popish Army"

When the English referred to the king's forces of 1639 as "popish" (the phrase predated the outbreak of the civil war and was used to describe the forces of 1639 and 1640),[35] they were not thinking primarily either of the Scottish Catholic peers or of Antrim's Irish clans. They were referring to the English and Welsh forces that marched north with the king to York, then on to Newcastle and Berwick-on-Tweed, and to the force carried north in Hamilton's ships to the Firth of Forth. The general of these forces in 1639 was the earl of Arundel, upon whom the English suspicions centered.

The secrecy shrouding the Scottish negotiations during much of 1638 had created uneasiness at court. Charles did not consult the privy council on Scottish policy until the end of June 1638, when he formed a junta consisting of Arundel, Cottington, Windebank, Coke, Northumberland, and Vane to handle Scottish affairs. The three crypto-Catholics (Arundel, Cottington, and Windebank) immediately adopted an aggressive military approach toward the Covenanters, whereas Coke, Vane, and Northumberland counseled compromise. The military approach prevailed with the king; as early as 9 June he contemplated the appointment of Arundel as general of a land force to be sent north, an appointment that Con warmly supported.[36]

The king's choice of Arundel as commander is difficult to explain. Clarendon described the earl as a man who was martial only in his demeanor, an assessment corroborated by his conduct as a general in 1639. But the king may have hoped that Arundel's rank as a member of the ancient nobility and the premier peer of the realm would evoke support from the nobility and prevent squabbles about precedence and prestige in the northern force, which was drawn largely from aristocratic volunteers.[37] Nor was Arundel merely a figurehead. In July 1638 Arundel was sent north to inspect border fortifications and review available troops in the area. He was one of the six lords-lieutenant of the three border counties and owed these northern lieutenancies (he also had three in the south) to the extensive Howard landholdings there. Arundel toured the garrisons at Berwick and Carlisle; he then stopped off to visit his Catholic uncle, Lord William Howard of Naworth, a substantial Cumberland landowner who was not only permitted but instructed to arm for the defense of the border.[38]

In succeeding months of the winter of 1638–39, Arundel's influence on policy seemed to be increasing. While the other privy councillors felt increasingly ineffectual and frustrated, the king was seen more and more often in consultation with Arundel, Hamilton, and also with Vane, who had been won over to an aggressive policy. All shared Con's views on the Scottish troubles, favoring the use of force and the employment of Catholics as part of that force.[39]

As Arundel's role in policy making seemed to expand and his friendship with Con became closer, muttering could be heard about the significance of his activities. When Arundel used Con's coach, emblazoned with the papal arms, to drive to his meetings with the king at court, the Puritans were scandalized.[40] If Arundel did not see himself as the head of an English Catholic party—and Con frequently remarked in despair that he did much less for Catholics than he might have—there were others who did. Despite his nominal conformity to the Church of England, Arundel was regarded by both papists and Puritans as the logical head of a Catholic faction in England. Baillie described him in mid-1639 as "a known papist, and the head of the Spanish and popish faction in England." Scottish propaganda alleged that the king "follows the advice and counsel of professed papists, and entrusts them with the chiefest offices of the arms now preparing." Barberini, influenced by Con's description of Arundel as a crypto-Catholic and a powerful one, urged that Arundel should undertake to "wipe out and beat down" all enemies of the Catholic religion in England and to work for the revival of Catholicism and the conversion of the king.[41]

The king's plans to take an army north to subdue the Scots were confirmed late in 1638 by the appointment of officers for the expeditionary force. The king looked to two very different sources to make up his army: trained bands of the counties and the peers of the realm with their attendants.[42] The appeal to the peers represented an attempt to economize, while at the same time making an impressive show of English unity and strength. Letters of 26 January 1639 called on the peers to attend the king with horse troops at their own charge, rather like latter-day tenants-in-chief summoned to the king's standard. The response from the nobility was varied and not wholly enthusiastic; some promised attendance, others "compounded" with gifts of money for their absence, others pleaded poverty, age, youth, or frailty. Summoning the aristocracy would prove to be a serious tactical blunder on the king's part. In this gathering of a greater body of the political nation than had met since the dissolution of parliament in 1629, the strongly disaffected had an opportunity to mobilize opposition to the king's policies among the hitherto merely disgruntled.[43]

As commander of the army, Arundel exercised some control over appointments; he did not use this to create any phalanx of Catholic officers, but neither did he exclude them as Puritans would have wished. Arundel's patronage, like the king's, had always been old-fashioned and nonsectarian.[44] In selecting auxiliary officers for the northern expedition, Arundel and his assistants adopted a similarly casual attitude toward religious affiliation. Of the veteran and professional soldiers employed to mobilize the north in the winter of 1638–39, two were Catholic: Roger Bradshaigh of Lancashire and Colonel Francis Trafford of county Denbigh.[45] Of all the Catholic officers, only the unfortunate Roger Widdrington, scout-master general to the expedition, drew unfavorable notice for his religion, and this was because he blundered at his job.

Aside from Arundel, the high command of the army was entirely, even conspicuously, Protestant. Sir Jacob Astley, George Goring, Henry Wilmot, and the earls of Essex and Lindsey, like most of the professional soldiers in the campaign, had served in the forces of the Protestant Netherlands. The second level of command, down through the captains in the regiments, was less exclusively Protestant; but the number of identifiable Catholics was not large. Even Arundel's intimates on the expedition, men who served as his personal attendants and assistants, were not Catholic, although most would later be royalists.[46]

Alarm about the "popish army," then, seems to have derived not from any actual preponderance of Catholics in the force but from suspicions about the influence of individuals, particularly Arundel but not him alone. Of the peers of the realm who contributed to the campaign either by money or by personal attendance, the Catholics were notable. The peer-age was proportionately far more Catholic than the general population (about one-third of the peers were Catholic) and Con had encouraged the Catholics to attend the king. The earl of Worcester sent the largest contri-bution, £1,500, and was represented in the army by his son, Lord Her-bert of Raglan, who brought a troop of cavalry. The very wealthy John Paulet, marquis of Winchester, was personally present.[47]

Several court Catholics who accompanied the expedition made them-selves conspicuous. The crypto-Catholic Endymion Porter was busy in the English army camp on behalf of his friend Secretary Windebank, who had been left in London. Porter's intrusions into state affairs and his attempts to get information from Coke threw into relief the tension between the Protestant and Catholic wings of the secretariat. Finally, there were priests in the camp. Con had quietly made sure of their pres-ence; there were, he explained to Barberini, many declared Catholics in the expedition and others who did not wish to die Protestant if they could help it.[48]

The Catholic Contribution

In addition to the use of Catholic forces in the First Bishops' War, Con sponsored the collection of a contribution for the king's needs from the

English Catholics. This was one of several extraparliamentary money-raising schemes developed in 1639 under the guise of "voluntary" levies; there were also contributions from the lawyers, the west-country gentry, and the Anglican clergy. None was very successful, but only the Catholic contribution was truly counterproductive. It became a focal point for the Long Parliament investigation of alleged Catholic conspiracy.

The origins of the Catholic contribution[49] are somewhat obscure; it certainly did not begin with Con, who became involved with it rather against his will. The initiative appears to have come from the Catholic nonjurors—those opposed to the oath of allegiance—as a response to the petition that the juring Catholics presented to the privy council late in 1638.[50] By the time the matter was drawn to Con's attention in December 1638, two groups were involved: the secular priests and certain Catholic lay courtiers.[51]

Anthony Champney, dean of the secular clergy, had already composed a circular letter to his priests and their penitents, directing them to pray for the success of the king's policies and to think how they might offer "an efficacious and real expression" of their loyalty. This may have represented the first stage of the scheme. The secular secretary, George Gage, would be the copyist for many of the letters about the contribution that went out from London to the counties.[52] If the contribution project originated among the seculars, they were probably moved by their desire to gain tacit approval from the king for their bishop; they had every reason to want to demonstrate their loyalty.

The organization of the contribution was difficult and long delayed. The king, who warmly supported the plan, sent Cottington and Windebank to work in conjunction with Con. They began to hold planning meetings in January, but Con refused to carry the matter further until February, when he got written permission from Rome to act as general organizer.[53] He was essential for this role, because the aim was to utilize the only national network of Catholic communications, the missionary priests, to organize the collection. Given the internal quarrels of the missionaries, Con was the only person who might succeed in persuading the heads of the various groups to cooperate.[54] In January the seculars and Jesuits were organizing independently, each group sending out letters to their men in the counties with instructions to prepare lay opinion and forward the names of possible collectors. Meanwhile, Con began what would be a long series of meetings in his London residence with the missionary superiors; by the end of February, a number of prominent London laymen had been drawn into the planning. Of these, Sir Kenelm Digby and Wat Montagu were the most active, and it was these two who drew up a letter on behalf of the London notables to Catholic gentry in one county, assuring them that the queen was supporting the endeavor and would protect them from recriminations.[55]

From its inception to the final planning stages in London, the organization of the collection consumed more than four months. When the king left for the north at the end of March, Con had not yet procured a joint statement of support for the project from the missionary superiors. Windebank wrote the king encouragingly of Catholic promises of "considerable supply," and court reporters estimated possible receipts of £40,000–£50,000. But so far all that the Catholic meetings produced was a good deal of unwelcome publicity.[56]

The London organization finally coalesced in April. The superiors of the missionary groups signed a joint letter that was sent to all their subordinates in the counties. To speed the appeal, the letter was accompanied by a campaign strategy paper entitled "Advices and Motives." The queen, who had done her best to hasten the effort in London by sending messages through Montagu and her secretary, Sir John Winter, added her own personal appeal on 17 April in a circular letter to the county Catholics.[57] In London, Sir Kenelm Digby and Sir Basil Brooke were named central collectors.

There is expressed in all the documents connected with the collection an assumption that the Catholics had a special interest in the king's success against Scotland. Champney told his clergy that "if the faction of those rebellious spirits should prevail (which God forbid) the Catholics will doubtless feel the ill effects of it more than others." The paper "Advices and Motives," like the London laymen's letter, emphasized the benefits enjoyed by Catholics under Charles's rule and depicted the expedition as providing an opportunity to prove the loyalty of English Catholics to the king and to further the Catholic cause. The queen's own letter of 17 April promised protection to the collectors and alluded to her interventions on behalf of English Catholics, delicately suggesting that a generous response on their part would be appropriate.[58]

The deliberately sectarian stance toward the war adopted by the queen and the collection organizers did not go unnoticed. After the king left London for the north, the queen ordered a weekly fast among the Catholics of her household for the king's success, encouraging Catholics throughout England to follow suit. The newswriter Rossingham reported on it to his clients: "The queen has appointed a fast amongst the Catholic people every Saturday with a solemn service and sermons to be in her chapel, for the king's happy progression in his design, and for his safe return; the queen does appear in it to require the Catholic party to expend their liberal contributions towards the king's expenses in this expedition against the rebellious Covenanters."[59]

The reference to the "Catholic party" is suggestive. As we shall see, the documents described here—"Advices and Motives" and the various letters—came into the hands of the parliamentary opposition and were used in the opening session of the Long Parliament as evidence of dangerous and far-reaching Catholic designs. There is no evidence of such hopes or intentions on the part of the country Catholics who responded to the queen's request; indeed, the Lancashire documents suggest that they felt great diffidence about appearing politically as a Catholic group. In this episode, as in others, court Catholicism was unrepresentative of, and dangerous to, country Catholicism.[60]

Spanish Men and Papal Money

The final proposal for Catholic party action was a plan to use against the Scots foreign Catholic mercenaries, who would be subsidized by a papal loan. Unlike the projects described above, this scheme was never put into operation; but it was pursued, with various modifications, from mid-1638 until the outbreak of civil war. The attempt to appeal to the continent to rectify the balance of political power in England was thus an important feature of the king's policies at an early date. The bid for Spanish soldiers never came fully under public scrutiny, although suspicions about it were voiced from time to time. In fact, when Baillie wrote about the threat of a "Spanish army in West Flanders to be employed where the king would direct,"[61] he was referring to the early phases of this plan.

The negotiations between England and Spain developed in an atmosphere of mounting crisis in both countries. Spain was entering the crucial period of its struggle to maintain control of Flanders, fend off blows from France, and regain a foothold on the Rhine. Dutch triumphs at sea in 1638 acutely threatened both the Spanish treasure routes from the Indies and the supply route to Flanders. The Spanish offers of troops to Charles I were strictly conditional; in exchange the Spanish ministers expected close protection for their troop convoys and a generally more vigorous English policing of the Channel.[62] Ministers in Madrid and Brussels had been following events in Britain with interest. In August 1638 the Cardinal Infante Fernando, acting governor of Flanders, pointed out to his brother the king the importance of the movement of opposition against Charles I, and received permission to correspond on the subject with Cárdenas in London. Philip IV agreed that the Scottish revolt would benefit Spain by restricting English activities on the continent and that it might provide a good occasion to strengthen Anglo-Spanish ties. When

first approached about aid for England, however, the Spanish king refused to authorize it; so long as Charles was occupied by northern troubles, he would be unable to ally with Spain's enemies. Noninterference
would be quite enough to ensure good relations with England, especially
since the French and Dutch were rumored to be giving the Scots active
assistance.[63]

The first overture to Spain appears to have been made by the Porter
family, presumably at the king's initiative, in the summer of 1638. When
the plan was revived later in the year, it was in the form of a proposal
from the secular priest George Gage and his brother Colonel Sir Henry
Gage. They came from an established Sussex Catholic family that was
traditionally associated with Spain, as were the Porters.[64] Colonel Gage
had been a mercenary in the service of Spain in Flanders since the 1620s.

In his memorandum to Windebank, George Gage suggested that the
king "borrow" an army of 10,000 men from Flanders under Gage's
command, which would be maintained by contributions from Catholics
and by a papal subsidy. In exchange Charles I would offer the Brussels
government a levy of double that number for service in Flanders (possibly
Irish soldiers were contemplated) and would thus give the pope "some
hope . . . of abrogating the severe laws against recusants, if not of an
absolute toleration of Catholic religion." An obvious objection to this
plan, that the recusant laws could not be changed without parliament's
consent, was answered by the suggestion (already put forward, as we
have seen, by the Spanish ambassador) that the army be used to overawe
a parliament after subduing the Scots. "So might the King, having a
foreign army of foot, subdue the Scots therewith, and at the same instant
keep the parliament in awe, that his Majesty might easily make them
come to what conditions he pleased. And by this means confirm his royal
prerogatives, and repeal such laws against recusants."[65]

By the time of Gage's proposal at the end of 1638, diplomatic and
military developments had changed the attitude of the Spanish government toward aid for England. Spain now had need, not merely of English
neutrality, but of substantial English assistance. The fall of Breisach in
December 1638, which cut off the Rhine valley route through which the
empire and Spanish Netherlands received men and supplies from the
Mediterranean; the successes of France and Sweden in the field; and the
increasing boldness of the Dutch fleet under Admiral Tromp in attacking
the naval lifeline between Spain and Flanders—all had eaten away at the
superiority enjoyed by the Habsburgs in 1636. During the last months of
1638, Spanish requests for Irish levies and Spanish diplomatic overtures
to England became more urgent. The tide of the Thirty Years War was
turning, and the potential role of Britain as a source of manpower and as
a naval ally in the Narrow Seas was becoming more important to Spain.

Encouraged by reports from Sir Arthur Hopton in Madrid and spurred by recognition of his own military needs, Charles I approved Windebank's continued negotiations with the Gage brothers in the early months of 1639. The queen's recovery from near-death in childbirth in February 1639 provided an opportunity for a journey by George Gage to the shrine of Our Lady of Sichem in Flanders. He carried a gift of thanksgiving from the queen, but he also took with him a commission for Colonel Gage to treat with the Cardinal Infante about troops.[66] This project, in which the queen, Father Philip, and Windebank were involved as well as the Gage brothers, was kept secret from both the official English agent in Flanders, Sir Balthazar Gerbier, and the privy council. One councillor, the earl of Northumberland, lamented in January that "to us that have the honor to be near about him [the king] no way is yet known, how he will find means either to maintain or to begin a war without the help of his people [i.e., parliament]."[67]

The plan was gradually reduced in scale from George Gage's proposal of an exchange of 10,000 Flemish soldiers for 20,000 Irish soldiers. In his preliminary negotiations with Prince Thomas of Savoy, Henry Gage had found him receptive, but noted that "their abilities are not so answerable to their desire." If the Spanish were assured that their Irish and English regiments could be kept up to the level of 2,000 men each, they would grant the English king 4,000 foot soldiers and 400 horsemen— "old soldiers and well-armed." After Prince Thomas left for Italy in February, the Cardinal Infante took up the talks, assuring the Spanish king that Charles I was now willing to enter an alliance with Spain and arguing that in general truce negotiations an English alliance would provide valuable leverage for Spain.[68]

The instructions that George Gage took with him to Flanders in mid-February were sufficiently detailed to suggest that Charles I took this negotiation seriously. There are indications that the force was to be put under Hamilton's charge and sent by sea to surprise Edinburgh, just as Hamilton had threatened in July 1638: "the readiness of the king's navy to set upon [the Covenanters] with 10,000 soldiers well-trained." Colonel Gage was warned to "use great secrecy, dexterity and expedition in this business." He entered into negotiations with the marquis of Ceralbo and the cardinal's confessor, "whom he hath authorized to treat with me in his name, and enjoined them seriously expedition and secrecy."[69]

The plan was aborted, but not for lack of interest in either London or Brussels. Negotiations were delayed by the habitually slow communications between Brussels and Madrid, by the distrust of the Cardinal Infante that had come to prevail in Madrid, and by the centralization of Habsburg military planning, which far outstripped both the ability of the

Spanish government to respond to crisis and the communications system through which it could make its decisions known.[70] At this point, moreover, the Madrid government was still mainly preoccupied with hiring English shipping to carry troops to Flanders.[71] A Dutch naval victory in February left Brussels destitute of men and ships. On the very day that George Gage crossed the Channel, Admiral Tromp destroyed the Dunkirk fleet near Gravelines, with a loss of nearly 1,500 seasoned Spanish troops.[72] Since replacements from Germany would have difficulty bypassing Baner's Franco-Swedish army, Brussels had an all the more acute need for British troops, but a corresponding inability to lend them.

In any case, nothing could be done without approval from Madrid, which was very slow in coming. When Gage insisted on an immediate reply, as he had been directed to do, the Cardinal Infante felt obliged to deny aid, following his brother's instructions of the previous summer. At the beginning of March, the Gages regretfully informed London that nothing could be expected from Flanders. As soon as the Spanish were resupplied from Germany or Spain (and ships had already been sent to Spain to pick up more troops), they were ready to help. Those in charge at Brussels continued to be sympathetic to the project; Colonel Gage emphasized that General Piccolomini, recently arrived in Brussels, would support it as strongly as Prince Thomas had done.[73]

Although the new policy at Madrid was evolving too slowly to affect the English campaign of 1639, it ensured the continuation of negotiations about this project during the next few years. At the English court, the scheme was viewed as a prelude to much closer ties between England and Spain. When Windebank wrote Hopton on 15 March 1639, outlining for the first time both the plan and its failure, he described it as an opportunity "which, if it had succeeded, might, in all possibility, have laid the grounds of a strait intelligence and firm friendship between these two crowns."[74]

The idea of a papal subsidy for the mercenaries from Flanders, part of George Gage's initial proposal, was not pursued in connection with the First Bishops' War. Gage's assumption that the pope would readily provide money may have been based on the rather vague offers of assistance from Rome in the winter of 1638–39. In October 1638 the Florentine agent Salvetti reported that the pope had sent an offer through Sir William Hamilton and Windebank to assist the king against the Scottish rebels. In December Barberini alluded to possible assistance "to the queen." Salvetti reported that the king made a show of displeasure at the talk of papal aid—merely, Salvetti was convinced, to ward off Puritan criticism. By January 1639 Windebank was only too aware of problems of financing the northern expedition and was keen to pursue the possibility of papal subsidy.[75] Evidence of negotiation on this matter during the next five months is lacking, but this project, like others emanating from the court Catholic party, remained very much alive in the succeeding three years.

Conclusion

The "popish plot" propaganda of the Covenanters was not merely paranoid fantasy; as we have seen, the king's policy provided only too much basis for fears of Catholic influence. By the beginning of 1639, Charles was already embarked on the Antrim project, was negotiating for foreign mercenaries, and was willing to consider papal subsidy. The instinct to turn to Ireland and to the continent to resolve domestic political problems was evident well before the Long Parliament; it was not a response to vindictive parliamentary opposition in 1640–41. And, despite abundant illustration during the Long Parliament that all such schemes were politically lethal to the king's cause, they would continue as part of royalist policy.

The next two chapters analyze the elaboration and failure of such policies in the eighteen months before the Long Parliament. Con's role in the genesis of the "Catholic loyalist" response to political crisis is clear; this orientation did not disappear when he left England at the end of 1639. The queen had made it her own, and in the years before the outbreak of war, her influence with the king increased.[76] She had interfered with army appointments for the First Bishops' War, she had sponsored her favorite Antrim, and she had so completely lent her name and support to the Catholic contribution that it became known as "the queen's contribution." The plan for Spanish men and papal money was devised in her entourage, and she provided a religious cover for George Gage's mission to Flanders. The project of a papal loan quickly became her favorite scheme for rescuing her husband from his political difficulties, and she would avidly pursue it in 1640–42. At every opportunity, Henrietta Maria was pushing the king toward just those policies that he should most scrupulously have avoided.[77]

The queen's influence on the king was remarked by her Puritan critics. George Walker, rector of St. John Evangelist in London, preached a series of sermons in the autumn of 1638 that were characterized by the government as "persuading the people to disobedience." Walker found himself in prison on 11 November 1638, after a particularly stirring sermon on the occasion of the annual Gunpowder Plot celebration. It was alleged that his sermon contained "things tending to faction and disobedience to authority." A Star Chamber case against him was prepared by Attorney General Bankes, and all this was reported by the newswriter Rossingham, who said that Walker had been "too bold against his Majesty in the pulpit."

Bankes claimed that, "instead of preaching subjection to the higher powers, [Walker] infuses false principles of disobedience into the ears and hearts of the people." In one sermon Walker was alleged to have said that it was *"scandalum magnatum"* in these days to speak in Christ's name; but, he allegedly continued, the people must not fear great men, kings, and potentates. All should question the commands they were given by superiors, for none would be excused by God for obedience to false human authority. The text on which he preached was Genesis 3:17: "And unto Adam he said, Because thou hast hearkened unto the voice of thy wife, and hast eaten of the tree, of which I commanded thee, saying, Thou shalt not eat of it; cursed is the ground for thy sake; in sorrow shalt thou eat of it all the days of thy life." Bankes argued that Walker had given "a cunning alarum to rebellion"; among the wicked princes Walker had mentioned were Saul, Ahab, Darius, and—to make his reference to Henrietta unmistakable—Jezebel. As Bankes pointed out, it was a dangerous sermon at a time "when the people of another kingdom are in a tumultuous disobedience against their sovereign."[78]

6. Catholic Action and the First Bishops' War

oth the king and the Covenanters accompanied their military preparations with propaganda campaigns during the months before the brief skirmish known as the First Bishops' War. By the end of the war in June 1639, there seems little doubt that the Scottish point of view had gained ground with the English, while the king's had lost credibility. As early as 1637, the Venetian ambassador reported on what he called the Puritan version of the prayer-book crisis:

> A report has got abroad that the pope's resident has had a hand
> in this [Scottish innovations] and that he has encouraged the efforts
> of the archbishop, hoping that either the people will yield to his
> ordinances, which approach closely to those of the Roman church,
> or by opposing them they will bring about a civil war between
> the Protestants with considerable advantage to the Catholic party,
> to whom the archbishop would have to approach more and more
> nearly in order to suppress the other. Such are the suspicions that
> the Puritans have about him not without reason.[1]

By mid-1639 this interpretation of the Scottish troubles had spread beyond Puritan circles.

For this development the persuasiveness of Scottish propaganda can take only partial credit, although in the person of the renegade Jesuit Thomas Abernethie they had a presumably expert witness on popish plotting. The utter conviction and consistency with which the Scots pressed their arguments must also have helped their case. But the king's own actions provided the best corroboration of Scottish propaganda. The secrecy with which Charles I handled his preparation for the war, the failure of his campaign and the sense of humiliation and frustration it induced in the English, and his patent (albeit unsuccessful) appeal to Catholic aid—all stimulated Protestant imaginations. Furthermore, the attempt to use Scottish and Irish Catholic arms, the reliance on advisors suspected of Catholic sympathies, and the permission given the queen to organize a Catholic contribution were all political errors that far outweighed the slight practical advantage they provided. Within the ranks of the aristocracy that gathered at the king's northern rendezvous in April, dissatisfaction was focused by the king's attempt to impose a new, non-parliamentary oath of allegiance on the army—an oath that was intended, as they may have suspected, to provide an alternative to the 1606 oath that many Catholics would not take. The refusal of leading Puritan lords to take this oath was a widely publicized incident, a preliminary clash of wills between the king and those who would lead the Lords' opposition to him in the Long Parliament.

The Propaganda War

During the winter of 1638–39, each side intensified its propaganda campaign and directed it toward both Scottish and English public opinion. The king's own explanation of the Scottish crisis, prepared for him by Dean Balcanquhal of Durham, depended on the comparison between Jesuits and Puritans that James I had frequently drawn. Studded with references to the "Jesuitical" proceedings and arguments of the Covenanters, the *Large Declaration* heaped scorn on the Covenanters' claim that their bond was divinely approved. It proclaimed that "no such Covenant or combination can come from heaven, but from hell, from whence cometh all faction and schism."[2]

The so-called reformers of Scotland

> have taken such a course to undermine and blow up the religion reformed, by the scandal of rebellion and disobedience . . . that if the conclave of Rome . . . had all their wits and devices concentrated into one conclusion and resolution, they could hardly have fallen upon such a way, as these pretended reformers have fallen upon, for turning all men out of the paths of the reformed religion. . . .
>
> For by their particular proceedings . . . it will plainly appear, that their maxims are the same with the Jesuits . . . their poor arguments, which they have delivered in their seditious pamphlets printed or written, are taken almost verbatim out of Bellarmine and Suarez . . . the means which they have used to induce a credit of their conclusions with their professions, are purely and merely Jesuitical fables, false reports, false prophecies, pretended inspirations and divinations of the weaker sex; as if now Herod and Pilate were once again reconciled for the ruin of Christ, and his true religion and worship.[3]

The king claimed, moreover, that the Covenant was greeted by Catholics abroad "with infinite joy, as hoping that now the time was come in which both we and our successors might be brought to abhor and detest that religion, whose professed zealots had been the authors of such an unsufferable Covenant, which could not consist with monarchy."

The *Declaration* continued in this rather dangerous and provocative vein, seeming to threaten that Charles I would abandon his allegiance to the reformed religion if resistance continued, and alluding to allegations that Jesuits and other priests were arriving in Scotland in large numbers because they were sure the king would turn to them and welcome them, in his revulsion from the Covenant. Foreign Protestants were said to have grieved over the Covenant, fearing it would bring "an indelible scandal" on the reformed cause generally.[4] Readers of the *Declaration* might well have had difficulty deciding whether the king was accusing the Scots of collaboration with Jesuits or was threatening to embrace the order himself if the "professed zealots" of reform did not cease to cause him trouble. But they would be left in little doubt that the Jesuits had played some role in the troubles; from this point of view, the *Declaration* may be seen as the starting point for later royalist historians' allegations of Catholic-Scottish collaboration.

On a more popular level, anti-Jesuit and loyalist sentiments were expressed in a satirical newsletter entitled *Pigges Corantoe*, written in the spring of 1639. Pigg was stoutly anti-Puritan, although he adopted a knowing and cynical perspective that left him free to aim his jibes in all directions. He alleged that the spirit of Loyola "hath crept into all assemblies and presbyteries" and said he "hath heard the old father laugh heartily out of purgatory to hear his disciples have brought the gospellers to his own lure to rebel against their own prince and prove it lawful by scripture and maintain it with the sword." He went on:

> There is a great question between the papists and Puritans, which are the best Christians and which are the best subjects, for the papist with his dark lantern would blow up all government and not be seen, and the Puritan like blind Bayard is so bold to summon all the brethren in New England and Nova Scotia to whine publicly in prayer, that with a safe conscience they may rebel against their prince and believe the Christian French king will relieve them when in his own kingdom he neither loves any Puritan nor any rebellion but say they, what he may do in his brother's kingdom, God knows.[5]

The argument is summarized in Pigg's comment that "disobedience is a fundamental point of papistry."

The Scots too, in the battle for the sympathy of the English public, hammered away relentlessly at their version of the popish plot theory. By early 1639 they had the benefit of the revelations of a renegade Scottish Jesuit, Thomas Abernethie. Abernethie had been in Rome in the early 1630s, where (so he alleged) he came to know of a scheme for the "reduction of Scotland to Rome," through the "perversion" of the king to Catholicism, failing which the Jesuits would bring their influence to bear on the young Prince of Wales. Abernethie claimed that a Scot involved in establishing the mutual agency had proposed England as Rome's first target, because it was spiritually closer to Catholicism. So Panzani was sent to England, "a great politician, well versed in the French tongue." Abernethie had traveled through England on his way to the Scottish mission in 1632 and claimed to have had a long interview in London with the queen about ways to relieve the sufferings of the Scottish Catholics; the queen supposedly said she would try to assure the king's cooperation. From 1632 to 1636, the whereabouts of this Scottish Jesuit are a mystery. According to his own account, he conferred with Panzani in London; others said he had consulted also with Con about sending the prayer book to Rome for revision by the Curia.[6]

By 1636 Thomas Abernethie was in Scotland serving as chaplain to the marquis of Huntley; when Huntley died that year, the Jesuit may have found himself without support. It was then that his period of irresolution set in; for a while, as a Scottish Catholic was later to write, "No honest man had a good opinion of him for he frequented heretics, went to heretic preaching, and lived with scandal." By mid-1637 Abernethie had certainly switched camps; the Jesuits attributed his defection to moral turpitude and the bribes offered him by Protestant officials to reveal the names and addresses of Catholic missionaries.[7]

Abernethie the apostate was quickly picked up by the Covenanters for propaganda purposes. At the first solemn subscription of the Covenant in early 1638, he was introduced to the assembled crowd by a Scottish minister; there he told the story of his life, his errors, his change of heart, "and what great attempts the pope and his conclave had been and was acting against Scotland and did as yet continue to act." Abernethie's propaganda value was all the greater because he made a good impression on even the more moderate supporters of the Covenant. The historian Burnet said that "Abernethie's story had a ready belief as well as a welcome hearing; though the lightness and weakness of the man became afterwards . . . visible."[8]

On 24 August 1638 Abernethie made a formal confession at Greyfriars Church in Edinburgh, entered the Church of Scotland, and himself subscribed the Covenant. His speech at Greyfriars was printed at the end of the year under the title *Abjuration of Popery*. In it he warned the Churches of England and Scotland against any compromise with Catholic ideas and practices; this would be the first step to the ruin of Protestant-ism in the British Isles. He described an international Catholic conspiracy against Protestantism. This conspiracy was centered at the Congregation for the Propagation of the Faith in Rome and used the Catholic seminar-ies abroad and an English fifth column supported by Roman pensions. He made much of the annual reports sent by the missionaries to Rome, "where the treasons are hatched." He greatly exaggerated the numbers of Jesuits in England and accused them of constant espionage.[9]

Although it was a less confident work than William Prynne would later produce, the *Abjuration* moved beyond the earlier generalized accusa-tions against Laud to a detailed exposé of popish activities in England and Scotland. Subsequent Scottish propaganda elaborated the details. On 4 February 1639 there appeared a Scottish pamphlet that linked the popish plot theory specifically to the threatened royal expedition against Scotland. *The Information to all good Christians within the Kingdom of England* accused "popishly affected prelates" of trying to force England and Scotland to war in order to extinguish or weaken the reformed religion, the better to introduce Catholicism.[10] Baillie said that this piece "did us good service for it satisfied so fully the hearts of that [English] nation that our adversaries being extremely galled with our success, moved the king to make this pitiful declaration [of 27 February 1639] . . . [but] our innocence was so well remonstrate in print, by these three or four dainty sheets of Mr. Henderson's that we, over all England, began to be much more pitied than before and our enraged party, the bishops, to be the more detested."[11]

Henderson's "three or four dainty sheets" contained the *Remonstrance* of 22 March 1639. Like the *Information*, the *Remonstrance* branded Laud as a cryptopapist who deliberately stimulated war between England and Scotland and negotiated with Rome about the new prayer book.[12] Laud described the reception of this libel in England: "The court, city, and country are presently full of it, that the archbishop of Canterbury had negotiated with Rome about the alteration of religion."[13] Scottish propaganda seems to have circulated widely in England, for in May 1639 the Venetian ambassador reported that "in order to keep the English Puritans steadfastly in their favor the Scots distribute many papers in this country, in which they point out that the steps taken by his Majesty were solely due to the interested advice of ministers, won over by the pope, who, under the pretence of reforming the liturgy of the churches of the two countries, proposed to introduce the mass as well, and to reduce these realms once more to the Roman court, which is most hateful to them."[14]

Scottish and Irish Catholic Action

The king's persistent although unsuccessful efforts to make use of Catholic military forces seemed to confirm Scottish propaganda. The Scottish party led by Douglas and Nithsdale was the first Catholic group to crumble.[15] Indeed, the war was initiated rather earlier than the king anticipated by the Covenanters' attack on Catholic strongholds in Scotland. Baillie tells the early part of the story: "Our Scottishmen were dismissed from court to come home, both to strengthen the king's party among us, and by their removal to hinder our intelligence. . . . The papists in the south, were lifting up their heads: Nithsdale and Herries, with some English forces from Carlisle, were feared to have joined with the marquis of Douglas, who might have reached out their hand to the marquis of Hamilton's followers."[16]

The Covenanters moved first; they took the royal castles of Edinburgh and Dunbarton (the latter under Abercorn's command) before the king was able to leave London. They followed this up with the capture of Dalkeith; and on 24 March they moved against Douglas Castle. Here, said Baillie, "they expected nothing but blows, and a shameful retreat from a rash enterprise, for the house was strong, and they had no cannon." But Douglas's courage failed him, and he fled.[17]

By the time the king reached York on 30 March, Nithsdale's castle of Carlaverock was the only royalist stronghold left south of the Tay. The Covenanters had made an attempt on this position too, but had retreated because of its strength.[18] When they were finally able to storm Carlaverock in early April, they tore down Nithsdale's house. They bore a special grudge against the earl, reported Rossingham, because they had no hope of winning him to their side: "Then they believe he exasperates his Majesty against them to invade their country; also he threatened to come against them, if they durst, saying he would have good his house against the whole power of the Covenant; lastly he is said to be a known recusant, and they hate popery with a perfect hatred."[19]

In London, Con heard the bad news in a letter from Nithsdale, who explained that he, Douglas, and Winton had been forced to flee Scotland and join the king. No royalist party of consequence was left in Scotland.[20] As Salvetti reported, "although some Scots, mostly Catholic, are with the king, and refuse the oath [i.e., the Covenant] they are not enough for a party and will be of little help to the king."[21] Nor could the king offer much help to Scottish Catholics, who were now in a very difficult situation. Harried by the kirk and offered the choice of joining the Covenanters or leaving the country, both lay Catholics and priests went into exile in England, France, and Belgium.[22]

The notion of a Scottish Catholic force had not been an entirely fanciful one; later, during the civil war, Montrose would be able to draw upon the support of highlanders, many of them Catholic, in the spectacular royalist rearguard action that ended at Philiphaugh. But the lowland lords were isolated and politically weak. Nor could they appeal to the military support of experienced mercenaries, as could Antrim or the king himself. Recruitment in Scotland for the armies of the Thirty Years War had been almost entirely by and for Protestant powers. During the early 1620s, the seventh earl of Argyll had raised a regiment for Spain, but Spanish recruiting in Scotland stopped after the French marriage. As France moved to ever more vigorous support of the German Protestants, Charles I permitted the French to resume their ancient practice of recruiting mercenaries from Scotland. As a result, France became the chief recruiting agent in Scotland between 1633 and 1640.[23] But in 1639 there was no large reserve of experienced officers; and, with their usual single-minded pursuit of self-interest, the French refused to release Scots to serve the king of England.[24]

Moreover, the king's failure to grant religious liberty to Scottish Catholics despite Con's efforts, coupled with the carrot-and-stick approach to the Catholics adopted by the Covenanters, seems to have disheartened the Scottish Catholics. Baillie thought that this was an important element in the failure of that party: "The papists did not much stir; at the beginning their offers were great, but finding that no open liberty of conscience was to be granted to them, they held in their hand."[25] A Jesuit missionary, writing in September 1639, revealed the mental wavering of some Scottish Catholics: "Even in this extremity there is a hope remaining. They [the Covenanters] are fighting, as they allege, for liberty of conscience, and have staked their lives and all they have on their opposition to the king. They would rather lose all they have in the world than incur the pangs of conscience by joining in a ritual which they think opposed to the truth, and this consideration may possibly induce them to desist from persecuting the Catholics."[26]

Antrim's plans for an Irish force met with no better success. While the earl's needs multiplied (needs that Wentworth passively resisted supplying), his projected forces dwindled from the 10,000 originally promised to 8,000 and then 5,000. As Wentworth had feared, Antrim contemplated an officer corps composed of his relatives in Spanish service and of leading members of the very Gaelic families (Maguire, MacMahon, O'Neill, Mageniss, and O'Hara) whom Wentworth most distrusted. But Colonel Owen Roe O'Neill, Antrim's intended second in command and the linchpin of the enterprise, vanished to Spain before any agreement could be made. By April Antrim was beginning to regret his ill-considered promises.[27] The Scots were, quite reasonably, more worried by Antrim's potential descent than by the Catholics in the lowlands. Baillie reported how some of the western clansmen had flocked to Antrim's standard because Argyll was unpopular and regarded as a usurper of MacDonald rights:

> Sir Donald Gorum, the Clanronald, and many others were hatching a mischief to join with the Earl of Antrim, the chief of the Clan Donald, who was with the king's money and authority, to come with forces from Ireland to Kintyre . . . Antrim's boats were ready on the Irish shore; Gorum and others of the Clan Donalds were gotten away to Ireland. . . .
>
> Also the coast [was] in no small fears for the Irish invasion; for the estate of that country we did not then understand; only we heard that Crowner Bruce was sent about with some officers to the earl of Antrim, who, after long disappointment, got money to levy flat-bottomed boats, that sundry troops of the trained bands were come down to the shore.[28]

Sir Henry ("Crowner") Bruce and his nephew Captain John Reade, two experienced Scottish soldiers, had indeed been sent by the king to Antrim to hasten his preparation. Moreover, the king offered Antrim bait, promising him possession of any conquered land in western Scotland to which he could claim some title. Reaching Ulster at the end of May 1639, Bruce and Reade found Antrim in disarray; he could do nothing to move his men without considerable royal funding, which Wentworth was neither willing nor authorized to provide. The king's orders in June to Antrim and Sir Donald MacDonald of Sleat to attack in the western highlands were of no avail. Bruce returned to his command in Flanders; Reade, a well-known Scottish court Catholic, remained in Ireland to accept a commission in the new Irish army.[29] Antrim, his ambitions not yet quenched, retired to nurse his project for another day.

The English Army of 1639: Arundel and the Army Oath

Stung by reports of the Covenanters' moves against Scottish loyalists in early March, the king departed from London on 27 March, leaving behind a number of privy councillors to run the government and continue the recruitment and dispatch of soldiers to the York rendezvous of 1 April. With the king traveled the commanding general, the earl of Arundel.

Late on the night before his departure, Arundel went with Windebank to make his farewells to Con. They discussed the king's affairs at some length, including the possibility of using the expedition as the occasion for introducing a new oath of allegiance. Windebank, who had been much disappointed at the failure of the earlier oath negotiation, had first proposed this new expedient in January; and Con had discussed it not only with Arundel but also with the heads of the missionaries in England.[30] The formula devised was satisfactory to Con and had even been provisionally approved by the Jesuits, who sent it to their theologians in Spain for examination. An "army oath" administered to those with the king, under the pressure of the Scottish crisis, would circumvent the problem of how to get a new oath devised without the approval of Parliament. It was to be hoped that the new oath would ultimately lead to the abolition of the old oath of allegiance.[31]

There was still uncertainty about whether and how the oath would be administered; but as the expedition got under way, the king's dependence on Arundel and Vane, already noticed in the preceding autumn, deepened. In a letter to Hamilton on 18 April, Charles stated that he was conferring only with Arundel and Vane, for he "could trust no other." He instructed Wentworth to channel all correspondence through Vane. Arundel and Vane, who had emerged as allies isolated from the king's other councillors, agreed on strategy: the king should advance vigorously and prepare to make war.[32]

Arundel's primacy and his policy were generally resented. The earl of Holland expressed his doubts of Arundel's "real intentions for accommodation of these troubles," but Holland could be expected to scoff at his court rival.[33] However, Sir Edmund Verney also suspected Arundel of plotting to lead the king deliberately to disaster. Verney's letter to his son from the English camp foreshadows the royalist version of the popish plot theory:

> Our army is but weak, our purse weaker, and if we fight with these forces and early in the year, we shall have our throats cut. . . . My lord marshall puts on the king to fight by all the ways and means he can possibly devise. . . . Then the king is persuaded to it, too, from Whitehall. . . . The Catholics make a large contribution, as they pretend, and indeed use all the means and ways they can to set us by the ears, and I think they will not fail of their plot. . . . My lord marshall himself, I dare say, will be safe, and then he cares not what becomes of the rest.[34]

Arundel was known to be the instigator of the "army oath," which was tendered on 21 April to the peers gathered at York with the idea that it would subsequently be taken by the rest of the army. Arundel admitted that he had helped compose it; it was he who approached the earls of

Northampton and Rutland to ask them to convene the rest of the peers at a special "afforced" meeting of the king's councillors. He was the first to take the oath and he administered it to the others. The incident served to isolate him further from the peers and gentry in the camp. The proposal of an oath-swearing was greeted with almost universal astonishment and some misgivings. The opposition it aroused in some quarters could scarcely have been greater had it been publicly identified as a means for the Catholics to dispense with the oath of allegiance.[35]

Two Puritan peers, Viscount Saye and Sele and Lord Brooke, actually refused to swear the oath; those who accepted it expressed such serious reservations that the king was obliged to modify its terms. As a result of their refusal, Brooke and Saye and Sele were taken into custody, interrogated, and dismissed from the king's camp to return to their homes. This ensured the widest possible publicity both for the oath and for the nonjurors. In London, Giustiniani reported a "very great murmuring" against the arrest of the two peers, "everyone freely saying that this severity will only hasten greater troubles in England." On 1 May, probably in connection with this incident, Samuel Hartlib was arrested for questioning in London.[36]

Considering its avowed purpose as a counter-Covenant, the army oath had a curious formula. Unlike other anti-Covenanting oaths, it made no specific renunciation of other covenants or bonds, but it did contain several phrases reminiscent of the 1606 oath of allegiance. In particular, it affirmed that Charles I was "lawful king" of his dominions, that the oath was taken "without any equivocation or mental reservation whatsoever," and that "no power on earth" could absolve the juror from his oath. On the other hand, the army oath did not venture on to any of the theologically dangerous territory of the 1606 oath, containing no reference to "deposition," "priests," or even "ecclesiastical persons"—omissions that probably account for Con's approval.[37]

Whether contemporaries suspected that this oath was particularly intended for Catholics remains unclear. The nonjurors and others who questioned the oath did not address this issue directly. Instead, they asked first how far they were obliged, by the oath's reference to "the utmost hazard of my life and fortune," to risk life and fortune for the campaign against the Scots.[38] Secondly, Saye and Sele and Brooke asked whether the peers were committing themselves not only to a defense of England but to an invasion of Scotland. Finally, the nonjurors and other peers questioned the legality of any oath not sanctioned by parliament and reminded the king that the 1606 oath of allegiance was available for his use on this occasion.[39] The last question was an oblique criticism of the king's policy in not summoning parliament to deal with the Scottish

crisis and in arming Catholics for his service. The questions about the
legality of the oath had more general implications as well. The only oaths
established by parliament since the Reformation were aimed primarily at
Catholics and, like the oaths of supremacy and allegiance, were framed
to support royal supremacy and the Protestant religion. As Saye and Sele
and Brooke were reminding their fellow peers, loyal Englishmen took
oaths against Catholics, not against Protestant Covenanters whose own
"band" was an anti-Catholic one.[40]

Unrest mounted after the oath-giving incident at York. In the first
week of May, when the royal army was at Newcastle, the king accepted
Arundel's assurances that the Scots' army was weak and that the royal
army should confront them. Arundel's optimism was not shared by the
other commanders; but they were overruled, as it was reported, because
Arundel "presseth it with so much earnestness" and evinced "such animosity and great desire, to begin the work."[41] Despite a second small
rebellion in the ranks of the peers on 16 May, the king continued to take
Arundel's advice, and the English moved up to the Scottish border where,
after only a week of inconclusive and bloodless skirmishes with the Scottish forces, the military confrontation was settled by the so-called Pacification of Berwick.[42]

Even this final phase of the expedition added a touch to the emerging
"popish-plot" nervousness. One of Arundel's appointments in the force
was that of the scoutmaster general, Roger Widdrington. Widdrington
was a member of an old family of Yorkshire and Northumberland gentry
that was notorious for its unabashed Catholic recusancy. When the Scottish army advanced unexpectedly to within sight of the royal camp at the
beginning of June, throwing the whole army into disarray, Widdrington
was blamed for inadequate intelligence. Rushworth described the suspicions the incident drew upon Widdrington and Arundel:

> In the opinion of the court and commanders, the Scoutmaster
> general bore the blame; and his crime was aggravated because he
> was a papist.
>   The Lord General made this reply . . . that he made choice of
> him . . . as the fittest man in England for the office of scout-master
> . . . one best acquainted with all the highlandmen upon the borders
> of Scotland, and who was best able . . . to gain intelligence from
> thence . . . that he was a person of integrity, and that he would
> justify himself.
>   In conclusion this business was hushed up, but great was the
> murmuring of the private soldiers in the camp.[43]

Catholic Money

The attempts to raise money from the pope and from English Catholics also continued without much success. As the king's difficulties became more acute in April and May of 1639, Windebank returned to the notion of a papal subsidy for the expedition. He reminded Con of the former offer of help, but Con was not optimistic about the chances of getting money from Rome for a schismatic ruler. Windebank persisted; the negotiation for reunion was not going quickly, but a sum of money might hasten it. Con replied that a way would be found to aid the king when he showed a clear determination to return to the Roman fold. Meanwhile, some smaller sum might be found to support a company of soldiers in the queen's name; this Windebank rejected as unacceptable.[44] There the matter rested for the time being, but it would be revived in the following years.

The results of the English Catholic contribution were proving that Con's doubts about it were well founded. Not only were there delays and difficulties in organizing it in London, but the country Catholics were also more fearful than enthusiastic and were unable, in any case, to organize rapidly on the scale imagined by the Londoners. In many instances, Catholic gentry who were expected to take the lead were preoccupied with raising the militia for the king's northern expedition.

Initial steps toward creating a county collection network had been taken by the Jesuits and seculars independently in January, when they asked their men to approach prominent laymen who might contribute.[45] The Digby-Montagu letter, sent out at the beginning of March to lay Catholics in the counties via their confessors, had urged them to nominate "such persons as shall in your opinion be agreed of for the ablest and best disposed in every several county, not only to solicit, but to collect such voluntary contributions, as everybody's conscience and duty shall proffer." The subsequent letter from the missionary superiors, sent out with the "Advices and Motives" paper on 11 April, assumed that lay collectors were already chosen. There is also a reference in Con's correspondence to a confirmation of the names of the collectors at a 4 April meeting in London. But evidence from Lancashire suggests that the county organization was not yet so definite. The total number of county collectors ultimately involved probably approximated the 120 that appear on a list subsequently published by parliament.[46]

The progress of the collection in Lancashire is well documented in the manuscripts of the chief collector for that county, Charles Towneley. These enable us to correct (at least for one county) the picture of the collection that was later drawn as part of the popish plot exposés.[47] Far from being a diabolically efficient, Jesuit-run operation, as later propaganda implied, the contribution in Lancashire was handled chiefly by local gentry and secular priests.[48] There is little sign in Lancashire of the disagreements between secular and regular missionaries that had so delayed the planning in London.

But other difficulties arose in Lancashire. The county was large, communications were sometimes difficult, and the collectors were poorly distributed around the county. The organization there did not get under way until mid-April, by which time several of the designated collectors were preoccupied with other aspects of the king's campaign. One of them, Sir Cecil Trafford, played no role at all in the collection, because as a deputy lieutenant he was busy raising the county militia. Most of the collectors and their assistants were men who by necessity or intent led retired lives, shielded from public attention outside their own provincial sphere of influence. They were deferential to the leadership emanating from London, but they were loath to involve themselves in a venture that was novel, expensive, and possibly dangerous. When civil war broke out later, they would join the king; but in 1639 they were not anxious to make themselves conspicuous. The hesitation of men such as these, who were distant from the court and who had safeguarded themselves and their families by a reticent loyalism, was in striking contrast to the activism that reigned at court.

When the king left for the north, the government still hoped that the Catholic contribution would amount to between £30,000 and £50,000. Even in early May, as much as £25,000 was anticipated.[49] But the money was trickling in very slowly indeed. The collectors in southern counties had been instructed to pay in their sums to London by Easter (14 April), and those in the northern counties by 14 July. Few met these deadlines, and on 17 May Con had to report that "purse strings remain tightly drawn."[50] It was said that some of the collectors were overbearing and that some had falsely alleged that it was necessary for Catholics to declare their income, as if for an assessment, which led contributors to fear the information would be passed on to the government and their recusancy fines raised. Moreover, attempts had been made to persuade Catholics to participate also in the general gentry contribution that was under way; many of them, along with their neighbors, were assessed for coat and conduct money and other charges connected with the mobilization of the king's army. In the middle of May, Sir Basil Brooke could promise Windebank no more than £10,000 by midsummer and a possible second installment of £10,000 in the autumn. Windebank told the king that he had "used all the persuasions I could to make him sensible of the great disservice, if it succeeded not, beside the danger to his party; and I am confident there shall be no failing in him."[51]

The first installment of about £10,000 was in fact ready by mid-July, but the Pacification of Berwick made it difficult to get further payments. In Lancashire the collectors sent out reminders of the "urgent occasions now required and the imminent danger as we are informed (we doubt) too certainly may happen unto us all if we show not ourselves free upon this occasion," but they were not able to draw up preliminary totals until the end of August. In the end, Lancashire Catholics provided a respectable proportion of the national contribution of £14,000, but they did so very slowly and with a sense that they were not well requited for their efforts. They accompanied their final payment with a formal complaint against extortions from recusants by the county sheriff, Sir Edward Stanley.[52]

There were complaints from Catholics in other counties too. In a move characteristic of the internal contradictions of the king's policies, a new and expanded commission for "quickening" the recusants of southern England to composition had been granted in January to the pursuivant John Pulford.[53] Con managed to get the commission suspended for the sake of the Catholic contribution, but in several areas the local authorities, under the reasonable assumption that the government was staging a crackdown on recusants, had already begun to move. Complaints poured in to Windebank and the queen from Berkshire, Norfolk, and elsewhere that recusants were under investigation. The queen was unable to do anything until the proceedings reached the central courts in London; there she simply quashed the cases by royal authority, a move that raised the eyebrows of Protestant observers.[54] Pulford naturally objected to this interference. Through the rest of 1639 and 1640 he would attempt unsuccessfully to put his commission into effect and in 1640 would finally turn to the Long Parliament for redress of his grievances.[55]

The contribution generated hostile publicity for the Catholics. It was said that despite the king's opposition to calling a true parliament, he permitted Con to convoke a "parliament of papists."[56] Public opinion about the contribution cannot have been sweetened by the claims apparently made by Jesuits in the summer of 1639 that whatever success the contribution had enjoyed was due to their own efforts. A forged brief from the pope, forbidding Catholics to make special offers of men and money and forbidding "mixed" congregations of priests and laymen such as had been meeting in London, was widely circulated in May and June, was considered genuine by many Catholics, and drew further attention to the contribution.[57]

Negotiations with Spain

Rumors of the government's continued negotiation for foreign troops contributed a further element to public apprehension. Madrid had finally responded positively to Gage's proposals; on 20 March Olivares unexpectedly informed Hopton that he would provide mercenaries in exchange for naval protection of the Flemish coast. Tromp's victory at Gravelines had shaken the Spanish government, but had not weakened its determination to transport large numbers of troops to Flanders. In succeeding months, ministers in both Spain and Flanders would several times offer five or six thousand troops in exchange for the assistance of the English fleet, but these offers were all contingent on the safe arrival in Flanders of the sizable reinforcements that were being prepared.[58]

By early June 1639 this Anglo-Spanish negotiation, hitherto only hinted at in Hamilton's warnings to the Scots, had become known in garbled form in court circles. The Venetian ambassador reported that "a Scottish captain of experience and reputation, has reached the court from Flanders, sent by Count Piccolomini . . . to offer his Majesty 4,000 German horse. . . . The king expressed his gratitude but did not accept the offer . . . as in addition to the scarcity of money, which makes fulfillment impossible, the exceeding jealousy of the people here does not allow him to entertain the idea of introducing foreign troops into the country."[59]

In reality, the king felt no such politic reservations; nor had he abandoned the plan to use troops from Flanders. They were simply not available in time for the 1639 campaign. Colonel Gage in Flanders and Windebank in London pursued the negotiation well into the summer. They now pressed the Spanish representatives for a large loan in exchange for the desired recruits and protection for Flanders.[60] Continued Dutch victories in the Channel kept alive the Spanish interest in this scheme. In June Tromp's fleet stopped a number of English ships that had been chartered by Spain to convey 1,500 troops to Dunkirk, and two-thirds of these soldiers were carried off.

English Response

Reflection of English opinion about the First Bishops' War is scattered in letters, pamphlets, broadsides, and reports of "seditious speeches." These give us some evidence, necessarily inconclusive, that the Scottish explanation of the crisis as part of a larger battle between Protestantism and Catholicism for control of the British Isles had taken hold in England.[61] Uneasiness about Catholic influence in the king's circle and the king's appeal for Catholic support was voiced along a wide segment of the political spectrum. The earl of Leicester wrote anxiously from Paris in February 1639 about the alleged activities of a Scottish Catholic priest, Thomas Chambers, who was a nephew of George Con and a chaplain of Richelieu. Chambers had traveled to Scotland several times in recent years to organize troop levies for France; a rumor circulated that his secret business now was to coordinate a league, headed by the pope and financed by the emperor, Louis XIII, and Philip IV, that would use British and foreign troops for some undisclosed operation in England. This story, perhaps a garbled version of the Gage plan, frightened Leicester sufficiently for him to warn the king that "it is to be suspected that no good is intended either to your person or state" and that, by accepting foreign aid, the king might find himself "reduced to exigents, very dishonorable, and full of danger." Leicester cautioned that although the Catholics acted "as if they would do great matters for your service," they would only serve the ends of foreign princes. The earl concluded that he was "confident that there is some very dangerous conspiracy against your majesty; for the contrivers of this practice are your mortal enemies; and I fear have their spies and agents in your court."[62] Thus had the Scottish troubles brought a relative moderate to believe in popish conspiracies.

More predictably, perhaps, the Puritan Harley family in Herefordshire had watched the rearming of the Catholics with deep suspicion. Lady Brilliana Harley mentioned early in March that there were various reports that "the papists will furnish themselves as well as they can be. There is a book, which is written by a papist that is converted; it discovers much."[63] Against such deepening suspicions of subversion the king's pronouncements and disclaimers had little effect. As the royal party moved north through Durham, Bishop Morton preached in the cathedral there on Romans 13:1: "Let every soul be subject to the higher powers." He repeated at some length the comparison drawn in the *Large Declaration* between Covenanters and papists, both of whom allegedly defended the legitimacy of rebellion. Georg Rudolph Weckherlin's reaction to the sermon was hostile; he noted tersely in his diary that the bishop had spoken "much against the reformed churches beyond the seas."[64] Later in May the king issued yet another proclamation; as the Venetian ambassador explained, it was intended "to dissipate the very general idea that he inclines to Catholicism." But in London the populace was "entirely favorable to the constancy and interests of the Scots"; only Catholics, Giustiniani reported, spoke out openly against the Scots.[65] The Harley family heard and believed that the king was deliberately reinforcing his army with Catholics.[66]

Broadsides and pamphlets, safely anonymous, gave a more pointed expression to notions of popish conspiracy. A poster tacked up by apprentices during the 1639 campaign focused on court Catholics and the danger they posed to reformed religion:

> Gentlemen and others that are Christians assist us for the truth
> of the Gospel that is like to be extinguished, viz, the pope's nuncio
> doth protest to make us all Roman Catholics, the ambassador of
> the Anti-Christ, Sir John Winter, (whose kindred were of the Gun-
> Powder treason) is his associate, and doth trust to work that
> treachery upon us.
>
> Sir Kenelm Digby a maintainer of that Society [the Jesuits] is going
> to Rome, and the ship-money must defray him, as the queen's
> mother and the frogs of hell in Somerset House.
>
> Finis Cotanet [sic] opus.[67]

Among the most widely circulated of satirical broadsides in 1639 was *Reasons that Ship and Conduct Money ought to be paid*; this drew a clear connection between court Catholicism and the nonparliamentary financial expedients of the 1630s. Its anonymous author portrayed the 1639 war as part of a full-fledged attempt to bring in popery, made Con the center of the plot, emphasized the sending of "intelligence" to Rome, named Sir John Winter and Sir Toby Mathew as prime conspirators, and put the Scots in the role of deliverers:

> [Ship and conduct money ought to be paid] first, for setting up
> of the mass and maintaining idolatry, as it is begun, but not yet, as
> was intended, brought to perfection, praise be to God and the Scots,
> whom he made an instrument. That the pope's nuncio takes, and
> has these five years taken great pains in perverting his Majesty's
> simple subjects . . . for he sends every week a packet of all affairs
> here to Rome; he must be well rewarded of ship and conduct money.
> . . . Sir John Winter whose kindred were some of the chief actors
> of the Gunpowder treason, and Sir Toby Mathew, do countenance
> the matter very well, and we must needs go against the Scots for
> not being idolatrous, and will have no mass amongst them, yet
> conduct and ship money must be had to go against them to reduce
> them to obedience. . . . That it is not permitted to talk of a
> parliament to redress these abuses, nor to hear the Scots, but ship
> and conduct money are the sinews wherewith we must go to war
> against them. And the papists in the meantime do make a laughing-
> stock of us; and, indeed, the captains and lieutenants must be
> all papists, for none will go but them. . . . Leave this where you
> find it.[68]

The Scottish Scouts' Discoveries by their London Intelligencer was an anonymous pro-Covenanter pamphlet composed during the First Bishops' War. The author saw Spanish and Roman intrigue behind the Scottish crisis, was highly suspicious about Catholic influence at court, and mentioned several specific aspects of Catholic action during the war. He pictured Arundel's Sussex castle ("kept by four priests, two porters, and a rat-catcher") and imagined the spirits of King James and Queen Elizabeth "conferring about the troubles in Scotland, which they said was plotted in Spain, ratified at Rome, and agitated by the Jesuits in England, to be acted in a tragical procession in Scotland." He referred to Antrim's soldiers and to an army of foreign Catholics that was to have been brought against the Scots, including "twenty thousand old soldiers offered by the King of Spain." Speaking of the court, the *Scottish Scout* said: "Since the king's departure from London, Whitehall is become an Amazonian castle, St. James [queen mother's court] an hospital for strangers, Somerset House a Catholic college, Westminster a receptacle for seminary priests and Jesuits."[69]

The author of *Scottish Scout* also knew a good deal about the Catholic contribution. He referred to the "Advices and Motives" paper sent to the counties, the activity of the queen in support of the contribution, and the forged letter of Urban VIII to the English Catholics. Finally, he discoursed on the "popish parliament": "The new council table [is] to be erected at London, where the Catholic lords, knights and superiors of the Roman clergy, meet to consult upon fitting means for raising of money towards maintenance of this holy war, which they hope will either procure a dissolution of your [Covenanters'] religion or a toleration of their own."[70]

Conclusion

Broadsides and pamphlets can provide only indirect and inconclusive evidence of opinion, but the *Scottish Scout* reads like a London production and suggests that by the summer of 1639 disaffected Englishmen were adopting and elaborating Scottish allegations about court Catholic activities. In September 1639 the house of a Puritan merchant of London, Samuel Vassall, was searched by government agents. The papers relating to public affairs that were found there provide a very interesting list, for Vassall was a confidant of those who would lead the Long Parliament. There were a copy of the *Scottish Scout*, a copy of the letter from the clergy superiors of 4 April 1639, and a copy of the queen's letter of 17 April 1639. There were also a remonstrance against ship money and a number of pro-Covenant documents.[71] Vassall's papers, of course, are but one sign; but they do suggest what information and propaganda were reaching interested Englishmen and how some of them might use it to find a pattern in the king's policies.

Meanwhile, royal policy continued along the lines initiated in 1638. After the king's return to London from the north, some of the leading figures on the court stage changed: Arundel began to fade from the political picture as Wentworth—recalled from Ireland by the king to become his chief adviser in the autumn of 1639 and raised to the dignity of earl of Strafford—moved into the ascendancy. In the northern campaign of 1640, Strafford would be commanding general, as Arundel had been in 1639. At the queen's court, George Con was replaced by Carlo Rossetti, who developed a particular intimacy with his Italian compatriot, the queen mother. Rossetti, who arrived in August 1639, would continue many of Con's endeavors. Despite the failure of the Catholic party schemes, most of them were retained and some expanded. The Scottish and Irish Catholic parties were joined in 1640 by what looked like a Welsh Catholic party. These groups pointed ahead to the "Celtic strategy" of the civil war, which was also, in reality, a Catholic strategy.

7. The Failure of Reform: From War to War

he Scottish crisis made a parliament almost inevitable, but it did not lead with the same inevitability to the outbreak of civil war in England. Possibilities for political readjustment still existed in late 1639, but had substantially diminished by the dissolution of the Short Parliament in May 1640. They lessened even further by the time of the convocation of the Long Parliament the following November. The reasons for this are varied and complex. In this chapter I shall trace two related strands: the continued prominence of the Catholic party at court and the king's willingness to take their advice, and the foreign orientation of the court, which continued pro-Spanish. These policies helped to alienate some ambitious court peers who wished to enter the inner circles of power and who were also in touch with Puritan country peers. On a wider front, the Catholic and Spanish activities at court sharpened public fears about the king's intentions, making English Protestants receptive to Catholic conspiracy theories. In addition, the exile component of the Spanish party was engaged in ceaseless intrigues against Richelieu's government and attempted to involve the English government in these machinations. Those who saw the court as full of conspirators were correct.

The period from the Pacification of Berwick to the convocation of the Long Parliament was filled with disappointment—for the king, one must add, as well as for those who would later be ranged against him. Although their hopes were initially raised by Strafford's accession to power, the members of the French party who were his friends did not achieve the political influence to which they aspired. The Palatine family was not able to profit from the Anglo-Scottish accommodation that was greeted joyfully in June 1639 or from the opportunity created in July by the death of Duke Bernard of Saxe-Weimar. For weeks in the autumn of 1639, the king held Spain to ransom as a crippled Spanish fleet lay in English waters; but he did not exploit this advantage, and the Dutch instead of the English became the popular heroes in this saga of the "second Armada." The court continued to seem more hospitable to the friends of Spain than to their enemies. The winter of 1639–40 witnessed icy relations between France and England, the rejection of Dutch overtures for a dynastic alliance, a continuing warm reception for Richelieu's French enemies, the renewal of Anglo-imperial contacts, and the cordial entertainment of an extraordinary Spanish embassy in London. Strafford, who was perceived as all-powerful at court, was blamed for these policies. Although this was an exaggeration, it was not wholly unfair. The failure of the Short Parliament in May 1640 was a turning point in English politics. Convinced by then that Strafford would fall from power and anxious to rid the English court of its Spanish sympathizers, the French agents courted his opponents within and outside the court, providing them with information about Anglo-Spanish negotiations.

A sinister light was thrown on the king's foreign policy by its association with the queen mother, the exile French, and the papal agent Rossetti, all of whom were identified as leading protectors of Catholic as well as Spanish interests. During the winter of 1639–40, the cardinalate negotiation revived, involving not only the queen's favorite, Wat Montagu, but also the king's cousin, Ludovick Stuart-d'Aubigny. Rossetti continued Con's policy of protecting the Jesuits from government reprisals. His unsuccessful attempts to resolve English Catholic problems such as the government of the secular clergy left him identified with Jesuit interests. There were scattered but violent verbal attacks on the court Catholic circle during the winter of 1639–40, and the Short Parliament was expected to launch a violently anti-Catholic crusade. This did not occur; but Rossetti's orchestration of defenses against it added to the impression of an activist Catholic party at court, and his attitudes may well have contributed to the king's diffidence about this parliament and the next.

In the summer of 1640 the anticipated anti-Catholic reaction set in strongly, aggravated by the king's reliance on Scottish, English, Welsh, and Irish Catholics in the Second Bishops' War. Both sympathizers and critics of the court were coming ever more to picture it as the sole support and embattled defender of Catholicism, and popish-plot rumors proliferated in the months before the Long Parliament. The most extended exposé, the so-called Habernfeld Plot, was sympathetic to Laud and the king, but pictured London and the court as swarming with subversive Catholic elements. It was now that the language of "popish conspiracy" came to dominate the political rhetoric of English parliamentary leaders. Prominent members of the Short Parliament took independent initiatives after its dissolution. They met in London while the king was in the north and prepared a petition for a new parliament. The petition emphasized the political dangers of popery, thus foreshadowing the rhetoric of the Long Parliament. Popish conspiracy would be a central theme uniting and dominating many other grievances; the ministers who came under attack, notably Strafford and Laud, would be vilified as popish sympathizers, and this label would be used to explain why and how they were a danger to English liberty and religion.

Disappointed Hopes: Strafford, the Prince Palatine, and the Falling Out with France

Strafford's return to England as the king's chief minister in the autumn of 1639 created the possibility of new domestic and foreign political configurations. His previous attachment to the "peace party" or Spanish party, which had aligned him with Arundel, Cottington, and Laud, was based as much on practical considerations, not all of them still as weighty, as on a network of personal relationships. Arundel was no personal friend; in any case, he had financial difficulties at the end of 1639 and would no longer count for much in court politics, despite the king's continued partiality for him.[1] Of the two secretaries of state, Strafford preferred the anti-Spanish Coke to Windebank, despite the latter's courtship of him. From a political point of view, the peace policy might seem less essential to Strafford as chief minister than as lord lieutenant of Ireland. In Ireland he had depended on English neutrality to keep the country quiet and profitable; moreover, the peace party dominated the Irish committee of the privy council whose cooperation he needed to give him a free hand in Ireland. Now, moving into the larger task of advising the king on policy for all three kingdoms, Strafford had reason to reconsider England's international stance.

Strafford's cordial relations with most of the French party created an opening for these men to attain the dominance they had been seeking. From Ireland, Strafford had carried on a continuous correspondence with Northumberland, Henry Percy, and the countess of Carlisle; he was also on friendly terms with Conway, Leicester, and Jermyn. Of the entire group, only the earl of Holland was his avowed enemy.[2] So, in the autumn of 1639, the French connection saw an opportunity to rise to higher office with the assistance of Strafford and the queen. In June Leicester had come home from France in great haste and been sworn a privy councillor; he now sought either the office of deputy of Ireland or that of secretary of state, which was clearly dropping from the hands of the aged and ailing Coke.[3] Northumberland, lord admiral since 1638, had been frustrated by the king's failure to seek or follow his advice in the winter of 1638–39; with Strafford at the helm, he might hope to exercise more real influence. Northumberland moved into the inner circle of the council along with Hamilton and Strafford in November 1639; in 1640 he would be named general of the king's army for the Second

Bishops' War. On a lower level, Henry Percy was promoted within the royal household in September 1639.[4]

Friends of the Palatine family had their hopes raised, too, by the end of the First Bishops' War and the beginning of a new regime. The defeat of the prince Palatine's forces in Germany in the autumn of 1638 had not ended his efforts to get into the field. In December 1638 he had journeyed to Hamburg, where Roe continued negotiations on his behalf, and had been welcomed and encouraged by both his great uncle, the king of Denmark, and Melander, general of the Hessian troops. The project of hiring Hessians for the prince's use was revived. Despite Elizabeth's fears that "the business of Scotland and queen mother being in England will hinder much," the king granted his nephew £15,000 early in 1639, with the hope that France would also contribute to support this force.[5] Both Elizabeth and Roe favored overtures to Bernard of Saxe-Weimar, master of the Rhine after his capture of Breisach in December 1638. Presently in French pay, Bernard had more common interests with the Palatine house, which a marriage with one of the Palatine princesses might consolidate.[6] Impatient of the delays in England and Hamburg, Charles Lewis had begun to make levies of men and to stockpile arms and ammunition provided by the Dutch.

The Pacification of Berwick had been greeted joyfully by Elizabeth because it removed the major impediment to British aid at a crucial moment. Both Melander and Rakoczi of Hungary were declaring their reluctance to serve France except in association with the prince Palatine. "The business of Scotland doth hinder all," Elizabeth had complained to Roe in February 1639; and "all would be well if Scotland were well," she lamented in May. Hearing of the pacification, she exulted: "My dear brother did all himself in spite of papists and clergy who did all they could to disturb it." She also noted the concern for the prince's cause expressed by the Scottish Covenanters: "Lesley [general of the Scots] doth offer to go with his troops to the Prince Elector."[7] She continued through the summer to hope that the English or Scottish army, or both, might be deployed on her son's behalf.[8]

In July 1639 the death of Bernard of Saxe-Weimar opened further possibilities to the prince. Sir Oliver Fleming, who as agent to Switzerland had watched Bernard's triumphant progress up the Rhine, returned to England to urge the king to put his nephew at the head of the Weimarian army, whose officers would prefer him to a French general. Charles Lewis sent agents to the Weimarian officers, made overtures for Swedish support, and went immediately to England—crossing with the king's message begging him not to come. Con's comment on the prince's arrival indicates again how the Palatine house could be viewed as a potential rival to the king's family in times of crisis: "There would be very much to ponder in it did not his good nature put him above suspicion."[9] The French ambassador was glad to see him coming and hoped that he would "confuse" the Spanish faction at court; the French government offered him command of the Weimar army if he got an English subsidy.[10] The Spanish agents there and abroad, under this threat of military action, pressed for resumption of negotiation on the Palatinate.[11] There were council meetings in August on Palatine affairs, but nothing substantial was decided.[12] When the king had the Spanish fleet at his mercy later in the year, it provided another occasion for proposals on the prince's behalf. The Dutch urged him to seize the whole fleet, fill it with English troops, and send it against Spain under the prince's command. The French again offered the Weimar army, this time with financial support, in exchange for a free hand to wipe out the Spanish fleet.[13] But, as before, the king allowed to slip through his grasp the opportunity to extract major concessions from any side; he thus lost the best chance he had to aid his nephew.

Perhaps anxious to be rid of the young prince and the challenge of Protestant politics he embodied, Charles I managed to get together a further payment of £10,000 for him in October 1639, with promises of further supply if he succeeded in winning the Weimar army. Agents were dispatched to Switzerland and Germany, and the prince himself set out to travel through France to the army—scarcely secretly, since all the diplomatic community knew of his plans, but formally incognito.[14]

Tensions between England and France had been aggravated by the king's rejection of French proposals and the prince's plan to detach the Weimarian army from French control. On the English side, there was suspicion of French involvement in Scotland, expressed even by those who had sponsored a French alliance eighteen months earlier. The queen was openly resentful of French refusal to release officers for the northern expedition. Elizabeth of Bohemia also believed that the French encouraged the Covenanters.[15] There had been alarms all during the summer about possible French attacks on the south coast. The French were equally suspicious of English intentions and wondered whether the forces raised for the Scottish campaign might soon be turned against them. Bellièvre saw the court leadership in the autumn of 1639 as anti-French in orientation; his efforts to win over Cottington had failed, and without Cottington there was no hope of gaining Windebank. Only the earl of Holland, at odds with Montagu in the queen's court and with Strafford in the king's, remained a firm and sometimes influential friend of France.[16]

These mutual suspicions cast doubt on the likelihood of any effective joint action, and Richelieu would never allow the seasoned and powerful Weimarian force to fall into the hands of an independent agent. As Charles Lewis passed by Moulins early in November, he was politely detained by French government agents. He would not be set free until the Weimarian army was firmly in French control. Neither Leicester's efforts nor those of young Thomas Windebank, who was sent to France in December to negotiate the prince's release, were successful. The French made the prince's release conditional on promises of English funding for the army; Charles I refused to negotiate that or any other issue prior to the prince's release.[17]

These dramatic events did much to frustrate those at the English court who had formerly been counted among the friends of France. In the winter of 1639–40, no courtier could comfortably express sympathy for France, and policies based on collaboration with France were unlikely to receive a cordial hearing. At the same time, the individual ambitions of these men were disappointed, in part because Strafford was not always able to help them, in part because his orientation remained, as it had been in Ireland, firmly toward Spain. Leicester continued to be favored by the queen, but neither her efforts nor Strafford's sufficed to win him appointment as secretary of state. Laud was not his friend, regarding him as unsound in religion, namely, too sympathetic to Puritans. Strafford was able neither to persuade the king to retain his old friend Coke in the secretaryship nor to prevent the king from appointing Sir Henry Vane in January 1640.[18] While Coke had been generally regarded as a staunch supporter of French and Dutch interests, Vane's standpoint was still unclear, with some regarding him as pro-Spanish.[19] Over the winter, the perception that Strafford was "wholly Spanish" in his sympathies led to speculation about a reshuffling of ministers, in which any suspected of partiality toward the Scots, the Dutch, or the French would be replaced— the cases of Coke and Vane doubtless fed these rumors. A mutual recall of ambassadors between England and France was anticipated, and when Bellièvre departed in January 1640, he was not soon replaced.[20]

The agents of France increasingly cultivated their contacts with the king's critics in England and Scotland. Bellièvre had already started to negotiate independently with the Covenanters for troop levies in Scotland. He reported that they would appeal to France for aid if the English king made another expedition against them, and that in exchange for support they were willing to insist on the inclusion in the English privy council of Scottish members who could effectively balance the power of the friends of Spain.[21] As the political crisis deepened in the early months of 1640, the French secretary Montreuil hovered in the wings, waiting for disaffected English courtiers who might be used to his king's advantage.[22]

The king's decision in December to call a parliament evoked both uneasiness and some hope in French observers. A successful parliament might provide Charles I with an army and the means to foment trouble in Normandy in retaliation for the arrest of the prince Palatine and the supposed French assistance to the Covenanters. "They [the king's ministers] cherish dark designs here," the Venetian ambassador reported, and "these are vigorously supported by the suggestions of the queen mother and by the malcontents of France who sojourn at this court."[23] This apprehension was heightened by the news of a special Spanish embassy coming to England; it was said that these representatives were eagerly awaited by the king and Strafford, who perhaps hoped for serious proposals of dynastic and military alliance. The French redoubled their efforts to detach the duchess of Chevreuse from the English court, since "from her more than from any other cause they apprehend that precipitous movements may find encouragement."[24]

At the same time, the new parliament might give a positive opening to France's friends at court, in conjunction with friends of the Palatine family, to mediate the quarrel with Scotland and direct English attention to the Palatine cause. The Venetian ambassador reported that the French would try to conciliate parliamentary leaders to this end. Indeed, the French released Prince Charles Lewis in March, on the eve of the parliament. The gesture displeased Charles I because it was not a triumph for his own diplomacy but was clearly meant to placate the prince's supporters in the coming parliament.[25]

Dutch and Habsburg Rivalry at the English Court: The Role of the Queen Mother

Meanwhile, rivalry between ambassadors from the United Provinces and the Habsburg powers dominated the diplomatic scene at court. Despite the predominance of peace party councillors, the Dutch had friends at court, and they would need them.[26] The Spanish had finally assembled the great fleet that had been so long in the planning; with it they hoped to damage the French fleet and eliminate the Dutch one, while simultaneously reinforcing Flanders and collecting soldiers for service in Spain.[27] Composed partly of English transport ships, this fleet left the northern coast of Spain on 26 August, carrying 10,000 troops and a large sum of money destined for Dunkirk. The Spanish government apparently believed that it had assurance of naval protection from Charles I. Upon reaching the Channel, the Spanish fleet hugged the southern coast of England, but on 6 September it was intercepted by the Dutch. As the Spanish ambassador desperately negotiated with the king over the price he would accept to protect the Spanish fleet, the Dutch gathered in strength; after several days' battle, the Spanish took refuge in the Downs. While opposing ambassadors tried to buy English support, the English fleet under Sir John Pennington played an uneasy role as truce-enforcer between the two fleets.

Details of these negotiations remain rather murky, but the results were disastrous for Spain. It is certain that Charles I asked a very high price (one source says £150,000) and it seems that the delayed Spanish response permitted the Dutch and French to place a winning bid. At any rate, Admiral Tromp became impatient of delay when he saw the Spaniards being reinforced from Dunkirk; on the night of 11 October, he loosed his one hundred armed vessels on the hapless Spanish ships. Three quarters of them were destroyed, run aground, or taken by the Dutch as the English watched passively.[28]

This high drama on the seas that brought the Thirty Years War so close to England greatly impressed public opinion. Well before the battle, the gathering of the fleets in the Channel had evoked memories of the Armada of 1588, and, judging from the detail with which the incident was reported in contemporary correspondence, it absorbed the attention of the public for weeks on end.[29] The Dutch ambassador played on English fears of Spanish invasion. From the start he claimed that the Spanish fleet had "pernicious designs" on the British Isles. After Tromp's victory, when the king expressed righteous indignation at the violation of English territorial waters, the Dutch ambassador pressed his attempt to rally sympathy, claiming that the Spanish fleet had been part of a great design upon England.[30] These allegations seemed to be borne out by stories of a dying English Catholic on board one of the Spanish ships, who told his confessor a tale of Spanish intrigue involving a fifth column of English Catholic nobles. Such tales confirmed fears that the fleet was somehow part of the king's rumored negotiations with Spain for aid against the Scots.[31] It was later remembered that Strafford reached London to take up his new role as chief minister on 2 October in the midst of the crisis; he would later be suspected as an instigator of it.[32]

The king's complaints about the Downs battle (whether his anger was real or simulated, none could decide) prompted the Dutch to make a conciliatory gesture; moreover, they genuinely feared an Anglo-Spanish alliance. An ambassador extraordinary was sent to London carrying proposals for the renewal and broadening of the 1628 Anglo-Dutch alliance and suggestions of new dynastic ties between the Orange and Stuart houses.[33] Henrietta Maria was invited to be godmother to the newborn son of the prince of Orange. In January 1640 Heenvliet came as a second ambassador extraordinary to England. But the king reacted coldly to both political and dynastic proposals; diplomatic gossip had it that the Dutch were being entertained only to push up the Spanish bid. Both Dutch agents left England in mid-March 1640, much discouraged by what they perceived as ever-tightening bonds between England and Spain.[34]

Spanish outrage at their humiliation in the Downs had not prevented Madrid from recognizing the necessity of conciliating, not alienating, the English government. Military reversals had already persuaded the Habsburgs to continue throughout 1639 their negotiations with England on three or four fronts, principally Madrid and London. Sir Arthur Hopton in Madrid was anxious to get an agreement. After a slow start, he had begun to feel by June 1639 that there was progress toward settling the Palatine issue, the question of defending Flanders, and perhaps even an Anglo-Spanish marriage. Although the unpopularity of the Spanish agent Cárdenas at the court hampered London negotiations, Marie de Chevreuse represented Spanish interests there and persuaded her royal hosts of the desirability of an Anglo-Spanish match. They wrote to Hopton, encouraging him to pursue the matter.[35]

Brussels continued to serve as a convenient sounding board for Anglo-Habsburg overtures. It might have seemed a natural arena for serious negotiations, with its proximity to England and the presence there of the Spanish king's own brother. But Balthazar Gerbier, the English agent on the spot, was as unpopular in Brussels as Cárdenas was in England; in any case, Charles I and Olivares were never prepared at the same moment to delegate binding authority to others. However, the unavowed exchanges at Brussels between Princess Phalzburg and Gerbier continued, and rumors of these talks naturally led to speculation about their content and import. In April 1639 John Taylor returned from Vienna, loudly protesting that all he had said of the Brussels talks was true; he soon found himself in the Tower. The emperor, aware of a quickening pace in Anglo-Spanish negotiations and unwilling to let Spain make decisions on his behalf, sent his own envoy to Brussels. The envoy corresponded with Laud and Windebank, but shortly returned to Vienna without having accomplished anything.[36]

These diplomatic flurries led to suggestions, all during the summer of 1639, that Marie de Medici and her friends and advisers were closely involved in Anglo-Habsburg negotiations at Brussels. The exile circle would indeed have been glad to play a major mediating role; that would have served their own interests.[37] The queen mother and others sought credit with Spain through diplomatic maneuvering in Brussels, some of it ostensibly on behalf of England. Marie de Medici was anxious to return to Brussels and tried, with little success, to ingratiate herself with her former hosts. The English court, weary of the expense she represented, supported this attempt while outwardly paying her every honor.[38] Moreover, the king and queen genuinely cared about the marriage negotiations with Spain, in which she might prove a useful intermediary. They therefore tolerated the intrigues that were generated about her in London, as well as the diplomatic machinations across the Channel. Elizabeth of Bohemia reacted quite differently. Outraged at tales of negotiations involving her son's interests (and very likely sacrificing some of them) about which she had not even been informed, she complained bitterly to Roe that "the queen mother hath strange people about her that are able to undertake or do any impertinence."[39]

The intrigues of the queen mother and her exile friends actually concerned the prince Palatine only indirectly; they aimed primarily at disrupting Richelieu's government. Mme de Chevreuse, Princess Phalzburg, and other associates of Lorraine were keeping afloat the idea of trading Lorraine for the Palatinate. Trouble for Richelieu at home might force him to terms. The exiles were encouraged by the popular discontent that pressures of war and taxation had created in France by the summer of 1639. When the Nu-Pieds revolt broke out in Normandy, they saw an opportunity to take advantage of civil turmoil.[40] Giustiniani reported that "the French malcontents hold very frequent meetings in the house of the queen mother, constantly discussing schemes for making trouble for that crown. Leading [English] ministers do not cease either, with the influential support of that queen [Marie de Medici] to induce the king to connive at this, so that they may get a good start with their ill devised and restless plans."[41] Bellièvre was informed of this plotting against his government and reported that the exiles planned an attack on Brittany. This did not mature, but throughout the summer the queen mother, her ministers, the Spanish resident Cárdenas, and such leading exiles as Madame de Chevreuse, the marquis of La Vieuville, and the duke of La Vallette were seen in constant consultation. Moreover, the English court was visibly drawn into these intrigues. The queen was known to be informed of them; Bellièvre suspected that English couriers had carried messages from Chevreuse to her friends in France; and Giustiniani thought that Charles I might well lend support to the conspirators, given the queen mother's "great confidence" with him and the "malicious advantage" that La Vallette was pressing.[42]

Over the winter of 1639–40 the courts of the queen and queen mother continued to swarm with anti-Richelieu elements, while the king eagerly awaited the arrival of a new ambassador extraordinary from Spain.[43] The disaster at the Downs, followed by the new Dutch initiatives, seems to have convinced the Spanish government that English affairs demanded a more effective agent than Cárdenas and a more official one than Marie de Chevreuse. In November the marquis of Velada was accredited to the English court, and early in 1640 he began the lengthy trip to England. Described by Giustiniani as "a man of great note owing to his high rank and his favor with the count duke [Olivares]," Velada was someone that Charles had met on his youthful trip to Spain. It was reported that he would bring marriage proposals, a large sum of money to bribe the court, and requests for English ships and English assistance in sustaining the Norman revolt. Soon, the court was astonished to hear that a second extraordinary ambassador, the Marquis Virgilio Malvezzi, was also on his way to England.[44]

Velada did not arrive until April, but other Habsburg agents were busy with the French exiles. Madame de Chevreuse was assisted by an agent of Prince Thomas of Savoy, who encouraged the king to foster rebellion in Normandy as a means of forcing Richelieu to release the prince Palatine and to permit Marie de Medici's reentry into France. Giustiniani believed that "they find the king and most influential ministers much inclined that way."[45] The imperial agent Lisola, arriving in London early in 1640, decided almost immediately that destabilizing French domestic politics was the easiest way to relieve pressure on imperial forces and that England was an ideal base for this. He soon made contact with the exile conspirators, as well as with their allies still in France, the count of Soissons[46] and Gaston d'Orléans. He heartily approved their plans, reporting to Vienna that La Vallette and Monsigot were in touch with the Norman rebels and the duke of Soubise with the "Croquants" of Poitou. He looked forward to another Norman uprising under La Vallette, as well as a rebellion in the southwest under Soubise and the duke d'Épernon, to be assisted by a British expedition to the Isle of Rhé; all of these would be coordinated with an imperial invasion of Burgundy. Charles I, he claimed, had assured La Vallette and Soubise that he would not stand in their way. Undaunted by the difficulty of getting firm promises of ships, men, and money from Brussels or Spain, let alone from the English king, Lisola pressed this ambitious plan upon the Spanish ambassadors after their arrival.[47]

On the eve of the Short Parliament, then, England's stance vis-à-vis other European powers afforded little comfort to committed English Protestants, including those arriving at Westminster as members of parliament. The prince Palatine was but recently released after a humiliating internment, from which his uncle had been either unwilling or unable to extricate him. The French party was in eclipse at court because of the wrangle over this issue and because of well-founded suspicions on both sides that each government was aiding and abetting the enemies of the other. The Dutch had failed in their most recent efforts to draw the English into an alliance, and the friends of Spain seemed entrenched in power. In ever-worsening financial straits, the king was reportedly authorizing disbursements for only two objects: the military preparations against the Covenanters and the support of the queen mother's establishment.[48] Not only one but two extraordinary ambassadors from Spain were daily expected at the English court—coming, it was said, with generous offers of men and money to help Charles I recover control of Scotland, in exchange for a binding English commitment to Spain.

On 20 April Velada made his first entrance to court with "great pomp," and his initial audience with the king was attended by "all the leading lords and ladies of the court . . . as well as a large crowd of people."[49] His colleague Malvezzi arrived within the week. The Venetian ambassador reported their long and frequent conferences with the duchess of Chevreuse and their close contacts with other French exiles. He noted that they especially worked to induce the queen mother to make trouble in the French provinces by arguing that this was the only means to pave a way for her own return to France. These developments, he remarked, were opposed by "those who are attached at once to the public cause and to France."[50] It was a scene well calculated to disturb the M.P.s gathering at Westminster.

Rossetti and the Court Catholic Party

Nor did the development of court Catholicism during the winter of 1639–40 offer any cause for relief. The important developments in the court Catholic party during the winter of 1639–40 were the revival of the cardinalate negotiation and the increasing prominence of the queen mother as a protector of English Catholics. The former was the result of Con's death; the latter was largely due to the natural affinity between Marie de Medici and her compatriot Count Carlo Rossetti, the Ferrarese nobleman and prelate who succeeded Con as papal agent at the queen's court.

Con left England in August 1639 on a royal ship, laden with gifts from the queen and court. His successor inherited the sympathy Con had evoked in some quarters, the animosity he had aroused in others, and the unsolved problems of the English Catholic community. Although Rossetti had left his clerical robes in Italy, his arrival was preceded by rumors that he was a prelate and came as a nuncio to England.[51] The king received him warmly and gave him audience almost immediately; but Rossetti spoke no English and had no prior contacts at the English court.[52] He therefore enjoyed less scope for creative interference in English politics, although he had the freedom of the court and attempted to continue Con's policies.

Rossetti was much less intimate with the king than Con had been; like Panzani, he worked through Windebank, Father Philip, and the queen. He was also a close companion of the queen mother and her advisor Fabbroni, both of whom were interested in cultivating the pope and the Curia. The Barberini family, who hoped to use Marie de Medici to smooth over the ruffled relations between Spain and the Holy See, encouraged the relationship.[53] Depending on intermediaries for much of his information about the court and the king's views, Rossetti was more credulous and optimistic than Con had become; in his early days he reported happily to Rome that Charles secretly leaned to Catholicism. Six months later Rossetti was still repeating optimistically the reports he received about the king's views on matters such as the position of the altar, use of crucifixes, auricular confession, and the marriage of bishops.[54]

During the months between his arrival and the opening of the Short Parliament, Rossetti continued Con's role as leader of the English Catholics, intervening energetically and successfully with the queen on their behalf. He was no more able than Con had been to heal the rifts among the more vocal segments of the clergy, especially the Jesuits and the seculars. The royal and ambassadorial chapels continued as hives of Catholic activity and devotion. Rossetti made special mention of the attendance at his and the queen mother's chapels and of the occasions when her Jesuit confessor, John Suffren, preached.[55]

Rossetti took over from Con the half-finished business of the Catholic contribution and continued Con's practice of meeting with gentry and clergy at his home. His first task was to answer the complaints of Catholics in various counties that official harassment was hindering the contribution. At Rossetti's request, Windebank intervened to stop this and ordered an end to the activities of the pursuivant Pulford. Continuing problems in the north were dealt with by the friendly intervention of Strafford. The last £4,000 of the contribution was turned over in April 1640.[56]

The Catholic meetings in London were protested by what Rossetti called "Puritan" and "Protestant" courtiers, and in particular by Archbishop Laud. But Rossetti was protected by the queen and her circle (Winter, Philip, Montagu, and Digby), who fended off complaints. In December 1639 the meetings were stopped for a time, but Laud's objections were overridden by the queen and her friends. Rossetti used the gatherings to discuss not only the contribution but also means of mitigating the effects of the penal laws and other concerns of the Catholics.[57]

Quarrels among the missionaries plagued Rossetti as they had Con. The French Capuchins serving the queen's chapel enjoyed special privileges; for this reason and because they were foreigners, they were envied by other clergy. The mission of their superior, Father Jean Marie Trélon, to Italy in the spring of 1639 (ostensibly to carry the queen's gift to the Loreto shrine, but also to plead for papal assistance for the king) aroused suspicion. Some claimed that Trélon traveled to Rome to procure permission from the pope for Catholics to attend Protestant services. Some missionaries tolerated this practice, as Rossetti had complained, and Laud never lost an opportunity to argue that the papal agents were unnecessarily unyielding on this point.[58]

It also fell to Rossetti's lot to defend the Jesuits, who had again angered the government, this time by appointing the controversial Edward Knott as English provincial in June 1639. The king at first demanded that the appointment be rescinded, but neither Barberini nor the Jesuit general would budge. Instead they wrote to Rossetti, to Knott's predecessor More, to Father Philip, and to the queen mother's confessor, as well as to both queens, in an effort to change the king's mind.[59] By the end of February 1640, a compromise had been arranged whereby Knott would retain his position but remain out of the country, in Flanders. The former provincial, Henry More, and the rector of London, Henry Bedingfield (alias Silisden), remained to manage the English province with the advice and assistance of the queen mother's confessor, Father John Suffren.[60]

Nor was the question of secular clergy organization yet settled to anyone's satisfaction. In the months before he left, Con had frequently urged upon the Curia the importance of giving the seculars an approved superior and the wisdom of appointing Champney, already serving de facto in the position and recognized by the English government.[61] Rossetti inherited the problem and the resentment that Roman delay and intransigence had created among the seculars. Rome finally decided to appoint not a dean, but a "praepositus"; moreover, it nominated neither Champney nor anyone else acceptable to the chapter, but an aged and relatively obscure cleric named Cuthbert Trollope, who worked in Durham county.[62] Rossetti felt that the outcome was even worse than the inordinate delay and attempted to conceal from the clergy how rudely their hopes had been dashed; at the same time, he tried to persuade the Curia to change its decision. But when he invited Trollope to London in March 1640, the members of the chapter were instantly suspicious. They blamed the Jesuits, whom they saw as seeking revenge for Knott's exclusion; they referred bitterly to Rossetti's attempts to destroy their chapter; and they looked to their court friends Montagu and Philip to save the situation.[63] Their agent, Peter Fitton (*vere* Biddulph), soon returned to

Rome to represent the queen between Hamilton's departure and Digby's arrival as agent. He carried not only the queen's recommendation of Montagu for the biretta, but also a number of letters from English Catholics that had been solicited by Champney on behalf of Montagu, who was regarded by the chapter as their one constant friend with influence at Rome. Fitton would make it his business, Rossetti reported, to do all he could for Champney with the Roman officials.[64] This rivalry, intrigue, and competition for the patronage of the Catholic queen had little to do with English politics, but there were few Protestants in a position to be sure of this. Meanwhile, all the activity added to the impression that the court was teeming with busy priests, and the immunity enjoyed by the priests naturally gave rise to questions about their objectives and the king's intentions.

More politically relevant was the direction taken by the cardinalate negotiations, which came to focus on a highly placed English courtier and a member of the king's own family—Wat Montagu and Ludovick Stuart d'Aubigny. The negotiation had never completely lapsed, but the optimistic days of 1637 had given way to months of stalemate and weary disillusionment. Reports reaching England from Rome portrayed the delay as the result of sordid political intrigue, and there was speculation at court that Rome was using the agency only for political ends (to gather English state secrets and arouse the jealousy of other European powers), with no real intention of assisting English Catholics.[65]

As early as 1638, alternative candidates for the biretta had begun to be canvassed. Wat Montagu had his ambitions and expected the assistance of Sir Kenelm Digby as Roman agent. There was also a member of the royal family in contention. The king's cousin Ludovick Stuart d'Aubigny, brother to the duke of Lennox, had been educated in France for Catholic ecclesiastical preferment. While scarcely more than a child, he had been suggested by Panzani for the role of British cardinal; and his arrival in England in May 1637 for an extended visit had revived talk of his candidacy. The Lennox-d'Aubigny branch of the Stuarts had a long history of barely concealed Catholicism—a "courtier-like Erastianism grafted upon a Catholic past," as David Mathew has put it.[66] In March 1639 Lennox had suddenly confronted the queen with a seemingly serious request that she nominate Ludovick for the cardinal's cap. But Henrietta had never cared for the Lennox family; and in any case, she had not then given up hope of Con's promotion. Montagu began at about the same time to mount a subtle campaign. He talked of retiring from the world to enter the Roman Oratory, but put off his departure from month to month—first to help with the Catholic contribution, then to attend the queen until the king returned from the north. Meanwhile, he intrigued to have Hamilton replaced by Sir Kenelm Digby as agent in Rome; with a man on the spot to support him, he would be better placed to make his bid. Hamilton's relatives fought to keep him in the position and a compromise was reached whereby Hamilton would remain until the spring of 1640, when Digby would replace him. The nomination of Digby was understood to indicate the queen's support for Montagu, should Con's candidacy fail.[67]

After Con's death in January 1640, the negotiation revived, with the various candidates enlisting support at court, abroad, and in Rome. Montagu could count on the queen's backing; she had indicated it in the very letters of condolence she wrote the pope on Con's death. The duchess of Chevreuse, Henry Jermyn, the English abbess Mary Ward, and many of the secular clergy favored his candidacy. The king, however, was adamantly opposed and conveyed to Rossetti a warning that Montagu's elevation would have "pernicious consequences for the Catholic religion" in England.[68] Nor was Montagu highly regarded at Rome. The French government, which had its own candidate in the person of DuPerron, did not trust him.[69] Rossetti alleged (with what accuracy it is difficult to say) that Montagu was suspect to many English Catholics because of his Puritan relatives.[70]

Ludovick's main support came from the king. Windebank spoke to Rossetti on his behalf, and Rossetti's report to Rome was favorable. Apart from his youth, Ludovick was in every way qualified, he said—by birth, wealth, education, and the king's favor. He had, however, influential enemies. Marie de Medici thought him a client of Richelieu, while the cardinal regarded him as pro-Spanish.[71] The queen's distaste for him was pronounced, and Rossetti heard that the king and queen were quite at odds over the issue.[72] Whatever its outcome would be, the introduction of a Stuart candidate for cardinal made an impression at court. The Venetian ambassador referred to Ludovick as "one of the most conspicuous persons at the court from his close connection with the royal house." Later that year he reported that the king's negotiations with the pope on behalf of Ludovick did not go unnoticed.[73]

By the time Peter Fitton left for Rome in March 1640 with the queen's new nominations, a compromise had been reached and the names of both Montagu and Ludovick were included. But there was little doubt of the queen's real wishes, and Fitton stopped on his way in Paris to see Mazarin, who might, it was hoped, induce the French king to send a letter of recommendation for Montagu.[74] There were other candidates as well. Digby had his own ambitions, although he kept them quiet while Montagu was in the limelight; and Father Philip had been mentioned just after Con's death. Rome was inclined to look favorably on Philip and on Ludovick, but thought DuPerron unsuitable because of his close association with France.[75] Discussions on this subject were still being pursued as late as May 1641, but the adamant opposition to Montagu in Rome ended any immediate possibilities of a promotion.[76]

Criticism and Defense of Court Catholicism on the Eve of the Short Parliament

During the 1639 campaign there had been expressions of anti-Catholicism in print. These proliferated and intensified in hostility in the summer of 1640 after the Short Parliament failed. In the interim there was a relative lull, a moderation perhaps induced by anticipation of parliament and the hope for redress of grievances there.

Of course this restraint was not universal. From Edinburgh, Baillie sent out a violently anti-Laudian tract entitled *Canterburian's Self-Conviction*. He connected Laud with an intricate popish conspiracy at the English court and blamed him for the king's failure to pursue an aggressively Protestant foreign policy. Haranguing against the mutual agency and the queen's chapels, he mocked the loyalist pamphlet published in Dublin with Strafford's encouragement by "the personate Jesuit Lysimachus Nicanor, a prime Canterburian."[77] He exhorted the English parliament to renounce war with the Scots, which only weakened both parties and left them vulnerable to a papal-Franco-Spanish invasion: "The pope hath a pretty confidence to join England to Scotland, that so the reduction of the whole isle, and your Ireland with it, to the see of Rome, may be set up as an eternal trophy to the honor of this pope's family; surely the ground stones of this hope are laid on to deep plots, that except the hand of God and the king in this present Parliament pull them up, Pope Urban, for all his age, may yet live to put the triumphal copestone upon that building."[78]

English Puritan voices were also raised. The Gunpowder Day sermons of Richard Heyricke, dean of Manchester, alluded first guardedly and then more bluntly to the toleration of Catholicism at court. On 5 November 1638 Heyricke had preached on the text "Therefore (brethren) stand fast" (2 Thess. 2:15). Emphasizing the "bloodthirstiness" of "such papists that adhere to the pope of Rome as to their head, Italian, Spanish, Jesuited, Gunpowder papists," he lamented the increase of popery in England and argued that neither Rome nor individual Catholics should be offered concessions: "Cruelty for Christ is godliness." Heyricke described the pope's agents as behind every plot against the crown—"crafty, subtle, base and impudent," like the frogs that came into Pharaoh's house.[79]

In November 1639 Heyricke spoke more boldly on current events in the text "Simeon and Levi are brethren, instruments of cruelty are in their habitations" (Gen. 49:5-7). Heyricke threw the whole blame for the First Bishops' War on Jesuits and their supporters in a sermon "laying open the perjuries, treacheries, treasons, the murders, massacres, cruelties of Rome-Christians." He compared Simeon and Levi, the king-killers, not to the rebellious Scots, but to the papists. So, while making a strong statement against rebellion—"it is against the law of nations, against the law of nature, against the royal law of God, to kill, smite, to touch a king, yea to revile him, or in our secret chambers to think evil against him"—Heyricke sidestepped any criticism of the Scots. The danger to the king, he argued, came from the Catholics and Jesuits who were shown clemency and even allowed into his presence: "How ever for the present they may strive to appear good subjects, traitors will ever be traitors." Conventional allusions to Catholic dependence on the will of the pope ("a rotten thread . . . to hang so sharp a pointed sword in, over the head of kings"), to mistreatment of Protestants in Europe, and to Jesuit teaching against the oath of allegiance culminated in the warning that no compromise with Catholicism must be tolerated. "It hath been the desire of many, the endeavor of some, to work a reconciliation betwixt the Church of Rome and us," but such a reunion could not be.[80]

In London, Rossetti reported some anti-Catholic sentiment in the winter of 1639–40 accompanying the Puritan pressure for a parliament. He expected measures against Catholics, and especially against the mutual agency, to be near the top of any parliamentary agenda. The countess of Holland had been heard to say that parliament must destroy the Catholics, who had attained "excessive power" in England.[81] He went on to report that Secretary Coke had imprisoned a secular priest for refusing the oath of allegiance, as well as two Scottish Minims, one of whom had preached against the oath in the Venetian ambassador's chapel. After Coke lost office, Rossetti reported that he blamed Catholics for the loss and agitated among his Puritan friends for the end of the agency and the closing of the Capuchin chapel.[82]

Rossetti's reports reflect a rigid and hostile attitude at court toward the upcoming parliament. Apparently convinced that the Covenanters were abetted by France and by sympathetic English councillors, the king claimed the Scots wanted to take away from him all but the "appearance and title" of royal authority. As Con had done, Rossetti encouraged this wary and fearful stance, the more so as he regarded parliament as a serious threat to English Catholicism. He reported to Rome that parliaments were "always hateful" to English kings and urged on the king his own view that there was an imminent threat to the monarchy itself. Rossetti suggested that the "Protestants"[83] should ally with the Catholics to counterbalance the powerful faction of Puritans who aimed to subvert the monarchy. He and his court friends schemed to get Catholics into the Commons and exempted from the usual oaths, in order to protect the Catholic cause against the anticipated attacks on the agency, the chapels, and the lax enforcement of recusancy laws.[84]

In April Rossetti got both Henrietta Maria and Marie de Medici to lecture the king at length on the need to protect Catholics from parliamentary attack, and he reported that Charles had promised not to give in to "the will of the Puritans." The queen also urged Strafford to protect Irish Catholics from Puritans in the Irish parliament who complained about them. As he left for Dublin in March with Toby Mathew, Strafford was said to have promised "every moderation." In anticipation of the parliament, the privy council issued an order for the arrest of English Catholics attending ambassadorial chapels; Rossetti hurried to the queen, who promised to nullify the order.[85]

On the eve of the Short Parliament, then, court Catholicism presented as sinister an aspect to English Protestants as it had a year before. Rossetti had continued Con's aggressive protection of Catholics and had become to some extent identified with the Jesuit order. The revival of the cardinalate negotiation had placed in the limelight the figures of Ludovick Stuart, the king's own cousin, and Wat Montagu, friend of the French exiles. Because of his assumptions about Calvinists and his fears for English Catholics, Rossetti had fed the king's anxieties about the upcoming parliament and encouraged him, as Con had done previously, to depend on extraparliamentary resources ranging from a domestic Catholic party to a papal loan.

The Short Parliament and Its Aftermath

The king's diffidence toward the approaching parliament and his schemes to overawe, outwit, or even overpower it were not merely Rossetti's imaginings. They seem to be corroborated by Windebank and other witnesses. In December 1639 Windebank had described the attitude taken by the king and some of his ministers toward the parliament: "The lords were desirous that the king and his people should meet if it were possible, in the ancient and ordinary way of parliament . . . that so he might leave his people without excuse, and have wherewithal to justify himself to

God and the world . . . but that if his people should not cheerfully according to their duties meet him in that . . . the world might see he is
forced contrary to his own inclination to use extraordinary means, rather
than by the peevishness of some few factious spirits to suffer his state and
government to be lost."[86] By raising a large sum of money in advance
through the loans of privy councillors and gathering together a large
army, the king might be able to keep order around London, dissolve parliament at the first sign of trouble, and enforce the collection of needed
revenue should parliament prove recalcitrant.

Bellièvre reported the king's intention "to hold a parliament in his own
fashion, and by this means render himself absolute in this country."[87]
The Venetian ambassador heard from the king's "more confidential ministers," as he called them, that the army being mobilized ostensibly for a
second northern expedition was intended to "keep within bounds, by the
fear of these forces, the parliament which they have decided to open on
the 13th April."[88] During the March elections Giustiniani reported that
the king was discouraged by the returns and that he secretly intended to
use the army "to bridle the insolent demands of parliament and make
them do their duty." Should he be forced to dissolve parliament, the king
contemplated using force to get considerable sums of money from the
people by nonparliamentary means. As the opening of parliament drew
near, Rossetti said that the king planned to get a subsidy quickly and
then prorogue the parliament until September, although this might not
prove easy.[89]

Perhaps because of rumors such as these, the leaders of the Short
Parliament focused on the immediate and urgent tasks of ensuring that
redress of grievances precede supply and of registering in the strongest
terms their insistence that the king follow a parliamentary route for
supply. The full-scale parliamentary assault on English Catholicism that
Rossetti and others had feared did not come about. Indeed, treatment of
the religious issue was very restrained in comparison with the feverishly
ideological rhetoric of the Long Parliament six months later. Foreign
ambassadors reported that Catholicism was raised as an important grievance, but the debates as recorded did not pursue this as a major theme.[90]

The Speaker's oration on 15 April proclaimed that the government
was concerned about "Jesuited foreign states who look perchance with
envious and malignant eyes upon us and would be glad to rejoice in our
divisions . . . and their wicked hopes and expectations to render us, if
their endeavors might prevail, a people inconsiderable at home and con-
temptible abroad." But this speech was in the context of a government
appeal for "a knot of love and true affection betwixt the head [the king]
and the members," in short, for deferring grievances and supplying the
king immediately.[91]

Several members did speak bitterly of Catholic activity in the early days of the parliament. On 16 April Sir Benjamin Rudyerd accused the papists of having a role in the breakup of the 1629 parliament, "who now by the discontinuance of parliaments are come to that arrogancy and boldness that they intend [contend?] who are the greatest subjects." Sir Francis Seymour complained of seminary priests at Somerset House and St. James's Palace with "too much countenance," behaving like "varnished sepulchres."[92] On 17 April Francis Rous of Truro made a long speech alleging that "the root of all our grievances I think to be an intended union betwixt us and Rome." He complained especially of Davenport's book, which outlined how the doctrine of the Church of England was reconcilable with that of Rome. He also expounded on the ecclesiastical and secular grievances to which the "intended union" had given rise.[93]

But Pym and other parliamentary leaders kept the session focused on the immediate practical grievances arising from the Bishops' Wars (coat and conduct money, purveyance of ammunition and of transport) and on venerable issues of parliamentary privilege, tonnage and poundage, and impositions. An attempt by Littleton to bring up the subject of "a nursery of Jesuits . . . here in England" was not followed up because (one diarist said) "this by them [the government] was laid as a mere plot to see if it could divide the House, to make some of them fall one way, and some another."[94] Pym's speech of 17 April outlining the plan of action for the House of Commons[95] admitted that, "although religion is in truth the greatest grievance to be looked into . . . before either of the other generals [property and parliamentary privilege] yet in so much as that verity in religion receives an influence from the free debates in Parliament without which men will be afraid to speak, I think it fit in order to privileges in parliament to have priority."[96]

The references to papists in Pym's 17 April speech are nevertheless interesting because they suggest some of the approaches he would develop in his Long Parliament rhetoric. Initially striking a moderate note, he complained of encouragement to papists but said, "I desire no new laws, nor a rigid execution of these we have but only so far forth as may tend to the safety of his Majesty." He rapidly warmed to his subject, warning of "an unrestrained and mutual communication of or counsel with them by the frequent access of those who are active men, amongst them, to the tables and company of great men, and under subtle pretences and disguises, they want not means of cherishing their own projects, and of endeavoring to mold and bias the public affairs to the great advantage of that party. . . . They are encouraged by admitting them to great places of trust in the church and commonwealth." The nuncio intended to "reduce our land to the pope," for which purpose popish books, doctrines, and ceremonies were introduced, while true religion was discouraged.[97]

Pym did not at this time pursue the question of popish councillors and popish influence on politics that he would develop in the Long Parliament. But he ended with a motif that would become familiar, namely, the notion that grievances of all kinds were prejudicial to the king because they bred divisions and prevented understanding between the king and his people, harming the body politic, discouraging the people from giving subsidies, causing subjects to emigrate, and damaging religious alliances abroad "because our change is feared."[98]

The dissolution of the Short Parliament was followed by an intense public reaction in the form of broadsides, riots, and rumors that brought a turbulent summer to London and the counties and contributed to the tense suspicious atmosphere in which the Long Parliament was convoked in November. As Robin Clifton has shown, this agitation was strongly anti-Catholic in character and was the first important manifestation of this kind since the 1620s. As disappointed members of parliament returned to their localities while the Scots threatened the north of England, panic broke out in Colchester and Oxford over supposed papist gatherings; later in the summer, rumors about popish plots stirred York, Berkshire, and Lichfield.[99]

In London the situation in late May and early June was indeed serious. The Venetian ambassador referred to "an open revolt against the present government," and Salvetti reported that the court feared a popular uprising.[100] Placards appeared urging mass meetings to preserve liberty and true religion, to "secure in union the death of many leading ministers, reputed enemies of the commonweal."[101] The chief target of the rioters was Laud; his house was under virtual siege for a time, and the king had to lend him guards. He was a predictable target, blamed for the sustained campaign against the Scots and long smeared with the popish label. In June Salvetti commented upon Laud's political isolation, saying that only the king still supported him. The discovery that summer of Bishop Goodman's conversion to Catholicism further discredited the Laudian episcopacy. Laud's efforts to clear himself sometimes backfired; in May he captured a priest, only to have the priest claim that Laud himself was a papist.[102] In June Toby Mathew was arrested, much to the amazement of London Catholics, but soon released. In July Laud ordered a search of Catholic houses in London, but nothing was found. All this was to little avail; Salvetti thought the king would be unable to run the country so long as Laud was part of the government, so intense was the popular hatred for him. By September Laud was forced to withdraw to the queen's residence for safety against the mobs, whence he emerged only cautiously and infrequently.[103]

The agitation in the capital was anti-Catholic as well as antigovernment. Salvetti lumped together the objects of popular ire (Strafford, Laud, Rossetti, the Capuchins and Catholics in general) as though their connection were obvious. Citizens from London presented a petition against Catholics to the king. There was an attempt to attack Arundel House in the Strand, where guns were said to have been stored.[104] The queen was maligned; someone scratched a motto on a windowpane in the king's own chamber: "God save the King; God confound the queen and all her party; God grant rule in this kingdom to the count Palatine."[105] Animosity against the queen mother was so pronounced that she renewed her attempts (stimulated also by her financial difficulties) to find another refuge on the continent. It cannot have added to her popularity when one of the Spanish ambassador's priests, preaching at her chapel in July, compared her sufferings with those of Jesus Christ.[106]

Attacks on Catholics and on the symbols of Catholic influence at court were more than reflex reactions to political crisis. The king was negotiating with the pope and with Spain for financial support that would enable him to govern without parliament; and the two queens were identified with these negotiations. Montreuil and Giustiniani, who had friends among the parliamentary leaders, probably revealed their information about these negotiations to other enemies of Spain and the queen mother; it was in their interest to do so.

It was rumored that the Spanish ambassadors, the queen, the queen mother, and the French exiles had banded together to persuade the king to dissolve parliament, arguing that with Spanish aid the king would be able to subdue Scotland and govern without parliament. According to Salvetti, "The Puritans say publicly that this was the reason why the king resolved to end the parliament," a story that was repeated by the Puritan Walter Yonge in Devon.[107] The queen mother was said to have a financial interest, a commission, in the promised Spanish subsidy. Giustiniani also reported the complaints of "Puritans and others" that Spain had bribed the king to dissolve parliament. The French agent believed this and noted that the Spanish ambassadors had made no secret of their offers of money for use against the Covenanters.[108]

The queen was fully identified with these Spanish counsels and was blamed both for the wars against the Scots and for the dissolution of parliament. Giustiniani heard that the queen wanted a second Scottish war and that she held out hopes of obtaining large contributions from the Catholics and even from the pope. In the latter project she was assisted by Rossetti, who "adroitly encourages such vain intimations" to improve the position of the Catholics and win the king's favor.[109]

In fact, negotiations between Windebank and Rossetti for a papal loan had resumed after the Short Parliament. Rome made concrete offers of men and money, but all were contingent on the king's conversion, for which Rossetti could offer little immediate hope. Nevertheless, the talks continued and indeed intensified in the autumn of 1640.[110] Against this background, as Giustiniani commented, it was difficult for the king to "disabuse the minds of those who profess the greatest hostility to Catholicism of the notion, hateful here, that in secret he leans to the Catholic faith."[111]

On the popular level, suspicions of the queen mother and Spain were expressed in gossip and in print. *The Devill's Letter Sent to Rome*,[112] a heavily satirical, antiepiscopal, and antipapal broadside, pictured Lucifer congratulating the bishops for "sowing discord" among the English and provoking the Scots to rebellion. He announced that he had instructed Richelieu to invade while the king was in the north of England, and described the battle of the Downs as, "the service endeavoured for the confusion of the heretics by the last conceived invincible armada procured from Spain . . . notwithstanding that the main intention of the plot was unfortunately crossed by the divine providence above and Hans Van Tromp here below." The devil concluded by complimenting "our well-beloved cousin and councillor, Signor Con" and his successor Rossetti.[113] The queen mother was popularly represented as a corrupting influence in the royal family. One Henry Wheeler of Ruislip, Middlesex, allegedly remarked during a discussion of the "danger of the times and of the increase of popish recusants in this realm" that "it was no marvel in that, as he heard (and did verily believe it) that the king did go to Mass in Lent last . . . he was verily persuaded that the queen-mother was a witch in that all the time she was in France her son, the king of France could have no issue, but since her departure from thence the king of France had had a goodly son."[114]

The Second Bishops' War, the "Welsh Popish Army," and the "Irish Army of Papists"

As the Short Parliament sat and the king negotiated with Spain, preparations for the second campaign against the Covenanters got under way. In 1640, as in 1639, the king called on Catholics for support, but with no better success.[115]

In Scotland Catholics under Nithsdale made a second valiant but futile stand. The Covenanters' siege of his castle Carlaverock, which lasted from July until its capitulation in September, was the key to their control of Scottish territory. The capture of Carlaverock and the mistreatment of its defenders symbolized the Covenanters' ferocious feelings against Catholics. The singling out of Catholics for reprisals was a policy of the invading Scottish army as well; after his troops entered England, General Leslie carefully instructed them to spare all property but that of the papists and prelates.[116]

The English army that gathered slowly over the summer might be labeled popish in 1640 with somewhat more justification than in 1639, although there was nothing approaching Catholic dominance in the army. Rossetti claimed that many Catholics had enlisted and that they, rather than the Puritans, were given commissions because the latter were suspected of sympathy with the Scots.[117] The soldiers apparently agreed with Rossetti, for the discontent pervading the forces that summer took a violently anti-Catholic form. At Berwick the troops mutinied and murdered an allegedly Catholic lieutenant; pressed men from Dorset mutinied while passing through Berkshire and killed a Catholic officer; in Devon yet another lieutenant was killed, as Yonge reported, "for that he was a papist."[118] The queen's attitude encouraged such jealousies; as in 1639, Henrietta asked the English Catholics to fast during the king's absence and to pray for divine aid to his cause—"on which the continuation of our religion also depends," Salvetti dolefully remarked.[119]

A new element in the military picture was the activity of the Somerset family in rallying a force for the king from Wales and the Marches. It was natural for the government to turn to Wales for soldiers; like Scotland and Ireland, the country had a strong military tradition and an economic backwardness that pushed Welshmen into mercenary service. Wales had regularly contributed to Irish wars and Irish garrisons, and the Welsh had been supportive of the military efforts of the reign. Even before the civil war, Wales might be called "the nursery of the king's infantry."[120]

Although plans to raise a substantial force from Wales during the First Bishops' War were cut back, so that the serving soldiers came from border areas rather than inland Wales, there had been a large number of Welsh officers, especially in Hamilton's naval force.[121] Rumors had circulated then about the activities of certain prominent Catholics in Wales and the Marches. Lady Brilliana Harley had repeated a story that "my lord of Worcester's son shall be general of the horse." This was not true, but the king was keeping in close touch with Lord Herbert of Raglan, and in the following year he carved out a special role for the Somerset family in his military plans.[122]

Concern about Welsh Catholics was nothing new. The mid-1620s had brought scares about weapons and ammunition in their hands. But in the 1630s the evolution of local politics placed the Somersets in an unusually powerful position; they had recently come to dominate the local scene in south Wales and the Marches. They were faithful Catholics; Con described them accurately as "very prominent and greatly Catholic."[123] The family seat at Raglan enjoyed dispensation from recusancy fines throughout the 1630s and became a refuge for Catholics from every part of Wales. Although the fifth earl of Worcester tried to avoid the appearance of favoring Catholics in local offices, he was, as Dodd says, thrust "willy-nilly" into the role of leader of a religious faction.[124] The Somersets were not merely Catholic, as Clarendon pointed out, but adhered to a religious style "of that sort . . . the people rendered odious by accusing it to be most Jesuited." Raglan Castle became the headquarters of the Jesuit mission in Wales in the early seventeenth century. Neither the mission nor the Welsh Catholic population was large, but Monmouthshire was generally deemed as Catholic as Lancashire.[125]

The fortunes of the aristocracy of the region had left the Somersets as the only significant local interest in south Wales. Since the turn of the century, the local ties of the great Protestant families of the region (Essex, Pembroke, Herbert of Cherbury) had loosened, while Ludlow was no longer the center of Welsh political life it had been when presidents of the Council of Wales resided there. The earl of Bridgewater, president since 1631, had administrative experience to offset his slight territorial influence, but he conducted most of the business from London through deputies.[126]

While his father maintained the authority of Raglan during the 1630s, the young Somerset heir, Lord Herbert of Raglan, played the courtier. He spent much of his time at Worcester House in the Strand, which became a center of London Catholic life, and cultivated Catholic courtiers such as Sir Kenelm Digby, his cousin Sir John Winter, and his uncle Sir Thomas Somerset, Viscount Cashel.[127] Lord Herbert failed to regain for his father the lords-lieutenancies lost because of his Catholicism to the president of the Council of Wales, but he secured for him the right to nominate men to all county offices in Glamorgan and Monmouthshire, and became himself a deputy lieutenant in the latter county.

When he received the king's letter to the nobility in January 1639, Worcester replied that he was "wholly out of his element in military affairs and raising of forces." He claimed that his loss of office and deprivation of arms had so damaged his prestige that the "hearts and good wills of most of those that made fair semblance of love and respect towards me and my house are in this necessity discovered to be alienated and disaffected." But he sent the king a large donation.[128] This pitiful description of Worcester's standing and resources was to prove quite inaccurate. In 1640 Wales was called upon to provide 2,000 men, the largest army amassed in Wales since the Act of Union and thrice the number called up the previous year.[129] Worcester was given sweeping authority over much of the area normally administered by Bridgewater, and the president and the earl of Pembroke were specifically directed to assist him, along with their friends and tenants and local officials of the counties. The nature of Worcester's commission was not clearly specified, and it is not surprising that it aroused comment.[130] At the same time, it was rumored that the Somerset family was on the brink of an exalted new role in British Catholic life. The secular clergy believed that one of the Somersets—perhaps Sir Thomas, younger brother of Lord Herbert— might be nominated for the cardinal's cap. The seculars brooded darkly over what they thought a Jesuit maneuver to displace their friend Wat Montagu.[131]

In Ireland, too, Catholic forces were raised against the Scots, not this time by the earl of Antrim, but by the lord lieutenant himself. Strafford undertook to provide by July 9,000 men, who would be freed from the usual anti-Catholic religious tests for this occasion.[132] Why did Strafford adopt this plan, when he had so vigorously resisted Antrim's projected Catholic force in 1639? He must have known that it was politically risky, for he had participated in the parliamentary debates of 1628 when Irish troops had been portrayed as a threat to English liberty. Moreover, there was in 1640 some cause for anxiety about Irish discontent and exile activity. Over the winter, Hopton had warned from Spain of intrigue between the exile mercenaries and Irish clergy.[133] An Irish Dominican named by Hopton was arrested when he came to England in January 1640, on charges of spying for Spain.

Strafford's conviction of his ability to control the force may have outweighed, in his mind, the risk of employing disaffected men. Perhaps his faith in the cooperation of the English parliament waned as its convocation approached; and without supply from England, only Ireland could balance the Covenanters' army. Moreover, the king was offering Irish Catholic soldiers as part of the bargaining with Spain; the demonstration of the thousands that would be available for recruiting when the Scottish troubles ended might tempt the Spanish ambassadors and loosen Spanish purse strings.

Preparation of the Irish force lagged behind schedule, as did the rest of the king's military preparations. But the gathering Irish army made quite an impression on the English and Scots. Giustiniani reported that the Irish were expected to give "the best service and prompt obedience" of all the king's soldiers, because they were Catholics and hated the Covenanters. Baillie commented on the apprehension that this force had created in the west of Scotland among Argyll and his men.[134] The king's intentions for this army aroused misgivings well before the Short Parliament; it was rumored that both this and the English army were to be used to keep order or quell unrest in England. "The king of Great Britain," asserted Montreuil, "thinks of using 10,000 Irish, as much to obtain satisfaction from his English subjects as for the Scottish war." Salvetti said in June that Colonel Henry Bruce was being sent to Ireland to bring 10,000 infantry "to this country," ready for use against the Scots "or in whatever else might occur." In September both the French and the Florentine agents remarked that the Irish Catholic army had been expected to land in England that summer, and no one knew why they had not come.[135]

Anxiety about Ireland was woven into stories of Catholic conspiracy in the summer of 1640. An Irish woman in London, Anne Hussey, announced in August that there was an Irish popish plot to overcome the country. She said she had heard it from the queen mother's confessor—Marie de Medici was the mastermind, assisted by the Spanish, Venetian and French ambassadors, and all were in league with the pope. Windebank's skeptical reaction to this tale would later be raised in parliament against him. He was suspicious of the woman because she was an apostate from Catholicism, "a convert and zealous sister," as he put it. Moreover, he alleged she had some relationship to a Puritan peer, the earl of Warwick. Windebank did send for one of the queen mother's chaplains, one O'Connor, and put him in the Gatehouse for a week; when Mrs. Hussey continued to complain that Windebank "smothered the business," the privy council summoned O'Connor for interrogation. However, the priest was soon released on the queen's warrant and with the king's explicit approval, although at that very moment the king was hearing even more elaborate stories of Catholic conspiracy.[136]

During the Second Bishops' War, both the Scots and observers of the court associated the king's war policy with Catholic aims and fortunes. In the manifestos they issued when they invaded England, the Scots harped on the popery issue, linking Strafford, Laud, the prelates, and the Catholics as instigators of the troubles. Courtiers saw continuation of the war effort as serving the interests chiefly of the king's leading ministers and the Catholics, both of which would be threatened if the English made common cause with the Scots. Salvetti declared in September that the king's only friends were the Catholics, while the English Puritans and Covenanters were united in their determination to extirpate Catholicism and alter the government.[137]

Looking at the events of 1640 in retrospect, it is natural to assume the king realized that calling another parliament was the price he would have to pay for a second war against Scotland. At the time, however, the court saw the matter differently. The prosecution of the war against the Scots, if necessary even with a Catholic army, appeared as an alternative to recalling parliament or at least as a vital prelude to it. Victory over the Scots and the maintenance of an army without parliamentary support were achievements that might put the king and his advisors in a position strong enough to risk another parliament, a parliament that might then be conducted "à sa mode," as Bellièvre had phrased it. A parliament on any other terms would be ruinous for the king's ministers, for the Catholics, and possibly for the king himself. Laud and Strafford, Montreuil explained, urged on the war because they dared not face a parliament; their lives were at stake. Giustiniani recounted how Scottish propaganda aimed at increasing the unpopularity of Laud and Strafford, associating them with the bishops and the Catholics and appealing to an English parliament against them.[138]

The Habernfeld Plot

The conviction that the king was a dupe in the hands of Catholic conspirators, who had manufactured the Scottish crisis for their own ends, was no longer, if it ever had been, a monopoly of the Covenanters. It was expressed in August 1640 in the most detailed popish-plot account to date, one that clearly was not of Scottish inspiration. It came from across the Channel and seemed to reflect the viewpoint of someone familiar with, and not hostile to, the court. The "Habernfeld Plot," as it was called after the informant, is a rather agitated elaboration of the fears expressed by Leicester the year before, "that there is some very dangerous conspiracy against your Majesty."[139]

The king was in the north with his army when Sir William Boswell, ambassador to the Netherlands, wrote in distress to Laud about a plot against the king's life he had heard about from "a friend of good quality and worth in this place," one Andreas ab Habernfeld. Habernfeld, a Bohemian Protestant exile and publicist in the anti-Habsburg cause, professed to find the story convincing because it illustrated the Jesuits behaving in the same evil ways as they had in Germany and Bohemia.[140]

Boswell took the information seriously and begged Laud to keep it secret so as to catch the guilty parties. The "General Overture and Discovery" enclosed in his letter described the plot, alleging that the Scottish troubles had been provoked specifically to effect a double murder. Both the king and Laud were to be killed by the Jesuits, who had a network of spies in England. Many unidentified intimates of the king "corrupted with a foreign pension" were alluded to, and hints were dropped of a way "whereby the villainy may be discovered in one moment, the chief conspirators circumvented, and the primary members of the conjuration apprehended in the very act." Boswell asked for directions on how to proceed with the informant and enclosed a cipher for correspondence on the subject.[141]

Laud took the revelations as seriously as Boswell had and instructed the ambassador to "hold on the treaty with these men." He forwarded the documents to the king, who at first seemed disposed to believe in the plot, although his credulity may have ended when the detailed accusations involving so many of his trusted associates reached him.[142] A mass of information soon arrived from The Hague. Habernfeld wrote directly to Laud, describing how he had met his informant, a lapsed Catholic priest: "Who when he heard me discoursing of these Scottish stirs, said that I knew not the nerve of the business. . . . From that hour he every day became more familiar to me . . . with a full breast poured forth the burdens of his heart into my bosom, supposing that he had discharged a burden of conscience."[143]

Habernfeld enclosed a "Large Particular Discovery" of the plot by this anonymous informant.[144] It began with a conventional polemical description of the Jesuits, who were alleged to be composed of four orders and to be responsible for "all those factions with which all Christendom is at this day shaken." Britain, it was said, was swarming with Jesuits, "scarce all Spain, France and Italy can yield so great a multitude of Jesuits as London alone, where there are found more than fifty Scottish Jesuits." All were part of an international conspiracy based in Rome and supervised by the Congregation for the Propagation of the Faith, which was headed by Cardinal Barberini; its representative in England was George Con. Con forwarded secrets to Rome every week and worked on the chief men of the kingdom to corrupt or convert them, enticing the king himself with trinkets brought from Rome. He promised the king to arrange help for the prince Palatine at the Cologne conference, but underhandedly hurt the prince's cause instead. He tried unsuccessfully to bribe Laud with the offer of a cardinal's cap. When Secretary Coke tried to thwart these designs, Con and the Jesuits had him removed from office.

Having failed to win over the king or the archbishop, the informant went on, Con and his party began to plot assassination. The trial and punishment of Puritans in 1637 and the introduction of the Scottish prayer book were part of a plan to create a political crisis that would mask and facilitate the assassination. The first stages succeeded, and the Scots were goaded into action. "A certain Scottish earl, called Maxfield [i.e., Maxwell, earl of Nithsdale], if I mistake not was expedited to the Scots by the popish party, with whom two other Scottish earls, papists, held correspondence; he sought to stir up the people to commotion, and rub over the injury afresh, that he might inflame their minds, by which the hurtful disturber of the Scottish liberty [i.e., the king] might be slain."[145] The English were encouraged by the conspirators to support the Scots, so that the king might remain "inferior in arms who (thereupon) would be compelled to crave assistance from the papist; which yet he should not obtain, unless he would descend into conditions, by which he should permit universal liberty of the exercise of the popish religion."[146] If he refused these conditions, Charles I would be assassinated by means of "an Indian nut stuffed with most sharp poison," and his son, now being educated "from his tender age, that he might accustom himself to the popish party," would be put in his place. The attempts before the First Bishops' War to settle the quarrel by negotiation were subverted by Con and by Richelieu's agents, both of whom wanted the crisis to lead to war and the king's death.[147]

Moving on from the Scottish crisis to the broader Catholic conspiracy, the "Discovery" described the chief conspirators. It gave the standard "diabolical" presentation of Sir Toby Mathew:

> A Jesuited priest . . . a most vigilant man of the chief heads . . . neither day nor night spared his machinations . . . who flies to all banquets and feasts, called or not called; never quiet, always in action and perpetual motion; he urgeth conference familiarly, that he may fish out the minds of men; whatever he observeth thence . . . he communicates to the pope's legate; the more secret things he himself writes to the pope, or to Cardinal Barberino . . . whatever he hath fished out, he . . . carrieth it to the general consistory of the Jesuits Politics, which secretly meets together in the province of Wales. . . . There councils are secretly hammered out which are most meet for the convulsion of the ecclesiastical and political estate of both kingdoms.[148]

From the spy at court, the "Discovery" moved on to the agent in London, "Captain Reade,[149] a Scot, dwelling in Long Acre Street, near the Angel Tavern, a secular Jesuit . . . in his house the business of the whole plot is concluded, where the Society, which hath conspired against the king, the archbishop, and both kingdoms, meet together . . . on the day of the carrier's (or post's) despatch."[150] This information was forwarded by Reade or Mathew to Con, and by Con to Rome. Reade acted as deposit for mail from Rome, which he distributed throughout England.

From Reade, the "Discovery" moved on to other figures: the countess of Arundel, who told Con "whatsoever she hears at the king's court, that is done secretly or openly in words or deeds"; the earl of Arundel and Endymion Porter, both described as crypto-Catholics and maintainers of

Jesuits; and Windebank, who revealed "even the king's greatest secrets" to Con, along with advice on advancing the conspiracy. Finally, in an orgy of identification, the informer threw in the names of "Sir [Kenelm] Digby, Sir [John] Winter, Mr. Montagu the younger, who hath been at Rome, my Lord Stirling, a cousin of the earl of Arundel's a knight [Sir William Howard?], the countess of Newport, the duchess of Buckingham and many others who have sworn into this conspiracy. . . . Some of these are enticed with the hope of court; others of political offices; others attend to the sixteen cardinals' caps that are vacant, which are therefore detained idle for some years, that they may impose a vain hope on those that expect them."[151]

In conclusion, the informant suggested that the Scottish troubles might shortly be calmed. For when, by means of his revelations, "the Scots shall know by whom and to what end their minds are incensed, they will speedily look to themselves; neither will they suffer the forces of both parts to be subdued, lest a middle party interpose, which seeks (the ruin) of both." Habernfeld, in a cover letter to Laud, recommended interception of the secret weekly correspondence between the papal agent, the Brussels nuncio Stravio, and Rome. The government should raid the weekly gathering at Reade's house, arrest and interrogate Reade, and force someone to decipher the coded letters.[152]

Laud and the privy council investigated the allegations, although not as dramatically as Habernfeld had urged. Toby Mathew, who had been arrested and released in July, was arrested again in October and taken before the Court of High Commission but not detained. Laud asked for more information from Boswell and a privy council committee was created to deal with the matter. The council was apparently still gathering information when the Long Parliament convened.[153]

The identity of Habernfeld's informant (if indeed there was one) has remained a mystery. In the "Discovery" he identified himself as a Catholic priest sent by Barberini to assist Con, "by whom he was found so diligent and sedulous in his office, that hope of great promotion was given him," but who had since apostatized. Boswell, who may never have met the man, told Laud that the informant, "thinks his Majesty and your Grace, by the character he gives of himself, will easily imagine who he is, having been known so generally through court and city, as he was for three or four years."[154] Laud clearly had no idea who the informant was or who Andreas ab Habernfeld was. Some of the Habernfeld story followed Abernethie's *Abjuration*; details about the court and London Catholic scene might have been added by anyone familiar with the court. Several disgruntled Catholic priests were to apostatize in the next few years and provide the Long Parliament with "inside information" about popish plotting;[155] the "Large Particular Discovery" may represent a first attempt by one of these to profit from his knowledge.

The "Discovery" contains little new information. Its exaggerations, half-truths, and occasionally hysterical tone, capped by the story of the poisoned nut, tempt one to discount it altogether. But it is circumstantial, in a sense predictable, and this lends it significance. It echoes the concerns and efforts of Con himself and reads at some points like a satire on one of Con's letters to Rome. Where the agent boasted of his progress, the "Discovery" deplored it; the contacts he valued (the Howards, Porter, and Windebank), the "Discovery" lamented. Few secrets are actually revealed, although details such as the correspondence with Stravio suggest familiarity with Catholic organization. But for the most part, the material was common knowledge or easily available to an interested observer, common knowledge that was woven together, for the first time comprehensively, into a conspiratorial pattern.

The Habernfeld Plot may well have been known to the parliamentary leaders of 1640–41 (in early 1641, Laud alluded to it in his own defense), although it was not put in print until Prynne's 1643 publication of *Rome's Masterpiece*. It was part of a tradition of Protestant propaganda that went back at least to the Gunpowder Plot, and it was conventional in such points as its portrayal of the Jesuits. But the story also wove together various threads that had appeared in earlier seditious speeches and broadsides of the late 1630s that concerned specific court figures and events of that period.[156] It represented a damaging criticism of the court, despite its professions of loyalism.

Yet, unlike several other English publications, the Habernfeld exposé clearly owed little to specifically Scottish inspiration; and its emphases differed in important respects from the popish-plot stories that the English parliamentary leadership exploited in 1640–42. Their version of the plot was anticipated in Calybute Downing's sermon of 1 September 1640. Downing also made much of a "Jesuited faction" that fomented treason, rebellions, invasions, divisions, and civil wars in England as elsewhere in Europe; but by drawing a parallel between the Jesuits and the Amalekites of old, Downing sketched a defense of a just war in which English Protestants featured as modern Israelites and Scottish resistance to the government was vindicated on religious grounds.[157] In the Habernfeld Plot, on the other hand, Laud was portrayed as a potential victim, Strafford remained unmentioned, and the resisting Covenanters were pictured as dupes of Catholic plotting. These attitudes were consistent with those of Elizabeth of Bohemia's circle, but not with the views of Pym or other members of the parliamentary leadership who sympathized with the Covenanters, were totally hostile to Laud, associated Strafford with the popish threat, and were deeply suspicious of the king himself. The Habernfeld account is the first detailed articulation of the royalist version of the popish plot.

A more garbled and popular version was apparently circulating in London by November, under the title *Jubilee of the Society of Jesus*. This, like *The Devill's Letter*, was a Protestant production in Catholic guise. It described how "the king having wars in Scotland they [the Jesuits] would fish in troubled waters. They had given a potion but it would not work. But the king should have such a potion as should work." The Spanish sailors who suffered at the Downs were described as "holy martyrs that suffered in the fleet sent against the heretics in England."[158] Such stories about attempts on the king's life may explain Salvetti's rather obscure comment in September that the Catholics were anxious about the king's trip to Scotland, fearing reprisals should the king personally meet with "some misfortune."[159]

The Prelude to the Long Parliament

If the Habernfeld Plot reflects views held in Elizabeth of Bohemia's circle, this would not be surprising.[160] The queen had been quick to see "papists and clergy" behind the First Bishops' War; and events in England during the summer of 1640 left her and her English friends disappointed and worried. The release of Charles Lewis, followed by Roe's appointment as privy councillor in June 1640, had seemed to augur well for the Palatine family. As late as August, the Venetian ambassador described Roe as enjoying "great credit" at court and in council. But Roe's appointment had been made because of his long experience with the London merchant community, from which the king hoped to raise money after the Short Parliament was dissolved. His hope was disappointed; and when the king threatened to seize the bullion in the Tower mint and debase the coinage, Roe opposed this violently. He quarreled sharply with Strafford at the council table in July. By the end of the summer, the watchful French agent had concluded that Roe was "very well disposed to the better faction, an enemy of the lieutenant."[161] He and his friends—Boswell, in England trying to persuade the king to send an agent for the prince to the Diet of Ratisbon; the prince's agent, Sir Richard Cave; and Georg Weckherlin, the German émigré in the secretariat—looked on as the king, following Strafford's advice, conducted domestic and foreign policy in ways that alienated his people and left his sister's family forlorn of hope.[162]

For the opponents of the Spanish alliance, the dissolution of the Short Parliament seems to have been a turning point. Heenvliet's renewed negotiations for an Orange-Stuart marriage got nowhere; and his attempts with his colleague Joachimi to thwart the continuing Anglo-Spanish negotiations "do not make the impression that he and those interested in the public cause would desire, because the most important affairs of state here are in the hands of ministers disposed to assist at all costs the success of the Catholic's plans."[163] The French secretary and his friends (in particular, Strafford's inveterate enemy, the earl of Holland), the friends of the Palatine family, the friends at court of the Dutch and the prince of Orange—groups that often overlapped—began to disengage from the king's policies and to look to another parliament as the arena from which they might force a change of policy and of councillors.[164]

Although the arrival of the Spanish ambassadors had coincided with the Short Parliament, serious negotiations were postponed until the dissolution. Meanwhile, speculation about the scope of Spanish offers intensified. The ambassadors were observed to confer constantly with the duchess of Chevreuse and other French exiles. The day after the dissolution, negotiations began between the Spaniards and a commission of English councillors headed by Strafford. Of the five committee members, Strafford and Cottington were key figures; Windebank, Hamilton, and Northumberland made up the remainder.[165] The dynastic marriage between England and Spain, of which so much had been said and hinted in previous months, was never seriously treated. An agreement between England and the Netherlands on East Indian trade forestalled Spanish ambitions of protecting their trade in that area by giving the English limited trading rights.[166] But English and Spanish ministers came to an agreement late in May for Spanish loans to the king to repress the Covenanters. In exchange, England would grant Spanish recruiting rights in Ireland, English protection of Spanish men, money, and trade in the Channel, protection of Dunkirk and the coastal towns, and ultimately a definite English break with Holland. The loan of £300,000 to Charles I would be gradually discounted after the break with Holland, and further Spanish financial support for the English fleet would be provided.[167]

This Anglo-Spanish treaty never took effect. Strafford's illness in June, and perhaps the king's fear of public reaction, caused delay on the English side, and the revolt of Catalonia in May created an immediate need for Spanish resources that outweighed Olivares's concern for Flanders. The king resented the promotion of Cárdenas to the status of full ambassador in July, and this provided him with a diplomatic explanation for the failure of the treaty. The king and his court began to speak of Spanish "insincerity" and to hint to the French agent that English friendship was again available for a price.[168] After the king left for the north in August, Toby Mathew went to the Spanish ambassador on Strafford's request to ask for an immediate loan of £40,000–50,000 from the Brussels government. The Irish customs were offered as security, and twenty war ships were promised for Spanish use within eight months; but it was to no avail. By September, the Spanish ambassadors talked of leaving England;[169] they would linger on until February 1641, accomplishing nothing.

The king, Strafford, and Windebank apparently thought that this negotiation could be kept secret. It is difficult to imagine why, given the publicity of the ambassadors' arrival, their exalted rank, the king's obvious financial straits, the hostility to the negotiation on the part of councillors like Roe and Northumberland who were in a position to find out about it, and the clear advantage for the French agent in doing all he could to frustrate the scheme.[170] In mid-May foreign ambassadors were already giving reasonably accurate accounts of the transactions, and a connection had been drawn between Spanish money and the repression of the Covenanters.[171]

The intrigues of the French exiles, in concert with the Spanish ambassadors and the imperial agent Lisola, gave Montreuil a good motive to upset the power balance at the English court. Richelieu's ministers had managed to get the duchess of Chevreuse out of England in May, much to the regret of the queen and the Spanish agents.[172] But the duke of La Vallette remained a dangerous figure. Lisola persuaded the Spanish ambassadors to participate in La Vallette's plans for a revolt in Normandy and Poitou; by August Montreuil knew something of this plotting. Early in November he discovered its full extent and the involvement of Soubise and Chevreuse. He speculated that Olivares, seeking revenge for French meddling in Catalonia, might have sent his extraordinary ambassadors to England for this purpose alone.[173] In fact, Montreuil was right to take the matter seriously. Although it came to little in 1640, it was the prelude to the wider and more dangerous Soissons conspiracy of 1641.

In order to discredit, and preferably remove from court, the Spanish party and the exiles, the French moved toward a working partnership with the leaders of parliament. Convinced that the present ministers of England would not last long, they felt that a timely alliance with the likely heirs to power would profit France. Strafford thus found a very lukewarm response to his approaches to the French government about a loan. Montreuil pointed out in his letters home that Strafford was too pro-Spanish at heart to be trusted and was unlikely to retain power much longer. He counseled his masters against trying to buy the English court; it would provide no real advantage now and would anger the Scots. In any case, he noted, suspicion of France at the English court was deeply rooted; many remained convinced that France aided the Scottish rebels, a persuasion nourished by the Spanish agents.[174]

As hope for relief from Spain faded, the king and queen pressed France to appoint a regular ambassador, the king going so far in October as to threaten the recall of Leicester if no French counterpart arrived. But Richelieu had decided that the wind was blowing against the court. He explained to the Venetian ambassador in Paris that England toyed with France only to tease Spain and that in its present state England was both useless and harmless. So long as the king negotiated with Spain and neglected France, he added, the Puritans and the Scots would, "keep up their agitation, from their fear that something may be arranged with the Spaniards to their prejudice. This agitation will make the king hesitate and render it certain that in order not to incite them to declared hostility he will not take any steps with the Spaniards to the prejudice of us or the common business."[175]

The English opponents of Strafford's policies were withdrawing from their association with the court in the summer of 1640 and forming alliances in anticipation of another parliament. In August Northumberland delayed his departure for the north of England, hoping (as the Venetian ambassador believed) that the king would give up his war plans; eventually his illness (many thought it feigned) forced the king to nominate Strafford to replace him. The French agent reported that Northumberland was spoken of as a Puritan and "very forward on behalf of the people."[176] Pembroke and Holland, he said, had withdrawn from court, perhaps to avoid identification with unpopular policies. Holland remained potentially powerful, but Strafford's ascendancy thwarted him, and his position with the queen was temporarily eclipsed by his Catholic rival Montagu.[177] In the aftermath of the Short Parliament, leaders confidently expected a recall of parliament, and "such as resided about London met together frequently and gave intelligence by Mr. Samuel Hartlib and Mr. Frost, to those in the country of affairs. Ere long they gave them a more general summons to come all up, who not only came themselves, but brought up also such country gentlemen as they could confide in."[178] It is difficult to believe that the new privy councillor, Sir Thomas Roe, had no contact with this group.

At the end of August, as Mrs. Hussey made her plot revelations to Windebank and Habernfeld told his story to Boswell, a number of the country peers, many of whom were in London, sent a petition to the king complaining of grievances and calling for a parliament.[179] Among the seven grievances were innovations in religion, the "great increase in popery and the employing of popish recusants and other ill-affected to [religion] in places of power and trust especially in commanding of men and arms," and the "great mischiefs" that would follow the reported plan to bring Irish and foreign soldiers into England. The peers called for the punishment of those responsible for these policies, so that England and Scotland might unite "against the common enemies of their Reformed Religion." Salvetti and Giustiniani both remarked upon the anti-Catholic tone of the petition.[180] In response to the petition, the king summoned a great council of peers to meet at York on 24 September; by the time this convened, both he and the peers realized that a parliament would have to be called.[181] He announced that it would begin on 3 November 1640.

In the weeks just before the Long Parliament, the ambassadors took the gravest view of the position of British Catholics, whom they saw, with Strafford and Laud, as the likeliest targets of parliamentary action. A parliament, said Giustiniani, "will mean the total dissolution of the Catholic faith in this country, with a notable diminution of the king's authority, and the final ruin of his most confidential ministers." Rossetti harped on his old theme that a threat to royal authority was a threat to the interests and cause of the Catholics.[182] The Scots, for their part, continued relentlessly in their proclamations to link Strafford, Laud, and the Catholic party as the sources of grievances.[183]

Popular agitation in London against Catholics, the queen, and the queen mother, which had somewhat calmed over the summer months, resumed early in October. The night before parliament opened, Catholic homes in London were searched for arms.[184] The queen mother and her advisors were blamed, it was said, "for having secretly given the king advice against the religion and liberty of the realm."[185] The expense she represented was resented, as were her protection of Catholics, her influence on the king through the queen, and her alleged proposals for taxes and monopolies from which she would personally benefit. Windebank told the king of a rumor sweeping country and city that Marie de Medici "hath procured a grant from your Majesty concerning an imposition upon leather," which heightened popular resentment. Salvetti feared that she would be personally identified as a grievance by parliament; Montreuil reported that some M.P.s would provoke mob action against her ministers. The Venetian ambassador said that both the queen mother and the papal agent were likely to be forced out of England.[186]

The French agent welcomed the attack upon the friends of Spain, seeing in the king's troubles nothing but benefit for France. He regarded the new parliament chiefly as an occasion for purging the English court of the Spanish party. He realized the gravity of the political crisis, even as he intrigued to turn it to French advantage, urging that a French ambassador be in England when parliament met. The king, he reported, was in real danger; some members of his own council had wanted to join the petitioning lords. Strafford and all the members of the "Spanish party"— Laud, Windebank, and Cottington in particular—would be destroyed by parliament, since Strafford's "apparent design to kindle war between England and Scotland has failed."[187]

The last phrase is telling; Montreuil was calling Strafford an "incendiary," which was the tactic that Pym would adopt. As he predicted Strafford's downfall, Montreuil was fashioning the alliance with Pym and other parliamentary leaders that would help to bring this about. Among other charges, Strafford would be accused of inciting war between England and Scotland. In October Montreuil referred to Pym ("a very eloquent man of great credit among the people") as someone who would help topple the Spanish party and get the queen mother out of England. Pym was "a great Puritan," Montreuil reported in early November, and recognized that English and French interests ran parallel. He would serve both countries by making political capital of Montreuil's information about how Spain had "tried to deceive its neighbors, especially France and England."[188]

The convocation of the Long Parliament was recognized as the death knell of the Spanish party and a symbolic triumph for anti-Habsburg forces. It was also seen as a triumph for Protestant anger over Catholic privilege. Finally, it raised the possibility, perhaps remote but not inconceivable, that the royal family itself was at risk. Catholics "are hurriedly selling their goods with the intention of going to live quietly in some other country," reported Giustiniani. In London the rumor circulated that the king was to be deposed and Elizabeth of Bohemia put in his place.[189]

8. The Long Parliament and the Popish Plot: Part I

As anticipated, the Long Parliament opened with rousing attacks on Catholics and Catholicism: rhetorical diatribes, judicial measures, political investigation, and popular agitation. The conviction that popish conspiracy was somehow to blame for the ills of the nation provided a recurring motif from November 1640 until the Grand Remonstrance a year later. In the first phase, which culminated in Strafford's execution, the accusation of advancing popery was a weapon used against the king's chief ministers, who were imprisoned or forced to flee the country. The parliamentary investigations of this period focused on the Catholic contribution of 1639 and the supposed popish hierarchy behind it, the Irish Catholic army that Strafford had formed in 1640, and the Welsh popish army that was to join the Irish in an attack on England. The activities of court Catholics, lay and ecclesiastical, began to be scrutinized. From the spring of 1641, fears of popery centered ever more closely on the royal family and its household friends and unofficial advisors.

In the course of ridding the government of "evil counsellors" in 1640–41, parliament destroyed official support for the Spanish party. The royal marriage alliance with the house of Orange symbolized a change in foreign policy, but this proved to be too late and too ambiguous to help the king in domestic politics. The French meanwhile tried to play a balancing act and gave the king as little assistance as possible; but the flight of English courtiers to France and the apparent confidence of the king and queen that France would help them unnerved even the friends of France in parliament. In the fright over the army plot in May 1641, France played much the role of alien popish force that Spain normally enjoyed.

While the agitation over popish conspiracy was certainly a useful tool in the hands of the court's opponents, it would be wrong to dismiss the fears expressed as either hypocritical or groundless. The activities of the court in the winter of 1640–41 continued to arouse suspicions that the king planned a coup d'etat in which domestic and foreign Catholics would participate. Negotiations for a papal loan began anew between Rossetti and Father Philip; the money was intended for the support of English, Irish, French, and possibly Dutch troops to enable the king to regain independent authority.

Intrigue quite distinct from the king's own plans also continued to flourish at court. Within the circle of court Catholics, Montagu and DuPerron contended for the queen's favor and the precious nomination for a cardinal's cap. Montagu encouraged the queen to defend her religious prerogatives and her friends and to develop rash schemes for extricating the king from his difficulties. DuPerron befriended the French secretary Montreuil, to whom he divulged any secrets of the queen's court that had not already been revealed by the earl of Holland. The queen mother and other French exiles remained at court and persisted in their double game of negotiating with Richelieu and with Spain. The Soissons conspiracy saw much of its long gestation on English soil, and the conspirators hoped for English assistance. However peripheral all this was to Charles I's own plans, it created an atmosphere at court.

Salvetti, Giustiniani, and Rossetti repeatedly identified the royal and the Catholic cause; a threat to one was a threat to the other.[1] This was more than a rhetorical convention. In the first place, it reflected the ambassadors' perception, shared by other observers, that protection of Catholics was the king's own policy and would dissolve without his constant support. It also reflected the common Catholic assumption that Calvinism was inherently subversive and antimonarchical. How far the rest of the court or the king himself shared this notion is difficult to say. The obvious sympathy of many English for the Scots seems to have caused the king to wonder whether the monarchy itself was in danger, a fear that Rossetti encouraged. Giustiniani reported in November that "the palace" believed parliament aimed to leave the king nothing but his title, that Charles realized he must bow for a time to necessity, but that he awaited the opportunity to regain power. "Their far-reaching designs," reported the Venetian ambassador of the parliamentary leaders, were "all alike opposed to the true worship of God and to the rights of the royal sovereignty." In January he reported that "the most seditious among the Puritans" aimed at complete democracy, a view that he said the king encouraged (whether or not he believed it) in order to win support from moderates, especially in the House of Lords.[2]

The parliamentary leaders, especially Pym, were equally persuaded of an intimate connection between Catholicism and royal authority. They consistently alleged that there was a popish conspiracy at court, in which the ministers they wished to remove were implicated and which explained almost every detested feature of royal policy in the 1630s. For those like Pym who saw Arminianism as scarcely better than popery, the Laudian regime and bishops were at best dupes, and possibly agents, of the campaign to return England to the Roman fold. In the area of secular policy, the popish plot theory of the personal rule was also relevant, albeit more indirectly. The connection between subversion of religion and subversion of the constitution was no novelty in parliamentary rhetoric; it had appeared as early as 1625, as Sir John Eliot recalled: "Wherever that mention does break of the fears or dangers of religion, and the increase of popery, their [the Commons'] affections are much stirred, and whatever is obnoxious in the state, it is then reckoned as an incident to that."[3] This was not as confused an idea as it sounds. If the government contemplated a change of religion (so reason and common sense revealed), it would be forced to resort to arbitrary power. The allegedly arbitrary or illegal acts of the personal rule thus acquired a very sinister significance. If these acts were symptomatic of a developing tyranny, might they not also indicate religious perversion at the core of government? Moreover, as Conrad Russell has pointed out, "It was often supposed that any ruler of false religion must be a tyrant."[4] In this perspective, ship money, impositions, and unpopular monopolies could all be seen as popishly motivated tyranny. The Scottish crisis was perceived as an attempt, all too typical of Jesuit political tricks, to divide and thus conquer British Protestants. Therefore all "incendiaries" who had encouraged the king to take arms against the Scots, who had "created divisions" between England and Scotland or between the king and his people, were branded as accessories to the popish plot.

The "Design to Alter the Kingdom"

On 7 November Pym delivered his opening speech to a House of Commons that would shortly be purged of hidden Catholics by compulsory communion.[5] It was a ringing call to antipapist action. He proclaimed the existence of a "design to alter the kingdom both in religion and government." Members of the government and higher clergy, although none were yet named, were understood to be willing or unwitting accomplices to the popish conspiracy. Throughout his speech, Pym emphasized that the blame lay not with the king but with those whom he had unwisely trusted, and that "to abuse the king's trust is the high point of treason."[6]

Pym outlined four "heads of grievances," all of which concerned papists. First, there was a design to alter religion by "setting differences between the king and his subjects" and admitting popish tenets into the Church of England. Second, there was a plan for union with Rome supported by the "corrupt part of our clergy." Next, there was the activity of agents for Spain and other Catholic powers, distributing pensions to Englishmen to corrupt religion and government. Finally, there were the activities of Englishmen greedy for promotion and preferment who were willing to "run into popery."

Pym then proceeded to connect the Catholic conspiracy with every unpopular government policy, "steps of these things that have proceeded in motion first softly now by strides which are near their ends if they be not prevented." The design rested on four "feet": ecclesiastical policy, state and judicial policy, policy to parliament, and military policy. Each could be connected with the plot to bring in popery. The objective of ecclesiastical policy, the promotion of Arminians, and the agency with Rome was "to extirpate our religion, proof will appear." Secular policy included illegal taxation and interference in justice; the latter heading probably included Windebank's interventions for recusants. Policy toward Scotland was also part of the plot: "To make a difference between England and Scotland (that when we had well wearied ourselves against one another we might be both brought to what scorn they pleased.) A sermon preached in the north before the king to make an agreement between popery and our religion, the partition wall must be pulled down, which was the puritans."[7]

Even in discussing the third "foot of the design," that of parliament, Pym slipped into the argument an allusion to the "ingratiating of papists and saying they are the best subjects to bring the king in love with them." In the fourth (or military) foot, he deplored the appointment of papists, suspected papists, and Irish to command in the king's armies. There was even, he said, a plan to bring in and billet foreign and Irish soldiers for the 1639–40 campaigns. Referring to the uneasiness caused by the Spanish fleet in the Downs, Pym concluded by hinting darkly of the circulation of "papistical books" and popish agents—"Many active men live here and are agents."[8]

The heavily antipapist tone of Pym's speech represented a departure from his Short Parliament rhetoric.[9] The popish conspiracy motif would appear repeatedly in his attacks on the king's councillors in 1640–41. There can be little question of his genuine concern with the issue; how widely his perspective was shared by his fellow M.P.s, especially in the early months of the parliament, is more difficult to assess. It was certainly shared, as we have already seen, by many of the Scots. Scottish pronouncements were full of diatribes against Catholics and advocated the harshest possible anti-Catholic measures.[10] Baillie picked up and seemed to accept much of the Catholic exposé material introduced into parliament.

Pym's call on 7 November for a "settled committee to find out the danger the king and the kingdom is in" and a petition from the City of London complaining of the "concourse of papists" led on 9 November to the formation of a committee to investigate papists (especially those in London), disarm them, and inquire into the "dispensation, discharges, or immunities" that had been granted recusants.[11] Leaders of the Commons were members of this, and of subsequent recusant committees, and the committee reports often provided the occasion for connecting anxieties about popish plotting with other important matters of debate.

It was predictable that the attack on the Laudian regime would be framed in terms of popery. Pym and others of his persuasion thought Arminianism was little better than popery, perhaps even more dangerous, because it purported to be the orthodox doctrine of the Church of England. Catholic reunionists like Christopher Davenport who minimized the differences between the Churches of England and Rome in the 1630s confirmed the suspicions of many that Laud was "soft on popery."[12]

During the autumn of 1640, moreover, there was a very curious series of meetings in London involving the queen's Franciscan chaplain Giles Chaissy, Rossetti, Laud, and James Ussher, archbishop of Armagh. According to Rossetti, Chaissy introduced him to Laud in the chapel of the Venetian ambassador (with whom Chaissy resided), and they had several discussions about Laud's possible conversion and flight to Rome before the archbishop's arrest in December. Again through Chaissy's intervention, Rossetti twice met secretly with Ussher, possibly at Arundel House, to discuss the Irish primate's possible conversion. Unlikely as these contacts may seem to those acquainted with the views of these bishops, they are described in independent sources by Chaissy and Rossetti.[13] One wonders whether these meetings became known, and, if so, how they were understood.

Cosin of Durham was accused of "seducing to Catholicism" and Bishop Wren of "bringing in popery and seducing the king's subjects in their religion," in the charges against them.[14] The articles brought against Laud on 24 February 1641 included the claim that he had advanced popery by various means that were tantamount to treason.[15] Proponents of the "root and branch" extirpation of episcopacy also appealed, not surprisingly, to fears of popery. Their petition was presented on 11 December 1640 and listed the following items among the many "evils, pressures and grievances" caused by the bishops: "the publishing of popish, Arminian, and other dangerous books and tenets"; "the growth of popery and increase of papists, priests and Jesuits in sundry places, but especially about London"; and "the great conformity and likeness both continued and increased of our church to the church of Rome, in vestures, postures, ceremonies and administrations." The conclusion alluded to "the general hope and expectation of the Romish party, that their superstitious religion will ere long be fully planted in this kingdom again, and so they are encouraged to persist therein, and to practise the same openly in divers places, to the high dishonour of God, and contrary to the laws of the realm."[16]

The Attack on Strafford

Secular as well as ecclesiastical advisors were attacked for alleged popish associations. The propaganda campaign against Strafford that preceded his trial linked him with an intricate web of Catholic conspiracy in Ireland, Wales, and England. Charges of "favoring popery" were never proven, and after their appearance in the initial indictment they faded from the legal proceedings. But they reflected a powerful association of ideas about popery and tyranny, the notion of a "design to alter the kingdom both in religion and in government."[17]

Throughout the 1640–41 session, Strafford's name would seldom be mentioned without an accompanying reference to some new evidence of popish plots. Nor did it take long for the more serious accusations to surface. On 21 November 1640, Sir Henry Anderson suggested that Strafford "was brought into this great place [his office] by Jesuits" and that "probably the Spanish navy was to this end [the destruction of laws and religion] and did proceed from him."[18] It was reported that the Catholic peers in the House of Lords would be among Strafford's supporters when he came to trial.[19]

On 11 November the revelations about Strafford began. When the day's debate ended, Strafford and the Irish army had been connected with an alleged plan to invade England, supported by a fifth column of English Catholics and by foreign powers. Pym reported on "the jealousies we have of some violent courses, to be taken for the advancement of popery," and alluded to the organization of Catholics within England and to Strafford's Irish army. Had Windebank sufficiently investigated the rumors that Irish landings were imminent?[20]

Sir John Clotworthy, a Puritan with Irish lands who had a key role in the campaign against Strafford, expanded on the plan to bring in Irish soldiers. Sir George Radcliffe, Strafford's aide, was implicated and he was summoned from Ireland to answer charges.[21] Pym and others speculated on the support the Irish would receive from British and continental Catholics. It was said that the earl of Worcester had arms for 500 men, that papists in Berkshire and Dorset had commissions and were stockpiling arms. Large sums of money had been collected abroad by English Catholics, as a letter from Sir Kenelm Digby proved, and "prayers beyond seas for the success in England and money is here gathered and powder provided." Arms had been found in the City of London itself, in Chancery Lane where numerous Catholics lived.[22]

Alexander Rigby, M.P. for Wigan, Lancashire, elaborated upon the Catholic contribution. He declared that "there was a popish ecclesiastical hierarchy and government over the whole government of this kingdom"; as evidence, he pulled out a letter circulated by Champney and Rossetti "requiring a fast among the papists towards the queen's pious intentions." Lancashire papists, he claimed, were fasting weekly and were well furnished with arms. Such news from Lancashire was particularly alarming because it was a strongly Catholic county and an obvious landing point for troops from Ireland.[23]

The Catholic contribution and the question of the popish hierarchy would be further pursued in later months. Montagu, Mathew, and Digby were already worried by the disclosures in parliament, the first two sufficiently to get themselves sworn in as the queen's servants for their own protection.[24] But on 11 November Pym pulled the debate back to its immediate object and summarized the day's revelations by proclaiming that Strafford was "a main instrument to provoke the king to make a war between us and the Scots that thereby we might consume one another that he might the better bring in the papist party." A general accusation against Strafford was pushed through the Commons that very day. The small committee for formulating the charges was unable yet to present details; for the present they stipulated only "my Lord Mountnorris' cause and the papists suffered in England to increase in arms."[25]

On 25 November the seven articles of preliminary charges were sent to the Lords. The fourth was perhaps a significant variation on Pym's charge of 7 November; then he had described the Bishops' Wars as Strafford's means to "bring in the papist party." On 25 November the charge was that Strafford had "traitorously abused the power and authority of his government, to the increasing, continuancing, and encouraging of papists, that so he might settle a mutual dependance and confidence betwixt himself and that party, and by their help prosecute and accomplish his malicious and tyrannical designs."[26] With respect to Strafford, at least, the emphasis had shifted from popery as the objective to popery as a means to tyranny.

Strafford's case would not again hold center stage until January 1641. But while the committee on his impeachment compiled evidence, the House of Commons was kept alive to the danger of Catholic activities. Fast sermons emphasized the dangers of popery. Windebank, who had been questioned on 11 and 12 November about his warrants for releasing priests, was the object of further investigation; the testimony of pursuivants was taken.[27] On 21 November a demented Catholic, John James, attacked a London J.P., Peter Heywood, who was on his way to parliament with a list of Catholics. The Committee on Religion agreed that "the execrable malice was in part discovered to us, of the papists." When James was examined, he refused to take the oath of supremacy, although he took the oath of allegiance, and Sir Walter Erle "shewed that the party had been in Flanders at Brussels as he confessed."[28] On 24 November a correspondent from London reported that Windebank "shrinks, for shrewd matters are come in against him" and that Endymion Porter was likely to be ejected from parliament as a projector and papist. The City of London petitioned for the removal of papists from the City, proposing that those remaining be required to wear identifying badges.[29] On 28 November, John Glynn, M.P. for Westminster and one of the managers of Strafford's impeachment, reported from the Committee on Recusants that the king's proclamation of 11 November ordering Catholics to leave London was proving ineffectual. Many papists had residences in and around the capital. Discussion ensued of the "number and danger of the papists" before the Commons returned briefly to debate the treason charges against Strafford.[30]

On 1 December, the Committee for Religion presented a list of the names of prominent recusants, including nineteen peers.[31] On the same day, the case against Windebank was presented, with Glynne providing detailed statistics on the secretary's protection of priests and recusants from the testimony of John Pulford and other disgruntled pursuivants. Special mention was made of the case of the Jesuit Henry Morse.[32] Sir John Colepepper widened the debate, attacking Rossetti, proposing a remonstrance and parliamentary act about the growth of popery, and urging that a charge be drawn up against Windebank. He claimed that "the priests and Jesuits have reference to the secretaries as the iron to the loadstone" and that "the papists do generally flock to Denmark House [Somerset House] with as much boldness as any Protestants do to the church."[33] The proposed act and the matter of Rossetti were referred to the Committee of Twenty-four. This activity made the court Catholics nervous. After his house was searched, Rossetti moved to the more protected residence of St. James's Palace, where he stayed as guest of Marie de Medici. The queen's servants, including members of her French choir, found themselves presented for recusancy, a procedure against which Henrietta Maria protested vigorously to parliament.[34]

Windebank's case was acted upon, but not quite promptly enough. Several days after Glynne's report, the Commons commanded the secretary to appear to answer charges. Their messenger found that Windebank had fled to France, never to return. His escape presented no danger to his accusers, but it deprived them of the evidence he might have been forced to give against Strafford and Laud. The sluggish inattention of the House of Commons in letting him escape despite the already considerable evidence against him has thus surprised historians.[35] Perhaps, as has been suggested, his speedy departure was welcomed as an opportunity to fill his post with a more trusted figure, although this ambition was not realized. Or his accusers may have wished to avoid examining the activities of his fellow secretary, Sir Henry Vane.[36]

The Dissolution of the Spanish Party
and the Dutch Marriage

Windebank's flight, following Strafford's arrest and soon to be followed
by Laud's imprisonment, removed the most important English supporters
of Spain from the council. Salvetti, whose sympathies were basically pro-
Spanish, remarked that "we have lost a good friend in this court." Giustiniani, whose loyalties were different, decided that "that [Spanish] party
is now completely overthrown."[37]

Windebank's paradoxical choice to go to France was probably due to
the queen's advice, for she sent with him a letter asking her brother's
protection. It was a favor she repeated for several later victims of parliament's ire, and it served to draw suspicion both on her court and on
France. The French secretary, Montreuil, gave a cynical explanation of
Windebank's arrival in France; he thought the secretary hoped eventually
to return to England and wanted to avoid Spanish territory so as not to
add to his unpopularity. Windebank was accompanied in his flight by his
nephew and assistant, the crypto-Catholic Robert Reade, who was described by the French agent as "openly pro-Spanish."[38]

The remaining court Catholics were regarded by Montreuil as equally
friendly to Spain, and those most powerful with the queen were especially
so—Montagu, Winter, and Father Philip. Mathew, fearing he might be
rearrested, retired from public view in December, possibly to the Spanish
embassy. He escaped a sergeant at arms sent after him in February and
decamped to Raglan Castle.[39] Thus, the fortunes of Spain and the Spanish ambassadors languished at the English court. As the king's hopes for
substantial Spanish loans disappeared, so did his willingness to permit
Spanish recruiting in Ireland. In February the special ambassadors left
for home, much embittered.[40] The following month, ambassadors from
newly independent Portugal were warmly received at the English court,
and negotiations for an alliance began.[41] At the same time, the oft-
rejected Dutch alliance was accepted, and the marriage between the
prince of Orange and the king's eldest daughter Mary ensured that no
English princess would be accepted by Spain.[42]

The Stuart-Orange marriage negotiation was carried on very secretly,
and the news that an agreement was near surprised the court in December. The Dutch hoped for an offensive and defensive league, possibly
involving France, and that the marriage would unite king and parliament
and lead to "vigorous assistance" for the prince Palatine. None of this
materialized. Indeed, the initial speculation that the queen of Bohemia
supported the alliance shortly gave way to the realization that she vio-

lently opposed it, having hoped for the princess for her own son. She also resented the failure of the treaty to include assurances of aid for him from both sides.[43]

Charles Lewis hurried across the Channel in March in a last-minute attempt either to snatch the princess or to ensure that the treaty served his interests. He failed in both aims, and sulked. Nor did parliament, despite the Palatine's friends there, seem inclined to support his efforts. The king was annoyed by his presence, and the Venetian ambassador reported that Charles would try to get rid of his nephew soon "because of the danger amid the present agitations of the sojourn in the kingdom of a prince so near to the succession, the son of a mother acclaimed by the people, and one for whom they have always displayed the greatest affection."[44] To placate Elizabeth and her son, the king named Sir Thomas Roe as ambassador to the Diet of Ratisbon; but Roe's departure was delayed by his illness and no one at court, including the dauntless Roe himself, hoped for much from this embassy. His instructions, which included substantial concessions to the emperor, were unlikely to meet with Elizabeth's approval.[45]

Far from allaying anxieties, the Dutch marriage seems positively to have increased them. The proposal had originated with the queen mother, and she was thought to have had a hand in the final stages as well. The king's motives in seeking the alliance were given a sinister interpretation; he was thought to be hoping for substantial aid from the United Provinces with which to suppress the Scots and "curb the English parliament." When the negotiations had reached a serious stage in December, it was noted that the king spoke more confidently of his authority and said parliament would not succeed in punishing his ministers. The queen, who had warned Rossetti that he must leave soon, now assured him that he could stay. In February Rossetti reported that the king hoped to procure a mercenary force from the United Provinces to dissolve parliament and release Strafford.[46]

The Queen's Plans

Henrietta Maria had responded vigorously, sometimes angrily, to parliament's attacks on Catholics, especially those who were her courtiers. She so much resented all slights on the king's authority that she was even reported to be upset at the arrest of her rival Laud. The Venetian ambassador added that "she never ceases to urge [the king] to throw himself into desperate courses."[47] Very much in the style of her mother, she continued to plot the use of force against parliament even as she tried to negotiate with its leaders over the "bridge" appointments of early 1641 and the passage of the Triennial Act.

By the end of 1640, Henrietta Maria, with the encouragement of Rossetti, was looking specifically to France for assistance.[48] In December she sent an agent there to ask refuge for Rossetti and for any court Catholics who had to flee England. Speculation began at court that she would retreat to France herself, an alternative urged upon her by Montagu and by Jermyn—the former fearing parliamentary attack for his religion and the latter for his monopolies.[49] In February 1641 the queen's servant, Sir Richard Forster, who had served Montreuil well as an informer, was forced to leave England; he was a nonjuror. He had been useful because he associated with Strafford, Windebank, and Cottington. Montreuil hoped he would reveal details of the negotiations with Spain to the ministers in France. Forster took with him a very secret request for aid from Henrietta Maria to her brother.[50]

French response to these overtures was ambivalent. On the one hand, Richelieu and his agents were willing to use English parliamentary contacts to help oust the Spanish party at court; on the other, they did not want to abandon efforts to strengthen their position at court more directly. With both court and parliament, they relied chiefly on the earl of Holland, although the influence of his rival Montagu left Holland on equivocal terms with the royal couple. From December onwards, at Montreuil's instigation, Holland pressed upon the king the advantages of a league with France. Montreuil then felt that the political situation in England was very favorable for French interests; the court was on the defensive and would agree more readily to French terms. He urged that an ambassador be sent immediately. DuPerron, who wanted French support in his rivalry with Montagu for a cardinal's cap, was providing him with information from the queen's court; in return, Montreuil attempted to protect Rossetti, hoping to impress Rome and better DuPerron's choices.[51] As was often the case, French policy making was complicated by the need to take account of a French queen who was not always pro-French and of the Catholic community in England as well.

The passage in February 1641 of the Triennial Act shifted French attitudes yet again; persuaded that the king was now helpless to do good or ill, Montreuil advised that little would be gained by special favors to the royal family. The queen's proposal that she might withdraw into France "for the sake of her health"—a plan correctly interpreted by the parliamentary leaders as a cover for seeking military aid against parliament—was rebuffed by Louis XIII in polite but unmistakable terms, much to the queen's and Father Philip's displeasure.[52]

Concealing her outrage, the queen continued to boast of the help she expected from overseas. She portrayed the new French ambassador La Ferté-Imbaud (appointed in January although he did not arrive until May) as a man who would protect Catholics from Puritans and abandon Montreuil's collaboration with parliamentary leaders. She spoke of an impending peace in Europe and of a league between France and Spain that would bail out the English monarchy and English Catholics. She continued to make apparent preparations for a trip to France, although some at court already suspected she had been snubbed and would not go.[53]

The queen's elaborate bluff made it difficult for the French agent to persuade his friends in parliament, let alone a wider circle of English opinion, that the French were not in fact offering military aid to Charles I. Montreuil did his best with Holland and Pym, but the continuing trickle of court and Catholic refugees into France as the winter progressed provided an irritating contradiction. Finch, Windebank, and Reade crossed over in December, Forster in February. Montagu's departure in April would cause acute suspicion.

Meanwhile, the court pursued the plan for a loan from the pope that had originated over a year before. Negotiations between Windebank and Rossetti in the fall of 1640 were continued by Father Philip after Windebank's flight. Word of these endeavors seeped out. The Venetian ambassador reported that the queen had written personally to Barberini begging for £150,000 "under the plea that the Catholic faith, protected from that quarter, will derive great benefits."[54] Both Rossetti and Father Philip used the king's difficulties as an argument in favor of his conversion to Catholicism. In a long letter to Windebank, Rossetti developed his arguments for the king. He referred to the danger of the Puritan sect, which had been an implacable enemy from the beginning and "has always professed that it is most hostile to the ruling monarch"; he urged the king to "bid farewell to his religion, which is not a good one," and to depend on the Catholic Irish and other Catholic princes "to vanquish and break the arrogance of the Puritans."[55]

The royal response was a temporizing one. The queen pointed out that the king's conversion might well lead to deposition, but held out the hope that money and soldiers to strengthen his position might change his mind.[56] By January Charles I had become personally involved in the negotiations and went so far as to promise that he would grant liberty of conscience in his three kingdoms in exchange for papal aid. On the question of his own conversion, he remained silent; Father Philip appended to the king's message an optimistic comment of his own. But the reply from Rome in March 1641 was adamant: conversion, even if private, must precede any aid from Rome.[57]

These court schemes help to explain parliament's continuing anxieties, which were not calmed by the arrest or flight of many "incendiaries." That several of these ventures (the papal loan and French assistance) were foundering by March and that others such as the Dutch soldiers would never materialize mattered less than well-founded suspicions that the king was seeking forceful solutions to the political crisis that would enable him to reverse the concessions he had made. The presence of armed forces within the kingdom that might be available to him heightened these anxieties.

Concerned about Catholics in the northern army, parliament ordered it purged in December. It removed all known recusants and offered the oaths to suspected Catholics, because, as Salvetti bitterly said, "they were too zealous for the king against the Scots."[58] Montreuil attempted to recruit some of these experienced Catholic troops for French service, especially the Scottish element that had joined the king's forces. The earl of Crawford, who had commanded the Scots under Hamilton, offered 1,000 cavalry; Nithsdale thought he could muster three or four regiments. Falkland and other commanders from the "old" Irish army also offered men and officers. Montreuil pressed unsuccessfully for a French commitment to these commanders that would keep them from Spanish service. Nithsdale's plans are particularly interesting. He told the French agent that "he hoped to return with these same men for the conquest of this country."[59] Reinforcement of the king's army in the spring by trained bands from the northern counties renewed uneasiness in London, for the men were rumored to be "for the most part Catholics."[60]

Catholic dominance of the Irish army was not rumor but a fact that could never be ignored by those who pondered its potential role in English politics. The king's continued refusal to disband the Irish force in early 1641 alarmed many, especially those who knew or suspected that Charles I was in communication with Irish Catholic leaders such as the earl of Antrim and Sir Phelim O'Neill, to whom he promised religious concessions in exchange for armed assistance. In March, after the queen had lost hope of going to France, she began to talk of a trip to Ireland. Father Philip told Rossetti that the Irish Catholics were ready to serve the king if the pope could provide financial support.[61]

The Exiles and the Queen Mother

The exile community continued active in London, still largely unaffected by the English political crisis. Although some of its members made conciliatory gestures to France as Spain's military situation worsened, most had not abandoned their double game of negotiation and intrigue. The duke of Vendôme, fleeing from Richelieu, arrived in February 1641 and was welcomed by the king and queen. Salvetti commented that "he will find here others of the same rank taking refuge for the same reasons, so that England is nowadays obliged to France for sending her such grand guests."[62] Vendôme was soon seen in conference with the queen mother.

Salvetti's fears that Marie de Medici would be immediately attacked for political meddling when the Long Parliament convened had not been realized.[63] But by the end of 1640 her financial situation was very precarious, and it soon became untenable. The king could offer her no further support; she would have to come to terms, however disagreeable, with Richelieu. When the king stopped her pension in January 1641, Henrietta Maria told Montreuil that her husband had already contributed £800,000 to his mother-in-law's support. As the money dried up, Marie de Medici dismissed most of her household and sold her jewels. Her advisors, Fabbroni, Le Coigneux, and Monsigot, were quarreling about where she should go; her Jesuit confessor Suffren, who had his own interests to protect, was passing information to Montreuil. Ill, destitute, no longer welcome in England, surrounded by intriguers and by Richelieu's spies, the queen mother was ready to capitulate.[64]

Convinced by his informants in her household that the queen mother's attitude toward Richelieu had not changed, Montreuil nonetheless assured his masters that this was the time to come to an agreement with her. After a long interview between them in February, Marie de Medici sent one of her chaplains to Richelieu. He came back in March with money and a promise of more if she would retire to Florence. The queen appeared to agree and broke off her public association with Vendôme and other suspect persons. But Montreuil knew that the French exiles, and perhaps Marie herself, posed a continuing danger to France. In late February he heard a long and garbled tale from one of her agents about the intrigues between the Spanish ambassadors and her household, involving a plan for the joint invasion of France, perhaps with English help or even that of Savoy. He heard that Soubise and La Vallette were coming to an understanding with the duke of La Force,[65] the duke of Candale,[66] and other powerful figures within France and that within a month of his arrival Vendôme was deep in intrigue with them and the Spanish.[67] Montreuil was inclined to discount part of the tale as diplomatic bluff, but he was wise not to discount it entirely, for he was listening to the rumblings of the Soisson conspiracy gathering momentum.

The Goodman Case

It was against this background of court intrigue that anti-Catholic agitation revived in late January 1641. The new inquiries began with the case of John Goodman, a secular priest. They branched out to include the Catholic contribution, the "popish hierarchy" that had managed it, and the so-called Welsh popish army. The investigations coincided with the next important stage in the prosecution of Strafford's case, the debate on the detailed charges of impeachment.

The king, as usual, had inadvertently assisted his parliamentary critics by giving them a cause. Yielding to the persuasions of Henrietta Maria and Rossetti, the king reprieved John Goodman from a death sentence. Goodman was a former Anglican clergyman and cousin to the bishop of Gloucester; the bishop's Catholic sympathies had become a public scandal the previous summer. Goodman's background, and perhaps his position as chaplain to the marquis of La Vieuville, aggravated his offense in Protestant eyes, and he had been in and out of prison during the 1630s. Yet his conviction, simply for being a priest in England, was based on a little-used section of the Elizabethan treason legislation; this inclined the king to mercy.[68]

There was immediate reaction in Parliament to the king's pardon. Isaac Penington, M.P. and alderman for the City of London and closely connected with the Commons leaders, rose to announce dramatically that the City would withhold its £60,000 loan for payment of the northern army until Goodman was executed. This initiative was welcomed in the house. Goodman was perceived as a test case; if the king could pardon him for treason, against the will of parliament, might he not do likewise for Strafford and Laud?[69]

From 23 January to 5 February, parliament struggled with the king over the body of Goodman. In the debate of 26 January, John Glynne took a major part, providing details of Goodman's career and instances of other priests pardoned for treason in recent years. D'Ewes spoke as a fiery spirit, proclaiming that "the sparing of this one malefactor justly condemned, may hazard the safety of the kingdom."[70] Several Catholic peers in the Lords (Wardour, Brudenell, Montagu, and Winchester) bravely spoke on Goodman's behalf, but their voices were drowned.[71] The two houses presented a petition to the king calling for Goodman's execution and, under continued financial pressure, he yielded, remitting the case to parliament but warning that severity might have unpleasant consequences for Protestants abroad. He also promised strict execution of the laws against priests and assured parliament that Rossetti would soon leave. Having won the test of strength, the leaders of parliament seemed content to leave the matter, and Goodman's execution was indefinitely postponed.[72]

The concern about popery stimulated by the Goodman case led to debate on two matters quite unconnected with that unfortunate man, except that they also revealed the presence of Catholic influence at court —"ill-wishing spirits," as Rigby had described them on 26 January. There was inquiry into the Catholic contribution, which raised questions about the status and powers of the papal agents and the activities of the queen's Catholic friends. Then there was a scrutiny of the actions of the earl of Worcester and other Catholics in Wales and the Marches, which raised the specter of a "Welsh popish army," an army intended to act in concert with Strafford's Irish force. Although no evidence of Strafford's contacts with court Catholics or Con was adduced (although such contacts did exist, as we have seen), the deputy's enemies traced a tenuous connection from the papal agent and the "popish hierarchy" to the Welsh and Lancashire coasts, and thus to Ireland.

The Catholic Contribution and the "Popish Hierarchy"

Documents relating to the 1639 contribution had been in the hands of Puritan notables almost as soon as it occurred, and allusions to it were made at the beginning of the Long Parliament. But the matter was not brought to the fore until late in January. Glynne's report from the Goodman committee on 27 January included complaints of "the great increase of papists and popery," of the "boldness" of priests in and around London, of the Catholic chapels of the queen and the ambassadors. All these obnoxious phenomena were attributed to the presence of the papal agent. Glynne dramatically produced a copy of the "Advices and Motives" paper for the Catholic contribution as proof that the Catholics were secretly organizing for evil purposes.[73]

In the subsequent debate on the document, D'Ewes seized upon two points as particularly significant. Echoing Rigby's remarks in November, he mentioned with concern the "secret hierarchy of a popish church in England" that the "Advices and Motives" implied. He knew that such a hierarchy had been constructed in Ireland, but said he had thought it had not yet appeared in England. Anxiety about the intrusion of a foreign authority into England, with the head of a shadow church government ready to assume control in the event of a religious coup d'etat, was behind the intense questioning that would ensue over the exact status of Con and Rossetti—whether legates, nuncios, or simple agents.

In the second part of his speech, D'Ewes pointed out how the "Advices and Motives" paper contradicted the king's own explanation of the Bishops' Wars. Royal propaganda had portrayed the conflict as secular in character, with the rebels using religion as a cloak to hide designs upon the civil authority of an orthodox Protestant prince. But the "Advices and Motives" paper brought the religious issue to the fore and painted the conflict as decisive for the future of English Catholicism. As a result, D'Ewes said, "great dishonour redounds to his Majestie and jealousies and suspicions are bred in the hearts and heads of his Majestie's subjects." As Gardiner noted, the information about the contribution impressed the Commons with the frightening belief that "the Catholics had been acting as a political party"; and, given Con's activities in 1638 and 1639, this fear was quite justified.[74]

The links between the Catholic party at court and Catholics in the provinces were explored through information about the contribution in Lancashire. John Moore, M.P. for Liverpool, described how "there had been collectors appointed in that county; and that one of the Roman Catholics there complained to him that he was greatly oppressed by the payment of the contribution." Other Lancashire M.P.s, representing a wide political spectrum, expressed concern over Catholic activities in the county, where a strong Catholic community and an outspoken Puritan minority created a constant potential for religious conflict. Roger Kirkby, knight of the shire, "understood that there had been 15,000 indicted in one hundred, called Amounderness hundred; being not the largest hundred in that county." Naturally, this grossly inflated figure left "the house itself . . . much startled."[75]

Names of the collectors in various counties were provided by other speakers, but the members were less interested in pursuing their recusant neighbors than in focusing on the men around the queen whom they saw as the prime movers of the contribution: her secretary Sir John Winter, Sir Kenelm Digby, Wat Montagu, and Sir Basil Brooke. These were summoned to testify, Winter as the author of the letter, Digby and Montagu as "treasurers here in London."[76] Winter was out of the city, but Digby and Montagu appeared.

Questioned by the Commons on 28 and 29 January,[77] both Digby and Montagu were anxious to minimize their own role in the contribution, which had begun to loom as a threatening issue. Digby spoke rather more freely than Montagu, admitting that he had participated in the collection and paid money in to the exchequer.[78] He described the project as an innocent imitation of the other voluntary contributions for the campaign, which had been extended to the counties only because of a disappointing response from London Catholics. Since, as Digby claimed, he "had little correspondency among the Catholics of this kingdom,"

Con had offered to organize the effort, henceforth took most of the initiatives, and was chief author of the "Motives." Admitting that he had at first been chief collector, Digby claimed he had been replaced by Brooke in that office. When questioned about other participants, Digby named Montagu, Winter, and Richard Forster, "a person Seigneur Con had particular confidence in."[79]

Wat Montagu "spake nothing so fully" as Digby, according to D'Ewes, and in several points his statements were inconsistent with those of his friend. A secular priest reported to Rome that Montagu "was so sparing and wary they thought he equivocated."[80] It was dangerous ground for Montagu; the easiest means of escape was to follow Digby's example and shift all responsibility on to Con, who was not only out of the country but safely dead. Yet magnifying Con's role might make the contribution look more sinister; and his own prospects for promotion could be harmed by anything he said. In the end Montagu threw the responsibility on the king, claiming that the meetings had been held at the king's suggestion. D'Ewes observed that "they had answered subtly and warily, and it was wished that this business might be more thoroughly sifted into." Hampden's motion for a committee of inquiry was accepted, and he and other leaders of the Commons were named to it.[81]

When the examination resumed on 29 January, the committee picked up the subject of the Catholic ecclesiastical authorities in England and the nature of the papal agent's powers.[82] If Con and Rossetti came as nuncios or legates, they came with delegated jurisdiction from the pope, contrary to English law. In fact, the two agents had come with certain powers of jurisdiction, but without the title of nuncio; Montagu and Digby did their best to conceal this. They emphasized that the agents came to attend the queen and help maintain her "civil correspondency" with the head of her church.[83]

Con had sponsored the contribution, they suggested, because he knew the missionary priests and the recusant community in England and was thus "fittest to distribute the 'Motives.'" On being asked "how it came to pass, [Con] coming immediately from the pope, should be the principal in that business, and should so willingly undertake the engagement of two kingdoms in a bloody war," Digby professed that he was "willing to keep himself ignorant as much as he might of many things, having much less acquaintance with Catholics, than is imagined he had."[84] His obvious alarm was justified, for the charge that Con had instigated the wars with Scotland resembled one of the treason charges against Strafford. A secular priest who reported on this investigation specified that the collectors were being treated as incendiaries.[85]

The interrogation of Digby and Montagu convinced the Commons that "there was enough in it to discover great machinations against religion" and to warrant further inquiries. The two were ordered to reappear, together with Brooke and Winter, and to bring books and accounts of the collection.[86] The inquiry now retreated into committee, where we hear little of it; but the committee was continued as "the committee on the popish hierarchy"; as further Catholic issues were raised, they were added to its tasks.

These investigations, together with the sweeps of recusants being conducted in London (Salvetti reported that both he and the duke of La Vallette had been presented for recusancy, although they were foreigners) alarmed the queen and her court.[87] The king had promised to banish all priests save for the queen's chaplains. It was initially thought that these chaplains would include only her Oratorian Father Philip with his companion Father Viette, her almoner DuPerron, her Capuchins, and a few others such as the seculars Leybourne and Gage and the Franciscan William Thomson.[88] Montagu eventually was able to lengthen this list considerably, but for the moment the queen attempted a conciliatory retreat. On 4 February she sent a message to the Commons expressing her concern for a "good correspondency" between the king and his people. She promised to control attendance of English Catholics at her chapel in Somerset House and to send Rossetti away, concessions that only upset the parties concerned.[89] She ended with an explanation of the Catholic contribution, which was intended "only to join in advancing his Majestie's service with divers other persons Protestants that did contribute at the same time." The letter ended with "great expressions of her good will to us," reported D'Ewes, but it was met with a silence in the house. Sir Hugh Cholmley's plea for a message of thanks to her went unheeded.[90] The investigations of the previous week had turned up too much information on court Catholicism for the queen's concessions to be effective.

The "Welsh Popish Army"

At the same time that Digby and Montagu were being questioned, attention returned to the alleged "Welsh popish army" that Worcester was said to have created by special commission in 1639–40.[91] This army was not only worrisome in itself; it also acquired a sinister significance in relation to the "Irish popish army." This is evident from the way in which the debate on 29 January swung back and forth between the alleged Welsh forces and the actual Irish forces.

John Bodvile, M.P. for Anglesea, was first to speak. He "stood up and showed that in the year 1638 there was a commission granted under the great seal of England to the earl of Worcester and the Lord Herbert his son was joined with him in it, being both papists for the levying of forces in divers shires in England and Wales where great numbers of papists inhabited."[92] Sir Thomas Middleton, M.P. for Denbigh, interrupted to contribute an inaccurate list of the shires over which Worcester's commission had extended. Then Sir John Price, M.P. for Montgomery, continued the story, describing how letters from the privy council to deputy lieutenants in those shires had charged them to give Worcester all possible assistance. Price referred to grants of subcommissions from Worcester for the levy of large forces. He alleged that Sir Percy Herbert, heir to the Catholic earl of Powis, had in 1638 gathered in corn from around the county and taken all the arms and powder from the county magazine at night and stored them in one of Worcester's castles.[93]

Clotworthy suggested a link between Wales and Ireland, stating that "the popish army now levied in Ireland . . . consisting of about eight thousand all of the Romish religion, were to have landed in some part of those counties where the earl of Worcester was to levy his forces." John Moore of Liverpool rounded out the picture by adding Lancashire; he described the situation there in 1638: "When the Irish army was expected to have landed there, the wealthier papists provided themselves of a greater number of attendants than formerly; and . . . ships were then pressed at some sea towns in Lancashire and awhile stayed."[94]

The Welsh popish army was taken seriously by the House of Commons. To the Welsh members, it revived the fear of an Irish Catholic landing on the coast that had haunted the principality since the break with Rome. Here, as in Lancashire, the issue united men across the political spectrum; of those who spoke on the subject, only Middleton would be a parliamentarian. Middleton and Price, it is true, had private motives for seizing on the papist issue. Middleton was a rival for power in Montgomery County with the Herberts of Powis Castle, and Price too had been at odds with the earl of Powis. None of the speakers was close to the parliamentary leadership, except perhaps through their compatriot John Glynne, whose family in Carnarvon struggled for influence with the Wynns of Gwydir, courtiers in the queen's circle.[95]

Stories from Wales were more readily accepted because that area, like Lancashire, was remote enough to make verification difficult. The Commons considered the Welsh popish army "a matter of great danger and consequence" and referred it to the committee on Strafford, adding temporary members from the M.P.s of Wales, the Marches, and Lancashire. The committee was charged to consider not only the specific actions of Worcester and Herbert, but also the general issue of disarming recusants.[96]

Like the Catholic contribution and the popish hierarchy, this issue soon subsided from debate into committee, where it is hard to trace. Worcester and Herbert were summoned; Worcester was questioned on 11 February and one of Leicester's correspondents averred that "both his lordship and Sir Percy Herbert are like to receive some trouble." The committee on Strafford transferred the matter back to the committee on the popish hierarchy.[97] The question of the Welsh popish army merged with anxiety about the Irish army, with which it was always linked in debate. Robert Reynolds, M.P. for Hindon, Wiltshire, and the man who had first produced a copy of "Advices and Motives," reported on 11 February from "the two committees now joined in one, viz., the committee touching the Welsh popish army, and the popish hierarchy." His report followed long accounts by Erle and Clotworthy of the Irish army, its cost, and the danger it posed. Reynolds proclaimed: "The army . . . was raised in Ireland but the scene thereof was appointed in south Wales. And the sole power of command there was transferred unto the earl of Worcester and the Lord Herbert his son both papists. The haven where the Irish army should have landed was Milford Haven in Pembrokeshire."[98] The issues of disbanding the Irish army and disarming recusants were henceforth firmly joined in parliamentary rhetoric, together with the problem of the court papists who had not yet been chased away. Of these issues, only the Irish army was directly connected with Strafford's trial, but the others provided a wider conspiratorial context that must have influenced the M.P.s as they weighed the danger Strafford posed to English liberty and religion.

The Irish Army and the Trial of Strafford

In the detailed charges brought against Strafford to the House of Lords on 30 January 1641, the charge of encouraging popery, so prominent in the parliamentary charges and in the propaganda against him, had quietly been dropped.[99] It had been funneled, as it were, into the issue of the Irish army, which had become the key element in the accusation. D'Ewes summed up the charge: "That he had persuaded the oppression of true religion in Scotland, fomented the war undertaken against [the Scots] and endeavoured to embark and embroil all the three kingdoms in the same; and in the issue by the Irish army of papists to subvert the laws and liberties of England."[100] The "Irish army of papists" was a phrase that would be monotonously repeated in the coming months.

The intense focus on Strafford's intentions for the Irish army was not merely retrospective; it was also aroused by the continued presence of the army and by fears about what role was planned for it in the spring of

1641. The subject had been raised as early as November 1640 by Pym and Clotworthy, who suggested that Irish soldiers might yet be intended for England.[101] On 4 January 1641 Sir Walter Erle warned that the still standing Irish army "might speedily draw themselves into a body." D'Ewes chimed in that the soldiers "were wholly guided by their popish priests and Jesuits" and subject to the commands of the pope. The Strafford committee prepared a conference with the Lords on a petition for disbandment of the army. Erle's committee report on 7 January found the army even larger than previously thought. It possessed the port towns of northern Ireland and its commanders enjoyed "daily access" to Strafford, from whom they received orders. Erle wanted speedy disbandment, but some members feared leaving Ireland vulnerable to foreign attack.[102]

Debate on the army revived during the battle over Goodman, when Anne Hussey's story of Irish Catholic plotting was repeated. In a slightly different version of her August 1640 allegations (in wording that suggests coaching), she spoke of the Irish Jesuit O'Connor's revelations that "the new army in Ireland was prepared to subvert the laws of England, and that he himself meant to kill the king."[103]

During the first days of February, Erle worked to get a petition on disbandment through the Commons, pointing out that "we had been formerly advertised of the dangers that threatened religion from the Irish popish army; and that lately we heard of a Welsh army of papists which should doubtless have been enjoined with the Irish." He pictured hoards of arms and ammunition in Irish Catholic hands, and reported disruption of Protestant services in Ireland and the open celebration of mass there. The army was concentrated in Ulster, "the ancient seat of rebellion," and "the lieutenant is yet general, and all to subdue the kingdom of England."[104] When four members went to the House of Lords on 10 February to "discover" the popish plot in Ireland, Wales, and England, they described "15,000 in arms in Lancashire, 8,000 in Ireland, and many thousands in south Wales and north Wales well paid and provided for by the earl of Strafford, the earl of Worcester and others. . . . And there was a letter sent from Secretary Windebank in the queen's name to have all the papists fast every Saturday for the good success of that design."[105] In the succession of conferences between the Commons and the Lords that followed, the issue of the Irish army was frequently linked with that of the Welsh army. On 13 February Clotworthy insisted that the Irish army was intended for England and echoed the earlier warnings: "Then there are letters to the President of Wales to submit all to the Earl Worcester in Wales, and the like to the earl of Pembroke. The lieutenant had power to land his men in Wales." Reynolds also insisted on the threat posed by Worcester, "who in 1639 should have raised an army of English and

Welsh papists," and urged that the recusants of England and Wales be altogether disarmed.[106]

Henceforth, the Irish army was also rhetorically connected with the court papists. The Commons' committee on the Welsh army and the popish hierarchy had no apparent success in unveiling either mystery, but it had no doubt of the identity of the friends of popery at court. In the middle of the 13 February debate on the Irish army, Sir John Hotham dramatically interrupted to present a paper that showed "there were dangerous instruments in the queen's court, had daily near access to her Majesty being English papists; and did by their converse with the superiors of the Romish priests and Jesuits here, and their intimation to foreign states abroad, give great cause to all good subjects [to fear] that their continuance in the court was full of danger. Those were Mr. Walter Montagu who had lately been employed at Rome, Sir Kenelm Digby who was suspected to be in orders himself, Sir John Winter the queen's secretary and Sir Toby Mathew."[107] A committee headed by Edmund Waller withdrew to examine the document, and the petition on the Irish army that was presented to the Lords that day stipulated not only the disarmament of papists but also the banishment of English and Scottish papists from court. Waller declared that "the papists hold the face of a parliament in England, where the pope's nuncio, the Speaker, the Nobles, Commons [are] present." He asked for the removal of court papists, specifying Montagu, Mathew, Winter, and Digby.[108]

The inquiry into court popery and the queen's friends would not be expanded for a few months; the removal of Strafford was a first priority, and the queen's attempts to play a mediatory role between the king and the parliamentary leaders had won her a little support, especially in the Lords. But the assault on the court circle had been launched, and a final element had been added to the conspiratorial context in which Strafford's policy had been placed: the popish plotters at the heart of the court. The interweaving of three themes that had no proven connection—the popish plot, the Irish army, and Strafford's intention to subvert the fundamental law of England—gave a propaganda victory to his opponents before the trial began. This was apparent in late February when Strafford replied to the impeachment articles. He explained that the Irish army had been formed at the king's order for use against Argyll and that he had never advised the king to use it in England. D'Ewes, for one, was not convinced. He admitted that the army might have first been intended for legitimate purposes, "but what was even at first plotted by this great man may well be suspected. Armies we know have been converted to other designs than those for which they were raised." Robert Baillie reported that "the combination of the papists with Strafford's Irish army, to have landed, not in Scotland, but Wales, where the Earl Worcester, a prime head of the popish faction, had commission to receive them; these things are more and more spoken of."[109]

Negotiations between the two houses over the Irish army, disarmament of papists, and the court papist issue in the weeks before Strafford's trial opened on 22 March revealed divisions on each issue. The Lords agreed in principle to disbandment of the Irish force, but wanted first to reinforce the "old Irish army" of Protestants. Likewise, they wished to limit disarmament of Catholics to convicted recusants and to exclude peers (such as the nineteen who had been named on the Commons list of December). They objected to interference with the queen's household, replying to the Commons that "there were but ten English papists in the queen's service." They agreed that Digby and Montagu should leave, but defended Sir John Winter, whom they thought a safer occupant of his office than any foreigner would be who might replace him.[110] Holland, supported by Dorset and Bristol, attempted to achieve a compromise, singling out Lady Savage and Winter as the only court Catholics in office whom the queen wished to protect. Montagu, Digby, and Mathew, he stated (and we may imagine his satisfaction at the opportunity to cite his old rival), were not her domestics. Winter also had supporters in the House of Commons, who referred to his "good parts and integrity, though he be a great papist."[111]

The stalemate on these issues between the more radical group in the Commons, led by Erle, Clotworthy, Reynolds, and Waller, and the more conciliatory members of the House of Lords persisted until a few days after the Strafford trial opened. But the actions of Wat Montagu, in particular, contributed to breaking the deadlock and producing a united anti-Catholic front. Montagu had managed to expand the list of those who would be exempt from the March proclamation ordering arrest of all priests who did not leave England before 7 April. In contrast to the fourteen or fifteen priests initially expected to be given this immunity, the final list had a total of twenty-eight. There was one member of each of the orders, including Dade of the Dominicans and Henry Bedingfield, London rector of the Jesuits (Toby Mathew's "great oracle," as one secular called him), together with Leybourne, Gage, Champney, and six other seculars from the chapter.[112] Furthermore, Montagu appeared in Westminster Hall with the queen's party on the first days of Strafford's trial, talking loudly and laughing. An enraged House of Commons called for the familiar trio of Irish army disbandment, recusant disarmament, and the banishment of court papists (specifically, Montagu, Digby, and Winter). On 27 March the Lords finally joined in a petition embodying these three points, the most important still being the dissolution of the Irish army.[113]

Montagu quickly departed for France on business for the queen; his ultimate destination was Rome. Mathew left Raglan Castle, where he had been in retirement since February, and by mid-April he had reached the Flemish convent where he spent the rest of his life. On 24 April Brooke was summoned a second time, but he had fled the city. When he failed to appear, he was named a traitor. Digby shortly left to take up his appointment as the queen's new agent in Rome.[114]

The king's continuing refusal to grant the joint petition on the Irish army, Catholic disarmament, and court Catholics provided a motive for anxiety about popish conspiracies that is otherwise not reflected in the Strafford trial proceedings. The managers of the trial (Pym, Glynne, Maynard, Erle, Geoffrey Palmer, and Whitelocke) had all been members of the early recusant committees and several had been prominent reporters from committees on Catholicism. But few elements of the original charge of aiding and abetting popery remained in the case argued against Strafford. Bulstrode Whitelocke, in arguing the article on the "Black Oath" tendered the Ulster Scots in 1639, implied in several ways that this was an un-Protestant as well as an unparliamentary oath.[115] Article 18 of the original indictment had charged that "Strafford had restored mass houses; raised an army of papists, about 8,000, and they were duly paid, but the Protestant army was not in twelve months. He compounded with papists at easy rates."[116] But Strafford had so successfully replied to these charges in February that only the issue of the Irish army was argued at the trial. Article 23, accusing him of the intent to use the Irish army against the English, had become the crucial charge.

The seven weeks' trial of Strafford is a gripping story that has often been told and will not be reiterated here. The arguments over the Irish army of papists did not repeat the association with court Catholicism, Welsh and Lancashire Catholics, and the popish hierarchy that had been established in the pretrial debates; but these cannot have disappeared from the minds of the members. Just before the trial began, an incident occurred in the House of Lords that suggests that the Catholic lords were expected to support Strafford and that continuing attempts were being made to get them out of the house. It was proposed that the Lords should enter in their official records the petition of September 1640 made to the king at York and that members of the house should individually subscribe to it. This was interpreted as an attempt to force the Catholic lords away, because the petition was strongly anti-Catholic in tone. Brudenell made a strong speech claiming that the Catholic peers supported the substantive sections of the petition, but led a contingent of them out of the house before subscription.[117]

Nevertheless, the evidence concerning the Irish army, as presented by Secretary Vane on 5 April, seemed insufficiently compelling to cost Strafford his life. His eloquent concluding speech on 13 April left observers doubting whether the Lords would convict him. In this speech he acknowledged the damage done by the charge that he had favored popery:

> But it is that which sticks very heavy upon me; and wherein I find myself as much afflicted, as in any one part of the charge . . . I am charged up and down to endeavour to draw upon myself a dependence of the papists. . . .
>
> This is a very heavy and grievous charge, and hath raised a great deal of ill opinion against me in the world . . . a greater and fouler crime there cannot be against God and man . . . and when there comes to the point, here is no proof, nor any part of the charge made good.[118]

In Pym's closing speech he alluded once more to the "increase of popery, and the favours and encouragement of papists," as a "great evil in the kingdom," to which Strafford was party. But he did not enlarge upon this theme. Within the context of the trial itself, the popery charge had become entirely distilled in the Irish army issue.[119] When the leaders of the House of Commons, alarmed by the possibility that their quarry would escape, finally resolved to proceed by attainder, the bill contained no charges at all relating to church policy. As Conrad Russell has demonstrated, however, Article 23 on the Irish army was one of the two crucial points in the bill.[120]

The Army Plot and the Protestation

The attainder also might have failed had not the king allowed the Irish and English armies to play just the role that Strafford's opponents had predicted. Despite an urgent request from the Lords, the king did not even deign to reply to the joint petition on the Irish army until the trial was over and the attainder under way. His unsatisfactory reply on 14 April was clearly a delaying tactic; he said he would "take some time (after these great businesses [trial of Strafford] now in agitation are over) to give an answer from his own mouth to both houses." The Commons passed the attainder on 21 April and Strafford's fate now rested with the Lords, where at least one Catholic peer, Lord Herbert of Raglan, was prepared to defend him. On 28 April the king again refused to disband the Irish army; his appearance before both houses on 1 May to assure them that he had never been counseled to bring the Irish army into England could not alleviate the continuing anxiety about the king's present intentions for that army.[121]

These suspicions seemed to be confirmed by Pym's revelations about the "army plot" on 5 May 1641. The plan to bring the English army south for a show of force that would intimidate parliament and save Strafford had been known to Pym early in April. Why he did not make it public earlier has never been entirely clear.[122] Pym's first guarded reference to the plot accompanied his introduction of the Protestation on 3 May, the "English Covenant," as Baillie called it. Declaring that he was "persuaded that there was some great design in hand by the papists to subvert and overthrow this kingdom," Pym suggested that a loyalty oath be drawn up. The resulting Protestation and its preamble were explicitly antipapal. The preamble alleged that "the designs of the priests and Jesuits, and other adherents to the see of Rome have . . . of late been more boldly and frequently put in practice than formerly, to the undermining and danger of the true reformed Protestant religion."[123] The document went on to mention the Irish army and referred to certain plans "to bring the English army into a misunderstanding of this Parliament, thereby to incline that army with force to bring to pass those wicked counsels." The suggestion of popish proceedings in the army was picked up quickly by members, one of whom recorded that day "some plots in agitation of the Jesuitical party to [word missing] our army in the north and to harbour a great dislike of the House of Commons."[124]

On 4 May the House of Commons presented the Protestation to the Lords, explaining that "they find popery to grow; the laws to be subverted, and arbitrary government, innovation, and superstitions to be introduced, jealousies to be raised, two armies to be in the heart of the kingdom, and a bad understanding of the parliament to be bred in our English army."[125] The same day, both houses subscribed individually to the Protestation, swearing to "maintain and defend, as far as lawfully I may with my life, power and estate, the true reformed Protestant religion . . . against all popery and popish innovation within this realm."[126] They then sent the oath out for national subscription. Reservations about the Protestation were voiced by both Puritan M.P.s and Catholic peers. The Puritans wished to avoid endorsing the present liturgy and church government; they were given assurances that the gist of the oath was antipopery, not pro-Laudianism.[127] The Catholic peers, unwilling to subscribe to the religious clauses of the oath, were eventually permitted to take it in a modified form that expressed their loyalty to king and country.[128]

The oath was generally understood as an anti-Catholic covenant, and the lists of those in the counties who refused it are sometimes used to identify nonrecusant Catholics. Salvetti reported that the Protestation aimed to destroy English Catholics.[129] In the short term, one of its purposes was to prevent Strafford's escape by temporarily removing the Catholic lords so that they would not vote on the attainder. Essex, Mandeville, and Saye and Sele argued that all nonjurors should be excluded from that vote. It was finally arranged, wrote the bishop of Rochester, "that who refused the Protestation only in point of doctrine of religion might vote, but who upon any other point, should not."[130] Several lords took the modified oath on 10 May, but the attainder had already passed.[131]

The passage of the attainder in the House of Lords on 8 May owed much to the revelations about the army plot made on 5 May. As the preamble to the Protestation suggested, the plot was to be treated as a popish plot, although almost every one of the chief actors in it was Protestant: Percy, Davenant, Wilmot, Goring, Ashburnham, Suckling, and Jermyn. Holles's first speech to the Lords about the army plot spoke of "Jesuits and priests conspiring with ill ministers of state, to destroy our religion" as well as English laws, liberties, and justice. Holles called for a common resolve to "defeat the counsels of these Achitophels, which would involve us, our religion, our king, our laws, our liberties, all that can be near and dear unto an honest soul, in one universal and general desolation."[132] The association of the plotters with the queen's court, the rumored intention to join the English army (reinforced, as was thought, with "popish" trained bands from the north) with the Irish army, and the conviction that the king and queen had induced the French to give them military assistance—all lent themselves to the popish conspiracy interpretation.[133] Throughout the first weeks of May, there were rumors in the capital and in parliament of Catholic plots and of the movement of French troops and ships. London was in great disorder, as mobs attacked the Spanish and Portuguese embassies where armed Catholics were thought to be gathering.[134] In the Commons Pym "declared the great scorn the papist made of us, and how they have rejected and condemned the king's proclamations, and what danger we would be in until the papists should be both disarmed, and severely punished . . . [Parliament must make a list of all their names] . . . and that some course may be taken to make an order to count them as *hostis publicus* which shall offer to bring in any foreign forces into this kingdom."[135] A general search and arrest of priests and Jesuits in London was ordered on 7 May.[136]

The activities of the queen's circle and the sort of talk that could be heard there lent plausibility to Pym's allegations. By May the queen was dreaming of a coup d'etat by English, French, and Dutch troops, all financed by a papal loan.[137] The king, it was said, contemplated joining his army in the north. Meanwhile, Montagu was in Paris begging assistance from the French government. Although the French distrusted him, they gave him an outwardly warm reception to smooth the way for La Ferté-Imbaud in London. The French fleet gathering on the Breton coast, actually bound for Portugal, provided a tangible focus for fears of French invasion. Montreuil lamented that "even the more judicious" of the parliamentary leaders began to believe that France was party to the army plot; when Jermyn and Percy fled there, the suspicions seemed to be confirmed.[138]

The queen mother lingered in England; around her clustered French exiles who were indeed deep in conspiracy, although not against England. Gerbier had come from Brussels late in April, sparking talk of new negotiations between the English and Spanish governments; he was observed to spend much time in consultation with La Vieuville and Vendôme. Cárdenas still hoped for levies in Ireland and sent a special courier to Spain, reportedly carrying the king's offer of 10,000 Irish in exchange for a substantial loan.[139] The young prince of Orange had just arrived, not with the 20,000 soldiers to save the English monarchy that the queen mother had predicted he would bring, but with a handsome sum of money to brighten the new alliance. Giustiniani reported that much of this was sent secretly to the troops in York "with the idea of winning their favor and bias them in favor of impressions which time and opportunity may present."[140]

Nothing about the court scene was calculated to reassure even the moderate peers. When the king finally ordered the long-awaited disbandment of the Irish army on 7 May, it was too late to save Strafford. The next day the Lords passed the attainder, and four days later the lieutenant was dead.

9. The Long Parliament and the Popish Plot: Part II

The death of Strafford, the dissolution of the Spanish party, and the revelations of the army plot made it increasingly difficult to keep parliamentary rhetoric within the tradition of attack on evil counselors. Unofficial advisors and courtiers could still be attacked, attempts to purge the court continued, and the queen's malevolent role was more openly criticized. A new revelation by a Catholic priest about court Catholic intrigue seemed to corroborate suspicions about the queen's friends. In June 1641 the Ten Propositions called for purging the court of Catholicism. Anger could be deflected onto Catholics generally, and during the summer attacks on Catholic priests and laymen throughout England grew bolder and broader. In London priests were seized even in private homes, and reports from the countryside spoke of attacks by mobs of "peasants" on Catholic residences. Giustiniani worried about "the increasing peril to the royal house and to all the Catholics."[1]

But the king's personal involvement in the most threatening of court intrigues could not be ignored; and he seemed willing neither to abandon them nor to disavow them. There is doubtless some truth to the allegations by cynical observers of the scene that anxieties were calculatingly exploited by radical leaders in the summer and fall of 1641. But the activities of the royal family did not inspire calm and confidence in their good faith. The queen's preparation in July for a trip to Holland, where it was known she would seek military aid for the king; the hope at court for a third party in Scotland that caused parliament to fear and attempt to prevent the king's visit there; the Incident in Scotland that ensued—all were susceptible of popish-plot interpretations and did not fail to receive them.

The outbreak of the Irish Rebellion at the beginning of November provided final evidence of the king's willingness to reach outside the English political nation to redress the balance of power. The Grand Remonstrance that was then passed recapitulated in great detail the story of Catholic and alien influences on English politics from 1637 to 1641. The king's attempt to arrest five members of parliament in January 1642 would be placed in the same interpretive framework.

The configuration of foreign policy and the activities of foreigners at court played their part, as before, in raising questions about the safety of religion. There was a final burst of enthusiasm for the prince Palatine's cause as an issue that might unite king, English, and Scots in the summer of 1641; but efforts by the prince and his friends, by France, and by the United Provinces to turn rhetoric into action foundered on the domestic crisis. Meanwhile, in both Vienna and London, imperial agents worked to detach the royal family and the Palatine house from France, principally with the aim of using England as a staging point for attacks on Richelieu's domain, possibly with the assistance of the prince Palatine as well as the exile malcontents. As the Palatine house continued to demand the complete restitution of lands and title that the emperor would never grant, the Anglo-imperial negotiations were futile in their ostensible object. That they continued nonetheless is evidence of the intense suspicion of France that had developed in certain circles of the English court by the autumn of 1641.[2] It also indicates the division developing among the sympathizers of the Palatine house between those who would continue in the parliamentary party and those who would remain loyal to the Stuart family.

Prospects that England would play a truly active role in the European arena receded as the English became increasingly preoccupied at home. The continental powers were more and more viewed, not as potential allies, but as potential threats to English liberty and religion. As the persecution of priests got seriously under way in the summer of 1641, all the Catholic ambassadors became implicated as "harborers of priests." Leaders of parliament continued to differentiate in the summer of 1641 between the friendly governments of France and Venice on the one hand and the other Catholic powers on the other, but the mob did not. As the Irish Rebellion intensified the crisis, no Catholic, domestic or foreign, was entirely immune from attack. This phase of the crisis ended in the early months of 1642, when parliament attempted to secure the person of the prince of Wales, the royal family withdrew from London, and the queen fled from England to the continent.

John Browne's Story

In May and June of 1641, popular animus against the queen, the queen mother, and the papal agent was more violently expressed than it had been since the period just before the Long Parliament. Giustiniani reported that "disgraceful pasquinades" against the queen were posted in the streets of London and that she had begun to talk seriously of leaving England. The queen mother was once again accused of "having instilled evil counsels into her daughter" and of protecting many priests, notably Jesuits. As the agitation mounted, Marie de Medici advanced her plans for departure; meanwhile, she asked parliament for a guard at her residence. When the House of Commons agreed to this, they coupled it with their request that "she may, for her own safety, go away."[3]

As in September 1640, this popular excitement was accompanied by a new popish-plot exposé, the work of the Scottish Minim, John Browne.[4] In addition to his difficulties with fellow Catholics and the Roman authorities, Browne had come to the attention of the pursuivants and was several times picked up and questioned. On one occasion he was brought before Laud, who confiscated a large portion of his college fund.[5] Chafing under this pressure and feeling bitter at the indifference of the Roman authorities and the hostility of his fellow Catholics to his treasured projects, Browne seems to have lost heart and perhaps faith. In April 1641 he was caught by an apostate priest turned pursuivant, one William Carpenter, himself adept at tales of Roman and Spanish conspiracy. Browne began to make appropriate revelations, in the hope perhaps of retrieving some of his lost funds. Visited by a committee from the House of Commons in mid-April, he produced what a secular priest described as "a most pestiferous information," full of "arch knavery and flat roguery."[6]

Browne's account of Catholic plotting, reported to the House of Commons and subsequently printed in a pirated and inaccurate version, resembled Habernfeld's in many points.[7] It combined conventional English anti-Jesuit and anti-Spanish sentiments, Browne's particular historical perspective and grudges against individuals, and his responses to leading questions about Laud and court Catholics. Since we do not know how much or what part of Browne's alleged confession was dictated, or at least suggested, by his interrogators, we cannot assess how his revelations may have buttressed convictions already held by parliamentary leaders or how far they simply used him to whip up the fears of fellow M.P.s. But the outpourings of this disenchanted missionary priest, like those of Abernethie, gave persuasive coherence to suspicions about court activities. Browne's narrative covered five topics: the Jesuits, dangerous courtiers, Laud, the papal plot to take over England, and the meaning of recent Catholic emigration from England. His largely conventional discussion of the Jesuits emphasized their role in the Thirty Years War and in the "destruction of the Christian commonwealth" and how they were "the cause of the civil wars like to befall in these kingdoms." Among the friends of the Jesuits he named, the familiar figure of Captain John Reade reappeared.[8]

Browne's list of the queen's dangerous advisers who merited removal must have satisfied both his captors and his own grievances. The superior of the Capuchins was assigned a sinister role as a spy for Richelieu, sent to create dissension between the English and the Scots so that France might conquer them both. Father Philip, the queen's confessor, was treated ambiguously, at one point named as the "cornerstone" of all Catholic conspiracy, but elsewhere described as ruled either by the so-called cabinet council of Mathew, Winter, Montagu and Digby, or by the Franciscan William Thomson, "who hath intruded himself by degrees to be a clerk of her Majestie's chapel . . . a furious and unquiet spirit, by a nickname called Cacafugo," or even by his own servant Balfour. Among the undesirables in the queen's service, Browne threw in the name of his old colleague, the Minim John Francis Maitland, whom he identified as having "intelligence at Rome, France, Flanders and Spain." Philip and Thomson had "placed many persons not fit to be about her" in the queen's service, namely, Winter, Francis Con ("a man altogether un-worthy of that place and a most scandalous, having at this present three wives alive"), the secular priests Leybourne and Gage, and the Carmel-ite William Pendryck, a "Spaniard and intelligencer for Rome," whose brother Robert was the queen's present agent at the Holy See.[9]

Browne's allegations against Laud reflected his own unhappy experi-ence; that they were elicited in such detail at this time suggests the inten-tion of some M.P.s to bring Laud's case to trial as soon as Strafford was convicted. Browne portrayed Laud as the "sole special cause" of the Scottish troubles and went into some detail about the administration of the Scottish church after 1633; but his most heartfelt comments con-cerned the Court of High Commission. He charged Laud with using the powers of that court selectively to punish poor recusants, while "the fattest he protected and cherished out of all measure"—Leander Jones, William Price, various Jesuits, and Sir Kenelm Digby—"to what end you may conjecture." Leander's visit, alleged Browne, was a turning point, after which Laud favored recusants and began to change Anglican cere-monies to conform with those of Rome.[10]

Browne's account of how "the pope means to intrude himself into the temporal monarchy of this kingdom" added little to the Habernfeld version. There was an intriguing story of Urban VIII initiating the mu-tual agency with a request for English advice on fen drainage for the Roman Campagna; there was the customary reference, soon to become awkward for the Commons leadership, to Richelieu's role in the agency; there was some salacious nonsense about Con's relations with the court ladies. Up-to-date on court Catholic activities, Browne added that Mon-tagu had nourished hopes for the cardinal's cap since Con's death but in vain, also that Rossetti intended to leave an unofficial correspondent with the queen after he departed. In his last brief section, Browne warned that English Catholics were selling their property and fleeing to Europe with their treasure; this should be prevented.[11]

Browne's extended narrative of Jesuit activities in Europe had a corollary in John Dury's 1641 publications, whereas the details provided on Catholic finances seem to reflect not only Browne's preoccupations but a developing concern in parliament about Catholic emigration at a time when the queen was herself considering a trip to Europe. Compared with Habernfeld, Browne minimized the role of the papal nuncios and increased the emphasis on the queen's court Catholics, both lay and ecclesiastical. The reiteration of the familiar names of Digby, Mathew, Montagu, and Winter smacks of coaching, but reference to relatively little known figures such as the Pendryck brothers confirms that Browne was no ignorant dupe of the Commons committee. It seems, indeed, that he tried to repay an old grudge against an otherwise obscure court figure, the Franciscan William Thomson. Thomson had been a chaplain to the queen since the late 1620s and was one of the Scots introduced into the queen's patronage through her confessor, Robert Philip. He had been instrumental in founding the English Franciscan chapter, which was now flourishing; it may be the success of this rival order that so aroused Browne's ire that he named Thomson as "eminence grise" behind Father Philip.[12]

As a result of Browne's information, Thomson was arrested and questioned by the committee investigating the army plot. He was asked particularly about the collectors for overseas Catholic colleges, as well as about the identity of priests in England, of whom the committee chairman reckoned there must be at least 3,000. Several attempts were made to elicit damaging statements from Thomson, but, according to his own account, he revealed nothing of importance and was released.[13]

The first use made of Browne's testimony in parliament was during the army plot investigations at the beginning of May. Sir Henry Anderson reported that Browne believed the lay court Catholics to be plotters, naming Brooke, Winter, Sir Richard Weston of Surrey, a Mr. Plowden, and the queen's cupbearer, Francis Con.[14] On 7 May Evelyn gave further details of Browne's testimony, this time on the popish hierarchy, the existence of which Browne had corroborated: "there was *ecclesia inter ecclesiam*, a Romish church within our church, and *republica inter rem publicam.*" It was shocking that priests with subversive aims were everywhere at court, for "religion is the apple of our eye, and the stay of the kingdom."[15]

The spotlight cast on Father Philip by Browne's version of the popish plot was unlucky for the court. Philip was by then deeply involved in negotiations for a papal loan to the king; moreover, he was corresponding with Montagu in France, as parliament discovered when the foreign mail was seized in May. One letter from Philip that particularly offended the Commons referred to the Protestation as "rather worse than the Scottish Covenant." More seriously, Philip's letter confirmed that the court was actively seeking aid from France; in it, Philip described the queen as being in grave danger and urged that her brother Louis XIII intervene to help her.[16]

Browne's revelations and Father Philip's letter were brought forward as evidence at the end of June to strengthen support for the Ten Propositions. On 24 June Pym produced the documents; Philip was arrested the next day and ordered to testify to the committee on the army plot.[17] The content of the Ten Propositions indicates the extent of anxiety about court Catholicism. Four of the eight substantive demands related to court popery: removal of Catholics from court and from attendance on the queen; expulsion of the Capuchins; expulsion of Rossetti; and safeguarding the royal children from Catholic influences.[18]

These demands were only partially satisfied. Newcastle's implication in the army plot had ended his career as the prince of Wales's governor; he had already been replaced by the earl of Hertford. The prince's tutor, Bishop Duppa, had long worried the House of Commons because of his dependence on the queen and the alleged fear that he might convert, but for the time being he kept his position.[19] The king stalled on the question of expelling the Capuchins, who had been the object of mob agitation for two months, but he agreed that Rossetti should leave England.

Rossetti already understood that his departure was inevitable. He had been badly frightened by the interception of his correspondence in May, which put him in grave danger. Even letters sent through the Venetian ambassador were no long guaranteed safe passage.[20] Puritan propaganda branded him a tool of Spain, an accusation that would haunt him in his later role as papal delegate to the Cologne peace conference. When he was summoned to testify before parliament on 24 June, Rossetti hurried to the Venetian embassy, where Giustiniani procured a safe-conduct for him and a royal ship to take him to Flanders. In his haste, Rossetti left some of his belongings with the Somerset family's Jesuit chaplains.[21] He reported to Rome from Cologne that, at his last interview with the king, Charles had spoken more like a Catholic than a heretic.[22] Rossetti hoped his place would be taken by an unofficial representative with the queen, an Italian canon who would be financed through the assistance of William Thomson.[23]

The queen mother, too, would soon leave England. She had been attacked in the Commons during the debate on the Ten Propositions; but her departure was delayed by the difficulty of finding a safe route to Italy for her entourage and by her financial difficulties. Ultimately, parliament had to underwrite her trip to the extent of £10,000. When she left, Marie de Medici was accompanied by the countess of Arundel and several Howard children, a number of English priests, and her Jesuit confessor, Father Suffren. Ailing and unable to withstand the rigors of the voyage, she got no further than Cologne, where she died before the English civil war began.[24]

During the summer, articles of impeachment based on Browne's accusations were drawn up against Father Philip. Like Browne, the framers of the articles seemed unable to decide whether the priest was the mastermind of Catholic conspiracy or merely a tool of others. He was blamed for the establishment of the mutual agency and identified as the patron of unsuitable persons placed in the queen's household: Francis Con, Sir John Winter, Sir William Hamilton, George Gage, and George Leybourne. At the same time, he was said to be "much ruled by Sir Toby Mathew, Sir John Winter, and Mr. Walter Montagu," as well as by the Capuchin superior and the Franciscan William Thomson. More dangerously, he was labeled a Jesuit, accused of attempting to convert the Prince of Wales, and "hath been observed to be a great cause, both in himself and his adherents, of a great part of the unquietness of this state."[25] But for the time being, he was left unmolested.

Anti-Catholic Activity in the Summer of 1641

The summer of 1641 was difficult not only for court Catholics but for less prominent ones as well, and it was indeed among the latter that the first martyrs of the civil-war period were found. Rather naively perhaps, the lay Catholics had hoped that parliament might provide them with relief from harassment by local officials, and a petition on the subject had been drawn up. Presentation to parliament was postponed, first until the Strafford-Worcester furor with its anti-Catholic overtones died down, then until the Scottish commissioners with their violently anti-Catholic attitudes had gone away.[26] In the meantime, the situation of the Catholics became more and more precarious. On 12 May the pursuivants were unleashed to do their worst, and the oaths—both the oath of allegiance, which some Catholics would take, and the oath of supremacy, which they could not—were more widely and stringently applied. The Commons ordered that lists of all recusants in the counties be prepared by the exchequer and local officials, so that they might be disarmed. In June the Commons passed an act to seize the arms of any papists who refused to take the two oaths and an act "for the better regulating of the two parts of recusants lands due to the king."[27] The Lords proved reluctant to accede to sweeping disarmament measures, but on 30 July they concurred in a resolution that those refusing to take the Protestation were not to have office in church or commonwealth. Lord Saye and Sele, as the new master of the Court of Wards, was reported to be taking children away from Catholic guardians and putting them in Protestant households.[28]

In July the Catholic petition was finally presented and read in the House of Lords, where it met with some sympathy;[29] but Giustiniani was not optimistic about its reception in the House of Commons. The momentum of anti-Catholic agitation was too far advanced. Despite the opposition of the Lords to the disarmament of prominent recusants, some of whom belonged to their own house, commissioners for disarmament of recusants were appointed in several counties at the end of August. Faced with this pressure on all fronts, Catholics began to leave England—not only prominent court Catholics, but many others who feared the onset of a general persecution.[30]

The English missionary priests suffered most, especially those without ambassadorial protection. The sweep of foreign correspondence in early May had caught several secular clergy carrying messages to the bishop of Chalcedon in France; they were questioned on the "popish hierarchy" that the letters implied.[31] Moreover, the reauthorization of the pursuivants in May posed a particular danger to the clergy. They were subject to the March proclamation requiring their departure from England, and the new enforcement of the oaths of supremacy and allegiance hit them hard, as few priests were prepared to take either. Two priests were condemned in April and July (one of them the convert nephew of the late archbishop of Canterbury), although neither was then executed.[32] William Webster (alias Ward), an aged scholar who was captured in the summer of 1641, was not so lucky. Condemned to death at the Old Bailey, he refused every inducement to renounce his faith and was executed on 26 July 1641.[33] Other priests, both secular and regular, were in prison during the summer of 1641 and several were condemned, although no others were executed.[34] The condemned priests, including the martyr Webster, were mainly men who had worked in the London area for some time and were known to the pursuivants, but lacked special royal or ambassadorial protection.[35] One condemned priest, however, did have such protection and his case because a cause célèbre over the summer. Cuthbert Clopton (alias Green) had been chaplain since 1638 to the Venetian ambassador, who had brought him from France. Captured by the pursuivant Carpenter, Clopton was tried with Webster at the Old Bailey and condemned on 23 July 1641. Giustiniani intervened and saved his life, but only on the condition that Clopton immediately leave England.[36]

The embassies of the Catholic ambassadors provided particularly attractive targets for both the London mobs and the pursuivants, and they lost most of the immunity they formerly enjoyed. Already in May, placards called on Londoners to march on the embassies and destroy idolatry. The Spanish and Portuguese embassies were hard besieged, for there were rumors of military preparations there as well as "idolatry." English Catholics attending services were attacked; eighty persons were arrested in May at the Portuguese residence. The lord mayor was ordered to prevent "the great resort of the common people" to mass at the Iberian embassies; a priest was taken from the Spanish embassy and thrust in the Gatehouse. On 16 May the Commons decreed that papists frequenting the Spanish ambassador's residence were to be taken and tried as delinquents in the court of King's Bench.[37] As a result of Clopton's case, parliament passed a resolution in July barring any of the king's subjects from residing with ambassadors, a measure aimed at the English and Scottish priests who were maintained there. The Spanish and Portuguese ambassadors did not respond to the warning; the concourse of people around their residences continued, and in August and September members of their households, including two English chaplains of the Portuguese ambassador, were arrested.[38]

Even the queen's Capuchins were not wholly exempt from the mounting attack on priests. The Ten Propositions had called for their expulsion; the matter was taken up again in the Commons in July. In August their superior, Father Jean Marie de Trélon, was arrested, and a motion was made in parliament that the whole group be expelled. The issue was only temporarily quieted on 13 August when the Lords sent Dorset to ask the queen to keep her Capuchins from "going abroad to pervert, and the English may not be suffered to come unto them." Secretary Nicholas, aware of the depth of sentiment against the Capuchins, advised the king in September to dissolve their house, but his advice was not heeded.[39]

Rival Ambassadors and Foreign Policy in the Summer of 1641

As the incidents at the ambassadorial chapels indicate, none of the Catholic ambassadors were exempt from the effects of xenophobia in the period between the army plot and the Irish Rebellion. The likelihood of English intervention on the continent seemed increasingly remote, but foreign agents were nonetheless busy in the capital. The presence of three mobilized armies in the king's territories provided more than enough incentive for diplomatic rivalry between France and Spain, both hungry for hired soldiers. In June the Spanish ambassador swallowed his outrage at the king's reception of the Portuguese emissary and resumed audiences, hoping to acquire up to six regiments from the disbanding Irish army and beguiling the king with his usual advice about regaining royal authority by force and foreign aid.[40]

The new French ambassador, La Ferté-Imbaud, expected permission to recruit English and Scottish troops, as well as Irish, as soon as the Anglo-Scottish accord took effect. But the attitude of M.P.s toward France was very ambivalent. Some suspected that French forces had been part of the army plot, despite the apparent sympathy between Montreuil and the parliamentary leaders.[41] In May and again in June, mail from France was opened at parliamentary order. The French agent's residence, owned by a prominent Catholic laywoman, was searched; there had been rumors of plots hatching there. These fears persisted through June.[42] One M.P. reported in his diary the continuing rumors about French activity: that the French would join with the army, that a Capuchin had alleged "we were sold to the French by the queen." Letters from Wat Montagu to Percy and Jermyn, and to Montagu from the court, were intercepted by parliamentary commissioners and given a sinister interpretation. In September there were riots in Lincoln's Inn Fields near the French embassy.[43]

Because of hostility to Spain and suspicion of France, neither government received the recruits it wanted. In midsummer parliament suspended all levies. At that time, some M.P.s expressed concern about the increase of French power in the European war theater. Despite the king's worried insistence that he had given his word to Spain for four regiments, the House of Commons balked. The matter dragged on into September, tentative promises being made and then rescinded. The soldiers never received permission to go, although in October some Irish troops departed for Spain on their own initiative.[44]

The arrival of a new French ambassador in July at first brought "unspeakable consolation to their Majesties," Giustiniani reported, for they expected him to be more sympathetic to the court than Montreuil.[45] This seems to have been the case, but it did not provide the king with an effective intermediary with parliament. Initially, the ambassador's intimacy with the royal family made him suspect to parliament; by the time these suspicions abated, the royal family had cooled to La Ferté because he got on well with the parliamentary leadership. The appointment of George Digby to replace Leicester at the Paris embassy kept alive the anxiety of M.P.s about court negotiations with France. In fact, the king and queen had not given up hope of aid from that quarter; the queen's unsuccessful nomination of her former almoner DuPerron for a cardinal's hat was not just a favor for an old servant; it was a service to the French government that had always supported his nomination.[46] By the time parliament reconvened in October, however, Pym and his circle were sufficiently persuaded of either the amity or the possible utility of France to devote considerable effort to pleasing La Ferté and his masters.

As the popular excitement over Catholicism mounted in the summer, even the Venetian ambassador, long sympathetic to the "public cause," began to deplore the direction of events in terms not unlike those of Salvetti. Giustiniani found himself in an ambiguous position; not only had he intervened to assist Rossetti safely out of the country, but his diplomatic couriers were being used clandestinely for correspondence between the queen and her friends in France (notably Montagu) and for Catholic correspondence in and out of England.[47]

The Retreat of the Prince Palatine

Reaction against parliamentary proceedings can also be seen among the supporters of the Palatine house, for by the end of 1641 their ranks would split as parliament divided with the approach of war. For a time in the summer of 1641, however, the fortunes of the prince seemed brighter, and the possibility of English intervention on the continent was raised again. For the first time since the 1620s, the king asked for parliamentary assistance for his nephew. His cause might prove a rallying point for loyalist sentiment and a pretext to keep afoot the English army that parliament was so anxious to disband. The French ambassador seconded the appeal.[48]

The rhetorical response, at least, was hearty. In the first part of July, both houses of parliament passed votes of support for the king's manifesto on behalf of Charles Lewis. Sir Benjamin Rudyerd and Sir Simonds D'Ewes made ringing speeches, declaring that the king should take his rightful place as leader of the Protestant party in Europe. Denzil Holles argued that English Protestantism could not survive a Habsburg triumph in Europe and that the Catholic menace must be stopped on Austria's frontiers, not on the shores of England. Some observers were skeptical that this rhetoric could have much effect, but the prince's cause was duly recommended to the attention of the Scottish parliament.[49]

Meanwhile, apostles of Protestant unity and activism were summoned to England by Samuel Hartlib and others, who saw in the Long Parliament the opportunity they had awaited for a *renovatio mundi*. Warwick's chaplain had recommended Dury and Comenius to the House of Commons in November 1640, and a small group of M.P.s invited the two to visit England. Dury arrived in early 1641, bringing his enthusiasm for Anglo-Scottish unity as the core of an anti-Habsburg alliance.[50] He petitioned the Commons to support his plans for ecclesiastical union and began to publish works on related subjects: Protestant unity against the Habsburgs, restoration of the Palatine house, and domestic social, religious, and educational reform.[51] In June Dury was appointed chaplain to the new lord lieutenant of Ireland, the earl of Leicester. In September Comenius arrived, to be greeted by Hartlib, Dury, Hübner, Pell, and Haak. The publication of *Macaria*, a vision of an ideal society based on Christian brotherhood, reflected the ideas of Hartlib and the influence of European utopian thought. An English translation of Comenius's first pansophical work was completed and published early in 1642, along with Hartlib's *England's Thankfulness*, publicizing the reform schemes he shared with Dury and Comenius.[52]

Similar ideas were expressed in English publications in 1641. In his *Sounding of the Two Last Trumpets*, Henry Burton returned to themes of foreign policy that he had not enunciated since the 1620s, namely, the defeat of the Habsburg-popish forces by a Protestant league joined to France.[53] Calybute Downing published a long defense of the Palatine cause, dedicated to the House of Commons and embodying conventional anti-Jesuit and anti-Habsburg motifs. Joseph Mede's millennial writings appeared for the first time in English translation with the publication of *The Apostasy of the Latter Times*.[54] The breakdown of government censorship of printing in 1640–41 permitted not only a proliferation of anti-Catholic and popish-plot literature that helped sustain the themes of parliamentary propaganda,[55] but also a flowering of millenarian speculation that was to prove a source of agitated controversy among Protestants. Pamphlets appeared that pointed to the fulfillment of John Brightman's prophecies for Protestant England, Scotland, and Germany.

Heralded by Dury's *Memorial concerning Peace Ecclesiastical*, which was addressed to the king and to the parliament and assembly of Scotland, the prince Palatine set off for the north with the king in August 1641.[56] Giustiniani suggested that the king wanted Charles Lewis at his side, "possibly in order to relieve his mind of the suspicions which the presence of a prince so near to the succession quite naturally excite"; for some in the Commons suggested "depriving [Charles I] of the crown and giving it to the prince or the Palatine, or else to set up a democratic government." A reference in the bishop of Rochester's diary to a plan by Newport, Mandeville, and "others at the Lord Mandeville's table on Sunday last" to "take and keep the queen and the prince [of Wales]" may be connected with this report.[57] If any overtures were made to Charles Lewis himself regarding a coup d'etat, however, they were either rejected or thwarted. Nor was his visit to Scotland successful; the king's position there would be ruined by the Incident, and Charles Lewis's hopes with it.[58]

The prince's loyalty to his uncle alienated him in the winter of 1641–42 from the parliamentary leadership. Frustrated in his attempts to get aid from within the British Isles, Charles Lewis toyed with offers held out to him by imperial agents. The negotiations at Ratisbon were getting no further than previous efforts. The release of Prince Rupert at Christmas was the only tangible result of Sir Thomas Roe's efforts. Yet Lisola in London had some success in wooing the prince Palatine. The failure of the Soissons conspiracy did not end his attempts to disrupt Richelieu's government. Thus, when he returned to England in October 1641, he explored the possibility of gaining Charles I's support through the prince Palatine. During his continued negotiations with La Vallette and Soubise (both by now on Spanish pensions), Lisola discovered that they would welcome the cooperation of Charles Lewis. Perhaps the duke of Vendôme, a recent refugee from Richelieu's regime, could be used to approach the prince. Anything that could be used to further Stuart distrust of the French government was welcome to Lisola, who observed the intimacy of the French ambassador with the earl of Holland and other parliamentary figures and the vigor with which the French attempted to detach England from Spanish and imperial interests.[59]

When, in January 1642, the prince Palatine accompanied Charles I into the chamber of the House of Commons in the attempt to arrest the five members, the action symbolized his retreat from the possibilities opened for him by the convocation of the Long Parliament.[60] A number of his supporters beat a similar retreat. Sir William Boswell would become a royalist.[61] Dury, perhaps because he was away from England during the 1630s, had remained relatively immune to the fears and suspicions of the court that had then developed. He had solicited support as eagerly from Laud and the bishops as from the Puritan peers of Hartlib's acquaintance; these contacts aroused distrust in men like Baillie, who had unfairly accused him of being Laud's tool to reconcile both foreign Protestants and the Church of England to Rome. After publishing a pamphlet urging moderation and conciliation on the emerging parties in parliament, Dury withdrew to the Hague early in 1642, where Boswell had arranged his appointment as tutor to the Princess Mary.[62] Comenius withdrew from the fray at the same time. Hartlib, who had worked so hard for parliamentary support for his friends, was more reluctant to abandon his reform projects in the face of the growing divisions within parliament. Less unsympathetic than Dury to religious radicalism, he would remain in England throughout the war years.

The division within this group exposed an ambiguity in the Palatine position that had been evident also in the Habernfeld exposé, namely, a conviction that the Catholic threat was real, coupled with an unwillingness to associate it with the royal family. Dury, an example of the loyalist party, was irenic in outlook, with a positive view of the role of England and the English king in Europe and a positive plan for reform. Other millenarians, like Prynne, also viewed England in a European looking glass, but their distrust of the government compelled them to sacrifice unity at home, and possible efficacy in Europe, to domestic housecleaning under the banner of antipopery. Although Prynne was to build his popish-plot story on Habernfeld's disclosures, the spirit he represented was better served by Browne's testimony, with its strongly anti-Laudian orientation and emphasis on the queen's friends.[63] The division among the Palatine's supporters may have owed something to differences in theological positions or to the degree and character of millenarian convictions, but it can be explained with equal plausibility by the behavior of the royal family in the period 1640–42. Those who looked closely at the king's policies were afraid; those who were afraid to look closely remained loyal.

The Court Seeks Help

Throughout the summer and early autumn of 1641, the king and queen sought help outside England for the restoration of royal authority that seemed less and less possible in a purely English context. These efforts went far to justify the suspicions raised by the army plot, in which the king was thought to be fully implicated and of which the queen was described as the "very author." Already in June, the Venetian ambassador had reported that parliament members were searching for legal precedents for initiating proceedings against the queen for political meddling.[64]

Frustrated in her attempt to muster support in France and frightened by the hostility of parliament, the queen began to talk of a trip to Holland, accompanying Marie de Medici and taking Princess Mary to her new husband. Rightly suspecting that the queen intended to pawn the royal jewels and intimating that they would intervene to stop her trip by force if necessary, parliament petitioned the king to dissuade her from leaving in mid-July.[65] Pym's statement on the subject, presented to the Lords and by them to the king, referred to the liquidation of assets and departure of Catholics from the country. He suggested that the papists had a "design upon her Majesty's journey," that they would cluster about her and give her "evil counsels" and use their funds "to the fomenting some mischievous attempts."[66] A diarist in the House of Lords picked up the reference to papist sale of lands, "which makes divers suspect that they will join themselves unto the queen." There is no trace of ironic realization that the policies of parliament were a major reason for these Catholic activities. On 21 July the queen gave in to parliamentary pressure and agreed to postpone her trip.[67]

Henrietta Maria's ingenuity, however, was far from exhausted; she continued negotiation for a papal loan that might be used in conjunction with the Irish troops on which she secretly rested her hopes. Rossetti's departure had not ended these Anglo-Roman negotiations. They were carried on for a time through papal representatives on the continent until Sir Kenelm Digby arrived in Rome as the queen's new representative. In June and July 1641, the queen reiterated her earlier assurances that £150,000 from the pope would bring immediate religious liberty for Ireland and free access to the chapels in London for English Catholics, followed in time by free exercise of the Catholic faith in England.[68]

The new Irish army was not being disbanded quickly; continuing Spanish requests to levy recruits gave the king an excuse to delay its dissolution.[69] In July he seems to have sent a verbal message to Antrim and Ormonde, instructing them not only to keep the army together but to increase its size, with a view to securing Ireland under royal, not parliamentary, control. This maneuvering over the Irish army was independent of plans being made at the same time by Gaelic Catholic aristocrats for a rising in Ulster; but the two projects would merge in the Irish rebellion.[70] The officers commissioned in May to convey recruits from Ireland to Spanish service included friends and agents of Owen Roe O'Neill (Maguire, MacMahon, Rory O'More and Sir Phelim O'Neill). O'Neill was negotiating independently with the pope, as well as with Spain and Richelieu, for help in an armed intervention to safeguard Irish Catholics against the increasingly threatening posture of the English parliament. Antrim was also in touch with Owen Roe O'Neill, as was Daniel O'Neill, one of the queen's courtiers. This network of contacts helped to explain why the Irish army still raised "great jealousies on this side," as Sir Edward Nicholas reported to the king's governors in Ireland in August. Giustiniani recorded a report at court that the Irish deputies had offered the king 15,000 men, ready to embark for England at a moment's notice.[71]

Plans for a new and more effective royalist party in Scotland that could be detached from the Covenanters also included Catholic figures. Suspecting that the king hoped to unite the Scottish and English armies, parliament attempted unsuccessfully to delay his trip to Scotland until the English forces were disbanded. The king's departure for Edinburgh in mid-August was attended by talk of a "third party" in Scotland that would include the ever-loyal Catholics. Secretary Nicholas reported to the king from London on the continued damage to his reputation from suspicions that he favored popery: "The alarm of popish plots amuse and fright the people here, more than anything, and therefore that is the drum that is so frequently beaten upon all occasions; and the noise of an intention to introduce popery was that which first brought into dislike with the people the government both of the church and commonwealth."[72]

In Scotland, the king's welcome soon dissolved in a storm of accusations and counteraccusations between Scottish and English courtiers on the one hand and Covenanting leaders on the other. The discovery of the so-called Incident on 11 October ruined the king's position in Scotland. It was alleged that the king's supporters intended to seize or assassinate Hamilton, Argyll, and Lanerick. One of the most prominent plotters was, unfortunately for the king, the Catholic earl of Crawford, already a focus of parliamentary suspicion.[73]

The Incident fed the flames tended by parliamentary leaders during the recess. Secretary Nicholas, aware of their unofficial meetings in the London area, warned the king that they were likely to renew antipapist agitation when parliament reopened. The king's personal presence in London, he said, was urgently needed. But parliament reconvened without the king, and Pym took immediate advantage of the reports from Scotland to proclaim that there had been dangerous conspiracies against the "good proceedings" of parliament and that these were connected with the army plot. Troops were summoned to London to protect the city and parliament against the supposed Catholic threat.[74]

Pym noted that "the principal party [Crawford] named in that design in Scotland is a person suspected to be popishly affected; and therefore may have correspondency with the like party here."[75] He introduced further evidence of plotting in the English army to support his thesis of a general conspiracy. Again, he was aided by the king's indiscretions. Before his departure for Scotland, Charles appears to have commissioned William Legge and Daniel O'Neill to sound out officers in the northern army about joint action with the Scottish army to overwhelm parliamentary opposition, a project that depended on the king's success in Scotland and was doomed by the Incident. O'Neill was imprisoned and closely questioned. In addition to the information he provided Pym, O'Neill was a figure of some symbolic significance in his own right; although a Protestant, he was a professional soldier who shared his family's ambition to regain family lands and position in Ulster. He was in touch with his uncle, Owen Roe O'Neill, and other Catholic exiles in Flanders and, through his brother, Con Oge O'Neill, with the Gaelic malcontents in Ulster.[76]

On 30 October Pym made a preliminary report on the second army plot. He cited Father Philip and the queen mother's agent, Monsigot, as "dangerous persons [who] held correspondence with some dangerous

persons fled from home, and did thereby daily contrive new and mischievous plots"; he alluded to "sundry great recusants" who gathered
forces and held secret meetings. The safety of the Prince of Wales was
questioned: "We might well doubt by reason of those persons about the
queen he should receive no good there neither for soul nor body." Pym
concluded "that he feared the conspiracy went round and that there was
a compliance in this new design both in Scotland and England." Philip
and Monsigot were summoned to appear in the House of Commons.
Before they were found, however, news of the Irish Rebellion had provided evidence of Catholic conspiracy that was far more persuasive and
frightening than the army plots, the Incident, or the revelations of Father
Browne.[77]

The Irish Rebellion and the Grand Remonstrance

News of the rebellion reached London on Sunday, 31 October, and was
reported to parliament the following day. The rebellion seemed to substantiate all that the opposition had said about popish plotting. The
rebels themselves claimed that they had royal authority for their activities
and that they were in arms not against the king but against his enemies.
They asserted that Charles I planned to come to Ulster to lead them and
would land at Antrim's castle at Dunluce, and that the queen had encouraged them to rise in defense of their religion. Sir Phelim O'Neill produced
what he said was a commission under the great seal, made in Edinburgh
on 1 October, ordering the Irish lords to seize the castles, houses, and
property of Protestant settlers.[78]

The queen and all those thought to be her allies came under immediate
scrutiny. Spain was suspected of playing a leading role, for the leaders of
the rising had been in Spanish employ and were reputed to have boasted
that they expected Spanish help. The Spanish ambassador's correspondence was intercepted and read. Monsigot, the queen mother's agent,
who was already marked in parliament as a "dangerous man," was
sought for questioning as a Spanish plotter.[79] This anti-Spanish animus
owed something to tradition, something to known and suspected Irish
appeals to Spain, and doubtless something to the French ambassador.
Cardinal Barberini had naively let the French government know of his
desire to help the royal couple and of the efforts he and Rossetti were
making on their behalf with Spanish agents. Rossetti, better aware of the
political line France was taking in England, stopped this flow of politically damaging information, but it was too late.[80] The leaders of parliament, said Giustiniani, feared direct papal intervention through the send-

ing of troops from the continent to Ireland. The Venetian ambassador's correspondence was seized, on the correct assumption that the queen was using Giustiniani's couriers to correspond with her friends in France. Within a few months, the long-festering suspicions of the queen were generalized, and she was seen as the primary inspiration of all the successive crises between the king and his parliament. Salvetti reported that the parliament leaders "dare to name her the principal author of that [Irish] revolt, calling it the queen's rebellion."[81]

The authenticity of the royal commission to the Irish rebels has been disputed, but the king's involvement with the rebels can no longer reasonably be questioned, although the details remain hazy. Charles I had sent Lord Dillon to Ireland in October, apparently to ask the Catholic lords of the Pale to seize and hold Dublin Castle and to raise the royal standard in Ireland. Dillon helped persuade the Ulster rebels to join with the lords of the Pale and returned to assure the king that all were ready to support him in exchange for complete liberty of religion. Arrested and examined by parliament on his return in England, Dillon said enough to convince them of royal complicity in the rebellion.[82] The king had not troubled to hide his relief at the Irish distraction, expressing in a letter to Nicholas his hope that "these ill news from Ireland may hinder some of these follies in England."[83] The agents he had used as early as 1638–39 reappeared on the Irish stage, lending credibility to the idea of a long-nurtured royal alliance with the Irish Catholics. Among many suspect travelers seized in passage between England and Ireland was one Arthur Progers, servant to Sir Henry Bruce. Bruce had newly returned to London from Ireland, leaving behind his nephew John Reade, one of the major protagonists in both the Habernfeld and the Browne exposés. Progers helpfully deposed to the Chester authorities that "he was employed by Col. Bruce on the king's behalf unto Col. Reade, living in Tredagh and a great papist . . . [that] he was going to Dublin to receive hundreds of money for his master's use."[84]

The Irish Rebellion was the catalyst for the outbreak of civil war in England, because the struggle for control over the army being sent to Ireland was the context in which two armed forces were created, one under royal and one under parliamentary control. The rebellion also contributed largely to parliament's justification for taking arms against the king. This was detailed in the Grand Remonstrance, whose passage through the Commons in November was facilitated by the Irish crisis. This lengthy parade of grievances exploited to the hilt the king's refusal to disentangle himself from Catholic party activity. It was as drenched with the spirit of "no popery" as Pym's opening speech of 7 November 1640.[85] In a conference with the Lords on the Remonstrance early in

November, Pym harped on the twin themes of alteration of religion and government and on the choice of evil advisers. He concluded that "there hath been one common counsel at Rome and in Spain, to reduce us to popery; if good counsel at home, we shall be the better prepared to preserve peace and union, and better respect from Ireland. It will also make us fit for any noble design abroad."[86]

In the last heated debate on the Remonstrance, Pym came close to accusing the king himself, claiming that "the honour of the king is the safety of his people. That he had thrust home all the plots and designs to the court, and it's time to speak plain English, least posterity shall say that England was lost and no man durst speak truth." The petition that accompanied the Remonstrance when it was presented to the king on 1 December urged the popish-plot theme and referred to parliament's fear of "malignant parties" in "employments of trust and nearness about your Majesty, the prince and the rest of your royal children."[87]

The preamble to the Remonstrance returned to the theme so familiar since the opening of the Long Parliament, namely, the "malignant and pernicious design of subverting the fundamental laws and principles of government, upon which the religion and justice of this kingdom are firmly established." The chief promoters of the design were the "Jesuited papists," the bishops and "corrupt part of the clergy," and "such councillors and courtiers as for private ends have engaged themselves to further the interests of some foreign princes or states." Their method was to perpetuate continual dissension between the king and his people so that "they might have the advantage of siding with him, and under the notion of men addicted to his service gain to themselves and the party the places of greatest trust and power in the kingdom"; to suppress pure religion; to unite papists, Arminians, and "libertines" while isolating those they called "Puritan"; and to "disaffect the king to parliaments by slander and false imputations, and by putting him upon other ways of supply."[88]

The Remonstrance that followed was an analysis and history of the activities of this party from the beginning of the king's reign. The revival of their influence at the beginning of the reign was associated with the break with France ("the interests and counsels of that state being not so contrary to the good of religion and the prosperity of this kingdom as those of Spain") and the ensuing peace with Spain, "whereby the Palatine's cause was deserted." Among the enumerated grievances between 1625 and 1637 was the retention of "many noble personages" as councillors, but in name only; "the power and authority remained in a few of such as were most addicted to this [malignant] party," whose suggestions were passed without real debate. The ultimate aims of the malignant plot were described as (1) freeing the government "from all restraint of laws concerning our persons and estates"; (2) joining papists and Protestants in doctrine, discipline, and ceremonies, "only it must not yet be called popery"; and (3) uprooting the Puritans "under which name they include all those that desire to preserve the laws and liberties of the kingdom and to maintain religion in the power of it."[89]

After this general list of grievances up to 1637, the Remonstrance launched upon a more detailed account of the period 1637–41, portrayed as the final stage of a campaign for revolution in church and state. The prayer book and Scottish wars "towards which the clergy and papists were very forward in their contribution," were fomented by "the malignant party; whereof the archbishop and the earl of Strafford [were] heads." The Irish popish army, the dissolution of the Short Parliament, and the financial expedients of the summer of 1640 were described as the prelude to the triumph of the popish party by mid-1640. Its triumph was marked by favor at court and exemption from the penal laws, by the activity of Windebank and Rossetti, by the intercession of foreign Catholic princes on its behalf, by the existence of the "popish parliament" and popish hierarchy, by the weekly prayers "for the prosperity of some great design," and by the secret commissions from court to "some great men of the profession for the levying of soldiers."[90]

This was the state of the kingdom when the Scots invaded and the Long Parliament was called; and this condition, claimed the Remonstrance, justified the measures that parliament had taken. The achievements of the first session were recounted with pride in the Remonstrance; but these were followed by the lament that "the malignant party . . . have taken heart again," now rising to positions of trust and slandering to the king the actions and motives of his parliament. The party counterattacked through the Catholic peers and the bishops, through agents in the House of Commons and in the armies of England and Scotland. In Ireland its subversion had succeeded. The remedy proposed by the Remonstrance was the purging of the "popishly affected" and those in the service of foreign princes from commonwealth, council, church, parliament, and universities. The widening of the definition of the popish party to include members of both houses of parliament and the bishops as a group; the description of impotent councillors that reflected the failure of the "bridge" appointments; and the reiteration in the accompanying petition and preamble of concern over popish influences on the royal family—all represented a more radical and more disillusioned mood than was evident in the rhetoric of the winter of 1640–41, when it was hoped that the removal of key ministers would change royal policy.

The Plot against Parliament

As their distrust of the king increased, so did the members' anxiety about the safety of parliament itself.[91] Some feared the Irish Rebellion foreshadowed a popish rising in England, and guards were put around the parliament house. Sir Henry Bedingfield of Oxborough Hall, Norfolk, a prominent recusant, was alleged to have said "that there would be great stirs or combustions in England and Ireland." He was arrested and examined, but soon released.[92]

Once again, a plot exposé was available to heighten these fears. A tailor, Thomas Beale, was led into the Commons on 15 November, with a tale of priestly conspiracy. He claimed to have overheard discussion of a plot to massacre many members of parliament, a deed that would precede a general popish uprising on 18 November. Discovered by the plotters as he listened, he had been wounded (he displayed his wounds to the M.P.s) and barely escaped with his life.[93] Several versions of Beale's story, of varying accuracy, appeared in print during November. Some of them implicated the French ambassador and Richelieu, to Pym's considerable embarrassment. In one case the printer was punished and a parliamentary declaration exonerating the ambassador was passed.[94] In all the Beale publications, parliament, not the king, appeared as the chief object of treasonous activity. Plots against the king were giving way to plots against parliament.

Ever clearer suggestions were made that the king himself was associated with plots against parliament. On 10 December Sir Walter Erle reported "that a papist of good rank and quality and one familiar at court had on Saturday last said, that there should shortly be a great change in this kingdom. It should be seen whether a king or no king. That the king had now the stronger party in the City of London." An emphasis on seditious activity directed against parliament can also be seen in prosecutions at Middlesex county sessions for treasonous or seditious utterances from the beginning of 1642.[95] The language of consensus between king and parliament was breaking down, to be replaced by expectations of hostile confrontation.

Sweeping measures against Catholics were called for in the House of Commons, to which the House of Lords was now prepared to accede. All English Catholics were ordered out of London within twenty-four hours, and all foreign Catholics were to put up bonds for good behavior or face imprisonment. The seizure of suspect figures and possible informants that had begun in the wake of the Irish Rebellion was intensified.[96]

On 2 November Father Philip had been summoned to testify before the Lords; refusing to swear on the English Bible because it was a heretical translation, he was held in the Tower for several months.[97] Fears that he was communicating with the Irish rebels (some even said directing them) led the Commons to send officials to tender his numerous visitors the oaths of supremacy and allegiance. He was forbidden any private conferences, and his trunk, which had been brought to him in the tower by two of the queen's Capuchins, was searched. *The Impeachment and Articles of Complaint against Father Philip* was clandestinely printed; again, much to the chagrin of Pym and La Ferté, France was alleged to be implicated in Catholic plotting and Father Philip was branded as an agent of Richelieu, sent to stir up trouble between England and Scotland so that France might conquer both. To placate the French, parliament ordered the pamphlet burnt by the public hangman in London. The Venetian ambassador was unimpressed by the parliamentary accusations against Philip, which he called a "malignant invention," but La Ferté thought the House of Commons had found enough material for a treason charge. Only at the end of 1641 were the entreaties of the queen, the French ambassador, and the House of Lords able to win Philip's release; even then, it was on the condition that he stay in Somerset House, away from the court, and appear when summoned by parliament.[98]

John Browne was also subjected to new questioning after the Irish Rebellion. The House of Lords sent justices to him in prison seeking information about the two priests, Jones and Andrews, whom Beale had named in his testimony. An unauthorized and inaccurate version of Browne's spring testimony was printed and circulated; like the *Impeachment against Father Philip* (and again to the great annoyance of Pym), it implicated the French ambassador in plotting against England.[99] These pamphlets that appeared late in 1641 were the first to bring to the reading public the names and accusations in the exposés that Habernfeld had initiated.

Not surprisingly, the Beale revelations renewed the hue and cry after priests who had stayed in England in defiance of the March proclamation. Pursuivants were instructed to search all suspect houses for Catholic books, religious objects, and priests. Two zealots broke into the residences of the agents of Florence and Lorraine, although diplomatic envoys were customarily immune from such treatment. Discovery of vestments, relics, and books in a dwelling near the Gatehouse suggested that priests lodged in the gaol had resorted there to say mass.[100]

The Capuchins became a bone of contention in the House of Commons. Their continued presence was noted and deplored in debate on 4 November; in a conference with the Lords on 6 November, the Commons requested the dissolution of their house and their expulsion from England, together with the delivery to the authorities of any priests who were subjects of the king and residing with foreign ambassadors.[101] The Capuchins posed a particular difficulty because they were part of the religious establishment permitted the queen by the marriage treaty, but on 17 November the Lords agreed to request the dissolution of their convent along with other measures against priests. In spite of all this agitation, the Capuchins remained. The House of Commons complained of them yet again in a message to the Lords on 3 January 1642, but although the monks gave their valuables to the French ambassador for safekeeping, and some seem to have withdrawn from London in January, they were not molested. Most returned to Somerset House after the queen left England. They were once more mentioned in debate on 26 February 1642, when Peard claimed that if they had erected a "college" in England by authority derived from the pope, they fell within the Elizabethan treason laws. Order was given to put them in custody, but the French ambassador intervened, offering to pay their transport to France. This was agreed on as "a very fair means to be rid of them." In fact, the Capuchins did not depart, and they were left alone until 1643, when their chapel and convent were ransacked and they fled the country.[102]

Other priests met with misfortune earlier. Two who were picked up on 11 November 1641 were bound over to King's Bench a few days later on orders of the House of Commons.[103] One of these became part of a group of seven condemned priests whose cases became notorious. The names of these seven were brought before the House of Commons on 11 December 1641, because the king, who wished to pardon them at the intercession of the French ambassador, desired parliamentary permission to do so. A Commons committee under Sir Gilbert Gerrard had already examined the priests about what they knew of the Irish Rebellion and the "design of the recusants" generally, and naturally they all "denied any knowledge."[104]

Of these seven priests, three were seculars, two Benedictines, one a Franciscan, and one a Bridgettine.[105] They included recently arrested court Catholics[106] as well as more obscure figures, two of whom had been in prison since before the convocation of the Long Parliament and thus could not have obeyed the recent proclamations. By 15 December the Commons decided to reject the king's plea and to call for the execution of all these men.[107] The matter dragged on. By early January the House of Lords had concurred in petitioning for the execution of the priests, but the king persisted in requesting a commutation to banishment. Several of the seven would eventually die in prison, but none were executed before the war began. As before, the bloodthirsty rhetoric of parliament proved to be more political than personal in its objective.[108] The second martyr priest of the period had indeed been executed, but in

Lancaster, not London. The Benedictine Ambrose Barlow was hanged there in September 1641. Not that London was spared entirely from such scenes of cruelty. At the end of January 1642, an aged secular priest, Thomas Green (alias Reynolds), and a Benedictine, Alban Roe, were executed at Tyburn.[109]

As the winter of 1641–42 progressed, lay Catholics also found themselves personally and financially harassed. The City of London attached to its loan for an Irish army the demand that the Catholic lords "and other persons of quality here in England, might be secured; lest some design be in them here as they have cause to fear"; the House of Commons agreed. As a result of the 16 November order for Catholics to leave London, many of the Catholic peers had already retired to their homes.[110] A royalist historian later voiced his suspicion that the Beale plot was an artifice to force the remaining popish lords out of the upper house; pressure in that direction during the winter of 1641–42 lends plausibility to his argument. Beale had implicated prominent Catholics, but not by name. He had reported that the conspirators were to meet at "My Lord's," but he could not say which lord. Guards were sent to the houses of the earl of Worcester, Sir Basil Brooke, Lord Petre, and other prominent Catholics; Worcester's house was searched, but to no effect.[111]

The House of Commons began to draw up a list of "dangerous" English papists to be secured. This was no easy task, because almost every papist was considered harmless by his acquaintances in parliament. By 20 November, after much debate, the lower house had compiled a list of sixty-five Catholics, including some peers, in those counties that they thought "the most stored with papists and in that respect most dangerous." With their proximity to Ireland, Cheshire and Lancashire naturally received special attention and continued to feature in plot revelations through 1642. The Lords responded to the Commons' list with a bill forbidding the named persons to move around the country; but when the lower house pressed for actual arrests, a deadlock ensued that persisted until the summer outbreak of hostilities.[112]

Efforts to deprive the Catholic peers of their votes also foundered on the conservatism and sense of privilege in the upper house. The issue had been raised as early as November 1641, but, "after a long debate that business was let fall, only there was an order made that the laws against recusants should forthwith be put in execution."[113] In December the king invited the Catholic peers who had withdrawn to the country to return to parliament, whereas the wave of county petitions beginning that month urged their exclusion from parliament, a demand seconded by the House of Commons. Although the Bishops' Exclusion Bill passed the Lords in February, no official action was taken on Catholic peers.[114]

Among the nobility, the Somerset family fell under particular suspicion, for one of the conspirator priests named by Beale was reportedly at Worcester House in the Strand. The search by Commons' agents had not unearthed him, but several of the Beale pamphlets named Worcester as the noble director of the conspiracy. Sir Robert Harley, M.P. for Herefordshire, warned the Commons that a popish uprising was about to break out in Wales. Lord Herbert of Raglan felt obliged to invite M.P.s to inspect his engineering experiments at Vauxhall to assure themselves he was not manufacturing or storing weapons.[115]

These suspicions of the Somersets had some foundation in the realignments at court because the king was beginning to turn to the Somerset family for resources he could not find elsewhere. In December 1641 he asked Herbert of Raglan to return to court, to discover the authors of "these lying and scandalous pamphlets concerning your father and you" and to discuss some matters of high importance. By early 1642 the family had agreed to give £9,000 to the king "for use of the queen and the Catholics," as Catholic sources put it.[116] Indeed, the Somerset family would provide the king with very substantial sums of money in 1642 that made possible the deployment of a royalist army.

The Struggle over the Prince of Wales and the Flight of the Queen

The worries about the safety of the Prince of Wales that were voiced in parliament at the end of 1641 were further indications of deep suspicions about the activities of the king and queen. The earl of Hertford found himself unable to keep control of the prince, whose official residence was at Richmond, but who often stayed with the queen at Oatlands. In November the Lords asked to have the prince moved back to Richmond "for his safety and to follow his learning and that though we did not so conceive that her Majesty in her own person would withdraw him from the Protestant religion yet we did justly suspect that some about her would."[117] The queen refused to let him go.

Foiled in this direct approach, the House of Commons tried to purge the royal households of suspect elements and called for a list of the prince's servants and the queen's priests. The Lords compromised, joining in a petition for a list of all the servants of king, queen, and prince, so that the oaths of supremacy and allegiance might be administered to them.[118] The king employed his customary tactic of delay.

By December the mood of the capital was becoming violently hostile to Henrietta Maria. The London mob, perhaps egged on by parliament's friends in the City, became menacing. The inner circles of the court were persuaded that parliamentary leaders were preparing to impeach the queen. Since the Irish rebellion, it had become the fixed conviction of some M.P.s that the queen was plotting against parliament. Giustiniani reported that various M.P.s were meeting secretly in the Guildhall of London and planning to accuse the queen of conspiracy against the public and of maintaining "secret intelligence" with the Irish rebels. They believed, he said, that all the king's most disturbing acts and policies were inspired by her advice.[119]

The threat to the queen, coupled with the king's suspicions that some parliamentary leaders had been considering the seizure of the Prince of Wales, contributed to Charles I's decision to try to arrest five leaders of parliament on treason charges at the beginning of January 1642.[120] In turn, this incident was immediately explained as part of the popish conspiracy because of the "discovery" of letters to two M.P.s, in which they were warned as "Strafford's friends" to "withdraw lest you suffer among the Puritans," against whom a master stroke was planned. The letters were read in the House of Commons on 11 January. A letter purportedly sent from an Irish Catholic to an English Catholic proclaimed that "though I am of opinion the king's majesty be a good Protestant in his heart, yet I am persuaded that by the persuasions of the queen's majesty, and the advice of the Catholic lords and other gentlemen, the wished design may take full effect." There was talk of Catholic troops who would be brought into action against London and parliament. D'Ewes, in a speech of 13 January on the letters, described them as "one of the greatest discoveries we have had this parliament, I believe now that this was merely one step of a design or plot hatched by the papists and prelates." Like earlier alarms, this episode quickly found its way into print in pamphlets that, significantly, referred to conspiracies and treasons against parliament, not against the king.[121]

On 10 January 1642 the king and his family withdrew from London, thus separating geographically what would become two rival centers of government, the court and the parliament. As parliament moved toward the assumption of an independent initiative, it depended heavily for theoretical justifications on the now well-developed "popish court conspiracy" theme. On 13 January the House of Commons voted a declaration to the king "for putting the kingdom into a posture of defense." Intended for circulation throughout England to justify the mobilization of armed forces under parliament's authority, this document revolved entirely around the "wicked and traiterous designs" outlined in the Grand Remonstrance. It drew the attempted arrest of the five members into the same scheme and concluded that "all his Majesty's subjects of the reformed Protestant religion" should prepare arms and refuse any commands made "without his majesty's authority, signified by both houses of parliament." Although the Lords rejected the declaration, its tenor reflects the nature of appeals that would be made in the debate over control of the militia.[122]

The withdrawal of the royal family led to renewed agitation over the Prince of Wales. He was now altogether out of Hertford's control. The Lords, fearing he would be taken out of the country, directed Hertford to resume his charge, but the king ignored them. As Charles I traveled through England in February he kept the prince at his side, despite parliamentary protests; he may have believed the reports, mentioned in parliamentary debate, "that there was an intention to crown the prince and make him king."[123] Repeated efforts by the French ambassador to mediate between the king and the parliamentary leaders were unsuccessful. His friendship with the parliamentarians made him suspect to the king, who blamed French meddling in English politics for his difficulties. Giustiniani reported that the king thought La Ferté in complete sympathy with the policies of parliament.[124]

The queen left England for Holland on 23 February, taking with her Father Philip and some of her Capuchin priests. For many of the king's critics she had been a symbol of the evil counselors who surrounded him, and the attempt to remove these counselors continued. On 15 February parliament named five who should be removed, two of them specifically because of Catholic associations, but the king ignored this advice, as his answer to the Grand Remonstrance might have suggested he would.[125] Sir John Winter, the queen's secretary, joined the king after Henrietta Maria's departure; Endymion Porter (named as a grievance after a long debate, although he was an M.P.) was included because "his wife and many of his family were papists . . . his eldest son was a papist and in service under the king of Spain." William Murray had served constantly as courier between king and queen during the Scottish trip in 1641; William Crofts had been attached to the duchess of Chevreuse's circle and remained in correspondence with her.[126] George Digby would become the king's secretary and would later convert to the Catholicism that his cousin, Sir Kenelm Digby, had constantly urged upon him. The queen's departure thus brought no politically significant change to the king's circle of advisers and no amelioration of the political crisis. It had become clear in the preceding year that the king was personally committed to the measures that had been deplored in the Grand Remonstrance as the work of the "popish malignant faction."[127]

Popular rumor identified the king ever more closely with Catholicism. A woman in Middlesex was tried for saying "she hoped ere long there would be crucifixes in all houses and that the king's majesty had one crucifix in his chamber and did bow to it." The distinction that parliament had attempted to maintain between the king and the popish party was blurring. Addressing the Lords in a conference on 25 January, Pym used the familiar analogy of the body politic: "Diseases of the brain are most dangerous, because from thence sense and motion are derived to the whole body."[128]

As the tug of war over the militia intensified, parliament insisted on its belief in a plot against king and country, as elaborated in the Grand Remonstrance. A joint committee of both houses was appointed on 2 March "to lay down the just causes of the fears and jealousies" of parliament. Pym's report on the matter to the House of Commons on 4 March reiterated that "there have been a design to alter religion here, that the war in Scotland was fomented by papists, that the wars in Ireland were contrived in England," and so forth. It was claimed that the papal nuncio had tried to get men and money for the king from Catholic princes. The old complaints about the mutual agency, the Catholic contribution, and the "queen's pious intention of fasting for some design" were all repeated. D'Ewes thought that events in Ireland showed the popish plot was still very much alive: "I think that there is greater cause to fear it now than ever heretofore."[129]

The preamble to the militia ordinance itself, as passed on 5 March, took up the theme of "a most dangerous and desperate design upon the House of Commons, which we have just cause to believe to be an effect of the bloody counsels of papists and other ill-affected persons, who have already raised a rebellion in the kingdom of Ireland; and by reason of many discoveries we cannot but fear they will proceed not only to stir up the like rebellion and insurrections in this kingdom of England, but also to back them with forces from abroad."[130] The declaration of both houses emerging from the Lords on 7 March went into more detail on the design to alter religion "by those in greatest authority about you, for divers years altogether." It ran through the now-familiar litany about the mutual agency, the war with Scotland "fomented by the papists," the army plot, the Irish Rebellion plotted in England as a prelude to an English papist uprising, and the attempt on the five members. The possibility that the king was attempting to secure foreign aid was deplored, "which false and malicious counsel and advice, we have great cause to doubt, made too deep an impression in your majesty." The declaration ended with notice of the "manifold advertisements" from overseas that the king "has some great design in hand for the altering of religion, and breaking the neck of your parliament."[131] During the debate in the House of Commons on this declaration, Sir Ralph Hopton protested that it seemed to charge the king himself with apostasy and subversion of religion; he was promptly sent to the Tower.[132]

Conclusion

Just as the king's plans and reactions in 1637–40 had laid a basis for the conspiracy theories expressed in the first session of the Long Parliament, so his continued attempts to enlist Catholic and foreign support after the convocation of that parliament help to explain the continuing tide of anti-Catholicism in 1641 and 1642. Whereas in the earlier period parliamentary debate had been centered on the king's official advisers, the royal family itself now came under scrutiny at the same time that measures were taken against Catholics quite outside the court and government.

The Irish Rebellion was particularly and conclusively damaging. A recent study of the impact of the rebellion on England and Wales stresses not only "the great significance of the 1641 rebellion in the escalation into civil war in England—something about which contemporaries were virtually unanimous—but the probability that memories of that rebellion contributed to the ultimate defeat of the royalist cause." The rebellion was seen as part of a European design against Protestantism, and the Irish, in league with English and Welsh Catholics, were thought to be planning an invasion of England. The Irish Rebellion was thus "one of the most effective weapons in the parliament's propaganda arsenal," and this was true not only among "vulgar-spirited people," as Clarendon pointed out, but among "sober and moderate men."[133]

Moreover, the king continued to seek the support of the Catholic Irish and other suspect groups after the beginning of the war, for he was unable to rally sufficient numbers of loyal English Protestants to his ranks. In September 1643 he signed articles of cessation with the Irish rebels and began to bring to England soldiers (both Protestant and Catholic) who had been fighting in Ireland. Modern historians agree with contemporaries, in a political spectrum ranging from Vicars to Clarendon, that no other single act of the king had such a harmful effect on his fortunes. In the spring of 1643 he had again supported Antrim's project, a revival of the old scheme of 1638, to invade western Scotland from Ulster. The plan would finally be put into action in 1644–45 when Antrim's force joined Montrose's highlanders; until their defeat at Phillip-haugh in late 1645, this largely Catholic force would present a serious threat to parliament's control of Scotland.[134]

Nor was the Welsh popish army forgotten. The lavish support given by the Somerset family to the king early in the war would cause Lord

Herbert of Raglan to be named a public enemy of parliament in 1642. For the next three years, Herbert's career would be intimately connected with the Irish Rebellion and with the plans laid by both the pope and Charles I to utilize the rebellion for their own purposes.[135] Scarampi, the papal agent sent to Ireland in July 1643 to negotiate with the rebels, and his successor Rinuccini were both instructed to cooperate with the king's plans to use Irish Catholics against parliament. The scheme devised in 1644–45 for Irish aid to the king centered on a force of 10,000 that Herbert of Raglan was to land in north Wales under his own command, while another 10,000 landed in south Wales under Sir Henry Gage. A third force of 6,000 from the continent, including some Scottish and Irish mercenaries, would land on the east coast of England, where it would be assisted by the prince of Orange and supported by the pope and Catholic princes. The religious concessions demanded by the papal agents frustrated this grandiose scheme, and what might have come of it we shall never know. But it wonderfully illustrates the character and continuity of the king's planning. As a reward for his part in the campaign, Herbert was promised the earldom of Glamorgan immediately, and later elevation to the family's old dukedom of Somerset, as well as the hand of the king's youngest daughter (with a marriage portion of £300,000) for his son and heir, Henry.

Even within the ranks of the English army, the charge that the king headed a popish force had considerable justification. As early as December 1642, Newcastle publicly defended the employment of papists in the royal army, and the king did not object. Clarendon, among many others, saw this as very harmful to the king's cause. An analysis of royalist activity among the northern Catholic aristocracy indicates that the king's forces included a significant proportion of Catholics and that they were sufficiently prominent in status to provide some substance to the charge of a "popish army."[136] Thus, the character of the king's forces after the outbreak of hostilities kept alive the popish-plot explanations of the conflict. This aspect of parliamentary propaganda was neither trivial nor ad hoc. It was part of a long-gestated pattern of explanation that reflected a sustained pattern of royal policy.

10. Popish Plotting in Retrospect

he pattern of events in 1640–42, therefore, was neither novel nor unpredictable. There was novelty, it is true, in the hothouse atmosphere of the Long Parliament, during which increasing numbers of the political nation began to share Pym's conviction that England was threatened with an international popish conspiracy. New also was the weapon provided to the king's opponents by the presence of an occupying Scottish army in northern England. By the convocation of the Long Parliament, initiative had already shifted from the king and his ministers to their critics and the parliament. But the feeding of suspicion upon suspicion that is so marked a feature of the developing crisis of 1640–42 had begun with the policies and perceptions of the 1630s; neither the king's policies nor the fears of his chief critics were newly fashioned in the autumn of 1640.

The most striking impression one receives from a study of court Catholicism and royal policy in the years 1637 to 1642 is of a consistency in the king's response to political challenge. This statement may appear paradoxical, because historians of the reign have repeatedly characterized the king as weak, vacillating, and apt to accept the advice of whoever had most recently caught his ear. The king's reliance on, and apparent later abandonment of, Strafford and Laud are often cited in this connection. It is not always appreciated how thoroughly the king's hands were tied by the end of 1640, nor how desperately—nearly to the point of war—the king tried to save Strafford, fruitless and misguided as his efforts may have been. There are also consistent refusals that characterize the king's policies in the years 1637 to 1642. From the beginning of the Scottish crisis onwards, Charles failed to explore the possibility of joining forces with the group of moderates, mostly of the French party, who would abandon the privy council for the parliamentary side in 1642—notably Pembroke, Leicester, Northumberland, and Holland. Northumberland, who was nominally in the inner circle of councillors as early as 1638, is perhaps the key figure whose career should be closely examined. He had unusual access to information, he was already uneasy about the king's handling of the Scottish crisis in mid-1638, he opposed the dissolution of the Short Parliament and had become disaffected from the government before the Long Parliament opened. As in the case of Leicester, the king's relatively cool feelings toward Northumberland seem to have owed something to Laud's distrust of a man with "Puritan" sympathies.

The ruinous influence of Laud's narrow, fearful perspective on the king's policy (which we must suspect although we cannot fully prove it) seems here again apparent. It alienated the king from his potentially most useful and natural allies; it led him from the outset to adopt a rigorous, undiplomatic, and belligerent attitude to the Scottish protest. It committed him to pursue every solution to a problem but that of calling parliament. It thus pushed him into the arms of alien and unrepresentative factions who shared Laud's conviction that the king's and the archbishop's critics were part of an international Calvinist conspiracy against monarchy and authority.

Another consistent feature of the king's policy in these years is his profound distrust of France and the French agents in England, a distrust nourished by the anti-Richelieu exiles who frequented his court. This provided another motive for coolness between the royal family and the "French party." It appears, for example, that the more friendly the earl of Holland became with the French ambassador in 1641, the farther he slipped in the queen's good graces and the more reliance she placed on his Catholic rival, Montagu. From the outset of the Scottish crisis, despite the absence of supporting evidence, the king was persuaded that French intrigue was behind the northern troubles. This conviction distorted and undermined his handling of the crisis, ended the possibility of genuine rapprochement with France that had opened during the winter of 1636–37, and thwarted efforts to provide even diplomatic or symbolic assistance to the prince Palatine. French meddling in Scotland was not inherently improbable, but the king was strikingly ready to see Richelieu's agents under every bush at a time when many of his subjects were seeing papal agents there instead.

In this instance, as in other ways, the king's policies from 1637 to 1642, if not actually shaped by the queen, could only too easily be identified with her point of view and that of her circle. Henrietta Maria's influence prior to 1641 has often been dismissed as trivial or has been sketched in the vaguest of terms. But her interventions on behalf of Catholics, her interference in the Church of England, her sponsorship of the 1639 contribution that implied a view of the Bishops' War as a Catholic-Protestant struggle, and her interest in the schemes for foreign troops and papal loans had established a definite pattern before 1641. We have no conclusive evidence about how the queen herself understood all this activity, how far it was ad hoc or to what extent part of a "master plan" for the advance of Catholicism. But it was obviously conducted under the supervision of papal agents who were known to contemporaries, as they are to us, as proponents of grandiose schemes for the re-Catholicization of England. Whether a skeptic and realist like George Con really nurtured much hope for such schemes is a good question, but that is politically beside the point. As papal representative and aspirant to the cardinalate, he was obliged to support them, regardless of the chances of any practical application, just as he was obliged to maintain in theory the papal right to depose princes, for the dignity of the papacy and the good of the church. The language of the papal agent and the attitudes he encouraged among the court Catholics thus lent even more sinister character to the dangerous projects that began in the 1630s and were pursued in 1640–42.

The violent public reaction that such expedients as foreign soldiers, Catholic money, temporizing with the Irish, and plotting with the army would provoke have been as painfully clear to historians of the reign as they seem to have been invisible to the king and queen. The isolation of the royal couple in their palace world is never clearer than in the king's toleration and the queen's encouragement of a flamboyant, brazen court Catholicism that offended public opinion far more than the number of conversions alone would have merited. It is scarcely surprising that Puritan observers wondered how firmly the king was prepared to defend the line between the Church of England and the Church of Rome; the queen, the papal agents, and numerous foreigners believed that any such line was weak and could be easily breached. A tenacious Catholic belief about the Church of England is at the root of much of the Catholic activism of the period, namely, the conviction that members of the Church of England could be divided into "Puritans" and "Protestants," the former being Calvinists and fiercely anti-Catholic, the latter apathetic, moderate, open to persuasion. As there were few "Puritans" at court (that is, few who were noisily anti-Catholic) and many "Protestants," some of whom did convert, it was easy for Catholic observers to underestimate the strength of attachment to the Church of England. That there really could be a "via media" between Rome and reform was a notion that convinced few Catholics—the fewer, because it convinced so few Puritans.[1]

What, in retrospect, did members of the court Catholic party try to do? What did they succeed in doing? And what did Protestant observers believe had happened? The objectives of the court Catholics ranged from the modest aim of achieving relief from Catholic disabilities and more freedom for individual Catholics to the most visionary schemes for converting the king and thereby the realm. The most optimistic views emanated from those closest to the royal family. Although it is impossible to assess the sincerity with which Father Philip in early 1641 held out hopes of the king's conversion, it is noteworthy that he had voiced similar opinions as early as 1633.

In pursuit of their objectives, the papal agents and their friends encouraged the queen to intervene systematically on behalf of Catholics, proselytized among the courtiers, and exploited the papal, royal, ambassadorial, and private chapels in London as centers of Catholic worship and evangelism. They then embarked on a more daring maneuver, that of utilizing the Scottish crisis of 1637–40 to the advantage of English Catholics as a body. The queen herself, with the agents Con and Rossetti and the enthusiastic collaboration of Father Philip, were the main actors in this part of the drama. Wat Montagu, because of his own ambitions, was also drawn in. In exchange for aid from the British Catholics and perhaps from the pope and foreign Catholics, it was hoped to extract from the king concessions regarding the oath of allegiance and the penalties of recusancy. Further, some hoped that this Catholic aid, together with private propaganda about Catholic loyalty and Calvinist subversion, might bring the king into dependence on a Catholic party and thus provide, at the least, a guarantee of continued privileges. It was for this reason that Con and the queen urged the king to take a hard line with the Covenanters; Scottish Catholics could only suffer from a continuing Covenanting domination of Scotland, but a confrontation might work to their advantage.

Attempting to mobilize all available centers of Catholic power in support of the king, the queen and the agent drew figures like Nithsdale and Antrim into their overall program, men who had little to lose or much to gain from rallying against the Covenanters. However, purely English figures like Arundel, although they were enticed into a half-deliberate collaboration with the "Catholic strategy," began to withdraw from such forward positions by the beginning of 1640. They had much to lose from an English political debacle that would lead to a parliament, the possible impeachment of ministers, the very likely sterner measures against Catholics. During the first session of the Long Parliament, some of them, like Windebank, would flee; others, like Sir John Winter, would be forced very much on the defensive. The army plotters, although they were portrayed in parliamentary propaganda as part of a popish plot, were Protestant—schemers, indeed, but not popish ones. Only after the outbreak of civil war in 1642 would the English Catholics, left with little alternative because of parliamentary anti-Catholicism, rally behind the king.

A final objective of the court Catholic party in the late 1630s was to keep the king aligned with a foreign Catholic power, or at least in friendly neutrality, so that no anti-Catholic parliament need be called. Catholic powers could be relied upon, moreover, to speak up on behalf of English

Catholics (with varying degrees of conviction and effectiveness, however). The anti-Richelieu exiles at the court, with their English camp following, had an additional objective in view. They planned to use London as an offshore base for attempts to destabilize France. They even hoped to gain English support for these efforts by exploiting the old ties between the houses of Stuart and Lorraine established by the marriage of James V with Mary of Guise, ties that had been given new life when Marie de Medici joined the loose anti-Richelieu coalition of which the Lorraine house was a perennial center. As the domestic crisis worsened, the king's own financial needs did pull him in the direction of the Catholic powers, and he tried to come to terms alternately with Spain and France.

The successes of the Catholic party were more ephemeral than lasting, more apparent than real. In the period 1636 through 1638 they obtained privileges for individual Catholics without any across-the-board changes in recusant policy, making a useful tool of Windebank in the process. They ensured a de facto freedom of practice for large numbers of London Catholics. This was mainly a court phenomenon, but one that was widely publicized. They subverted Laud's authority over religious policy, but in such a way that he got the brunt of blame for their activities. They emphasized the Catholic character of much of the Stuart family and toyed with the sympathies of the Palatine princes.

As the Scottish crisis warmed up, the court Catholics persuaded the king to put into operation some of their plans (the Scottish Catholic party, the Catholic contribution) and to attempt others (the papal loan, the soldiers from Flanders). In the process, they nudged the king away from a defense against the Covenanters based on English patriotism and toward the Celtic strategy he would later adopt. How far Charles wished to rely on the Catholics and how much he felt forced to do so in the face of an inadequate Protestant response to his appeal are difficult questions to answer. No religious ideologue himself, he seems not to have realized that such a policy could only alienate his Protestant subjects. It is even possible that he proceeded on the model of his foreign diplomacy, persuading himself that support from the Catholics would spur on the Protestants to a competitive show of loyalty.

This process of appealing to the periphery—ethnic, foreign, and religious—was accelerated in the period August to November 1640 by the battle of Newbury, the truce at Ripon, and the opening of the Long Parliament. These effectively deprived the king of political initiative. However, parliament moved quickly to neutralize the English Catholics as possible royal allies. Officers were removed from the royal army, Catholics were ordered out of London, Windebank and other protectors of Catholics were hounded from office or action, and local Catholics were frightened into quiescence.

In return for their help between 1639 and 1641, ineffectual though it was, British Catholics received gratitude and fair promises from the king, but little more. They never succeeded in converting him or in extracting a promise of conversion conditional upon further support. At most they were given assurances that, if the pope provided substantial aid, Charles I would permit liberty of conscience in all his realm when his authority was restored. Of course, his authority never was restored, and all that was left to the Catholics in the end was the opportunity to sacrifice their lives and fortunes in defense of their monarch.

Finally, the court Catholics never succeeded in pushing the king into an active alliance with a Catholic power, although Charles I, for his own reasons, was not completely averse to the idea. He would try for help from Spain; when the revolts of Catalonia and Portugal ended that possibility, he would angle for aid from France and suggest that the pope might channel funds through France to avoid the appearance of aiding and abetting a heretic monarch.

When one tries to assess how much of all this activity was known outside the innermost circle of court Catholics, and to whom, one encounters difficult problems of inference. One reason for this is that Protestant suspicion and rumor, while they outran fact, did not outrun Catholic hopes and, in some cases, Catholic tongues. Over-optimistic Catholics fed Protestant fears, as did renegade Catholics retailing often specious stories about intrigue at Rome and in the court. Protestant opinion ranged from popular hysteria, through a relatively well-informed and very hostile Calvinist point of view represented by someone like Pym, to the views of the French party courtiers, who were still better informed but less obsessed than Pym about the danger of Catholicism and Arminianism. The most extreme opinions, at least before 1640, were voiced in popular "seditious rumors"; the most moderate views were expressed precisely by those who were best informed, and thus in a position to know about the ambitious plans of some court Catholics. In short, the closer one was to the royal family, the more uncomfortable evidence one had to worry about, but the less likely one was to give vent to it publicly.

For example, the view that the king was a Catholic was occasionally expressed by uninformed fanatics. This does not mean that there was no good reason to hope, fear, or suspect that the king would convert, only that those Protestants in the best position to know were likely to be most discreet. The implications of such a charge were very serious. A conscientious and responsible subject who believed that the king had converted or would convert to Rome was placed in a dreadful dilemma. So long as possible, he would thrust away such a thought and resort to a more palatable explanation—evil counsel.

A conviction that the king had somehow been taken captive, had become the victim of bad associates, was held in a sophisticated form by those who themselves had ambitions as early as the mid-1630s to become the king's chief advisers. Distrust of the king's advisers was accentuated and promulgated among a wider group of the political nation when the Scottish crisis and the campaigns of 1639 and 1640 brought the gentry rather halfheartedly together and gave them the opportunity to exchange views. The dissolution of the Short Parliament seems to have been a turning point that caused much of the political nation to lose confidence in the government. When the Long Parliament met, distrust was expressed in the effort to remove the king's chief councillors, a project that absorbed the energies of the first session.

The view that these evil advisers were either Catholic or very sympathetic to Catholics was especially characteristic of what I have called the "high Calvinist" group, of which Pym was the most vocal spokesman. This attitude was easier for them to adopt because of their assumptions that the proof of true Protestantism was unswerving vigilance against Catholics and that Arminianism was but a polite name for Catholicism, whatever its proponents believed. Thus, Pym and his cohorts who shared these convictions hammered home to the members of the Long Parliament the connection between "evil counsel" and "popish plotting." As the king continued to seek aid from those regarded as England's enemies (Spain, the Irish, the pope) and as the queen continued to protect her court Catholics and the papal agent himself, such arguments were more and more persuasive. The Irish rebels' claim that they fought for the king and queen capped the evidence that seemed to support this view. Its most detailed exposition was in the Grand Remonstrance.

The queen's ability to dominate the king on matters close to her heart cannot be more strikingly illustrated than in the king's refusal to send away the papal agent Rossetti until it was too late to do the royal cause any good. No response to the antipopery rhetoric of the Long Parliament would have been easier or more appropriate. The king owed Rossetti nothing; Rossetti offered the king no immediate advantage; no royal prerogative was at stake. Yet six months after the convocation of parliament, Rossetti was still at court.

A corollary of the belief that evil advisers were either Catholics or sympathetic to Catholicism was the notion that they were in willing or unwitting collaboration with the international Catholic strategy designed to divide and conquer the British Isles. A generalized belief in this Catholic scheme was both traditional and widespread. Even the earl of Leicester, who must generally be counted among the relative moderates, appealed to it in February of 1639 in his plea to the king not to be fooled by Catholic offers of aid, for they were only tools in the hands of foreign princes who planned to do England harm. The activities of the court Catholics, in conjunction with the Scottish crisis, brought the possible application of this historical scheme close in time and place to English politics; it was the work of Pym's party in the Long Parliament to argue in detail how the king's councillors and courtiers had formed a part of it.

Thus, the seizure of power by the parliamentary leaders in 1640 and the paralysis that they enforced upon the king's government must be seen against a background of fears that had solid foundation in the king's policies in England, Scotland, and Ireland. Equally, the development of the Covenanting movement in Scotland must be viewed in the light of the activities of the Scottish papal agent at the king's court and the high profile of the Scottish Catholics there. In neither case was the popish-plot theme merely paranoia; in neither case was it a pretext to put into inflammatory religious language what were basically constitutional worries. Worries about illegalities and worries about popery were inextricably tangled and had equally firm foundations.

At the same time, this seizure of the initiative by the parliamentary leaders in the autumn of 1640 left the king with little option save to continue and intensify his intrigues with the various actual or potential enemies of parliament. Rossetti repeatedly insisted in his reports in early 1641 that the aim of the Puritans was to subvert the monarchy completely and eventually establish a republic; he implied that this was the view of the king and queen, and in this he may have been right. In this context, it is worth recalling the reports of the French ambassador after the passage of the Triennial Act, in which he said that the king had been made powerless and that it could no longer do France any good to help him or any harm to ignore him. In this struggle for power, Strafford and Laud became symbols for the king as well as favored councillors. In attempting to save them, the king was increasingly drawn into a world of domestic and international intrigue ranging from the army plot to the continued negotiations for a papal loan.

The world of international intrigue was a world in which many court Catholics were already deeply immersed, for reasons having to do with their own religious status and the development of the European war. As a proscribed minority, the Catholics had necessarily to conduct their affairs, and most particularly their relations with overseas Catholicism, with the discretion and secrecy appropriate to illegal activities. Their transfers of money; conduct of students, priests, and couriers; and communications with Rome were traditionally facilitated by resident agents

of foreign Catholic powers. As religious dissidents, they had also frequently appealed to these foreign agents to bring pressure to bear on the
English court on their behalf—to Spain as the traditional protector of
British Catholics, to France for enforcement of the articles of the marriage treaty by which the new queen after 1625 was meant to help better
the lot of English Catholics. For their part, the foreign agents foresaw
utility in the English Catholics: leverage on the English government,
support within the king's circle for their own interests, and a possible
focus for any future attempt to destabilize the English government. The
increasing scope of European warfare after 1635 and the hunger of all
sides for men to replace their depleted army ranks had given a new and
accentuated importance to the Catholics of the British Isles, who had
typically provided more than their share of mercenary recruits to continental forces. The world of ambassadors in England was essentially a
Catholic world; with no Protestant power save the United Provinces
did England maintain regular diplomatic relations. The more the king
sought allies in that world, the more frantic the suspicions he aroused. In
the course of the year 1641, the distinctions between the more or less
"friendly" Catholic powers (between France and Venice on the one hand,
Spain and Florence on the other) were increasingly eroded in Protestant
minds, so that even those like Pym who had recognized and acted upon
those distinctions had moments of panic about what the French were
really doing.

In 1641 the conspiracy mentality that had been festering for years
began to dominate attitudes on both sides. The Puritans saw that the
king was treating with suspect persons; the king's suspicions about the
subversive intentions of his critics were reinforced by the Catholic ambassadors who did not hesitate to portray them as members of the Calvinist
international. English Protestants had talked of betrayals by Scots in the
king's entourage during 1639. As a sense of community between the
king's English critics and the Scottish Covenanters developed, the idea of
Scottish betrayal was supplanted by that of Catholic plots. On his side,
the king had used the analogy between Puritans and Jesuits to explain the
opposition he encountered in Scotland; in the *Large Declaration* of 1639
he had launched the royalist version of the popish plot. He later justified
his attempted arrest of the five members in January 1642 by references to
treason and conspiracy that echoed the parliamentary accusations against
Strafford and other ministers in the preceding year. Clarendon's account
of the war would perpetuate this royalist view of the opposition as a
conspiracy of *frondeurs*.[2] Conspiracy theory was the corollary of the
consensus politics that still ruled, at least as an ideal, on both sides of the
impending battle. Unresolved political conflict was regarded as evil and

generally attributed to the influence of malevolent outside agents. Traditionally, any political initiative that did not originate with the monarch ran the risk of acquiring an aura of faction, sedition, and conspiracy. The king and his supporters were not slow to exploit this polemically.

Conspiracy was a fact of political life in Europe as well as a part of the political vocabulary. As long as monarchical rule continued to be accepted as the norm and genuine political alternatives were not explored, major changes of policy would require the replacement of one favorite or even one monarch with another. Assassination was the violent extreme of this approach to politics. The murders of William of Orange and Henry IV of France were long remembered, as were a dozen unsuccessful plots against other princes, including English ones. Coup d'etat at the very highest level had made the Elector Palatine Frederick the "Winter King" of Bohemia. His heirs did not seize the English throne from an unsatisfactory Stuart in 1640, but nearly fifty years later another branch of the family would do just this.

The replacement of favorites was frequently accomplished by assassination. Contemporary French experience provided illustrations of both this technique and the frequency of conspiracy against ministers, even against the crown. Marie de Medici's seven-year regency had been one long turmoil of conspiracy and counterconspiracy among the nobles; Concini and his wife had lost their lives to human rivals and their successor Luynes might well have met the same fate had he not been carried off by scarlet fever in 1621. Richelieu, never quite a favorite of Louis XIII although he was chief minister, had acceded to power on the arrest of his predecessor, La Vieuville, in 1624. La Vieuville subsequently went into exile and devoted himself to anti-Richelieu conspiracies. After the famous Day of Dupes, Marie de Medici likewise schemed abroad for revenge. From the Chalais conspiracy in 1626 until that of Cinq-Mars in 1642 just before his death, Richelieu had little rest from intrigue by his enemies. In all, there were an estimated twenty important conspiracies and revolts by French nobles between 1602 and 1674.[3] The Cinq-Mars conspiracy aimed at the assassination of both Richelieu and Louis XIII, so that Gaston d'Orléans might be placed on the throne. Altogether, the Europe of 1640 offered rather more support for Henrietta Maria's vision of politics, and correspondingly for Pym's, than for the judicious optimism of S. R. Gardiner.

The global view of events in England that was shared by so many parties to the conflict and observers of it involved more than an application of European political lessons to English experience, more than the king's appeal to external aid to redress the balance of power in England. The English experience was seen as an integral part of the great European power struggle between Catholic and Protestant, Habsburg and Bourbon. Foreign observers could see that the British crisis was one element in the European drama of Habsburg collapse. The Battle of the Downs, which alarmed Protestants viewed with premonitions of a second Armada, told another story to outsiders, namely, that the English king either could not or would not provide the really decisive help the Spanish needed to retain their naval route through the Channel. The attempt to tie England into the Habsburg defense system had been only partially successful.

The king believed his problems were worsened if not caused by an international Calvinist conspiracy, a view that would be repeated by later royalist writers.[4] Despite the marriage alliance with the house of Orange, the English court continued to treat Dutch ambassadors with mistrust and sometimes outright contempt, not as equals. As rebels who had not even replaced the Spanish monarch with a proper monarch of their own, the Dutch were both déclassés and suspect.

The king's opponents saw their efforts as part of the struggle against anti-Christ, the king's policies as encouragements to the onslaught against Protestantism throughout Europe. Many of the Puritans who emigrated to North America in the 1620s and 1630s were moved by the fate of the Palatinate and the French Huguenots; they feared that similar blows were ahead for British Protestants. Given the religious situation of the Stuart family, the French example was particularly poignant and ominous. The conversion of Henry IV and the subsequent policy of pressure and bribery against the Protestant nobility were proving effective. Despite the Edict of Nantes, the Huguenot population dropped from a million and a quarter in 1600 to fewer than half a million eighty years later.[5] After 1620, in fact, the military defeat of the Huguenots had gone hand in hand with the consolidation of royal absolutism.[6]

French experience thus seemed to contemporaries to provide a clear example of how division in religion would lead either to tumult or to arbitrary government. Under Catherine de Medici, civil war had prevailed; under Richelieu, this threat had been countered only at the price of arbitrary government. Conrad Russell has explained how arbitrary government was seen as a natural consequence of religious division: "It was true that if religious division made political obligation ineffective, government must then be arbitrary and dependent on force, or else could not exist."[7]

The presence and protection of Catholics at the center of the English government aroused fears about Charles I's intentions in all aspects of his policy. It was a commonplace that God would punish a country that promoted or tolerated impiety, both with natural disasters such as plague and famine and (Ponet had suggested) with the degeneration of its government into tyranny. To many English Protestants, the government of Charles I seemed embarked on this twin corruption of government and religion in the 1630s.

Of the two slogans of "tyranny" and "popery" that would be raised against the king's government, if not against the king himself, "popery" was the more potent and the more universal. It appealed to the common people as well as to the parliamentary classes, rallying strata of society whose position, as Robin Clifton has pointed out, "made irrelevant talk of personal liberties and security of property."[8] The religious position of the Stuart family made it peculiarly vulnerable to suspicions of this kind. When England found itself in the 1670s with a professedly Catholic heir to the throne, it was but the culmination of eighty years of church popery within the royal family.[9] In the 1630s, as in the 1670s, the religious instability of the family was more than usually evident. It was, as Philip Hughes has said, "a distraction impossible to resist" for Rome.[10] For English Protestants, it was a nagging source of anxiety that played an important role in the bloodletting of mid-century.

Appendix: The Plot Tradition and Civil War Historiography

The belief in a Catholic conspiracy extended beyond the circle of parliamentary leaders and their contemporary defenders. The idea was elaborated by several quite different parties to the ensuing conflict. There was a Puritan, or parliamentarian, plot theory, and there was a royalist plot theory. In his political tergiversations, William Prynne helped to develop first one, then the other. The plot tradition persisted into the Restoration period and provided the ideological background for the better-known popish plot late in the reign of Charles II.

William Prynne and the Literary Foundation of the Plot Tradition

William Prynne was the first to take the information thrown up by the Long Parliament's investigations and plot exposés of the prewar period and transform them into an extended explanation of how the popish plot had led to the outbreak of war. From 1637 to 1640 this most vociferous critic of the government's religious policy had been silenced by imprisonment. Prynne did not, therefore, observe the court Catholic activities of that period or have occasion to comment on them at the time. Even after his release in November 1640, his attitude toward the king evolved slowly enough to justify William Lamont's claim that he was not a representative of the lunatic fringe of Protestant thinking.[1]

The radicalization of Prynne's thinking occurred first in 1641, in relation to the episcopacy and the royal supremacy. Whereas in 1636 and 1637 Prynne had criticized the Laudian episcopacy as a semipopish perversion of a valuable institution, in 1641 he moved into the root-and-branch party with *Antipathy of the English Lordly Prelates*. Neither in 1637 nor in 1641 did he have much to say about court Catholicism. *The Jesuits' Looking Glass* of 1636[2] warned of Con's mission to reconcile England with Rome and cited rumors that Laud had been promised a cardinal's cap. In this pamphlet, however, Prynne's main evidence had been drawn from those Catholic writers of the early and middle 1630s, writers such as Christopher Davenport who were optimistic about the

supposed movement of the English church toward Catholicism and believed that Cosin and various other Anglicans were Catholic at heart. In
1636–37 Prynne still confined himself mainly to inference—the Church
of England was becoming more like the Catholic church, and this left it
vulnerable to Catholic seduction and trickery. A *Quench-Coal* (1637)
was addressed to the king and embodied similar attitudes. In it Prynne
described "the general fear in the hearts and an overgreat jealousy in the
heads of your loyal subjects of an approaching alteration of religion, and
total apostasy unto the see of Rome," but he was really more worried by
the Catholic character of the Arminian movement than by the activities
of professed Catholics.[3] Prynne's emphases in 1637 support the hypothe-
sis sketched at the start of this study, that the loss of confidence in the
king was not widespread in 1637 and that its development would be
closely connected with court politics and Catholic activity from that time
forward.

Even in 1641 Prynne did not insist on the popish-plot ideas that dominated later pamphlets. His writings in that year continued his attacks on
the Laudians, with special emphasis on his own sufferings. By 1643,
however, he took a far more critical view of the king, a change that is
connected in his pamphlets with the religious issues that were always
most significant to him.[4] The crucial events that had occurred since 1641
were the Irish Rebellion and the subsequent cessation. For Prynne, as for
many others, the rebellion confirmed his suspicions about popish plotting, and the cessation seemed to implicate the king in it. In working
through his reaction to these events, Prynne found a new meaning in
information that had long been at his disposal. As one of parliament's
propaganda agents, Prynne must have been acquainted with the information on court Catholic activities gathered before the war began; moreover, much of this information had already appeared in print. Prynne's
discovery of the Habernfeld documents among Laud's papers in May
1643 provided him with the occasion for publication on popish plots,
but the allegations he repeated in these pamphlets were nothing new. The
fact that Prynne did not make use of popish-plot revelations earlier is
another reason to take him seriously as a representative of moderate
public opinion for whom the king's policies of 1641–43 were a sad
confirmation of suspicions aroused by the court politics of 1637–41.[5]

The three major pamphlets of 1643–45 show the evolution of Prynne's
thinking about the king and the Catholics.[6] *Rome's Masterpiece*, based
on the Habernfeld documents, was the first composed; it was meant not
only to unveil the papist conspiracy, but also to demonstrate that Laud,
ostensibly its intended victim, was actually one of the perpetrators. This
rather strained interpretation was developed in Prynne's marginal notes

and postscripts.[7] In the course of the argument, Prynne showed some familiarity with the court Catholic scene, arguing ingeniously that the Jesuits would naturally hate Laud because of his friendship with other Catholics, secular priests, and Benedictines. Aside from the accusations against Laud, the tale of the "poison nut," and the several instances of contemporary misreporting that Prynne accepted, the major distortion in this pamphlet was the attribution of all supposed Catholic triumphs to the Jesuits, from the removal of Secretary Coke to the Irish Rebellion. Prynne concluded that since the king was in the hands of the Catholics, who might force him "to what conditions they pleased," parliament must continue to struggle if English Protestantism were to survive.[8]

In *Popish Royal Favorite*, later in 1643, the king was no longer an innocent victim of Catholics but their accomplice, as the subtitle reveals: "a full discovery of his Majesty's extraordinary favors to, and protections of notorious papists, priests, and Jesuits . . . as likewise of a most desperate long prosecuted design to set up popery . . . in this our realm of England . . . manifested by sundry letters of grace, warrants, and other writings under the king's own sign manual . . . as likewise by the king's letter to the pope, his marriage articles, oath. . . ." The pamphlet was based partly on documents collected by the Long Parliament committees that had investigated Catholicism in 1640–41.[9] It also incorporated material about the Spanish and French marriage negotiations and the 1625 marriage contract, information gathered from foreign sources such as the *Mercure de France*. These revealed a "most strong cunning and desperate confederacy . . . to set up popery in perfection."[10] Prynne had begun collecting this information in the 1630s, and he now found in it an explanation for all the gains made by Catholicism during the king's reign: the proliferation of missionaries and colleges, the creation of provinces and local superiors for the regulars, the "popish hierarchy" of the secular clergy, and the suspension of legal proceedings against Catholics.[11] Prynne described the process by which Secretary Windebank—"a Jesuited secretary, who had a pension from the papists, and was a lay-Jesuit brought up by the archbishop of Canterbury"—transferred priests from provincial jails to London and released them. Following the historical scheme of the Habernfeld exposé and the Grand Remonstrance, Prynne identified the Scottish crisis of 1639–40 as the height of the papists' power, when they held a "parliament" in London to impose war taxation: "And were not the papists, then, think you, grown to an extraordinary exorbitant power, and the pope revealed in his long exploded usurped supremacy in our realm; when they should thus be permitted to hold and keep a parliament without interruption, when the Protestants and kingdom might hold none at all."[12] Moving through the arrival of the Spanish "armada" of 1639 and on to the Irish Rebellion, Prynne concluded that the king and his Catholic advisors would accept no pacification without liberty of conscience for Catholics and that if they won outright they would establish popery and extirpate Protestantism. The king's rewards and promises to Catholics, his peace in Ireland, his plan to use Irish troops in England, his preferment of Catholics in his English army—all destroyed faith in his Protestant orthodoxy.[13]

In 1645 *Hidden Works of Darkness* rehearsed a good deal of the same material, together with a more detailed account of Laud's iniquities.[14] As a result of his delving into Windebank's papers, Prynne placed a new emphasis on the queen's court, the papal agents, and the Anglo-Roman negotiations. The story of court Catholicism was carried forward into 1641, touching on the army plot and lengthily exploring the Irish Rebellion and its alleged Anglo-Roman origins. The publication of the pamphlet coincided with Rinuccini's mission to Ireland, and Prynne was able to quote correspondence illustrating the grandiose hopes entertained in Ireland and at Rome that an international Catholic crusade would emerge from the rebellion.[15] He could also exploit the court's continuing interest in nominating an English cardinal, exemplified in recent letters mentioning the names of Montagu and Ludovick. What hope could there be for genuine peace with such a powerful Catholic party at the king's side? "Doubtless we shall never enjoy any well-grounded peace with God, or with one another, till we utterly renounce and separate ourselves wholly from all communion, fellowship, agreement, concord with the idolatrous Anti-Christian Church of Rome, and execute summary justice on all those who have been active instruments to reconcile, seduce us to her."[16] Those who came to share these sentiments would be prepared to condemn not only Laud, Prynne's immediate target, but ultimately his master the king. Prynne himself would later reinterpret his plot theory, and would see the execution of Charles I as a Jesuit triumph and the sectarianism of the 1650s as a mask for Jesuit intrigue.[17] But his first achievement was the elaboration and popularization of a radical Puritan version of the popish-plot theory.

Puritan and Royalist Versions of the Popish Plot

Contemporary reaction to *Rome's Masterpiece* was mixed, but sufficiently positive to confirm that Prynne was no isolated monomaniac. Elements of the story were rejected by some readers, but the existence of the plot itself was widely accepted.[18] Henry Parker, in his *Contra Replicant* of 1643, thought the popish plot a good explanation of the outbreak of war: "The main engineers in this civil war are papists, the most poisonous, serpentine, Jesuited papists of the world." *London's Weekly Intelligencer* of 8–15 August 1643 declared that Prynne had shown how "the wars against Scotland, the rebellion in Ireland, and this war against the parliament, is set on foot by the Jesuits."[19]

Other Puritan writers announced their belief in a plot. In *Jehovah Jireh* (1642), the polemicist John Vicars described the politics of the late 1630s as dominated by "a pernicious woven knot of malignant active spirits combining and confederating together for the supplanting and utter subverting of the fundamental laws and principles of government." Vicars appears to have based his commentary on the historical section of the Grand Remonstrance. His "woven knot" comprised Jesuited papists, perfidious prelates, and atheistical courtiers who were pensioners of foreign Catholic princes. Aiming to seduce Scotland to "Romish harmony," the prelates and papists generously supported the First Bishops' War. Until the convocation of the Long Parliament, the papists enjoyed toleration and favors from Windebank and aid from the papal nuncio and foreign princes; they convened in a private parliament, introduced a popish hierarchy, and sought the opportunity to destroy those whom they could not seduce. Thus they attempted to set England and Scotland at odds, preparatory to conquering both.[20]

In a letter of 1650, Nehemiah Wallington, author of *Historical Notices*, referred to the Spanish fleet of 1639 as part of the Catholic plot: "The enemies of God that were among us, had so contrived after they had stirred up this war with the Scots, and the king and the strength of our land were in Scotland in fight . . . that so this navy should come suddenly upon us, we then being unprepared and unprovided for them." The armada was sent, he concluded "as most do conjecture, by the intention of the Spanish and pope's faction among us to surprise this our native country of England."[21]

Wallington and Vicars were Puritan enthusiasts writing in the midst of the conflict. But all along the political spectrum, contemporaries admitted the importance of Catholicism in the struggle. Almost every seventeenth-century historian alluded to contemporary fears of popery, or accusations that the king favored Catholicism, as vital elements in the prewar crisis. This was true even of those who did not fully subscribe to the plot theory.[22] A relative moderate like Richard Baxter, reflecting many years after the war on the choosing of sides in 1642, reckoned that the Irish Rebellion and English Catholic support for the king did more than anything else to win popular support for parliament.[23]

Royalist commentators were not inclined, for their part, to underestimate the importance of the Catholic issue. Philip Warwick went to some trouble to refute the accusation that Laud and the king were Catholic sympathizers, laying the blame for these slanders on papists and presbyterians.[24] William Dugdale, in *A Short View of the Late Troubles in England* (1681), described the "great noise made everywhere touching fear of popery," the accusations that the prayer book was a missal framed at Rome, and the suspicion that the king was secretly inclining to Catholicism.[25] He explained how little impression the king's repeated denials had made on this popular belief.

In his account of the origins of the Scottish crisis, Strafford's friend and advisor, Sir George Radcliffe, referred to the conviction that Laud had "an intention to alter religion and by insensible degrees to bring back popery into our islands," a notion made all the more plausible by Henrietta Maria's influence with her husband. Radcliffe himself thought there might be some truth in the idea and did not particularly care, stating that he could not "affirm or deny that there was an eye herein to some conformity with the church of Rome." He could not condemn such a policy, since the Roman church was "a member of the true Catholic church of Christ notwithstanding all new opinions or abuses crept in."[26]

Clarendon attached much importance to the antipopery scare in his *History of the Rebellion and Civil Wars in England*, devoting more space to church policy than to any other feature of the 1630s and returning time and time again to the Catholic question. Unlike Radcliffe, Clarendon hotly denied that there was any intention of reconciliation with Rome, but he observed that the people in 1633 "were not without a jealousy that popery was not enough discountenanced, and they were very adverse from admitting anything they had not been used to, which they called innovation, and were easily persuaded that anything of that kind was but to please the papists."[27] He contended that by 1640 the Catholics "were grown only a part of the revenue, looked upon as good subjects at court, and as good neighbors in the country," enjoying "protection and connivance" from officialdom. But court Catholics behaved imprudently, especially after Con's arrival, and the Catholic collection of 1639 was so injurious that it was "as if they had been suborned by the Scots to root out their own religion."[28] In a 1647 letter to Nicholas, Clarendon had been franker about the king's own role in the Anglo-Roman contacts: "I will offer no excuse for the entertaining of Con, who came after Panzani, and was succeeded by Rossetti; which was a business of so much folly, or worse, that I have mentioned it in my Prolegomenon . . . as an offense and scandal to religion in the same degree as ship money was to liberty and property." However damaging Clarendon thought the Anglo-Roman agency had been, he was almost alone among seventeenth-century writers in expressing contempt for the popish-plot revelations, treating them as foolish fabrications exploited by Pym for his own purposes.[29] Considering Clarendon's familiarity with the court, it seems reasonable to suspect in this lofty disdain a bit of retrospective royalist propagandizing and personal vindication.[30]

Other royalists exonerated the king in a different way, by developing a royalist version of the popish plot. Hamon L'Estrange, in his *Reign of Charles I* (1655), was only mildly critical of Laud's policies, although he thought some of the Laudians were too sympathetic to popery. He discounted the possibility that the Spanish fleet of 1639 was intended to land in England, but believed in a domestic popish plot. As in all major disturbances, he alleged, seemingly contrary factions (in this case papists and Puritans) were involved; and the Jesuits "were as diligent in their machinations as possibly they could be."[31] The insistence of stalwart Anglican royalists such as L'Estrange on the contribution of Jesuits to the outbreak of civil war must have owed something to the revelations of the apostate Jesuit Abernethie. By the time of these royalist writings, moreover, figures such as Prynne and Baxter had adopted a Jesuit-plot explanation of the execution of Charles I.

William Sanderson's *Compleat History* (1658) was crowded with documents, but had little coherent historical argument save for the author's anti-Covenanting and anti-Scottish bias. Sanderson provided some detail on court Catholic activities and the Scottish reaction to them. On the question of Jesuit involvement, Sanderson agreed with L'Estrange. The Jesuits were implicated "not in love to [the Covenanters] but in policy to ruin the right reformed religion by setting up the presbytery and so all schism to succeed; and a plot was pretended to bring it about."[32]

Both L'Estrange and Sanderson are casual and conventional in their acceptance of the papist-Puritan plot. Matthew Wren, son of the former bishop of Norwich and secretary to Clarendon, had another version of Catholic involvement in the civil war that is fascinating, albeit inconsistent. He saw Calvinism as imbued with "the spirit of disorder and sedition," and thus traced the origin of the conflict back to the sixteenth century.[33] The Scottish and English critics of Charles I—"seditious preachers and libellers," joined with a "pack of discontented noblemen and gentlemen"—agitated for a parliament by exploiting the alleged threat to Protestantism. The "Puritan faction," explained Wren, made the people think that "the Protestant religion lay a gasping; and that, unless a speedy course were taken, popery, which had now overspread the court and begun to creep into the kingdom, would suddenly overrun that also. The truth is, a revolt of the Puritan faction being then foreseen, it was an obvious and innocent policy to endeavour to balance them with the opposite faction."[34] This policy failed because the papal agent's conditions for cooperation with the king were too high.

After admitting that the king encouraged a Catholic "faction" to balance the Puritans, Wren turned about and said that "there are very strong arguments to induce belief, that the Romish party did cooperate with the Puritan to the ruin of the church. For, seeing they had lost their hopes of obtaining anything considerable from the king, the undermining the church . . . was the only probable way of gaining in time sure footing for their religion."[35] Wren reflects the anxiety about Protestant dissent among Anglicans of the 1670s and their desire to attribute it to outside influences. John Kenyon has remarked that the excesses of the popish-plot scare of Charles II's reign are not surprising "when educated men . . . were ready to believe that the Jesuits, by their influence on the Puritans, had caused the Great Rebellion, and were now the inspiration of the Protestant Dissenters."[36]

The treatment of the events of 1639–42 by John Nalson and William Dugdale, who experienced the later plot scare, was very likely influenced by hindsight. In the introduction to his *Impartial Collection*, Nalson argued that Puritans and Jesuits had combined to overthrow the established church. The papists realized that the surest means of subversion was to encourage discord, and, "entering in at the backdoor of schism and separation, [the papists] joined hands with the nonconforming Puritans, to bring ruin and desolation upon this church and kingdom." Thus, Nalson concluded his summary, "The chief rise and original of our unhappy divisions and separations is to be fetched from the devilish policy of the papists, counterfeiting a design to advance the reformation of the Protestant religion to a greater purity; that the pope, cardinals, and Jesuits, have been always instrumental in raising these divisions and separations, and that they judge this the most effectual way to introduce popery."[37] Except for a reference to Richelieu's involvement in the Scottish crisis, however, Nalson failed to follow this rousing introduction with any details on how the politics of 1637–42 were influenced by popish plotting. In his treatment of this period, he relied almost exclusively on the king's *Large Declaration*. The Titus Oates Plot affected his general interpretation—as it did that of Dugdale, who revised his history to draw a connection between nonconformist sects and popery—but did not lead him to an extended reexamination of the 1630s.

The comments of these Anglican historians show that belief in a Catholic conspiracy behind the civil war was more than a Puritan misunderstanding of the Laudian program. L'Estrange, Sanderson, Dugdale, and Nalson saw the "Catholic party" as a group independent of, and indeed inimical to, Laud. The royalist historians, however, did not explore the Catholic party much, because it was a dangerous topic. Wren's comment that Charles I encouraged a Catholic "counter-weight" to the Puritans was unusually blunt, and appeared in an unpublished tract. The references of the others are generalized accusations that drew on the old convention of associating Puritans with Jesuits.

As the Exclusion crisis developed in the 1670s, the Habernfeld Plot had a curious resurrection, and Prynne's version of it was reprinted in 1678 as *The Grand Designs of the Papists*. In 1680 *A True Narrative of the Popish Plot against King Charles and the Protestant Religion* drew explicit parallels between the Habernfeld Plot and the Titus Oates Plot, without Prynne's anti-Laudian glosses. The resemblances between the two stories are indeed so marked that it seems likely that Oates used the Habernfeld story as a model.[38]

Notes

The following list indicates abbreviations used for manuscript and printed primary sources and reference works.

AAW, A. and B.	Archives of the Archbishop of Westminster, Series A and B, London
Add.	Additional Manuscripts, British Museum, London
Anglia	Anglia Series, Jesuit General Archives, Rome (microfilm and notes at APSJ)
Anstruther	Godfrey Anstruther, *The Seminary Priests*, vol. 1, *Elizabethan 1558–1603* (Ware/Durham, 1968), and vol. 2, *Early Stuarts 1603–1659* (Great Wakering, Essex, 1975)
APSJ	Archives of the English Province of the Society of Jesus, Mount Street, London
Avenel	Georges d'Avenel, ed., *Lettres, instructions diplomatiques, et papiers d'État du Cardinal de Richelieu*, 8 vols. (Paris, 1853–77)
Baillie	Robert Baillie, *Letters and Journals*, ed. D. Laing, 3 vols. (Edinburgh, 1841–42)
Birch	Thomas Birch, ed., *The Court and Times of Charles I* (London, 1848)
Birt	Dom Henry Norbert Birt, *Obit Book of the English Benedictines, 1600–1912*, ed. David Lunn (London, 1970)
BL	Barberini Latini Manuscripts, Vatican Library, Rome
BM	British Museum, London
Bodl.	Bodleian Library, Oxford
CCSP	*Calendar of Clarendon State Papers*, ed. Octavius Ogle, W. H. Bliss, and W. D. Macray, 3 vols. (Oxford, 1869–76)
CJ	*Journals of the House of Commons, 1547–1714*, 17 vols. (London, 1742–)
Clar. MSS	Clarendon Manuscripts, Bodleian Library, Oxford
CRS	Publication of the Catholic Record Society
CSP	*Clarendon State Papers*, ed. Richard Scrope and Thomas Monkhouse, 3 vols. (Oxford, 1767–86)
CSPD	*Calendar of State Papers, Domestic*, ed. M. A. E. Green, John Bruce, et al., 27 vols. (London, 1857–97)
CSPVen	*Calendar of State Papers, Venetian*, ed. A. B. Hinds, 37 vols. (London, 1864–1939)

D'Ewes (C)   *Journal of Sir Simonds D'Ewes (1641–42)*, ed. W. H. Coates (New Haven, 1942)

D'Ewes (N)   *Journal of Sir Simonds D'Ewes*, ed. Wallace Notestein (New Haven, 1923)

DNB   *Dictionary of National Biography*, ed. Sir Leslie Stephen and Sir Sidney Lee, 63 vols. (London, 1885–1900)

DWB   *Dictionary of Welsh Biography*, ed. John Edward Lloyd and R. T. Jenkins (London, 1959)

Epist. Gen.   Epistolae Generalium Anglia: Letters of the Jesuit General to England,   Anglia   Jesuit General Archives, Rome (photocopy at APSJ)

Foedera   *Foedera*, ed. Thomas Rymer and Robert Sanderson, 20 vols. (London, 1704–32)

Foley   Henry Foley, ed., *Records of the English Province of the Society of Jesus . . . in the Sixteenth and Seventeenth Centuries*, 7 vols. (London, 1875–1900)

Gawdy 1641   Parliamentary Diary of Framlingham Gawdy, Additional Manuscripts   and 1642   14,828 (1641) and 14,827 (1642), British Museum, London

Gillow   Joseph Gillow, ed., *A Literary and Biographical History of the English Catholics from . . . 1534 to the Present Day*, 5 vols. (London, 1885–1902)

Harl. MSS   Harleian Manuscripts, British Museum, London

Hist. Reb.   Edward, earl of Clarendon, *History of the Rebellion and Civil Wars in England*, ed. W. D. Macray, 6 vols. (Oxford, 1888)

HMC   Historical Manuscripts Commission Report

HMCD   *Historical Manuscripts Commission, De L'Isle and Dudley Manuscripts*

Joachimi   Dispatches of Dutch agent Joachimi, transcripts in Additional Manuscript 17,677Q (1639), British Museum, London

Knowler   William Knowler, ed., *The Earl of Strafford's Letters and Dispatches*, 2 vols. (London, 1739)

L&C   Henri Lonchay and Joseph Cuvelier, eds., *Correspondance de la cour d'Espagne sur les affaires des Pays-Bas au XVIIe siècle*, 6 vols. (Brussels, 1923–27)

LJ   *Journals of the House of Lords, 1578–1714*, 19 vols. (London, 1767–)

MCR   *Middlesex County Records*, ed. John E. Jeaffreson and William LeHardy, 4 vols. (London, 1886–92)

Panzani, Diary   Manuscript Diary of Gregorio Panzani (being edited by D. M. Lunn)

Panzani, *Memoirs*   *Memoirs of Gregorio Panzani*, ed. Joseph Berington (Birmingham, England, 1793)

Peyton   Parliamentary Diary of Sir Thomas Peyton (1642), Gerould cat. no. 137, University of Wisconsin Library, Madison, Wisconsin

Powis   Parliamentary Diary, House of Commons (1640–41), in Powis Manu-
                     scripts, Public Record Office, London

PRO   Public Record Office, London

Prop. Acta   Acta, Archives of Propaganda Fide, Rome (from transcripts and notes
                     in Downside Abbey)

Prop. Scr.   Scritture Riferite, Archives of Propaganda Fide, Rome (from transcripts
    Rif.   and notes in Downside Abbey)

Rawl. MSS   Rawlinson Manuscripts, Bodleian Library, Oxford

Rochester   Parliamentary Diary of John Warner, bishop of Rochester, Harleian
                     Manuscript 6424, British Museum, London

Rushworth   John Rushworth, ed., *Historical Collections of Private Passages of
                     State, etc.*, 8 vols. (London, 1680–1701)

Salvetti, H and I   Dispatches of the Tuscan agent Salvetti, transcripts in Additional
                     Manuscripts 27,962H (1637–39) and 27,962I (1640–42), British
                     Museum, London

St. Anglia A.   Stonyhurst College Manuscripts, Anglia A., English Jesuit Papers
                     (photocopy at APSJ)

Strafford MSS   Strafford Manuscripts, Wentworth Woodhouse Collection, Sheffield
                     Central Library

SP   State Papers, Public Record Office, London

Somers Tracts   *Somers Tracts*, ed. Sir Walter Scott, 2d ed., 13 vols. (London, 1809–15)

Towneley MSS   Towneley Papers, English Manuscripts 736 and 737, John Rylands
    736 and 737   Library, Manchester

Weckherlin   Weckherlin Diary (1633–42), in Trumbull Manuscripts, Miscellaneous
    Diary   Correspondence, Berkshire Record Office, Reading

Weckherlin   Weckherlin Papers and Letters (1615–61), in Trumbull Manuscripts,
    Papers   Miscellaneous Correspondence, Berkshire Record Office, Reading

Wood   Anthony à Wood, *Athenae Oxonienses*, 4 vols. (London, 1813–20)

Wynn Calendar   *Calendar of Wynn (of Gwydir) Papers, 1515–1690* (National Library
                     of Wales, Aberystwyth, 1926)

Yonge   Diary of Walter Yonge, Additional Manuscript 35,331, British Mu-
                     seum, London

Chapter 1

1. For the latter approach, see Lake, "Elizabethan Identification of the Pope as Antichrist,"
   especially pp. 165–70.
2. Wiener, "Beleaguered Isle," pp. 60–62; Clifton, "Popular Fear," pp. 25, 37–38, 53–54.
   Clifton argues that insofar as "Catholic activities matter, it is in the provinces"; the
   disturbances were "essentially local, never national." He thus attributes the high

incidence of panics in London to contagion from the provinces.

3. Havran, "Informers," especially pp. 289–90, and "Sources," especially pp. 248–50; Lindley, "Lay Catholics," pp. 210–14, 220–21.
4. Lindley, "Part Played by the Catholics," p. 174.
5. Hibbard, "Early Stuart Catholicism," pp. 28–34.
6. Russell, "Career of John Pym," p. 151.
7. Gardiner, *History of England*, 8:231.
8. Tyacke, "Counter-Revolution," especially pp. 131–36; Russell, "Career of John Pym," pp. 160–61.
9. From Revelation 3:15–16 came the message to the church of Laodicea: "I know thy works, that thou art neither cold nor hot: I would thou wert cold or hot. So then because thou art lukewarm, and neither cold nor hot, I will spue thee out of my mouth."
10. For the Radcliffe citation, see Strafford MS 34, two unnumbered folios on the Scottish question.
11. Gardiner, *History of England*, 8:243.
12. Ibid., 9:227–29. Zagorin, *Court and Country*, pp. 245–46, argues that the king's behavior in 1641 fully justified the mistrust of the parliamentary leaders; whether the king was fully serious and whether he had a chance of success could only be seen in retrospect.
13. Gardiner, *History of England*, 9:251–52.
14. For this side of Windebank's work, see Haskell, "Sir Francis Windebank," chaps. 5, 6.
15. Gardiner, *History of England*, 9:251–52.
16. Miller, *Popery and Politics*, pp. 82–84 and discussion in his chap. 4.
17. Ibid., pp. 27, 50, 90.
18. See G. R. Elton, "Tudor Government," although he would almost certainly exclude foreigners from his definition of the court.
19. See Foster, *Caroline Underground*, especially chap. 1.
20. Russell, *Parliaments and Politics*, pp. 379–80.
21. Russell, "Theory of Treason," especially pp. 31–34.
22. As by the king against Sir John Eliot in 1629; see queries to the judges in *CSPD 1628–29*, p. 528.
23. Nalson, *Impartial Collection*, 1:1.
24. For James, see McIlwain, *Works of James I*, p. 126; for Charles, see Add. 15,390, ff. 273–74, 443–44.
25. Thomas Hughes, *Society of Jesus*, Text, 1:120; see also Rostenberg, *Minority Press*, chap. 5; and McGrath, *Papists and Puritans*, chap. 10.
26. *Somers Tracts*, 5:480–86.
27. Russell, "Religious Unity," especially pp. 219–20, 224–25.
28. Clancy, *Papist Pamphleteers*, pp. 99–106; Figgis, *Political Thought*, chap. 4; Sabine, *Political Theory*, pp. 385–91.
29. Add. 15,390, f. 141.

Chapter 2

1. Clarendon, *Hist. Reb.*, 1:93–94.
2. Laud lamented that his rival Cottington was likely to receive the appointment through the queen's help (Laud, *Works*, 7:145). See also Smuts, "Puritan Followers of Henrietta Maria," p. 35.
3. Taylor, "Trade, Neutrality, and the 'English Road,'" especially pp. 240–52.
4. Russell, "Parliament and Finances," pp. 115–16.

5. See Ashton, *City and Court*, pp. 142, 148, for Juxon's conservatism.

6. Russell, "Parliament and Finances," pp. 111–16.

7. Tyacke, "Counter-Revolution," pp. 119–43.

8. In the late 1620s Henry Burton was developing familiar theories of popery working to subvert the reformed church by dividing it against itself; see Hughes, "Henry Burton," chap. 2. Laud's treatment of him in the late 1630s persuaded Burton that the Church of England was actually allied with Catholicism, and he became an Independent; see Burton, *Reply to a Relation*: "The Consultation" and "Epistle Dedicatory."

9. Foster, *Caroline Underground*, pp. 33, 41–43; Trevor-Roper, *Laud*, p. 304. The French ambassador reported the same; see PRO 31/3/72, f. 11. Laud's convictions about Puritan subversion developed very early; his speech at the opening of the 1626 parliament referred to a presbyterian conspiracy aiming at the overthrow of church and state. "They, whoever they be, that would overthrow *sedes ecclesia*, the seats of ecclesiastical government, will not spare (if ever they get power) to have a pluck at the throne of David" (Kenyon, *Stuart Constitution*, pp. 153–54). Parliament's identification of the Arminians as antiparliamentary in the 1620s was thus confirmed in the 1630s; see Russell, *Parliaments and Politics*, pp. 404–5.

10. See appendix.

11. Cited in Russell, *Parliaments and Politics*, p. 407.

12. Rushworth, 3:1320; Hughes, "Conversion," pp. 115–16.

13. See Albion, *Charles I and Court of Rome*, pp. 233–34, 240–42.

14. The king's sister, Elizabeth, had married the Protestant prince Palatine; she had earlier been considered as a bride for Gustavus Adolphus of Sweden (Williams, *Anne*, pp. 153–54). Elizabeth hoped that her son might marry Charles I's eldest daughter, but the king seems never to have seriously considered this idea. His eagerness to marry even his daughter (whose religion would thus be put at risk) to a Catholic prince was a departure from his father's practice.

15. AAW A.27, p. 121 (20 April 1633): Southcote to Fitton, on the king speaking well of the pope and of auricular confession.

16. Trevor-Roper, *Laud*, pp. 69–70. Cf. Wormald, *Clarendon*, pp. 246–47, 306–8.

17. Peters, "Some Catholic Opinions," pp. 292–302; Loomie, "Catholic Consort," pp. 303–16. See also Williams, *Anne*, p. 11.

18. Hughes, "Conversion," pp. 113–25; Pastor, *History of Popes*, 29:314n, 316, 317n, 332n.

19. For Prynne's use of the *Mercure de France*, which circulated widely in England in translation, see, for example, *Popish Royal Favorite*, p. 52. A list of books and manuscripts in *Household Books of Lord William Howard of Naworth*, app. B, p. 481, includes *Mercurius Gallo-Belgicus* for 1625, 1629, and 1639.

20. For the Star Chamber case, see Knowler, 2:180; Salvetti H, ff. 155, 157; Add. 15,391, f. 165; *CSPD 1637–38*, pp. 473–74; and Yonge, f. 68v. In 1633 an Essex clergyman was fined in the Court of High Commission and degraded for praying publicly that God might convert or confound the queen; the king threatened to have him hanged (AAW A.27, p. 43 [15 February 1633]: Southcote to Fitton). Earlier instances of talk against the queen can be found in *CSPD 1628–29*, pp. 517–18, 539.

21. Elton, *Tudor Constitution*, pp. 61–63, 67–68, 73. In the Star Chamber trial of Burton, Bastwick, and Prynne in 1637, Laud asserted that "there is not a more cunning trick in the world, to withdraw a people's hearts from their sovereign," than to claim he is endangering religion (Howell, *State Trials*, 3:729).

22. Troops also followed this route, in both directions. See Alexander, *Sir Richard Weston*, pp. 182–83; and Kepler, *Exchange of Christendom*, chap. 2.

23. Yates, *Rosicrucian Enlightenment*, pp. 51–57, 156–60. Green, *Queen of Bohemia*, p.

260n, mentions dedications to Elizabeth of prophetic works. *Vox Populi* (1620) was dedicated to her; ibid., p. 193.

24. Green, *Queen of Bohemia*, p. 323.

25. As early as June 1628, John Rous related the report that it was Elizabeth of Bohemia who had pressed the king to accept the Petition of Right and that there was "a secret whispering of some looking towards the lady Elizabeth" (*Diary*, pp. 18–19).

26. *CSPD 1636–37*, p. 307. On the French agreement (October 1636) with Hesse-Cassel that the latter would be involved in any peace negotiations, see Dickmann, *Der Westfälische Frieden*, p. 87; on the French attitude to Palatine participation in such negotiations in the period 1635–41, see ibid., pp. 88, 90, 94.

27. Frederick IV of the Palatinate had married Louisa Juliana of Nassau, daughter of William the Silent.

28. See, for example, Sir Arthur Hopton's reports from Spain in *CCSP*, 1:64, 66.

29. The resilience of Spain, which again and again seemed to belie prophecies of her decline, has been recently emphasized by Stradling, in "Catastrophe and Recovery," pp. 205–19.

30. Alexander, *Sir Richard Weston*, pp. 214–17. The Spanish were quite aware of English government concern over Dunkirk and exploited it as best they could; see Alcalá-Zamora, *España, Flandes*, pp. 346, 350–51.

31. On the early attempts to organize a peace conference. see Dickmann, *Der Westfälische Frieden*, pp. 77–98; and Leman, "Origines du Congrès de Cologne," pp. 370–83.

32. Polisenský, *War and Society*, pp. 217–19, outlines the nature of Habsburg planning and Habsburg vulnerability by 1636, and Alcalá-Zamora, *España, Flandes*, pp. 345–46, 348, emphasizes that Spain recognized very clearly its dependence on English friendship and the damage England could do if it joined the anti-Habsburg alliance. Dickmann, *Der Westfälische Frieden*, pp. 93–94, observes that the emperor's negotiating position was softening under military pressure by late 1638, although not sufficiently to admit the Palatine house to a peace conference. Parker, *Army of Flanders*, pp. 77, 279, gives estimates of troops sent to the Netherlands by the sea route in the 1630s; Alcalá-Zamora, *España, Flandes*, pp. 365–66, argues that these figures, which disregard smaller shipping, substantially *underestimate* the importance of the naval route for troop reinforcements to Flanders in the late 1630s.

33. Gardiner, *History of England*, 8:158. On the naval policy, see *HMC Sixth Report*, app. I, p. 278; and *CSPD 1636–37*, pp. 554–55. About three thousand English were said to be held captive by the Moroccans as a result of piracy in the 1630s; see *HMC Twelfth Report*, app. II, p. 192.

34. Bireley, "Peace of Prague," pp. 31–69.

35. Wedgwood, *Thirty Years' War*, p. 396. The three Calvinist princes of the Palatinate, Hesse-Cassel, and Brunswick-Luneburg did not participate in this settlement. By the end of 1636, the birth of a son and heir to Maximilian of Bavaria had heightened his resolve to retain his new lands and dignities.

36. Richelieu apparently agreed with Windebank that Spain was the key to the return of the Palatinate; cf. *CSP*, 1:59; and Avenel, 5:855. Some of the proposals considered by Spanish ministers for offer to England in the late 1630s, in exchange for assistance to Flanders, suggest the Spanish believed they could bring a good deal of pressure to bear on the Palatinate question with the other interested parties; see Alcalá-Zamora, *España, Flandes*, pp. 345, 351.

37. There were also occasional references to the "Jesuit party," referring not to known Jesuits but to certain Catholics such as Toby Mathew and Lord Herbert of Raglan who were regarded as supporters of the Jesuits in matters concerning Catholics. Secretary

Windebank's ciphers for his correspondence with Strafford in Ireland and with the secular clergy's agent Peter Fitton (*vere* Biddulph) in Rome employed the following categories: "the papists," "the Protestants," "the Puritans," and "the Jesuits." See Clar. MS 19, ff. 202–3, 220–21.

38. Roe had married into the family of Sir Richard Cave, who acted as agent in England for the prince Palatine; see Brown, *Itinerant Ambassador*, p. 19. The official agent of the queen of Bohemia in England was Sir Abraham Williams.

39. Baker, *Letters of Elizabeth*, p. 95; Turnbull, *Hartlib, Dury and Comenius*, p. 173. Elizabeth's friend and advisor, Ludwig Camerarius, architect of the "Calvinist international" and Swedish ambassador to The Hague, was another to hold this view. See Schubert, *Ludwig Camerarius*, pp. 369–79, and "Pfälzische Exilregierung," pp. 575–680. Polišenský, in "Denmark-Norway and the Bohemian Cause," describes an earlier northern alliance.

40. Aylmer, *King's Servants*, p. 358.

41. Dury outlines his program in a letter of December 1638 in Rawl. MS C911, ff. 476–78.

42. The Rhine Palatinate had a traditional alliance with France, for which see Clasen, *Palatinate in European History*, p. 22.

43. Beatty, *Warwick and Holland*, pp. 81–97.

44. Smuts, "Puritan Followers of Henrietta Maria," pp. 35–38; Russell, "Parliament and Finances," pp. 110–16. See *CSPVen 1636–39*, p. 125 (January 1637), on the intent of the "parliamentarians" to get rid of Laud.

45. Adams, "Foreign Policy," especially pp. 143–48.

46. The correspondence among members of this group in the late 1630s is printed in *HMCD*, vol. 6, and in Collins, *Sydney Papers*, vol. 2.

47. Aylmer, *King's Servants*, pp. 154–55. Michael Young, in his forthcoming biography of Sir John Coke, argues persuasively that Coke's experiences with the military ventures of the 1620s had so disillusioned him that, religious convictions notwithstanding, he had little heart for open conflict with Spain. Another member of the connection was Viscount Conway, who may have been further impelled in this direction by frustrated ambition; he wanted the appointment of ambassador to Venice that was given to Feilding in 1638. See *CSPVen 1636–39*, pp. 351–52. The correspondence of Conway is in *HMC Fourteenth Report*, app. II (*Portland*, vol. 3).

48. The only important exception is Basil Feilding (later second earl of Denbigh), who became a parliamentarian, possibly because of disappointments at court; see *HMC Denbigh*, 5:61, and n. 56 below.

49. Stone, *Crisis of the Aristocracy*, pp. 759–60; Burnet, *History of My Own Time*, 1:2 1n1. Gregorio Panzani thought that Burleigh and Naunton had both applied this sort of pressure on wards (PRO 31/9/17, f. 278), but the standard secondary sources have little to say of it. Saye and Sele, however, when he became Master of the Court of Wards, showed the intention of exerting this sort of influence (St. Anglia A. VII, no. 48, 21 June [1641]).

50. Haskell, "Sir Francis Windebank," chap. 8. Windebank corresponded regularly with English Catholic representatives in Rome through the 1630s: the secular clergy's agent, Peter Fitton (*vere* Biddulph); the Benedictine agent, Richard Wilfrid Selby; and others. His ciphers for them are in Clar. MS 19, ff. 202–3, 208–9. Windebank died Catholic in exile in France.

51. For the Spanish party, see chap. 3 below; for the Spanish faction of the 1620s, see Loomie, *Spain and Jacobean Catholics*, 2:xvii–xviii. The Spanish party was never a group prepared to let England be used as a tool of Spanish interests, but a group that thought England's interests would be best served by cooperation with Spain. Spain

could thus be lamenting its lack of influence at the court, while France lamented the strength of anti-Richelieu sentiment (which was, in French terms, "pro-Spanish") and some zealous Protestants lamented that England had even amicable relations with Spain—all at the same moment.

52. On Arundel's career in the 1620s, see Kevin Sharpe, "Earl of Arundel," pp. 209–44. See Snow, "Arundel Case," p. 33, for Arundel holding the proxies of four Catholic peers in 1626. The parish in which Arundel's London palace was located, St. Clement Danes, recorded a number of burials of Catholics in the 1630s (Anstruther, "Recusant Burials," p. 104). On Arundel as potential Catholic leader, see Hervey, *Earl of Arundel*, pp. 10, 35, 115–16; *DNB*, s.v. "Thomas Howard, earl of Arundel"; Grun, "Note on William Howard," pp. 331–34; Panzani, *Memoirs*, p. 249; Add. 15,390, f. 31.

53. Anstruther, "Cardinal Howard," pp. 315–61; and Gillow, s.v. "Philip Thomas Howard." The countess had a Jesuit confessor, Edward Travers, in the late 1630s; Epist. Gen. Anglia I (2), f. 523. On the sons and their wives, see Hervey, *Earl of Arundel*, pp. 245–47, 408; Add. 15,390, ff. 174, 410, 459; Add. 15,391, f. 328.

54. Reinmuth, "Lord William Howard," pp. 226–34, on the family and its marriage connections with the Widdringtons, Winters, Prestons, and others.

55. The first duke's sons were raised with the royal children. For the Villiers family and its religious history, see Hibbard, "Popish Plot," pp. 60–64, 553–56; and Trevor-Roper, *Laud*, pp. 54–55, 59–60.

56. Basil Feilding, heir to the earldom of Denbigh, married Anne Weston, Catholic daughter of the first earl of Portland, and had a long tenure as ambassador at Venice and other Italian courts (*DNB*, s.v. "Basil Feilding, 2nd earl of Denbigh").

Chapter 3

1. The godparents of the Prince of Wales were Frederick V and Elizabeth of the Palatinate, and Louis XIII and Marie de Medici.

2. The countess of Roxborough had been first lady of the bedchamber to Queen Anne; on the family, see Mathew, *Scotland under Charles I*, pp. 148, 232, 302–3. Lady Roxborough was left in care of the princesses (Add. 15,390, f. 127). Edward Sackville, earl of Dorset, had come under suspicion of pro-Catholic sympathies in 1628 and was described by Con as a Catholic, but this is not otherwise supported (*DNB*, s.v. "Edward Sackville, 4th earl of Dorset"; Havran, *Catholics*, p. 73; Albion, *Charles I and Court of Rome*, p. 357). His antipathy to Puritanism can be seen in his correspondence in *HMC Fourth Report*, p. 295. His uncle Thomas (1571–1646) was a noted Catholic exile and patron of Jesuits. Dorset was regarded as a friend of the seculars in 1634 (AAW A.27, p. 461 [7 July 1634]: Leybourne to Chalcedon). Prince James was first given a Catholic nurse, then removed from her care, then returned to her by the queen on the pretext that the Protestant nurse was mad (*CSPVen 1636–39*, p. 160; AAW B.47, no. 68 [13 December 1633]: Southcote to Fitton).

3. AAW A.28, p. 147 (12 September 1635); Gardiner, *History of England*, 8:137, 140; ibid., 10:225.

4. Add. 15,390, ff. 95–96.

5. On Porter, Winter, Digby, and Mathew, see pp. 52–56 below.

6. *DNB*, s.v. "Walter Montagu."

7. On the Somerset family, see Hibbard, "Popish Plot," pp. 547–50. On the Welsh Jesuits, see ibid., pp. 578–80. The Somersets had made marriage alliances with the Morgans of Llantarnam, the Arundells of Wardour, and the Brownes of Cowdray (Viscounts

Montagu); in the next generation they allied with the Howards of Arundel and the Powis Herberts.

8. Anstruther, *Hundred Homeless Years*, pp. 94, 103.

9. See Trimble, "Embassy Chapel Question," pp. 98–99.

10. For more on the chapels, see below, pp. 56–62. *CSPVen 1640–42*, p. 189, outlines the various embassies and their English priests. The Venetian ambassador protected several priests, including Giles Chaissy, O.F.M.; at least one English Carmelite; and the Scottish Minim, Francis Maitland. The Spanish ambassador in 1639 harbored an Irish Dominican, Theodore de Pietate, who heard confessions (PRO 31/9/92, ff. 88–93; Prop. Scr. Rif., vol. 139, f. 184). Laud did arrest an English priest in 1636 for preaching at Somerset House, but this seems to have had little effect (Birch, 2:237).

11. On Gage, see Anstruther, vol. 2, s.v. "George Gage"; and Revill and Steer, "George Gage I and George Gage II." In 1635–37 the dean of the seculars was Edward Bennett; thereafter it was Anthony Champney.

12. On the Jesuits in the early Stuart period, see Bassett, *English Jesuits*, pp. 139–224. The notorious "discovery" of Jesuits in 1628 at Clerkenwell was a raid on their planning meeting for a London novitiate; see ibid., pp. 168–70. On More, see Edwards, "Henry More, S.I."; on the Petre family, see Clay, "Misfortunes of Lord Petre," pp. 87–116.

13. On the Benedictines, see Lunn, *English Benedictines*, chap. 5. On Price (*vere* William Benedict Jones), see Birt, s.v. "William Benedict Jones"; and Lunn, *English Benedictines*, pp. 101–5. David Codner was one of the court Benedictines; he was released from jail in 1631 through the mediation of the French ambassador, Fontenay (Prop. Scr. Rif., vol. 100, f. 159). On the Franciscans, see Dockery, *Christopher Davenport*, chaps. 1–2. A secular priest wrote the secular agent in Rome in 1633 that the friars "multiplied" in England and were becoming as "politic" as the Jesuits (AAW A.27, p. 121 [26 April 1633]: Southcote to Fitton).

14. Dockery's biography of Davenport is excellent on this otherwise obscure figure; on Chaissy, see Giblin, "Aegidius Chaissy," pp. 393–96. William Thomson, O.F.M. Conventual, was a member of the queen's household; see Anderson, "William Thomson," pp. 99–111.

15. Of the Dominicans, there were only two or three, and their superior was Thomas Dade (*vere* Middleton); see Anstruther, *Hundred Homeless Years*, pp. 148–69. After the expulsion of the queen's Oratorian chaplains, there were only a few Oratorians in England: her confessor, Robert Philip, and his companion, Pierre Viette. Two Scottish Minims, Francis Maitland and John Browne, drifted about London and the court in the 1630s; for additional information on them, see this chapter and chap. 9. There were about eight Carmelites on the mission. Their superior, William Pendryck (Eliseus of St. Michael), lived with his fellow Scot, Robert Philip. Another Carmelite lived with the Venetian ambassador. Thomas Doughty (Simon Stock), after serving as chaplain to the Spanish ambassador Gondomar and his successors, settled with the Roper family in Canterbury where he was in lively religious controversy with Sir Edward Dering at the end of the 1630s. See Zimmerman, *Carmel in England*, pp. 48–59; and Dering, *Four Cardinal Vertues of a Carmelite Friar* (1641).

16. Bossy, *Catholic Community*, p. 106. Some of the clergy apparently wore habits (the Capuchins certainly did) and Con complained of this "insupportable [i.e., imprudent] liberty" to the Roman authorities (BL 8646, ff. 45, 51).

17. For examples of Windebank's methods for rescuing priests, see Nurse, "Recusant History of Cheam," pp. 105–10; and Anstruther, *Hundred Homeless Years*, p. 140. Comparison of Windebank's papers with those of Coke is made by Lomas, "State Papers of Early Stuarts," p. 108.

18. "We never had a greater calm since the queen [Elizabeth] came in than now," wrote Southcote to Fitton, 19 July 1633, in AAW A.27, p. 222. "The Catholics do enjoy a far greater quietness and liberty for the exercise of their religion than ever before" (information [1635] for the clergy agent at Rome, AAW A.28, pp. 25–27).

19. Stoye, *English Travellers Abroad*, pp. 337–40. For an expression of this view, see Correr's report, *CSPVen 1636–39*, pp. 300–304. The secular Leybourne wrote to Rome in 1633, "Never was there so great a disposition in those two universities towards the Catholic religion as now there is" (AAW A.27, p. 239 [9 August 1633]).

20. Pastor, *History of Popes*, 29:325n2, for a list of some of Urban VIII's letters to Henrietta Maria (1625–40).

21. Oman, *Henrietta Maria*, p. 66; Albion, *Charles I and Court of Rome*, p. 147. Urban VIII told his agent going to England that Charles would convert to Rome were it not for his Palatine nephew, who was available as a Protestant alternative for the throne. On the birth of Prince Charles in 1630, the Venetian ambassador had reported that "many of the Puritans, indeed the majority, have shown their sorrow at the birth of the prince because of [Elizabeth of Bohemia]" (*CSPVen 1629–31*, p. 350).

22. Anson, *Catholic Church*, pp. 10–15; Hughes, "Conversion," pp. 113–25; Leith, *Memoirs of Scottish Catholics*, 1:5n1, 22; Hay, *Blairs Papers*, pp. 85n2, 190.

23. Huntley's heir conformed, Argyll's became a Covenanter.

24. See Albion, *Charles I and Court of Rome*, pp. 116–44, on this mission generally. The project of a British cardinal went back to 1603; see Lea, "Sir Anthony Standen," especially pp. 470–75.

25. Add. 15,390, f. 88; Add. 15,391, ff. 59, 65, 108–9.

26. Although the agents were not officially nuncios, they were generally regarded as such and called by that title by the English; see, for example, Yonge, f. 64v.

27. The instructions to the English agent from the king are in *CCSP*, 1:73–74.

28. Hughes, "Conversion," pp. 123–24; the correspondence among the cardinals, on which the following paragraphs are based, is in BL 8656.

29. Giovanni Francesco Guidi di Bagno was former nuncio to Brussels (1621–27) and Paris (1627–30); he was considered a likely successor to Urban VIII in the late 1630s; see Biaudet, *Nonciatures apostoliques*, p. 269. On the reports to Rome from DuPerron, Alexander of Hales, Leander Jones, David Codner, Christopher Davenport, and others, see Hughes, "Conversion," pp. 115–18. In the summer of 1633 DuPerron's opinions were reported through Bichi, the nuncio in France, to the effect that Weston, Windebank, and Cottington were all crypto-Catholics and that, "in the opinion of many, [Charles] would be easy of conversion if the archbishop of Canterbury and Lord Treasurer Weston would only take the lead" (Albion, *Charles I and Court of Rome*, p. 109). A secular priest wrote to Fitton in Rome on 1 March 1633, "I do assure you unfeignedly that I am of opinion that we shall see shortly an other face of religion in this country" (AAW A.27, p. 53).

30. Hughes paraphrases Father Leonard's report from the Propaganda archives and cites Ingoli's comment, "Now that we have this bishop of London so favorably inclined we should not delay this mission any longer" ("Conversion," p. 116).

31. It is still unknown who made this offer, which is recorded in Laud's diary (*Works*, 3:219). Albion suggested David Codner (*Charles I and Court of Rome*, pp. 148–49), but Philip Hughes suggested the Franciscan, Giles Chaissy ("Conversion," pp. 124–25).

32. See Lutz, "Rom und Europa," pp. 82–93.

33. On Panzani and his mission generally, see Pastor, *History of Popes*, 29:312–18; Albion, *Charles I and Court of Rome*, pp. 120–43.

34. Trevor-Roper, *Laud*, p. 127; and *CSPVen 1632–36*, p. 163.

35. Laud, *Works*, 3:222–23; Havran, *Catholics*, p. 114; Trevor-Roper, *Laud*, pp. 333–34.

36. Laud, *Works*, 4:331–32.

37. Dockery, *Christopher Davenport*, chap. 4.

38. Lunn, *English Benedictines*, p. 124; Sitwell, "Leander Jones's Mission," pp. 133–36.

39. Ibid., pp. 136–39; Trevor-Roper, *Laud*, pp. 107, 145.

40. On Con, see *DNB*, s.v. "George Con"; *Spicilegium Benedictinum*, no. 5 (March 1897), p. 12, for a copy of the inscription on Con's tomb with biographical information; and Fraser, *Carlaverock*, 2:67–70. Windebank began corresponding with him in May 1636 (*CSP*, 1:535), remarking then on his "good offices between this state and that." For Con's earlier oversight of British affairs, see Dagens, *Bérulle et les origines*, 3:83; BL 8619, f. 95 (letter of David Codner, 1627).

41. BL 8639, f. 28. The seculars claimed that the Jesuits said the same thing (AAW A.28, p. 657, December 1636, [Leybourne] to Chalcedon).

42. Albion, *Charles I and Court of Rome*, pp. 158–59.

43. Blet, "Congrégation des Affaires de France," pp. 61–62, and "Débuts de Mazarin," especially pp. 242–51.

44. The French party in the Curia included Bentivoglio, di Bagno, and Bichi. Francesco Barberini, cardinal protector of England, was also protector of Spain (Dethan, *Mazarin*, pp. 51, 71). Promotions were a matter of international politics; a favor to Henrietta Maria could be seen as "but a faintly disguised favor to France" (Albion, *Charles I and Court of Rome*, pp. 118–22, 142, 293–99, 308–14; Add. 15,390, f. 246).

45. Add. 15,390, ff. 55–61, 178–79, 189, 226–28, 272. Urban's successor, Innocent X, was anti-French.

46. Panzani, *Memoirs*, pp. 150–52, 163–64, 173–75; Anglia 33, pt. 1, f. 469; Epist. Gen. Anglia I (2), ff. 446v, 458r–v. Among the friends of the Jesuits in the Curia were Cardinals Spada and Mellini.

47. Con's faculties, dated 18 August 1636, in BL 2693, f. 61.

48. Apart from Con's own reports, described in Albion, *Charles I and Court of Rome*, pp. 232–37, this is confirmed by George Leybourne in AAW A.29, no. 6 (January 1637), and by David Codner in a letter of 23 December 1636 (*Spicilegium Benedictinum*, no. 5, p. 9).

49. Add. 15,390, ff. 24–25, 164–66; Add. 15,391, ff. 42, 108. See Albion, *Charles I and Court of Rome*, pp. 232–48.

50. Add. 15,390, ff. 257–58, 286–88. Con referred much more often to "Puritans" than to "Calvinists" when describing English Protestants, and the term seems most frequently to denote degree of anti-Catholic zeal.

51. Pastor, *History of Popes*, 29:310, 312, 314–17, 319–20.

52. Add. 15,390, ff. 6–7, 346–48; Add. 15,391, ff. 159, 301; Salvetti H, ff. 50–53; *CSPVen 1636–39*, p. 272; Knowler, 2:115.

53. Add. 15,390, f. 79.

54. "Con molto disgusto delli spettatori Puritani." Add. 15,391, ff. 44–45. Cf. Add. 15,390, ff. 250, 494; Add. 15,391, ff. 20–21. The "Brownist" was a servant of Olive Porter (Add. 15,390, f. 341).

55. *CSPVen 1636–39*, pp. 217–18, 300–304.

56. On Duppa's sermons, see AAW A.27, p. 427 (April 1634); and AAW A.28, p. 107 (27 May 1635). On the attempt to convert him, see *CSPVen 1636–39*, p. 150. On his career, see also Add. 15,391, ff. 103–4, 145. Duppa was dean of Christ Church and also tutor of Buckingham's children. He was promoted to Chichester in January 1638 with the queen's help and later (1641) to Norwich.

57. Add. 15,391, ff. 126, 184, 223, 241, 270; Aylmer, *King's Servants*, pp. 6–7. Newcastle

was a friend of Endymion Porter; see BL 8642, ff. 178–80.

58. Add. 15,390, ff. 47, 65, 84, 92–94, 101–4, 119. See Panzani, *Memoirs*, pp. 252–53, for earlier suggestions along this line.

59. "Di spirito e garbo assai superiore"; "giovane d'infinite capacità per l'età." See Add. 15,390, ff. 145–46, 234, 270–72, 331, 338–39, 375–76, 403. Elizabeth's fears were not groundless; two of her younger sons converted to Rome, as did her daughter Louisa Hollandia, who became an abbess (*DNB*, s.v. "Elizabeth, queen of Bohemia"; Morrah, *Prince Rupert*, pp. 54–55).

60. Laud, *Works*, 7:334, 380.

61. Add. 15,390, f. 216; *CSPVen 1636–39*, pp. 148–49, 266; Thibaudeau, *Collections of . . . Alfred Morrison*, 2:60. The younger DuPerron was an abbot when he first went to England; he was made bishop in 1636.

62. "The king and queen do love him, and so do all the courtiers" (AAW A.27, p. 57 [8 March 1633]). On Philip, see also Add. 15,390, ff. 23, 28, 79; PRO 31/9/135, f. 174; *CSPVen 1636–39*, pp. 69, 92, 119, 216; Bellesheim, *Catholic Church of Scotland*, 4:51; Hay, *Blairs Papers*, pp. 247–48; Batterel, *Congrégation de l'Oratoire*, 1:222–32.

63. Add. 15,390, ff. 72, 132, 208, 229, 275; Add. 15,391, ff. 261, 265, 308; Add. 15,392, ff. 22, 27–28, 43, 50, 55; Salvetti H, f. 21; Knowler, 2:67–73. Montagu had been secretly ordained during his travels abroad.

64. Add. 15,391, ff. 22, 51–52, 102, 203; Laud, *Works*, 4:345, 6:447–55; Petersson, *Kenelm Digby*, p. 142; *Letters between Lord George Digby and Sir Kenelm Digby . . . concerning Religion* (1651).

65. However, Mathew's executors reveal his connections with Oxfordshire Catholicism—the Plowden, Wake, and Chamberlayne families are represented; see Davidson, "Catholicism in Oxfordshire," p. 579.

66. See Gillow and *DNB*, s.v. "Toby Mathew"; Mathew, *Mathew*; Matthew and Calthrop, *Life of Matthew*, pp. 300–43; Add. 15,390, f. 295. Mathew was a strenuous nonjuror and opponent of Bishop Smith.

67. For the first full treatment of Windebank, see Haskell, "Sir Francis Windebank." Also see *DNB*, s.v. "Sir Francis Windebank" and "Thomas Reade"; Gillow, s.v. "Thomas Reade"; Aylmer, *King's Servants*, p. 358; *CCSP*, 1:41–81, for the 1634–36 period; and Havran, *Catholics*, pp. 128–32, 136, for his activities against pursuivants. Add. 15,390, ff. 61, 76; Add. 15,391, ff. 8, 52, 91, 128, 144, 156, 345–46, deal with Con's initial reactions and relations with Windebank. See also Laud, *Works*, 7:390.

68. Add. 15,390, ff. 10, 29–30, 52, 73–74, 120, 169, 180, 186, 190.

69. Add. 15,390, ff. 31, 35, 90, 94–95, 101–4, 112–15, 146, 226; Add. 15,391, ff. 61, 166, 170, 249–50, 290. Panzani too had been more friendly with the countess than with the earl.

70. Add. 15,390, ff. 50, 86, 210, 278, 316, 366, 369, 370.

71. Con attended at the deathbeds of both these men (BL 8641, f. 112).

72. Knowler, 2:171, 194. Joachimi reported home in December 1637 that "the reformed church loses openly" (Add. 17,677P, f. 294). On Mrs. Porter, see Add. 15,390, ff. 209–11, 341, 418, 463, 479, 488; Add. 15,391, f. 30; and Huxley, *Porter*, pp. 25–26, 236.

73. See Huxley, *Porter*, pp. 176, 230–31, 243; Townshend, *Life of Porter*, pp. 95–96; Add. 15,390, ff. 99–100, 418, 502–3; Add. 15,391, ff. 87, 123–24, 142; Laud, *Works*, 4:489.

74. In 1635 Porter was associated with other courtiers (Arundel, Maltravers, and Heath), as well as with the earl of Bedford, in a monopoly scheme for licensing pawnshops.

75. Add. 15,390, f. 492; Add. 15,391, f. 46; Huxley, *Porter*, pp. 38, 137–41, 167–70, 178–79, 195–96.

76. Add. 15,391, f. 282.

77. The memoirs of Father Cyprien de Gamache, one of these Capuchins, are in Birch, *Court and Times of Charles I*, vol. 2; they must be used with care, but give details about the missionaries' activities that are otherwise not available. On the character of the order and its work in France and the British Isles, see Hess, *Capuchins*, chaps. 9 and 11. The Capuchins enjoyed special access to the pope in the reign of Urban VIII because his brother Cardinal Antonio Barberini (1569–1646) was a member of the order.

78. A Capuchin historian described the chapel as "a goodly and spacious room" and reported a contemporary estimate (at the end of the 1630s) that as many as six thousand people had heard mass there on Sundays and holidays, when one mass after another was said (Archbold, "Evangelicall Fruict," in Harl. MS 3888, p. 146). Although exaggerated, this figure indicates the throng involved; the room was over one hundred feet long and had two small transepts; its opening was celebrated with an eight-part mass accompanied by organ and orchestra; see Hodgetts, "Liturgical Music," p. 151; Little, *Catholic Churches*, p. 22.

79. The opening of the Spanish chapel in December 1637 is noted in BL 8641, f. 238; see also Salvetti H, f. 86, on the opening of the Florentine chapel.

80. Add. 15,391, ff. 2, 122.

81. Add. 15,390, ff. 204, 207, 473; Add. 15,391, f. 102. Con reported that Catholics were buying up houses near his residence so as to more conveniently hear mass (BL 8644, f. 364).

82. Knowler, 2:165.

83. Ibid.; Add. 15,390, ff. 240–41, 471, 504; Add. 15,391, ff. 21, 119.

84. Albion, *Charles I and Court of Rome*, p. 203. Henrietta Maria introduced into England the Confraternity of the Holy Rosary, which met weekly for services (Birch, *Court and Times of Charles I*, 2:432–33); and Marie de Medici brought her special images of the Virgin Mary for these devotions.

85. Add. 15,390, f. 285. Martz, in *Poetry of Meditation*, traces the influence of these works on contemporary English literature; see pp. 5–13. Menteith, *History of the Troubles of Great Britain* (1735), p. 18, gave this explanation of Laud's program, and Laud himself alluded to it (*Works*, 3:408).

86. See Nurse, "Recusant History of Cheam," pp. 109–10; Clar. MS 11, ff. 174–75, for the examination of Morse, S.J., on pursuivants; see also Add. 15,390, f. 436; Add. 15,391, ff. 68–69, 184, 215.

87. Add. 15,390, f. 261; Add. 15,391, ff. 43–46, 284–85; Knowler, 2:147. On the Petre case, see Clay, "Misfortunes of Lord Petre," pp. 89, 94–95.

88. Add. 15,391, ff. 205–6; BL 8644, f. 364; Knowler, 2:73–74. Con officiated at the marriage of Lord Herbert of Raglan to the daughter of the Protestant earl of Thomond (the bride promising to convert) in July 1639.

89. Add. 15,391, ff. 68, 119; PRO 31/9/18, ff. 46–51; *CSPD 1637–38*, pp. 64–65; *CSPD 1639–40*, p. 142.

90. See Hibbard, "Strafford," for further detail on the queen's attempts to help Irish Catholics.

91. Kearney, *Strafford*, chap. 10; Clarke, *Old English*, chaps. 5 and 6.

92. BL 8640, ff. 157–58; Laud, *Works*, 6:441; Strafford MS 8, ff. 433–35; *CCSP*, 1:69; Jennings, *Wild Geese*, pp. 31, 34, 273, 282–95, 564.

93. SP 94/40, ff. 66–67, 79–80, 89–90, 111–12, 286–87, 327–28, 347–48; Knowler, 1:292; Laud, *Works*, 6:519–22.

94. Knowler, 2:53–66, 112.

95. Strafford MS 8, ff. 300–301; Knowler, 2:110–11, 122.

96. Add. 15,390, ff. 25–26, 70; Add. 15,392, ff. 133, 150, 186, 189, 207, 211, 240; Strafford MS 3, ff. 332–33, 342–43; ibid., 17, f. 275; ibid., 18, ff. 16, 34, 68, 72, 74, 138; ibid., 19, f. 81; Knowler, 2:132–37, 227, 257; HMC Twelfth Report, app. II, pp. 218, 238.
97. Add. 15,391, f. 147; Strafford MS 10a, ff. 171–73; ibid., 18, f. 138; Knowler, 2:221–22, 257; Laud, Works, 6:542; ibid., 7:508, 511–12.
98. CSP Ven 1636–39, p. 150; CSP, 2:66; CCSP, 1:191; Kearney, "Ecclesiastical Politics," pp. 205–8.
99. Add. 15,391, f. 49; AAW A.28, p. 365 (8 March 1636).
100. Add. 15,390, ff. 80, 174.
101. Laud, Works, 3:411–12, 418–19; ibid., 4:332–34; Salvetti H, f. 76; Trevor-Roper, Laud, pp. 310–12, 322, 420. The information in Con's papers (e.g., BL 8641, ff. 211, 214) is very sketchy.
102. Add. 15,390, ff. 360–71, 373, 469–73, 511; Add. 15,391, ff. 98, 128, 135, 148, 235, 237, 338; Laud, Works, 3:148; ibid., 4:332–34, 443; ibid., 7:572. See chap. 5 below for Scottish propaganda against Laud.
103. Add. 15,390, ff. 187, 247–48, 283–84; Knowler, 2:74. In Devon, the news about Devout Life reached Yonge, who referred excitedly to "divers" papist books having been printed (Yonge, f. 66v). The proclamation recalling Devout Life was issued 14 May 1637; see Steele, Royal Proclamations, 1:210.
104. Con described the proclamation effort as a response to rumors of the king's being converted to Catholicism (BL 8642, f. 23).
105. Add. 15,390, ff. 469–73, 476–81, 486, 495–96; Knowler, 2:257; CSP Ven 1636–39, pp. 358–59.
106. Add. 15,390, ff. 494, 498–501; Add. 15,391, ff. 1–3, 17, 31, 48; Knowler, 2:166. The proclamation is in Foedera, 20:180, and in Steele, Royal Proclamations, 1:212.
107. Add. 15,392, f. 6; Knowler, 2:152; Salvetti H, f. 136. The king stipulated that the new secretary should not be "Spagnuolo, Giésuita o fattioso" (BL 8642, f. 179).
108. Add. 15,390, ff. 33, 118; Add. 15,391, ff. 98, 123, 129, 148, 236.
109. Add. 15,391, f. 136; Knowler, 2:166. See Con's letter in BL 8642, f. 184: Winter is a "Cattolico ottimo" whose brother has been at Rome and whose sister is a nun at Brussels. Winter was regarded by the seculars as an enemy (AAW A.27, p. 521 [October 1634]), and Panzani described him as a confirmed antiepiscopal figure (Panzani, Diary, f. 87 [April 1635]).
110. Add. 15,390, ff. 247–48, 282–83, 307–8, 469–73, 477, 501; Add. 15,391, ff. 165, 176, 201–2; Add. 15,392, f. 153; CSP Ven 1636–39, pp. 216, 272, 358.
111. Albion, Charles I and Court of Rome, p. 220; Add. 15,390, ff. 307–11, 469–72, 511; Add. 15,392, f. 66.
112. Add. 15,390, ff. 274, 390–91; Add. 15,391, ff. 106–7, 148, 337, 340–41, 345; Add. 15,392, ff. 10, 41.
113. Vere William Benedict Jones.
114. Gage, Travels, p. 345; CSP, 1:133–37, for the memorandum.
115. CSP, 2:18–19; PRO 31/9/124, f. 235; Add. 15,390, f. 348; Add. 15,391, ff. 107, 545, 555; CSP Ven 1636–39, pp. 273–74.
116. See Hibbard, "Early Stuart Catholicism," for further detail.
117. Jesuit support for Spanish succession to the English throne in the 1590s had left a lasting impression that the Jesuits favored a violent approach to the conversion of England. See Hughes, Rome and Counter-Reformation, pp. 277–85; see also Pritchard, Catholic Loyalism, chap. 5; Clancy, Papist Pamphleteers, chaps. 3 and 4, especially pp. 62–70 and 96–106; Rostenberg, Minority Press, chap. 5.

118. Watson, *Sparing Discovery*, for which see McGrath, *Papists and Puritans*, pp. 283–92, 364–65. See Clancy, *Papist Pamphleteers*, pp. 166–67, on Watson.

119. For the quarrel over the episcopacy in the late 1620s and early 1630s, see Birrell, "Catholics without a Bishop" and "Dutch and English Catholicism"; on some of the leading controversialists, see Brady, *Annals of Catholic Hierarchy*, pp. 86, 92–100; Hughes, *Society of Jesus*, Text, 1:204–22, 227; Dodd, *Church History*, 3:105–106.

120. Panzani's views on Jesuits are evident in every section of his *Memoirs*; see also *CSP Ven 1636–39*, p. 303. Leander Jones also urged the government to proceed against the Jesuits and specifically against Toby Mathew, their friend and advocate; see Clar. MS 6, f. 270. One tradition of Catholic historiography has viewed these and all other attempts at negotiating the Jesuits out of England as a government ploy to divide and conquer English Catholics by inducing some to betray others.

121. Con told Barberini that Jesuit penitents were better behaved than those of the seculars (PRO 31/10/11, f. 118).

122. On Percy as theologian, see Tavard, "Scripture and Tradition," pp. 38–44. Percy's account of his conference with Laud was printed in 1626: *Answer unto the Nine Points of Controversy* (St. Omer). Percy's career is treated in some detail in Hanlon, "Effects of the Counter-Reformation upon the English Catholics," pp. 157–214. He was one of the figures who represented all about Catholicism that was most disquieting to the English; he had converted Sir Everard Digby, later Gunpowder plotter, and been his chaplain; and he was very successful in proselytizing in England. Percy died in London in December 1641, having dedicated several of his works to Queen Henrietta Maria. For further details, see AAW A.28, p. 195 (9 December 1635).

123. Vitelleschi to Knott, 20 December 1636, and Vitelleschi to Richard Blount, 5 September and 10 September 1637, all in Epist. Gen. Anglia I (2), ff. 446v, 458r–v. Fitton reported that Con's appointment as agent to England had been held up because he had been too much courted by the Jesuits while in Rome, and it was feared he would not be thought impartial (AAW A.28, p. 347 [January 1636]: Fitton to Southcote).

124. Knowler, 2:257; see Caraman, *Henry Morse*, pp. 104–35, on the incident, and *DNB*, s.v. "Henry Morse." Add. 21,203 also includes an account; it is Morse's diary for 1637, under his alias of Henry Claxton.

125. Knowler, 2:274; Add. 15,390, ff. 248, 265–69, 334; Add. 21,203, ff. 60–63; *CSPD 1639*, pp. 91, 219, 229.

126. Add. 15,390, ff. 94–95, 146; Add. 15,391, ff. 61, 166, 170, 249–50, 290. See Caraman, *Henry Morse*, p. 141.

127. For the seculars' views, see AAW A.27 passim. For their relations with Panzani and with Con, see BL 8639, ff. 280, 288; Panzani, *Memoirs*, p. 206; Brady, *Annals of Catholic Hierarchy*, pp. 100–103; *CSP Ven 1636–39*, pp. 68–69, 119–20; AAW A.27, p. 173.

128. On Leybourne, who was "provisor" of the queen's chapel, see Anstruther, vol. 2, s.v. "George Leybourne"; AAW A.28, p. 347 (January 1636); AAW A.29, no. 70 (n.d.); Add. 15,392, f. 204.

129. BL 8639, f. 45; BL 8640, ff. 11, 164–65, 359; BL 8642, f. 179; Add. 15,390, ff. 20, 29–30, 42–46, 72, 196, 212, 229, 249, 404–5, 488–89; Add. 15,391, ff. 54, 81; AAW A.28, p. 651 (20 December 1636). Among other problems, Con mentioned scandals arising out of grants of marriage faculties to missionaries; he suggested they be withdrawn from all but the superiors (BL 8642, f. 207). Con did not, however, favor the return to England of Richard Smith.

130. Add. 15,390, ff. 424–28, 447; Add. 15,391, ff. 101, 157, 167–68, 172–73, 232–33; PRO 31/10/11, f. 173. Champney had been an Appellant and had been elected by the

chapter in 1637 at Smith's suggestion; both features of his career were displeasing to Rome (BL 8644, ff. 292, 413).

131. Add. 15,391, ff. 242, 271, 324; Add. 15,392, ff. 105–9, 139, 204; PRO 31/9/130, ff. 52–54.

132. It was in 1638 that Christopher Davenport began to compose a new work on episcopal authority. Con attempted to prevent its publication and described Davenport to Windebank as semischismatic (BL 8642, f. 203). The work appeared in 1640; see chap. 8 below.

133. They spread rumors that there were to be three or four bishops, in order to frighten the English; see Add. 15,391, f. 267; Add. 15,392, ff. 14–15; *CSP*, 2:17–18.

134. The seculars were very quickly distrustful of his friendly relations with Knott; see AAW A.28, p. 355 (February 1637): Leybourne to Chalcedon.

135. On Knott, see Bassett, *English Jesuits*. pp. 187–88, 205–9; Tavard, "Scripture and Tradition," pp. 87–89; and Wood, 3:181, s.v. "Christopher Potter."

136. See Add. 15,390, ff. 129, 311; Add. 15,391, f. 148; Guilday, *Catholic Refugees*, p. 323; Waller, "Chillingworth," pp. 178–81.

137. Add. 15,390, ff. 26–28, 38–42, 127, 175, 202, 310–12, 340, 479, 489, 510; Add. 15,391, ff. 29–30, 161. In December 1637 Con was conferring with Knott about another reply to Chillingworth (BL 8641, f. 211).

138. Bassett, *English Jesuits*, pp. 187, 208–9; Hughes, *Society of Jesus*, Text, 1:72, 459.

139. See BL 8641, ff. 55, 60–64, concerning the king's complaint that the pope would approve the oath if the Jesuits did not prevent it. See also Albion, *Charles I and Court of Rome*, chap. 11; and Lunn, "Benedictines and Oath of Allegiance," especially pp. 155–57.

140. On the "Clinkers," or priests housed comfortably in the Clink Prison, Southwark, see Havran, *Catholics*, pp. 63–64. Preston's book was entitled *Patterne of Christian Loyaltie*; see Webb, "Preston," pp. 245–55; Grun, "Note on William Howard," p. 339; and AAW A.27, November–December 1634, for the documents in the case.

141. Leander took the oath in the form given in Clar. MS 6, ff. 128–29 (dated 17 December 1634); see Sitwell, "Leander Jones's Mission," pp. 148–49, 158–59, 174–75; and Albion, *Charles I and Court of Rome*, p. 257. Leander's suggestion to Rome was that the pope should withdraw his condemnation of the oath in exchange for the king's assurance that the oath was intended only to ensure civil obedience, not to intrude on the pope's spiritual jurisdiction.

142. Panzani, *Memoirs*, pp. 141–45, 156–59, 164, 171; Brady, *Annals of Catholic Hierarchy*, p. 88; Webb, "Preston," pp. 253–54; Grun, "Note on William Howard," p. 336. He reported, mainly on the basis of discussion with Windebank, that some of the privy council were in favor of changing the oath to make it acceptable to the pope. Perhaps alarmed at the compromises suggested by Jones and Panzani, the Curia refused to draw up any draft formula or to pursue the matter further.

143. See chap. 4 for a discussion of the earl of Arundel's mission in 1636. Howard had accompanied him. Probably in an attempt to lift the pressure on Leeds, the Jesuits had provided Arundel's mission with introductions to Jesuits in Vienna, including the emperor's confessor, Lamormaini; an English Jesuit, Henry Silesdon, actually accompanied the embassy. Lamormaini, however, was a hard-line anti-Protestant, and these overtures accomplished nothing but to draw suspicion on the English Jesuits. See Add. 15,390, ff. 116, 125–26; Hervey, *Earl of Arundel*, pp. 368–70; Grun, "Note on William Howard," pp. 332–33; and Bireley, "Peace of Prague," pp. 31–69.

144. Add. 15,390, ff. 36–37. The idea was to have two oaths, the 1606 oath established by statute and a new formula. The new oath could not carry penalties for nonjuring, because only parliament could impose those, but Catholics willing to take it might be

protected by royal dispensation from having to take the old oath. Those unwilling to take either would be subject to the penalties provided by the 1606 oath legislation.

145. The oath of allegiance is printed in Kenyon, *Stuart Constitution*, pp. 458–59. The two points on which Charles I had been adamant previously were the denial of the legitimacy of "deposition" and the identification of "priests" as among those whose sentences of deposition were invalid. Con persuaded the king to substitute the term "ecclesiastical persons" for "priests"; his account appears in Add. 15,390, ff. 73, 153, 219–20, 291, 335, 351; Add. 15,391, f. 57. See Albion, *Charles I and Court of Rome*, app. VIIb, for one revised version. Another undated (Latin) copy of an oath is in BL 8642, f. 82; it refers to mental equivocation but omits mention of priests or deposition. Two versions of an oath initialed and dated by the king in April and May 1637 appear in Clar. MS 11, ff. 162–63, 164–65; whether they were sent to Rome is not known. The problem of finding an oath for Catholics took on a wider significance in 1639 in connection with the Scottish crisis; see chap. 6 below.

146. Add. 15,390, ff. 94–95, 230–34, 251, 341, 390–91; Add. 15,391, f. 105.

147. Add. 15,391, ff. 97, 102, 126. It was rumored that Con wanted a new English Benedictine superior who would be sworn to oppose the oath; Selby wrote an anonymous letter attacking nonjurors, and by implication Con himself. See Albion, *Charles I and Court of Rome*, pp. 279–82.

148. Add. 15,391, ff. 337, 340–41, 345; Add. 15,392, f. 10; Salvetti H, ff. 219–20, 222.

149. On Browne, see Durkan, "Brown's Confession" and "Career of John Brown"; Giblin, "Brown and Maitland"; Whitmore, *Order of Minims*, pp. 47, 71.

150. Browne's activities and early efforts to get him out of England are mentioned by Panzani in his Diary, ff. 50, 51, 129. Browne's deposit of college money with various Catholics in England is recorded in Bodl., Bankes MS 6/24 (n.d.), which contains a list of his creditors. Bankes MS 23/16 is a Catholic ecclesiastical license to Anthony Metcalfe to proceed against Browne in the English courts. Maitland's critical views of Browne are clear from his letters to Propaganda Fide, e.g., Prop. Scr. Rif., vol. 105, f. 278; vol. 134, ff. 138, 140.

A major reason for Roman suspicion about Browne's orthodoxy was his friendship with the maverick Cassinese Benedictine, David Codner, who was an admirer of Christopher Davenport and his book *Deus, Natura, Gratia*. For Codner's approval of Browne and Davenport, see Prop. Scr. Rif., vol. 105, ff. 260, 263; vol. 134, f. 135.

151. Browne had shown Con apparently genuine documents granting him wide faculties; see BL 8642, ff. 194, 197–99; BL 8643, ff. 5, 187; PRO 31/9/92, ff. 68–69, 72, 75–76; Prop. Acta, vol. 11 (1637): no. 40, orders to Con; Prop. Acta, vol. 12 (1638): no. 39, on Browne's lack of faculties. Reference to Browne's certificate signed by David Codner is in Prop. Scr. Rif., vol. 106, f. 35; vol. 137, f. 226.

152. See chap. 9 below.

Chapter 4

1. With the obvious and important exceptions of Henry Percy and Henry Jermyn.

2. The idea seems to have originated with the agent in Vienna, John Taylor; see *CCSP*, 1:160, 162–63. The Stuart dynasty had old ties with the house of Lorraine through Mary of Guise. The attempt to help the Guises and their allies, Gaston d'Orléans and other rivals of Richelieu, is a persistent motif of the 1630s; a contemporary reason for this solicitude was that these were the friends of Marie de Medici, mother of Henrietta Maria (Gardiner, *History of England*, 8:98–99).

3. Walter Lord Aston, who became a convert to Catholicism, went to Madrid; Juan, count

of Oñate y Villa Mediana, was named for London, but did not arrive until July 1636.

4. John Taylor was brother to Henry Taylor, formerly secretary for English letters at the Spanish embassy in London, 1622–24, and canon of St. Gudule, Brussels. In November 1637 Henry Taylor was recommended by Oñate as a prospective agent in London to handle maritime affairs of the Spanish Netherlands in collaboration with the Spanish ambassador (Loomie, *Spain and Jacobean Catholics*, 2:xiii; L&C, 3:188; ibid., 6:460). On John Taylor, see Trappes-Lomax, "John Taylor," which corrects the account in *DNB*.

5. Salvetti H, ff. 4–6; *CSP*, 1:310; *CCSP*, 1:68, 80–92 passim. On the policy of Ferdinand II, see Bireley, "Peace of Prague," pp. 31–69. The exclusion of the prince Palatine from the Ratisbon conference and the inclusion of Maximilian of Bavaria would set an official seal on the transfer of the electoral vote.

6. The sum of £7,262 issued to Arundel in February 1637 (PRO, S.O. 3/11) was by no means the full cost of the embassy.

7. Necolalde, the Spanish agent in London and the main source of information for Spain in early 1636, thought Charles I was too distrustful of France to break with Spain, and Radolt in early 1637 also doubted a rupture would occur (Gardiner, *History of England*, 7:381; *CSPVen 1636–39*, p. 132). But Philip IV was apprehensive, as can be seen from L&C, 3:123. The Venetian agent thought Spain counted on Oñate to be able to control the negotiations (*CSPVen 1632–36*, p. 568; *CSPVen 1636–39*, p. 65). However, the Venetian outlook was generally hostile to Spain, as it had been in the 1620s, and this factor must be weighed when using the Venetian reports; see Loomie, *Spain and Jacobean Catholics*, 2:xviii.

8. Gardiner, *History of England*, 8:161–62, 205. During 1636–38 Leicester was also conducting, through the mediation of the Protestant duke of Soubise, a negotiation for marriage between Prince Rupert and Marguerite de Rohan; see Scott, *Rupert*, pp. 30–33.

9. Knowler, 2:53.

10. Salvetti H, ff. 30–31.

11. Add. 15,390, f. 84. Coventry and Juxon were mentioned among those favoring a parliament, and several peers were said to have sent inquiries out to "where they have most power to some of their intimate friends of quality to feel the disposition of the country"; see *HMC Fourth Report*, p. 292, and the original in Kent Archives Office, Cranfield Papers.

12. Bromley, *Original Royal Letters*, pp. 96–97.

13. *HMC Fourth Report*, pp. 278, 292; Bruce, *Verney Papers*, pp. 188–89. In memoranda of June 1637, the earl of Middlesex argued for the feasibility of this proposal; see Kent Archive Office, Cranfield Papers, "Political Memoranda."

14. "Hanno quasi tutto il governo nelle mani" (Salvetti H, f. 10). In 1628 Salvetti identified the "Puritans" with the "French party"; see *HMC Tenth Report*, app. I (Salvetti MSS), p. 167. In the present context he seems to refer to friends of the Palatine family generally, including both "French party" courtiers and their country allies.

15. Bromley, *Original Royal Letters*, pp. 91–92, 98. For Dury's reports and their influence on the king, see Roe's letter in September 1636, reported in Turnbull, *Hartlib, Dury and Comenius*, p. 185.

16. Gardiner, *History of England*, 8:210, 217. The French wanted England to issue an ultimatum to the emperor, fixing a date after which, failing satisfaction on the Palatinate, England would break off relations and enter the French alliance. The negotiation can be followed through Venetian reports from London and Paris in *CSPVen 1636–39*, especially pp. 179–80, 218–19, 260, 268.

The commissioned work *Mare Clausum* by John Selden had appeared in December
1635; this was followed in May 1636 by a royal proclamation claiming dominion over
the Channel and requiring that foreigners obtain fishing licenses.

17. Salvetti H, ff. 1, 30–31, 46–48; Add. 15,390, ff. 157–59, 270–71. The manifesto is in
Add. 38,091, f. 223. Volradus Frubach's *Evaporation of the Apple of Palestine* (1637)
was part of the prince's propaganda campaign. In the end, Charles Lewis spent the
summer with his uncle, the prince of Orange.

18. *CSPD 1637*, p. 82; Baker, *Letters of Elizabeth*, p. 96; Bromley, *Original Royal Letters*,
pp. 91–93. The agent to Hamburg was De Vic, although Elizabeth had hoped for Roe
(ibid., p. 93).

19. Salvetti H, f. 88. The Swedes soon made it clear that the English fleet would be of little
use to them and that they would require English subsidies; see the letter from Charles
Lewis to Elizabeth, 18 August 1638, in BM, Microfilm Deposit 325 (Duke of Northumberland, Alnwick MSS, vol. 725). See also *CSPD 1636–37*, pp. 82, 227–28.

20. Gardiner, *History of England*, 8:376.

21. Wentworth, for one, felt sufficiently worried about the possibility of war to risk a long
and vehement letter to the king arguing against it; see Knowler, 2:60–64. Philip
Burlamacchi reported from London to the earl of Middlesex in February 1637: "With
France, the treaty is as good as concluded" (letter of 7 February in Kent Archives Office,
Cranfield Papers). Dorset, writing to Middlesex on the same date, was more skeptical
both of the likelihood of war and of its possible success, as also was Newburgh:
"Tempers are lukewarm . . . we want the vital spirits and sinews that these occasions
require, power, and treasure" (letters in Kent Archives Office, Cranfield Papers).

22. For domestic pressures in the 1620s shaping French policy, see Russell, *Parliaments and
Politics*, p. 210. The Venetian agent at The Hague was puzzled by the French delay,
while his colleague in England speculated that France feared English hegemony in the
Channel (*CSPVen 1636–39*, pp. 181, 106). Salvetti too (H, f. 41) referred to the
"insolite dilazioni" of the French.

23. Necolalde had told the king of the Franco-Dutch agreement. The Dutch stressed
England's concern for Dunkirk in interpreting Charles I's policy (*CSPVen 1636–39*, p.
139), and Salvetti also thought the matter very important (Salvetti H, ff. 151, 156, 167).
Coke was presumably reflecting the king's own views in emphasizing the importance of
keeping France out of Flanders (SP 78/92, ff. 61–63, 207–8).

24. The English had the idea that if the Spanish seemed to be losing Dunkirk, they should
snap it up themselves; see *CSP*, 1:103; and Grose, "England and Dunkirk," pp. 2, 4.

25. Gardiner, *History of England*, 8:218; on the readiness of the fleet, see *CSPD 1636–37*,
pp. 5, 21, 22, 55, 63, 109; for the king's plans, see Knowler, 2:53, and the letter of
Dorset to Middlesex, 7 February 1636, in Kent Archives Office, Cranfield Papers.

26. The Scottish situation, of course, could not be ignored. But the king's pattern of
expenditure as the crisis developed in 1638 suggests no adjustment of ends to means;
for example, he received Marie de Medici in October, which he need not have done, and
it cost him very heavily. Lamenting the emptiness of the treasury in February 1637,
Newburgh noted that in addition to other unusual expenses, the king had committed
£20,000 to the redemption of jewels pawned in Holland in the 1620s (*HMC Fourth
Report*, p. 292). In fact, the total expended on redemption of those jewels in 1636–39
was £84,804 (PRO, S.O. 3/12, December 1639 discharge to Sir Job Harby).

27. See chap. 2 above for an analysis of the friends of France.

28. PRO 31/3/70, f. 231.

29. "Al forzare Sua Maestà di servirsi di loro per mezzo di un parlamento. Ma come il suo
artificio è molto bene conosciuto dalla Maestà Sua, non si vede perciò nessuna ap-

parenza che possa essere compiaciuto" (Salvetti H, ff. 34–35, 35–37). Correr said
much the same in February 1637, *CSPVen 1636–39*, p. 146.

30. *CSPVen 1636–39*, pp. 179–80. On French perceptions of Cottington, Laud, and
Windebank, see Avenel, 8:308. In the person of Sir Richard Forster, the French had a
valuable informant about Cottington's activities; see ibid., 5:855. Forster was a
Catholic native of Stokesley, Yorkshire, cupbearer and later treasurer to the queen; see
Foster, "Forster," pp. 163–74. The family was devoutly Catholic; Aveling, *Northern
Catholics*, pp. 232, 238, 256–67. Since the 1620s, Forster had figured in Anglo-French
contacts (Albion, *Charles I and Court of Rome*, p. 105n3); in the 1630s he had a French
pension and fed information to the French agents (PRO 31/3/69, 70, 71, for numerous
references).

31. Salvetti H, ff. 10, 41–42, 46–48; Add. 15,390, ff. 31–32, 178–79. Oñate used an
English Jesuit from Necolalde's household as his interpreter at his first audience with
the king (*CSPVen 1636–39*, p. 80; cf. p. 257). The king refused to let Oñate have Ely
House, used by previous Spanish ambassadors, as his residence in 1636; see Loomie,
Spain and Jacobean Catholics, 2:xxiii. Oñate reported gloomily in August 1637 that he
found Charles antipathetic, all his ministers opposed to Spain, and the Spanish interest
in London held in so little account that he could find no confidant. It is clear that in
1637 both Oñate and his masters thought English intervention on one or the other side
of the European war could have a powerful effect, so Oñate's pose of calculated disdain
must be seen as a piece of bravado that, luckily for the Spanish, did them no immediate
harm (L&C, 6:447–49, 452).

32. Add. 15,390, ff. 198, 226; PRO 31/3/70, f. 199. For Erskine's negotiations generally,
see *CSP*, 1:778–85 passim. Erskine, who was a cousin of the king and a lord of the
bedchamber, lived chiefly in London and Paris until his death in 1640 (*DNB*, s.v. "John
Erskine, earl of Buchan"). His brother Alexander was a mercenary for France. There are
many references to Buchan in the Clarendon MSS. He left England for Spain in
February 1638 (Add. 15,391, f. 72).

33. "A modo suo"; "un armata di fanteria spagnuola per spaventarli e farli fare a modo di
questo Re" (Add. 15,390, f. 272). See also Salvetti H, ff. 30–31. Spain wanted an
offensive alliance against the Dutch, and Charles I wanted the restoration of all the
Palatinate, together with the electoral dignity, to his sister's family. For the marriage
proposal, see Add. 15,390, ff. 243, 263–64; such an idea had been raised as early as
1633 by Necolalde.

34. "Molto grato e accetto a questo Re e stato" (Salvetti H, ff. 51–53). On Scaglia's
negotiations, see Avenel, 8:232, 235, 237.

35. L&C, 3:173; *CSPVen 1636–39*, pp. 227–28, 281.

36. For the subsequent negotiations through Brussels, see the last section of this chapter.

37. On Monsigot, see Add. 15,390, ff. 363, 375, 432–35; his safe conduct dated 31 July
1638 is entered in PRO, S.O. 3/11. Salvetti reported that the conspiracy involved the
count of Soissons (Salvetti H, ff. 62–63), while the Venetian agent added the names of
the Cardinal Infante, the duke of Orléans, and the queen mother (*CSPVen 1636–39*,
pp. 277–78).

38. Charles I did promise Monsigot to mediate with Richelieu on behalf of the queen
mother for her return to France and receipt of her revenues thence; this may have been
all she really expected from him. For the negotiations, see *CSPD 1636–37*, pp. 468,
469. There are further references in Weckherlin's diary for the second half of 1637.

39. Avenel, 5:834; *CSPVen 1636–39*, pp. 260–68; on Montagu, see Smuts, "Puritan
Followers of Henrietta Maria," pp. 30–35; and Dethan, *Mazarin*, pp. 132–34. In
September 1637 a rumor current at the English court associated the wayward Will

Crofts, who had sometime earlier fled to France, with involvement in Chevreuse's intrigues (*HMC Fourth Report*, p. 293).

40. In 1635 Montagu had helped to effect a temporary rapprochement between Richelieu and Henrietta Maria, for which see Smuts, "Puritan Followers of Henrietta Maria," pp. 35–36.

41. *CSPD 1637–38*, p. 7; *CSPVen 1636–39*, pp. 268, 272, 278.

42. *CSPVen 1636–39*, p. 126, for speculation that Spain was involved; more than one pamphleteer in 1640–41 took up this theme (e.g., Heywood, *Rat Trap*, 1641). But no evidence of this has come to light, and the notion of a Spanish-Covenanting league is inherently improbable. English commentators, not Scottish, had this notion; it was a conventional idea, common to those who saw the hand of the Jesuits and the Spanish monarchy behind every crisis. There was some tradition of contacts between Scottish Catholics and Spain that persisted into the 1630s through the Semple family; on this, see Taylor, *Scots College*, pp. 18–28. Father John Seton, S.J., who had been Father Hugh Semple's associate at the Scots College in Madrid, returned to Scotland in 1637.

43. The letters are in Prosper Merchant, ed., *Lettres, mémoires, et négotiations de M. le Comte d'Estrades*, 9 vols. (The Hague, 1743), 1:3–16. Ranke, in *History of England*, 5:457–63, discusses the question at length; and Gardiner, *History of England*, 8:382 and 9:91, pays some attention to it. Further light on the activities in Scotland of Thomas Chambers, almoner to Richelieu and nephew of George Con, is provided in Hay, *Blairs Papers*, app. 6. See also Add. 15,390, ff. 415–20. The letters in question refer to the damage done in England by the duchess of Chevreuse, to Richelieu's desire to be assured of a free hand in the attack on Dunkirk, to the hostile attitude of Henrietta Maria toward the French government, and to Richelieu's determination to be revenged for England's abandonment of the Anglo-French alliance by fomenting trouble in Scotland.

44. See the comments of George Radcliffe in Strafford MS 34, two unnumbered folios on the Scottish question. On Dunkirk, see PRO 31/9/92, f. 38 (L. Villerè in Paris to Barberini, 13 August 1638).

45. For example, the diarist Yonge, who recorded in June 1637 that the prince Palatine had interceded for Henry Burton (Yonge, f. 67r).

46. Baker, *Letters of Elizabeth*, p. 98.

47. The negotiation can be traced in SP 81/46 and in Elizabeth's letters. See also *CSPD 1637–38*, pp. 29, 47–48. The Hessian army was highly valued by those who competed for it. In late 1638 Richelieu expressed his willingness to contribute £20,000 to buy it, plus share its upkeep, if Charles I would make an equal commitment. In late 1639 Philip IV was contemplating spending up to £100,000 to win Melander and the army away from the French (L&C, 3:348).

48. Wedgwood, "Elector Palatine," p. 6.

49. *CSPVen 1636–39*, p. 219; *CSPD 1636–37*, pp. 553, 554–55.

50. Charles Lewis had paid the Swedish forces who held the town of Meppen in Westphalia to make it available as a rendezvous; he had raised some troops in Westphalia as well as in England. The sum of £20,000 (recorded in April 1638, PRO, S.O. 3/11), which was disbursed to Sir Richard Cave for the prince Palatine, was apparently intended to enable him to purchase the Hessian army, but was used primarily to purchase Meppen. The best account of the whole 1638 fiasco is in Scott, *Rupert*, pp. 34–41. For contemporary accounts, see Salvetti H, ff. 137, 141, 143; Baker, *Letters of Elizabeth*, p. 100; SP 78/105, f. 73; SP 77/28, ff. 104–5; and SP 81/44, f. 28.

51. Salvetti H, f. 119; Bernard was fighting imperialist forces on the Rhine, in a campaign that would culminate in his capture of Breisach in December 1639.

52. Wedgwood, "Elector Palatine," p. 5. See *CSPD 1637–38*, p. 535; Baker, *Letters of Elizabeth*, p. 100, for General Leslie's offer of service to the prince; see Yonge, f. 71, for a report of Scottish sentiment.

53. The Scottish commander was Sir Thomas Ruthven. See Baker, *Letters of Elizabeth*, pp. 104–5; Bromley, *Original Royal Letters*, p. 100; Salvetti H, ff. 121, 124, 127, 130. There is record in May 1638 of a repayment to Lord Goring of more than £6,000 that he had advanced to the prince (PRO, S.O. 3/11).

54. "Uomo che parla assai e conchiude poco, e non avere altro talento che quello di essere Puritano, e nemico di casa d'Austria" (Salvetti H, f. 140). See also Salvetti H, ff. 142, 145; *CSPD 1637–38*, pp. 7, 29. Salvetti, the Tuscan representative, was generally looked upon as a friend of Spain and of the Jesuits (AAW A.27, p. 121).

55. Add. 4,168, ff. 70–72, 79; see also ff. 116–19 ("Discourse concerning alliances for England"). For the persistent appeal of Protestant union ideas, see Kleinman, "Belated Crusaders," pp. 34–56; and Bowman, *Protestant Interest in Cromwell's Foreign Relations*.

56. See further expressions in Add. 4,169, f. 100; and Add. 4,170, f. 5. Roe saw England at the head of this Protestant league, with Denmark, Sweden, and the United Provinces as the other chief members.

57. Parker, "Dutch Revolt and International Politics," pp. 76–77. In the 1620s and 1630s, Bohemian émigré students were to be found at Emmanuel College, Cambridge (Polišenský, *War and Society*, p. 168).

58. The Transylvanian connection was not entirely ephemeral. Transylvanian Protestants sustained their links with western Europe, Dutch and English influences being particularly strong (Evans, *Habsburg Monarchy*, pp. 266–74). The 1650s saw the realization of a plan long cherished by Comenius, the marriage between the Transylvanian prince, Sigismund Rakoczi, and Frederick V's daughter, the princess Palatine Henrietta (b. 1626); see Rood, *Comenius and the Low Countries*, p. 57.

59. For obvious reasons, the French encouraged this line of polemic—they emphasized the murder of Wallenstein and portrayed it as an example of Spanish-Jesuit intrigue, abetted by the emperor; see Polišenský, *War and Society*, p. 213. This interpretation of the murder had, of course, a foundation in the facts of the power struggles at the imperial court, particularly the roles there of Father Lamormaini and of Oñate; see ibid., pp. 144–45, 150; and Polišenský, *Thirty Years War*, pp. 178, 194–99. The theme passed into English literature with Henry Glapthorne's *Tragedy of Albertus Wallenstein* (1639), which played at the Globe as early as 1636. In the printed version, Glapthorne gave the leading action in the murder scene to two Scots and two Irish, mercenary soldiers in Habsburg service.

60. A Bohemian émigré surgeon resident in The Hague, Andreas ab Habernfeld (Ondrej Habervesl), who had a long-standing interest in prophecies relating to the Palatine family, published a work on the fate of Bohemia entitled *Hierosolyma Restituta* (Leiden, 1622). He pursued the theme in *Bellum Bohemicum* (Leiden, 1645), where he depicted the Jesuit-Habsburg coalition that had destroyed Bohemian liberties: "Eadem Jesuitica persuasione falsissime eo audactur, ut in pactum cum Rege Hispaniarum consentiret," and "Nec num videtur malorum ex perverso isto Loyolistico consilio finis: eiusdem Anglia, Scotia, Hibernia Jesuiticis uritur flammis. Neque ipse Pontifici parcitur, ut Sipsius convellatur Maiestatis sedes, pestis ista Ecclesiastica invigilat diligentissimi" (*Bellum*, pp. 185, 187). On Habernfeld, whose intervention in English politics is described in chap. 7 below, see Mout, "Contacts of Comenius with the Netherlands," p. 223; Evans, *Habsburg Monarchy*, p. 395; and Blekastad, *Comenius*, pp. 68, 112, 131, 334, 337, 376.

61. Polišenský, *Anglie*, p. 201, makes the attribution. During his embassy to Constantinople

in the 1620s, Roe had already become convinced of the existence of a far-reaching Jesuit plan for world domination; see Brown, *Itinerant Ambassador*, pp. 156–57.

62. Add. 4,168, ff. 70–72; Add. 4,169, f. 100; Add. 4,170, f. 5; these preoccupations recur frequently in his correspondence, Add. 4,168–70.

63. Weckherlin was involved not only in the business of Protestant northern Europe, but also in some of the negotiations with southern Europe and Catholic powers. His diary includes information about negotiations with France, and he also had some familiarity with the negotiations of Marie de Medici and the duchess of Chevreuse (for the latter, see Trumbull MSS, Miscellaneous Correspondence, vol. 19, no. 133). In February 1640 Vane, the new secretary of state, asked him to hand over papers relating to Spain, Flanders, and Italy (Weckherlin Diary, 10 February 1640).

64. On Camerarius, see Parker, "Dutch Revolt and International Politics"; Schubert, "Pfäl-zische Exilregierung"; and Schubert, *Ludwig Camerarius*.

65. Weckherlin's correspondents can be traced through his diary and letters; in addition to Roe, Camerarius, Dury, Theodore Haak, and the prince Palatine himself, they include René Augier (one of the English embassy secretaries in Paris), Ziegler (with the Palatine household in The Hague), Henry Lehlin in Paris, John Joachim Rusdorf, and Joachim Hübner, a Prussian émigré scholar at Oxford. For Weckherlin's religious orientation to foreign policy, see *HMCD*, 6:160; in a letter to Haak in August 1638 (noted in his Diary), Weckherlin referred to "verses against the papists" that he had composed.

66. Trevor-Roper, "Three Foreigners," pp. 237–93.

67. See Rawl. MS C911, f. 472 (Dury to Hartlib, 1638), on the "worldly and spiritual conjunctions" that he and Roe sought; this would be developed in 1639 in Dury's *Motives to Induce the Protestant Princes*. See Batten, *John Dury*, pp. 65–70, for his activities; and *HMC Fourth Report*, pp. 159–62, for additional correspondence. Dury's father had been minister of the Scottish church in Leyden in 1609–17; he himself was minister at Elbing in Prussia, where he came under the influence of Swedish thinkers (Rood, *Comenius and the Low Countries*, pp. 71–73). Dury was encouraged in his negotiations by the Swedish chancellor, who was an advocate of Lutheran-Calvinist amity, and Dury in turn pressed on Oxenstierna the interests of the prince Palatine.

68. See Dury, *A Memorial Concerning Peace Ecclesiastical*, (1641), p. 10, on the papists' subversive activities and propagation of superstition; pp. 10–11, on their cunning attempts to divide and thus overthrow the Protestants. Dury thought one Jesuit strategy was to create divisions among Protestants on "non-essentials," and he was always trying to establish common ground on "fundamentals." Other expositions of Dury's ecumenical and political views appear in Rawl. MS C911, ff. 266–68 and 714–24.

69. Among the other future parliamentary leaders were Bedford, Sir William Waller, and Nathaniel Rich. For support from more conservative figures, such as Elizabeth of Bohemia, Bishop Ussher, and Sir William Boswell, see Turnbull, *Hartlib, Dury and Comenius*, pp. 187, 191.

70. Yonge, f. 66r.

71. On Dury and Hartlib and their continental background, see Webster, "*Macaria*," pp. 147–64, although Webster is most interested in the scientific aspects of their work. Hartlib lived under the protection of the Puritan, St. John.

72. Turnbull, *Hartlib, Dury and Comenius*, p. 342; Webster, *Hartlib and Advancement of Learning*, p. 25.

73. Haak kept in touch with his friend Sir William Boswell, English ambassador at The Hague; he visited England in 1638 as a semiofficial agent of the prince Palatine. On Haak, see Yates, *Rosicrucian Enlightenment*, pp. 176–77; Barnett, *Haak*, pp. 27–32; Webster, *Hartlib and Advancement of Learning*, pp. 31–32; and (for his relations with Boswell and Mersenne) Wood, 4:280. Another popularizer of Comenius's work, a

member of the circle of scholar-friends that included Hartlib, Weckherlin, and Bisterfeld, was Joachim Hübner (d. 1666), who had come to England in 1636 and worked in
Oxford; on Hübner, see Turnbull, "Pansophiae," p. 114; Blekastad, *Comenius*, pp.
249–51; Rood, *Comenius and the Low Countries*, pp. 288–90.

74. Mout, "Contacts of Comenius with the Netherlands," p. 221. The work was not
published until 1648, but Turnbull dates it to 1632 on the basis of the author's preface
(*Hartlib, Dury and Comenius*, p. 441). Some of Comenius's works are known to have
circulated in manuscript in England in the 1630s (ibid., p. 342). On Comenius's
relations with Frederick V, see Rood, *Comenius and the Low Countries*, p. 29.

75. Clouse, "Rebirth of Millenarianism," pp. 42–43. Several of Alsted's works were
published in English in the early 1640s: *The Worlds Proceeding Woes and Succeeding
Joys* (London, 1642); *Beloved City* (London, 1643).

76. On Bisterfeld, Hartlib, and Hungary, see Makkai, "Hungarian Puritans," pp. 20–24;
and Rood, *Comenius and the Low Countries*, p. 44. In 1638, when Sir Thomas Roe was
at Hamburg, and again in 1639–40, Bisterfeld was sent to Hamburg, Paris, and London
to promote an Anglo-Franco-Transylvanian alliance. I am indebted to Professor Keith
Hitchins for a number of references on eastern European members of the Comenian
circle.

77. Makkai, "Hungarian Puritans," pp. 23–24. The Hungarian student who took
Stoughton's work home with him had sworn, with nine of his compatriots in London, a
Covenant-like oath in February 1638 to work for the reform of the Hungarian church.

78. On the symbolism, see Yates, *Rosicrucian Enlightenment*, pp. 158–60; and Reeves,
Influence of Prophecy, p. 361. In 1640, after its author's death, Hartlib published the
book and contributed a foreword (dated November 1639). Stoughton's work was
dedicated to Rakoczi and contained references to Dury and Comenius (*Felicitas*, pp. 33,
34).

79. The following paragraph owes much to the discussion by Christianson in *Reformers
and Babylon*, especially pp. 97–99, 100–102, 116–22, 124–28, 138–43.

80. *Speculum Belli Sacri; Or, the Looking-Glasse of the Holy War* (Amsterdam, 1628) was
dedicated to the king and queen of Bohemia, to King Charles I, and to the English
parliament; *An Appeal to Parliament*, the antiepiscopal tract published later that year,
was dedicated to parliament alone.

81. On Mede, see Clouse, "Rebirth of Millenarianism," pp. 56–65. *Clavis* first appeared in
1627, was reissued in an enlarged edition in 1632, reprinted in 1642, and translated to
English in 1643; *Apostasy of the Latter Times* first appeared in English in 1641.

82. Holland and Jermyn were influential courtiers to whom Roe and Weckherlin could turn
for help and favors; see Smuts, "Puritan Followers of Henrietta Maria," p. 36, and
entries in the Weckherlin Diary for 1637–40.

83. Add. 15,390, ff. 140–41, 224–25, 246–51, 277–79, 410–11, 415–17; Add. 15,391,
ff. 72, 111, 136, 174, 186.

84. See Add. 15,391, ff. 249–50, where Con says, "da questa signora non manco di ricevere
quel lume che è necessario per la perfetta notitia di questo stato," a claim that should
probably be taken with a grain of salt. Norgate was part of Windebank's circle and a
client of the Howards; see *DNB*, s.v. "Edward Norgate"; and Hervey, *Earl of Arundel*,
pp. 215–16.

85. Stoye, *English Travellers Abroad*, p. 432; Salvetti H, f. 134; Add. 15,390, f. 223; Add.
15,391, ff. 222, 241. Richelieu resented Montagu's impassioned defense of the chevalier
de Jars and would not accept him as the queen's messenger to congratulate Louis XIII
on the birth of the Dauphin in 1638.

86. Charles I not only provided the duchess with support after her arrival in London, but

paid for expenses of her retinue on the trip from Portsmouth to London, a total of over £2,000 (PRO, E351/2803).

87. Bonney, *France under Richelieu and Mazarin*, pp. 285–92.

88. On Richelieu's reactions to this group and its activities, see Bigby, *Anglo-French Relations*, p. 21.

89. See Prawdin, *Duchesse de Chevreuse*, pp. 76–85, for her Spanish visit; *CSPD 1638–39*, p. 103, for the pension; Avenel, 5:665, 834–35, 837; and Oman, *Henrietta Maria*, p. 99, for the king's allowance to her of two hundred guineas a week. *CSPVen 1636–39*, p. 446, mentions the loan, but I was not able to substantiate this. SP 77/28, ff. 282–83, 296–97, gives a fairly circumstantial account of a loan to the queen mother that was arranged in May and June 1638, and the Venetian ambassador may have been confusing the two. Mme de Chevreuse continued to receive a pension from Spain, which was increased in early 1640 (L&C, 6:504).

90. Add. 15,391, ff. 162–63, 169, 171, 194–95, 222; PRO 31/3/70, f. 199; HMC *Denbigh*, 5:55, 57, for Spanish hopes from her visit; and *CSPVen 1636–39*, p. 464.

91. Negotiations were also carried on intermittently in Venice, where Basil Feilding, a member of the Villiers clan, negotiated with the conde de Roca and other Spanish and imperial agents (CCSP, 1:177).

92. The princess of Phalzburg (Henriette de Lorraine, sister of Duke Charles IV) was married to the illegitimate son of the cardinal of Lorraine.

93. The first letter from Phalzburg to Charles I was apparently in April 1636 (CCSP, 1:94). The negotiation is discussed in *CSPVen 1636–39*, p. 290; Baker, *Letters of Elizabeth*, pp. 109, 113; SP 81/46, ff. 84–85; Salvetti H, f. 219. The progress of the negotiation can be followed through CCSP, vol. 1, and in L&C, 3:233–71 and following pages. Weckherlin translated the Cárdenas letter to Casteñada for the king in late October (Weckherlin Diary, 22 October 1638).

94. See Avenel, 6:3–4; 7:183, 184; 8:122.

95. Oman, *Henrietta Maria*, pp. 96–97, 99.

96. The *tabouret* issue is discussed at length in HMCD, 6:143–45, 148.

97. On Montagu, see Add. 15,391, f. 241. For the French belief that Mme de Chevreuse was corresponding with friends in France under the cover of Father Philip, see Avenel, 6:70–71; PRO 31/3/70, f. 199.

98. Prawdin, *Duchesse de Chevreuse*, pp. 88–90.

99. Oman, *Henrietta Maria*, p. 99; PRO 31/10/11, f. 119; Add. 15,391, ff. 197, 212, 252, 313, 343. She used Con's coach to drive to visit the Spanish ambassador.

100. See Prawdin, *Duchesse de Chevreuse*, pp. 88–97; Avenel, 5:887; 6:70–71; 7:191, 208, 211–12, 216–17, 245; and Thibaudeau, *Collections of Alfred Morrison,*, 1:203.

101. Baker, *Letters of Elizabeth*, pp. 107–8, 109; Add. 15,391, ff. 197, 225–26, 259. There are numerous references to efforts to keep the queen mother away in SP 84/154 (Holland). Her chief advisers, Monsigot, Fabbroni, and Le Coigneux, were the object of particular suspicion, but in the end even they were admitted to England (HMCD, 6:151).

102. Laud, *Works*, 7:486. See also Add. 15,391, f. 284; *CSPD 1638–39*, p. 103; and Oman, *Henrietta Maria*, p. 101, for the allowance and the queen's expenditures. The allowance is corroborated in PRO, S.O. 3/11 for October 1638, recording a warrant to the exchequer to issue £2,000 to Sir Roger Palmer (cofferer of the king's household) for the entertainment of the queen mother and her retinue. This was supplemented by a warrant for £100 per day payable to Luca Fabbroni, beginning 4 November 1638 (S.O. 3/12); in December a warrant was given (S.O. 3/12, December) for advances on this pension. In February 1639 over £2,000 additional were disbursed to Denbigh, as

master of the great wardrobe, for "necessaries" and furniture for the queen mother
(S.O. 3/12). Strickland, *Queens of England*, pp. 267–68, says that fifty chambers
were reserved for her use.

103. *HMC Denbigh*, 5:148–50; for De La Serre's account of the fireworks on her entry, see
Hodgkin, *Rariora*, vol. 2.

104. Oman, *Henrietta Maria*, p. 100. The queen mother was surrounded, as she was until
the end of her life, by spies and agents of Richelieu and also by agents of the Dutch and
other interested parties (L&C, 3:200–201; Joachimi, ff. 14–19).

105. Add. 15,391, f. 304.

106. Her chapel was in what is now Marlborough House; it contained an organ (Little,
Catholic Churches, p. 21; Hodgetts, "Liturgical Music," pp. 151–52). Her Jesuit
confessor was John Suffren, S.J., a native of France and former confessor and preacher
to Louis XIII; see Foley, 7 (pt. 2): 748; and Prat, *Compagnie de Jésus*, 3:444ff., 739ff.
His preaching was mentioned a number of times by Con (BL 8643, ff. 206, 218; BL
8644, f. 114).

107. Oman, *Henrietta Maria*, p. 100; PRO 31/9/140, ff. 15–19. The letters of her representative in Rome are in PRO 31/9/136. She was particularly active on behalf of the
family of her Florentine adviser, Luca Fabbroni degli Asini; see, for example, Add.
15,391, ff. 23, 110, 114, 153.

108. See Add. 15,391, ff. 153, 203, 293, for his initial reaction; cf. Add. 15,391, ff. 301–2,
304, 319, 321; and Add. 15,392, ff. 223–24.

109. Salvetti H, f. 61: "il timore dei Puritani, che la sua presenza non potesse fare qualche
alterazione in materia di religione." On Jermyn's negotiation, see Add. 15,392, ff. 55,
88, 112, 120. An interesting twist on these apprehensions is provided by the report
from one Englishman in Flanders, before the queen mother went to England, that the
agents of Richelieu who surrounded her were likely to be employed by the French
minister to "incite" the Puritans and the Scots (SP 77/28, ff. 488–90).

110. Charles, duke of La Vieuville, former chief minister of France, was in England during
part of the 1630s (Salvetti H, f. 220; Add. 15,391, f. 88). For further details, see also
Clarke, *Huguenot Warrior*, p. 115. His eldest son, Vincent, died at Newbury in 1643,
where he served with the royalist army.

On La Vallette's arrival, see Add. 15,391, ff. 285, 303, 320, 341–42; it was
apparently Mme de Chevreuse who got permission for him to stay in England
(*HMCD*, 6:151). Bernard de Nogaret, duke of La Vallette, had been lieutenant-general
of Condé's army against Spain in 1638; blamed for the defeat at Fuentarrabia, he fled
to England (Avenel, 6:184n, 194). Add. 19,272, ff. 75–76, is a copy of his justification, dated 3 December 1638. In early 1639, La Vallette was assuring the Spanish that
he could deliver Metz into their hands, and there was a detailed correspondence on
this subject between Cárdenas and the Cardinal Infante (L&C, 6:490). For the further
activities of La Vieuville, La Vallette, and other French malcontents (Soissons, Vendôme, Soubise), see chap. 7.

111. Joannes Stella's *Bewailing of the Peace of Germany* (London, 1637) was a French-
sponsored publication against the Peace of Prague. Less substantial items published in
London in 1638 included Philip Vincent, *Lamentation of Germany . . . illustrated by
pictures*; *Lacrymae Germanae: or the tears of Germany*; *Invasions of Germany . . .
since 1618*; and *The Warnings of Germany*.

112. See Chap. 7.

Chapter 5

1. This propaganda was getting to the English countryside by October 1637, as can be seen from Yonge, f. 67.
2. The propaganda campaign has been studied by Vincent Hammond in an unpublished article, "Scottish Propaganda and the Origin of the English Civil War."
3. Add. 15,391, ff. 27, 47–48, 94–95, 110, 113, 181, 204–5, 274–75, 288–89.
4. I have attempted to explore these attitudes in an unpublished talk on "The Scottish Crisis Explained? Charles I, the Covenanters, and Belief in Plots."
5. See chap. 4 for the background to this.
6. The following paragraphs derive from a longer treatment in Hibbard, "Popish Plot," chap. 5.
7. By the late 1620s, Jesuits could be found serving as chaplains in the great Catholic households. The order also controlled the Scots colleges in Rome, Douai, and Madrid.
8. Salvetti H, f. 254; Mathew, *Scotland under Charles I*, p. 220.
9. Douglas, *Peerage of Scotland*, 1:4; Mathew, *Scotland under Charles I*, pp. 105, 211–12, 251, 259, 264. The marquis of Hamilton was the clan senior; Con said of him, "in sostanza, crede poco" (Add. 15,391, f. 455).
10. *DNB*, s.v. "George Seton, 3rd earl of Winton"; Mathew, *Scotland under Charles I*, pp. 113–16, 216–19, 267–68.
11. *DNB*, s.v. "Hugh Semple"; Anson, *Catholic Church*, pp. 155–56; Hay, *Blairs Papers*, p. 165.
12. Fraser, *Carlaverock*, 1:325–60; Bellesheim, *Catholic Church of Scotland*, 4:24–25; on Herries, see Mathew, *Scotland under Charles I*, pp. 211–14.
13. *CSPD 1639*, pp. 53–54. See appendix below.
14. Burrell, "Covenant Idea" and "Apocalyptic Vision."
15. Donaldson, *Scotland*, pp. 173–79, 315; Burrell, "Kirk, Crown, and Covenant," chap. 8, especially pp. 240–45, on this episode.
16. Dugdale, *Short View*, pp. 41, 45; Burnet, *History of My Own Time*, 1:29–38; Menteith, *History of the Troubles*, pp. 1–17; L'Estrange, *Reign of King Charles*, p. 135; Donaldson, *Scotland*, pp. 305–9.
17. Add. 15,390, f. 503; 15,391, ff. 7, 63, 180, 222–23; *CSPVen 1636–39*, p. 273. The proclamations were on 7 December 1637, 19 February 1638, and 28 June 1638 (Gardiner, *History of England*, 8:326–27).
18. Hardwicke, *Miscellaneous State Papers*, 2:99.
19. Joachimi, f. 4 (5 January 1639), to the effect that he hears no Catholics will be allowed to live in Scotland. See also BL 8641, f. 63, on Scottish "torment" of Catholics; Leith, *Memoirs of Scottish Catholics*, 1:189–90, 205–6; Anson, *Catholic Church*, pp. 48–52.
20. Add. 15,390, f. 368.
21. In September 1638 there were still complaints that the king was keeping councillors in the dark about his preparations (Lambeth MS 943, ff. 687–88).
22. The following three paragraphs depend on the weekly reports of Con to Rome in 1637 and 1638; specific references to Add. 15,390, ff. 113–14, 432–36, 442–43, 457, 462, 478, 498; Add. 15,391, ff. 1, 21, 26, 35, 77, 84, 113, 128, 144, 164–65, 171–72, 181, 187, 190–94, 196, 214–15, 222–23, 237, 239–40, 265, 288–89, 294–95; PRO 30/10/11, f. 177.
23. Add. 15,390, f. 454; Huxley, *Porter*, p. 236; Rubinstein, *Captain Luckless*, chap. 4.
24. Add. 15,391, f. 164.
25. Add. 15,391, ff. 164–65, 192–93, 222–23, 239–40, 244–46, 294–95.
26. Baillie, 1:65, 70, 71, 80.

27. *DNB*, s.v. "George Gordon, 2nd marquis of Huntley"; Mathew, *Scotland Under Charles I*, chap. 14. George Gordon was not Catholic; like Lennox, he and his son and heir were the only conformists in families of Catholics (see Hibbard, "Popish Plot," pp. 514–16).

28. Add. 15,391, ff. 128, 149, 214–15, 220–21; Baillie, 1:65.

29. Add. 15,391, ff. 203–4; Baillie, 1:71.

30. Add. 15,391, ff. 220–21, 244–46, 260, 274–75, 295; Knowler, 2:233–38.

31. *DNB*, s.v. "Randal McDonnell, 2nd earl and 1st marquis of Antrim"; Hibbard, "Popish Plot," pp. 527–29; Add. 15,390, f. 210; 15,391, f. 31; Clarke, "Antrim and the First Bishops' War." The McDonnells supported the Franciscan mission, which was militant and pro-Spanish; see Mathew, *Scotland Under Charles I*, pp. 193–96; Kearney, "Ecclesiastical Politics."

32. For Hamilton's support, see Gardiner, *Hamilton Papers*, pp. 12–13; *CSPD 1637–38*, pp. 524–25; *HMC Hamilton Supplement*, 2:50; and Strafford MS 10b, ff. 63–69. Hamilton and Antrim were already associated in an Irish land project; see Percival-Maxwell, *Scottish Immigration to Ulster*, p. 530; Laud, *Works*, 8:484.

33. Knowler, 2:184, 187, 210, 220–21, 225–26, 233, 246–47.

34. Clar. MS 16, ff. 78–81; SP 94/41, ff. 68–69, 93–94, 97–98, 110–11; *CSP*, 2:29–30; Knowler, 2:204, 207, 212, 248, 262–63; Laud, *Works*, 7:483; Add. 15,391, f. 215; *CSPD 1638–39*, p. 4. Alcalá-Zamora, *España, Flandes*, p. 410, gives details of Tyrone's proposal to the Spanish government for landing between 4,000 and 5,000 troops in Ireland, with arms for many thousands more, to liberate Ireland from English control.

35. Whitelocke, *Memorials*, 2:131.

36. Knowler, 2:181–86; Add. 15,390, ff. 191, 206, 317–18.

37. *Hist. Reb.*, 1:150; Add. 15,391, f. 381.

38. Salvetti H, ff. 165, 166, 168; Baillie, 1:72–73, 93; *CSPD 1637–38*, p. 584. Bossy, *Catholic Community*, p. 96, sees Howard of Naworth as an outsider with little influence locally. On the lieutenancies of Arundel and his son, Lord Maltravers, see Sainty, *Lieutenants of Counties*, pp. 15–16. Rumors of employment of papists in the king's forces began to circulate. Newburgh wrote Middlesex of his concern to hear that "a papist bred at Brussels, called Sergeant Major Shaw, [is] made choice of for the keeping of Berwick"; in the event, the earl of Lindsey was given this position. Shaw was one of Colonel Gage's subordinates (*HMC Fourth Report*, p. 293; *CSPD 1639*, pp. 6, 7).

39. Gardiner, *Hamilton Papers*, p. 62; Knowler, 2:186, 214; *HMCD*, 6:159; Laud, *Works*, 7:505; Add. 15,391, ff. 317–18. Vane's ascendancy in the autumn of 1638 is remarked by one of Middlesex's correspondents: "already lorded by report, made governor of Berwick, and president of York" (Nicholas Herman to Middlesex, 17 September 1638, in Kent Archives Office, Cranfield Papers).

40. Add. 15,392, f. 40.

41. Add. 15,391, f. 290; PRO 31/9/18, f. 58 ("espunger et abbatter"); Baillie, 1:216. The Scottish propaganda pamphlet was entitled *Information to all Good Christians in England* and was put out on 14 February 1639; see Rushworth, 7:798–800.

42. *CSPD 1638–39*, p. 440; see Gardiner, *History of England*, 8:382–89. Mark C. Fissel is preparing a study of the mobilization for the Bishops' Wars.

43. See Schwarz, "Aristocratic Protest," for a general picture of the unrest during the campaign.

44. This can be seen in the Norfolk county military organization, which he largely controlled and which had not been "purified" of its Catholic elements; see Bodl., Tanner MS 177, ff. 14–25; *HMC Various Collections*, 2:251–54; and Ketton-Cremer, *Norfolk in the Civil War*, pp. 22, 32–33, 48–50, 109–16.

45. Bradshaigh was used to organize the militia of Lincolnshire and Nottinghamshire and was a captain in Arundel's force; Trafford was commissioned to raise a body of six hundred "dragoons" from the tenants of the border magnates and later took command of the garrison at Carlisle. More information about these and other officers in the 1639 force can be found in Hibbard, "Popish Plot," pp. 224–29. On Widdrington's misfortune, see chap. 6.

46. The list of officers can be found in BM, Microfilm Deposit 285 (Duke of Northumberland, Alnwick MSS, vol. 14, ff. 292–97).

47. Add. 15,392, ff. 20–21, 81, 152–53. A list of the peers' replies received by 28 February is in Rushworth, 2:791–92.

48. Add. 15,392, f. 188; *CSPD 1639*, p. 210; Huxley, *Porter*, pp. 195–96.

49. I have made a more detailed study of the Catholic contribution in "Court and Country Catholicism: The Contribution of 1639," *Recusant History* 18 (May 1982): 42–60.

50. On this matter, see chap. 2.

51. Add. 15,391, f. 340; 15,392, f. 4; Salvetti H, f. 222; *CSPVen 1636–39*, p. 477. For the nonjurors, see chap. 3.

52. Add. 15,391, f. 345. The letter was apparently composed in late November; a copy in the hand of George Gage is in Clar. MS 15, ff. 54–55, endorsed by Windebank and dated 12 December 1638.

53. Add. 15,392, ff. 18–19, 20, 25, 55–56, 57–59.

54. There appears to have been some tension between Con and the Jesuit Provincial More over the contribution; see Epist. Gen. Anglia I (2), ff. 488–90.

55. Add. 15,392, ff. 67–68; PRO 31/9/124, f. 233; Towneley MSS 737/33, 737/2. The letter is reproduced in the 1641 pamphlet, *A Coppy of the Letter*, pp. 3–4.

56. Add. 15,392, ff. 61, 75, 81–82, 86; *CSPVen 1636–39*, pp. 5–6; *CSP*, 2:35.

57. Add. 15,392, ff. 104, 113–14. A copy of the joint letter is in ibid., ff. 97–99; it was printed in *A Coppy of the Letter*, pp. 5–6, as was the queen's letter (pp. 1–2). See Salvetti H, ff. 279–80.

58. Towneley MS 737/33; Add. 15,392, f. 120. Copies of the "Advices" paper can be found in various collections, such as the Towneley MS 737/6, 7, and BM, Sloane MS 1470.

59. *CSPD 1639*, pp. 3–4. See also Salvetti H, ff. 263, 265, 271; *CSPD 1638–39*, p. 673; and Towneley MS 737/34.

60. See study cited in n. 49 above.

61. Baillie, 1:81.

62. Alcalá-Zamora, *España, Flandes*, pp. 402–15, describes the position of Spain in late 1638 and early 1639.

63. Clar. MS 14, ff. 90–91; L&C, 3:256, 263, 267.

64. On the Gage family, see Revill and Steer, "George Gage I and George Gage II," and Hibbard, "Popish Plot," pp. 509–14. Colonel Sir Henry Gage had close Jesuit associations; Henry Morse, S.J., and Peter Wright, S.J., served with his troops in Flanders in the 1630s and returned with him to the king's army in the 1640s (Foley, 1:184–85, 589–90, 654).

65. *CSP*, 2:19–20, 21–22. The suggested intermediary with the pope seems to have been the secular priest Henry Holden. The idea behind the exchange of soldiers was that alien soldiers could be used more effectively in one's own territories, a maxim often cited by Olivares.

66. Clar. MS 15, ff. 121–22; *CSP*, 2:28; SP 77/29, f. 190. The shrine was three miles from Scorpen Heuvel (Fr: Montaigu); see Hardman, *English Carmelites*, p. 63. The pretext of the trip seems to have been widely accepted; see Salvetti H, ff. 245–46. A similar mission was undertaken later that year by the queen's Capuchin superior, who took an

ex-voto gift to the shrine of Loreto and was said to be going on to Rome (*CSP Ven 1636–39*, pp. 506–7; Chaney, "Ex-voto of Queen Henrietta Maria," pp. 837–38).

67. Knowler, 2:267, 276. On Gerbier, see Notestein, *Four Worthies*; he was very much disliked by the Brussels authorities. There is no hint of the negotiations in Gerbier's own papers (SP 105) or in SP 77/28, 29 (Flanders).

68. *CSP*, 2:21–22; L&C, 3:292–93.

69. *CSP*, 2:23–24. On the Hamilton force, see Clar. MS 15, ff. 121–22, and *CSP*, 2:29–30. The delay in getting it started suggests a change of plans connected with the failure to get Flemish soldiers (*CSP*, 2:50–52). Rodrigo Pachaco Ossorio, marquis of Ceralbo, was gentleman of the chamber to Philip IV, member of his council of war, and ambassador to Germany and the northern princes. He was serving in Flanders in 1638 and 1639.

70. See Elliott, "Statecraft of Olivares."

71. Alcalá-Zamora, *España, Flandes*, pp. 411–15. From April 1639 on, efforts by Spanish agents in London were bent on getting English guarantees of safety in the Channel; see ibid., pp. 417–22; and chap. 7 below.

72. *CCSP*, 1:168; Salvetti H, f. 248; *CSP Ven 1636–39*, p. 501.

73. Clar. MS 15, ff. 171–72, 173–74, 177–78; L&C, 3:297; *CSP*, 2:26–28. Piccolomini was already in correspondence with Arundel.

74. *CSP*, 2:29–30.

75. Add. 15,391, f. 335; 15,392, ff. 11, 34; Salvetti H, f. 105.

76. She was unofficially entrusted with much responsibility by the king during his absences in 1639 and 1640. There are evidences of vague public fears of a coup d'etat connected with this. A "Libell from Ware" in 1639 expressed the fear that in the king's absence England would be overthrown by the "bringers-in of idolatry" (*CSPD 1638–39*, pp. 632–33). Fear of French attack on the south coast was repeatedly expressed in spring 1639 (*HMC Ninth Report*, app. II, p. 498; *CSP Ven 1636–39*, pp. 486, 501, 510, 525–26, 546). See chap. 7 below.

77. Add. 15,391, ff. 330, 340–41; 15,392, ff. 39–40, 182, 185. In Bodl., Carte MS 63/36–37, there is an account of seditious rumors about the queen's activities that portrayed her as an instigator of the First Bishops' War and as trying to poison the marquis of Hamilton.

78. The case can be followed in Bodl., Bankes MSS 23/17 and 44/46 (Bankes's notes from Hilary Term, 1638–39), from which the preceding quotations are taken; *CSPD 1638–39*, pp. 98, 231, 432, 533; and *CSPD 1639*, p. 70. This was not the very first time that the Jezebel label had been cast at the queen.

Chapter 6

1. *CSP Ven 1636–39*, p. 273.

2. *Large Declaration*, p. 181.

3. Ibid., pp. 3–4.

4. Ibid., pp. 74–75.

5. The version used is that of Bodl., Ashmole MS 1153/46–53. Other manuscript copies exist. It was printed in revised version in 1642 as *Pigges Corantoe, or Newes from the North*.

6. On Abernethie, see Foley, 7:3; Gordon, *Scots Affairs*, 1:44–45 and n. 1; and his own biographical information in *Abjuration*, pp. 44–48. Abernethie was in Rome in May 1633, as seen in a letter to Richard Blount in Epist. Gen. Anglia I (2), f. 371. The

allegation that he had consulted with Con came to the latter's attention but is not in Abernethie's printed works. For Con's disavowal of contact with him, see BL 8643, ff. 140–41; see Add. 15,391, ff. 180, 239–40, 248, 260, 283, for other references.

7. Leith, *Memoirs of Scottish Catholics*, 1:119, 202n1, 203. One account had it that he got a woman pregnant.

8. Baillie, 1:82, 102, 222; Burnet, *Hamilton*, pp. 105–6.

9. *Abjuration*, pp. 16–17, 39–41; the work was reprinted in July 1641.

10. The *Information* was written by Alexander Gibson of Durie and other Covenanters; see Ogilvie, "Bishops' Wars," pp. 21–22.

11. Baillie, 1:188–89.

12. Ogilvie, "Bishops' Wars," pp. 24–25. Henderson also drew up a set of "Instructions" on the right of resistance; these were procured in manuscript by John Corbet in Dublin, who printed a rebuttal entitled *The Ungirding of the Scottish Armour.*

13. Laud, *Works*, 3:417.

14. *CSP Ven 1636–39*, p. 52. Laud's secretary Dell was busy investigating "seditious letters" from Scotland in April (*CSPD 1639*, p. 52). Yonge recorded in his diary (f. 73v, June 1639) that Laud was said to be the author of the prayer book and to have written the pope promising reunion with Rome within a year; also that several bishops had papal pensions.

15. Weckherlin said that Douglas had promised the king 6,000 men and Nithsdale 5,000 (Weckherlin Papers, f. 39).

16. Baillie, 1:194.

17. Ibid., 1:196.

18. Ibid., 1:196–97; *CSPD 1639*, p. 3; Add. 11,045, ff. 5–6.

19. *CSPD 1639*, p. 139.

20. Add. 15,392, f. 110; *CSPD 1639*, p. 99. Huntley surrendered Aberdeen to Montrose's superior forces on 29 March.

21. Salvetti H, ff. 263, 277–78.

22. Leith, *Memoirs of Scottish Catholics*, 1:186–89, 193–96, 206–12; Add. 11,045, ff. 50–51.

23. Anstruther, *Vaux*, pp. 432–36; Mathew, *Scotland under Charles I*, pp. 223–26; Loomie, "Gondomar's Selection of English Officers," pp. 575–81; Ferguson, *Scots Brigade*, pp. 429–36; Privy Council of Scotland, *Register*, 5:xxvii–xxviii, 6:xl–xli, lxii–lxiii.

24. Clar. MS 16, ff. 156–57.

25. Baillie, 1:199.

26. Leith, *Memoirs of Scottish Catholics*, 1:190–91.

27. Strafford MS 10, ff. 255–56, 257–58; Strafford MS 10b, ff. 19, 63–69; Clarke, "Antrim and the First Bishops' War," pp. 11–12. On Owen O'Neill, see Coonan, *Irish Catholic Confederacy*, pp. 91–94.

28. Baillie, 1:206. Sir Donald Gorum would be Sir Donnell Gore McDonnell, according to Wentworth a prime instigator of the project; see Strafford MS 10b, ff. 109–11. For the links between Antrim's group and the western clansmen, see Stevenson, "Franciscan Mission and Irish Rebellion."

29. Strafford MS 10, ff. 291–92, 329, 335–37; Strafford MS 10b, ff. 109–11; *CSP*, 2:40; *HMC Twelfth Report*, app. IV (Rutland MSS, vol. 1), p. 509; Knowler, 2:358–59; Add. 15,392, ff. 126, 161–62. Reade is identified as a relative ("parente") of Con in BL 8655, ff. 43–44; for further information, see Hibbard, "Popish Plot," pp. 542–43; and chap. 8 below.

30. Add. 15,392, ff. 13, 84, 100, 112, 135–40. It is possible that some of the army leaders

already knew of the plan for an army oath, because Con had discussed it in their presence in January.

31. The English Jesuits' consultation with Spain, and Rome's condemnation of this initiative and of the new oath itself, can be traced in Epist. Gen. Anglia I (2), f. 499; BL 8644, ff. 289, 291; and Clancy, "Jesuits and Independents," p. 75.

32. Knowler, 2:88, 318–19; CSPD 1639, pp. 38, 150, 221–22; HMC Eleventh Report, app. VI, p. 102; HMCD, 6:164.

33. HMC Twelfth Report, app. IV, p. 508.

34. Bruce, Verney Papers, pp. 228–29.

35. Accounts of the oath giving are in HMC Twelfth Report, app. IV, pp. 507–9; CSP, 2:99n3, 154; Lismore Papers, ser. 2, vol. 4, pp. 20–22; HMC Buccleuch, 3:386; Warner, Epistolary Curiosities, ser. 1, vol. 2, p. 195; Add. 11,043, ff. 95–96. The oath was never extended to the rest of the army.

36. CSPVen 1636–39, p. 538; CSPD 1639, p. 104. Hartlib's correspondence network, including as it did members of the Providence Island Company, may have brought him under suspicion. See chap. 4, n. 71.

37. Text of the army oath in HMC Twelfth Report, app. IV, p. 508, and elsewhere; the 1606 oath is in Kenyon, Stuart Constitution, pp. 458–59. The army oath differed from the oath offered to the Scots in England (CSPD 1639, pp. 323–24) and from that offered to the Scots in Ireland at the time (Rushworth, 8:494). Con referred to these other oaths as being for "Puritans," in contrast to the army oath (Add. 15,392, ff. 174, 201, 221). Late in 1639, an oath of allegiance (a much shortened version of the 1606 oath) was imposed on the Catholic colonists of Maryland; it contained the same reference to Charles as "lawful and rightful king," but did not mention equivocation or renounce the possibility of absolution from the oath. Like the army oath, it avoided the contentious terms of the 1606 oath; for the text of the Maryland oath, see Hughes, Society of Jesus, Text, 1:451.

38. The offending phrase was altered to "the utmost of my power and hazard of my life"; see PRO 31/3/71, f. 64. See Knowler, 2:351–52 and CSPVen 1636–39, p. 539, for reactions of the peers.

39. The interrogation of the peers Saye and Sele and Brooke is detailed in HMC Fourth Report, p. 23; and Harl. MS 1219, ff. 1–2. For details on this incident, see Schwartz, "Aristocratic Protest." One question raised was the authority of the king to order the militia out of their own counties into a general force. Schwarz does not deal with the religious context of the oath. In a letter of 19 April addressed to the earl of Essex, the Covenanters had specifically asked for the opportunity to present their case to an English parliament (CSPD 1639, pp. 98–99).

40. This point was not lost on contemporary observers. Yonge in his diary reported the peers' refusal of the oath and made reference to the oaths of allegiance and supremacy (Yonge, f. 72v). It was true, however, that many Catholics took the oath of allegiance.

41. Bruce, Verney Papers, pp. 232–33; HMCD, 6:164.

42. HMC Twelfth Report, app. IV, pp. 507–8, 511; CSPD 1639, pp. 248–49; Warner, Epistolary Curiosities, ser. I, vol. 2, p. 199. For a detailed account of the expedition, see Stevenson, Scottish Revolution, chap. 4.

43. Rushworth, 2:938. See also Firth, Cromwell's Army, p. 64.

44. Add. 15,392, ff. 162–63.

45. Champney's letter to the secular clergy is in Towneley MS 737/33.

46. Henrietta Maria, A Coppy of the Letter (1641) includes these documents on pp. 3–4, 5–6. Lists of the collectors are given in A Coppy of the Letter, pp. 7–10, and in Rushworth, 2:824–26.

47. The documents are at the John Rylands Library, Manchester, English MSS 736 and 737 (Towneley of Towneley MSS). See chap. 5, n. 49.
48. Towneley MS 737/11.
49. Add. 11,045, ff. 5–6; Salvetti H, f. 284; *CSPD 1639*, p. 74.
50. Add. 15,392, ff. 144, 151; *CSPVen, 1636–39*, p. 535.
51. PRO 31/9/124, f. 241; Add. 15,392, f. 153; *CSP*, 2:46–47. On Brooke, see chap. 8.
52. Add. 15,392, ff. 169, 174, 183–84, 189, 192, 202; Towneley MS 737/23, 27, 29, 47; *CSPVen 1636–39*, p. 545. The total sum is given in Anstruther, *Hundred Homeless Years*, p. 172.
53. PRO, S.O. 3/12 (January 1639) for Pulford's commission. On Pulford and his associates, Henry Stanley and Philip Darrell, see Aylmer, *King's Servants*, p. 139; *CSPD 1636–37*, p. 81; *CSPD 1637–38*, p. 11; *CSPD 1638–39*, pp. 171, 335; *CSPD 1639*, p. 481.
54. "I do hear, the queen hath prevailed with the three courts of justice . . . to suspend all proceedings against recusants" (Rossingham, 23 May 1639, in Add. 11,045, ff. 20–22). See also Add. 15,392, ff. 63–64, 69, 75; Clar. MS 18, f. 7v; *CSP*, 2:38.
55. See chap. 8. For the battle between Pulford and Windebank, see *CSPD 1639*, pp. 387–88, 427–28; *CSPD 1639–40*, p. 2; *CSPD 1640–41*, pp. 518–20; *CSP*, 2:46–47, 68, 69.
56. Add. 15,392, ff. 89–90.
57. Add. 15,392, ff. 1–3, 68; Towneley MS 737/38. For the forged brief, see PRO 31/9/124, f. 342; Baillie, 1:99. There are numerous copies in contemporary manuscripts. It is printed in Rushworth, 2:821.
58. SP 77/29, ff. 190–93; SP 94/41, ff. 70–71, 97–98; *CSP*, 2:31–32; CCSP, 1:173; L&C, 3:305. See chap. 5, pp. 104–8 above for the earlier stages of this negotiation.
59. *CSPVen 1636–39*, p. 545. This may very likely have been Captain John Reade or Sir Henry Bruce, who were sent to Ireland to assist Antrim; it seems to have been intended that the Spanish request for mercenaries should be met by Irish levies. Con referred (Add. 15,392, ff. 161–62) to a "Scottish Jesuit" from Flanders, offering 3,000 soldiers to the king, and asking for Bruce's speedy return to Flanders; this may be John Seton, S.J., who was in England in April 1637 on a recruiting trip to Scotland (Add. 15,390, f. 224).
60. SP 94/41, ff. 101–3; L&C 3:312, 321, 325; *CSPVen 1636–39*, pp. 552–53, 554–55, 560.
61. See, for example, seditious speeches described in Bodl., Bankes MSS, for expressions of pro-Scottish sentiments, especially those of John Fox of Rothwell, Northamptonshire (Bankes MS 42/78; *CSPD 1639*, p. 69), and Robert Wardner (Bankes MS 18/8, 9, 10).
62. Collins, *Sydney Papers*, 2:596–97; the letter printed on pp. 599–600 identifies Thomas Chambers as the suspected agent. Chambers was in England from March to June 1639; see Avenel, 8:135–36.
63. *Letters of Lady Brilliana Harley*, p. 131. The allusion to a converted papist may well refer to Abernethie.
64. *A Sermon Preached in the Cathedral Church of Durham 1639 5 May. Before the King* (London, 1639); Weckherlin Diary, entry under Sunday, 5 May 1639.
65. *CSPVen 1636–39*, pp. 536–38, 543–44.
66. *HMC Fourteenth Report*, app. II, p. 57; this may relate to the king's hopes for bringing Irish troops to Carlisle and Lancashire troops to reinforce the northern army.
67. Reprinted by Prynne in *Hidden Works of Darkness*, p. 196.
68. *CSPD 1639–40*, p. 246. This was popular enough to be reprinted in 1640; see *CSPD 1640–41*, p. 126.

69. The pamphlet was printed for William Sheares in London in 1642; references come from pp. 9, 14, 21, 22–23, 24, 25, 32, of the printed version. Internal evidence dates the original version to 1639. The *Scout* also speculated on which English courtier would receive a cardinal's cap.

70. *Scottish Scouts' Discoveries*, pp. 28–29. *A Second Discovery by the Northern Scout* (London, 1642) was probably also composed originally in 1639.

71. *CSPD 1639*, pp. 525–26; Glow, "Committee Men," pp. 3–4; Pearl, *London and the Outbreak of the Puritan Revolution*, pp. 108–9, 189–90. Vassall had been imprisoned in 1635 over ship money and was again in custody in July 1640 for his role in organizing a petition to the king from the city of London.

Chapter 7

1. Salvetti H, f. 362; Salvetti I, f. 18; PRO 31/9/18, f. 23. Henceforth, Thomas Wentworth will be identified as "Strafford," the title granted him at the beginning of 1640 and under which he is most commonly known.

2. The running feud with Holland, centered on the Piers Crosby case in the late 1630s, can be traced in Strafford MS 7.

3. *HMCD*, 6:192, 204, 208, 211.

4. Salvetti H, ff. 342, 369, 405; Collins, *Sydney Papers*, 2:604, 610–615.

5. Baker, *Letters of Elizabeth*, pp. 112–13, 115, 116–17; *HMC Twelfth Report*, app. II, p. 204; Bromley, *Original Royal Letters*, pp. 102–4.

6. SP 81/46, ff. 84–85, 97; Add. 4168, ff. 116–19 (Roe's discourse concerning alliances for England).

7. Baker, *Letters of Elizabeth*, pp. 117, 129, 132, 133; *CSPVen 1636–39*, p. 556. Weckherlin used similar language in reporting the peace, saying that, "in spite of all the papists, priests and other ill-affected persons," England and Scotland had come to an accord (Weckherlin Papers, letter of 19 June 1639 to Trumbull). Leslie had already known Dury's work while a mercenary on the continent. Bruce, *Verney Papers*, p. 251, notes the Scottish offer in June 1639 to send their army to the continent at no charge to the king, on an expedition for recovery of the Palatinate.

8. Baker, *Letters of Elizabeth*, pp. 134–35; *CSPVen 1636–39*, p. 560; Salvetti H, f. 343.

9. Add. 15,392, f. 212; *CSPVen 1636–39*, p. 566; Baker, *Letters of Elizabeth*, pp. 135–36, 137–38, 138–39; SP 81/47, ff. 200–201.

10. PRO 31/3/71, f. 98; *CSPVen 1636–39*, p. 567.

11. Baker, *Letters of Elizabeth*, pp. 139–41, HMCD, 6:205, 222.

12. PRO 31/9/18, ff. 12, 19–20.

13. The French also wanted permission to make substantial levies in England; see PRO 31/3/71, ff. 114–18; *HMCD*, 6:187.

14. Fleming was sent to Switzerland and Curtius to Germany. See PRO 31/3/71, ff. 118–19; Baker, *Letters of Elizabeth*, pp. 140–41, 141–42; Salvetti H, f. 359; *CSPVen 1636–39*, pp. 575, 584, 600. The money, an advance on his yearly pension of £12,000 that had been granted in mid-1637 (*HMCD*, 6:114), was drawn on the tobacco license farmers; see PRO, S.O. 3/12, October 1639.

15. Add. 15,392, f. 184. See Joachimi, ff. 87–93, for the queen's attitude in September. Cf. PRO 31/3/71, ff. 86–87; *CSPVen 1636–39*, p. 576; Salvetti H, ff. 329, 359; Baker, *Letters of Elizabeth*, pp. 124, 127.

16. For Henry Jermyn's high standing with the queen, see *HMCD*, 6:204. Bellièvre's report

on the chief ministers and courtiers, including the remark that Montagu and Jermyn were increasingly at odds, is in PRO 31/3/71, ff. 132, 139, 140–42, 150, 157–58. Cf. *CSPVen 1636–39*, pp. 605–6; *CSPVen 1640–42*, pp. 16–17, 19.

17. *CSP*, 1:82; *CSPVen 1636–39*, p. 596; *HMCD*, 6:225.

18. See *HMCD*, 6:201, 204, for disagreements between Northumberland and Strafford in the autumn of 1639. Collins, *Sydney Papers*, 2:618, 623; Salvetti H, f. 410; Salvetti I, f. 3; *CSPVen 1640–42*, p. 8.

19. *CSPVen 1640–42*, p. 17. See PRO 31/3/71, ff. 401–2, on Vane as a frequent visitor of Le Coigneux in January 1641. Roberts, *Gustavus Adolphus*, 2:609, identifies Vane as a "Spaniard," i.e., an isolationist.

20. *CSPVen 1636–39*, p. 571; *CSPVen 1640–42*, pp. 7, 12, 17–18; Salvetti H, f. 404.

21. See PRO 31/3/71, ff. 108, 139–40, for his contacts with Leslie, Argyll, Rothes, Loudun, and Dumferline. One go-between was a certain Sir Thomas Dishington in Paris, a contact of Buchan (*CCSP*, 1:150). For 1640, see PRO 31/3/72, ff. 26, 48, 55.

22. PRO 31/3/72, ff. 23, 39. Montreuil had been left in charge of the London residence. Weckherlin, for one, was fearful for his job when Coke was dismissed and approached Montreuil.

23. *CSPVen 1636–39*, pp. 605–6.

24. *CSPVen 1640–42*, p. 1; cf. pp. 5, 7, 40–42.

25. Ibid., pp. 7, 13; BL 8647, ff. 78, 129.

26. Joachimi, ff. 26–29, 30–31. Ibid., f. 89, specified Northumberland, Conway, and Goring as among these friends. Cf. Salvetti H, f. 366.

27. Alcalá-Zamora, *España, Flandes*, pp. 418–28, for a detailed account of the objectives of the armada; Wedgwood, *King's Peace*, pp. 299–301, describes the incident.

28. In *CSP*, 1:71–74, Windebank tells Hopton that the king wants £150,000. For the Anglo-Spanish negotiations, see also L&C, 3:336, 339, 342; and CCSP, 1:185–87. Joachimi, ff. 87–93; Salvetti H, f. 361; and PRO 31/3/71, ff. 114, 119–20, indicate the roles and views of other parties.

29. Yonge, f. 74; *CSPVen 1636–39*, p. 574; Add. 11,045, ff. 55–60 (Rossingham's newsletter). There were several pamphlets about the fight, for example, *An Extraordinary Curranto: wherein is related the late sea fight* (London, 1639); Laurence Price, *A New Spanish Tragedy, or, More Strange News from the Narrow Seas* (London, 1639); and *Two Famous Sea-Fights, lately made betwixt the fleets of the King of Spain and of the Hollanders* (1639).

30. *CSPVen 1636–39*, pp. 576–77. Salvetti H, f. 358, reported that "the French party" and the Puritans supported this.

31. *CSPVen 1636–39*, pp. 574, 576, 581; see Nalson, *Impartial Collection*, 1:258–60, on the alleged negotiations between Charles I and Spain on the "means to establish the Catholic religion in Scotland" by a Spanish landing in the Orkney Islands.

32. Spalding, *History of the Troubles*, 1:295–96, said that Strafford was accused by parliament "for being upon the council in bringing in the Spanish armada in defense of the prelates and papists." This reflects the gossip of the time, not the actual parliamentary charge against Strafford.

33. Salvetti H, ff. 377, 381–82; *CSPVen 1636–39*, pp. 595, 601, 603. Francis Aerssons, lord of Sommelsdyck, was the extraordinary ambassador.

34. Salvetti H, ff. 391–92, 408; Salvetti I, ff. 7, 18, 23; *CSPVen 1636–39*, pp. 603–6; *CSPVen 1640–42*, pp. 22, 25; Geyl, "Frederick Henry and Charles I," p. 49. The second ambassador was Jan van der Kerckhoven, lord of Heenvliet.

35. See Salvetti H, f. 108, on the unpopularity among "Puritans" of Hopton's 1638

appointment; Clar. MS 16, f. 110; *CCSP*, 1:194.

36. Clar. MS 17, ff. 100–101, 136–37, 138–39, 199–200. The envoy was Count Leslie, a friend of John Taylor.

37. *CSP*, 1:59–60, 65–66, for the efforts of the exiles and consequent rumors; cf. Clar. MS 17, ff. 8–9, 42–43.

38. The Venetian ambassador expressed surprise in January 1639 that, despite the costs of mobilizing against Scotland, the king continued to pay Marie de Medici's pension of £3,000 per month (*CSPVen 1636–39*, p. 484). See Salvetti H, f. 328; Clar. MS 17, ff. 50, 71, 163–64; *CSP*, 1:61, 71; *CSPVen 1636–39*, p. 566.

39. Baker, *Letters of Elizabeth*, pp. 137–38; and see pp. 125–38 generally.

40. The Nu-Pieds revolt was from July to November 1639, and the most serious phase was in August and September; see Foisil, *La révolte des Nu-Pieds*. On the "great crisis of 1639–40" in France, see Bonney, *France under Richelieu and Mazarin*, p. 218.

41. *CSPVen 1636–39*, p. 557.

42. PRO 31/3/71, ff. 85–86, 93, 95–96, 99; *CSPVen 1636–39*, p. 593; *CSPVen 1640–42*, p. 12; Add. 15,392, f. 192; Bonney, *France under Richelieu and Mazarin*, p. 368 (the Breton estates had tried to have Marie de Medici appointed their governor after 1627).

43. Don Antonio Sancho Dávila y Toledo, marquis of Velada. The embassy is described in detail in Elliott, "Year of the Three Ambassadors," pp. 165–81. An agent for Lorraine, the marquis of Villa accompanied the Spanish ambassadors to arrange recruitment and other assistance for the duke of Lorraine (*CSPVen 1640–42*, pp. 28, 34–35).

44. Salvetti H, ff. 353, 366, 372, 385; Salvetti I, ff. 13, 18; Clar. MS 17, ff. 193–94, for Velada's accreditation letters; *CCSP*, 1:193; *CSPVen 1640–42*, pp. 7, 15, 18, 31–32. On Malvezzi, see Marañón, *Olivares*, p. 144.

45. *CSPVen 1640–42*, p. 18.

46. Louis de Bourbon (1604–41), count of Soissons, brother of Condé.

47. See Reynald, "Le Baron de Lisola," for Lisola's mission, especially pp. 314–15. See also BL 8646, f. 427; BL 8647, ff. 96, 128; *CSPVen 1640–42*, p. 12.

48. According to Rossetti; see BL 8647, ff. 29, 96. The figures of £200 per day (incorrect) for the queen mother and £100 per week (correct) for Chevreuse were noted by Yonge in his diary in April 1640, along with an account of the king's preparations for war with Scotland (Yonge, f. 75v).

49. *CSPVen 1640–42*, pp. 34, 36.

50. PRO 31/3/72, ff. 91–92, 103, 130; *CSPVen 1640–42*, pp. 38–39, 43, 48; Salvetti I, f. 38; *HMCD*, 6:246.

51. Rossetti's faculties are listed in *HMC Ninth Report*, app. II, p. 348; for rumors about him, see Add. 15,392, f. 233.

52. See PRO 31/10/11, f. 117, for an indication that the queen did not speak Italian. For Rossetti's welcome, see Add. 15,392, ff. 232, 235, 247.

53. For Rossetti's contacts at court, see PRO 31/9/18, ff. 10, 18, 20, 28–29, 38–39, 64, 69–70, 77, 90; BL 8646, ff. 346, 412; BL 8647, ff. 27, 64–65.

54. PRO 31/9/18, f. 10; BL 8647, ff. 13, 95–96. His informant on such matters seems to have been Windebank.

55. PRO 31/9/18, ff. 7, 62; BL 8648, f. 101.

56. PRO 31/9/18, ff. 28–29, 40, 50; BL 8646, ff. 270, 271; BL 8647, f. 93.

57. PRO 31/9/18, ff. 59, 78–79; BL 8646, ff. 228–29, 435.

58. Add. 15,392, ff. 224, 239; BL 8646, ff. 356, 427. For Trélon's trip, see Birch, 2:330–31.

59. PRO 31/9/18, f. 70; Epist. Gen. Anglia I (2), ff. 501, 502; BL 8646, ff. 294, 361–62, 435.

60. BL 8646, f. 467. On Bedingfield (1583–1659), see Foley, 7:45. Son of John Bedingfield of Suffolk, he would be Jesuit rector of London from 1639 to 1641, then provincial for England in 1645.

61. Add 15,392, ff. 167, 172, 215.

62. BL 8644, ff. 292, 293; BL 8646, ff. 269, 371, 379, 414. Trollope had been an Appellant, which makes Rome's choice of him peculiar; he had been a member of the chapter since 1623 (Anstruther, 1:363–64). By July 1640, following Rossetti's report that Trollope was very deaf as well as very old, Rome made another shift and decided to nominate "John Ridman" (PRO 31/9/18, f. 286). If this is the Redman of Lancashire, he was even more aged and infirm than Trollope.

63. PRO 31/9/137, f. 27; AAW A.29, no. 91, 96, 103, 104, 105, 109; BL 8646, f. 438 (Fitton living in Montagu's house), and ff. 468, 470; BL 8647, f. 62.

64. BL 8647, f. 42.

65. Add. 15,391, ff. 31, 78.

66. Mathew, *Scotland under Charles I*, pp. 238–39. Of the brothers of James, fourth duke of Lennox, two (Bernard and John) were Protestants, but Ludovick, Henry, and George had all been raised as Catholics in France by their grandmother, Catherine de Balzac (d. 1632), and by their aunt, Henrietta Stuart, countess of Huntley, who had been instrumental in Queen Anne's conversion. See Loomie, "Catholic Consort," p. 305; Mathew, *Scotland under Charles I*, pp. 232–39; *DNB*, s.v. "Lord Bernard Stuart, titular earl of Lichfield"; "Esmé Stuart, first duke of Lennox"; "James Stuart, fourth duke of Lennox"; and "Ludovick Stuart, second duke of Lennox." There is a history of the family by Eileen Cassavetti, *Lion and Lilies*.

67. Add. 15,391, ff. 53, 77, 222, 241, 261, 265.

68. BL 8646, f. 470; BL 8647, ff. 10, 11, 12; Salvetti I, f. 13. For Ward's letters, see PRO 31/9/92, ff. 184–85; for the negotiations, see Albion, *Charles I and Court of Rome*, pp. 317–33.

69. PRO 31/3/72, ff. 19, 23, 87, 97; Add. 15,391, ff. 5–6, 22; Add. 15,392, ff. 14–15; Avenel, 6:705–6.

70. BL 8646, ff. 435–38.

71. *CSP*, 1:133–37, has a paper in favor of Ludovick's candidacy, apparently written by the Benedictine superior, Price. See also Salvetti H, f. 400; Mathew, *Scotland under Charles I*, p. 237.

72. BL 8647, ff. 10, 11.

73. *CSPVen* 1640–42, pp. 16, 52.

74. PRO 31/9/137, ff. 24–26; Albion, *Charles I and Court of Rome*, pp. 320–21.

75. PRO 31/3/72, ff. 19, 23, 72, 96, 194; Add. 15,391, ff. 5–6, 22; Add. 15,392, ff. 14–15; Avenel, 6:705–6.

76. Even when she was made to see that Montagu's candidacy was a hopeless cause, the queen was unwilling to offend him by shifting her support to another candidate; finally, in the latter part of 1641, she backed DuPerron. Rossetti's elevation in 1642 closed this phase of the competition.

77. Reid, *Presbyterian Church in Ireland*, 1:265. This was the *Epistle congratulatorie of Lysimachus Nicanor of the Societie of Jesu to the Covenanters in Scotland* (Dublin, 1640), which made the Puritan-Jesuit comparison. Reid attributes it to John Corbet.

78. Baillie, *Canterburian's Self-Conviction*, pp. 5–6.

79. Heyricke, *Three Sermons* (1641), pp. 55–57, 80, 81–82, 91–97, 103–5, 108–9.

80. Ibid., pp. 117, 127, 131, 138–39, 152, 163–65. Heyricke refers to Davenport's *Deus, Natura, Gratia*.

81. BL 8646, ff. 326–29, 429; BL 8647, f. 63.

82. BL 8646, ff. 346–47; BL 8647, f. 27; PRO 31/9/18, ff. 90, 121.
83. By this term he usually meant those who were not anti-Catholic zealots.
84. BL 8647, ff. 93, 156, 170, 410; PRO 31/9/18, ff. 13, 31, 42, 93.
85. BL 8647, ff. 26–27, 62, 94–95, 126, 149, 170.
86. *CSP*, 2:81. These expressions concerning the king's right to revenue closely resemble those of Strafford, Laud, and Cottington, as recorded in Vane's privy council notes of 5 May 1640 (*CSPD 1640*, pp. 112–13).
87. "De faire tenir un parlement à sa mode, et par ce moyen de se rendre absolu en ce pays" (PRO 31/3/72, f. 154). He goes on to say that some who know and disapprove these plans admit they are very well laid.
88. *CSPVen 1636–39*, p. 605. See also Rossetti in PRO 31/9/18, f. 93; BL 8647, ff. 66, 93, 127.
89. Salvetti I, ff. 11, 21, 30; *CSPVen 1640–42*, pp. 27 ("throwing aside all respect for the ancient laws"), 30; BL 8647, f. 148.
90. Salvetti I, f. 46; PRO 31/3/72, ff. 111–12, 119.
91. Cope, *Short Parliament*, p. 130.
92. Ibid., pp. 138–40, 140–43, 248, 251–53.
93. Ibid., pp. 145–58. For Davenport's *Deus, Natura, Gratia*, see chap. 3 above.
94. Cope, *Short Parliament*, p. 240.
95. Ibid., p. 300; compare (pp. 182–183) the list of grievances presented 28 April with his speech.
96. Ibid., p. 173.
97. Ibid., pp. 150–51; the Harleian version is on pp. 254–60.
98. Ibid., pp. 155–56.
99. Clifton, "Fear of Catholics," pp. 123–24; Clifton, "Popular Fear of Catholics," pp. 24–27.
100. Salvetti I, ff. 47, 58, 62; *CSPVen 1640–42*, p. 47; HMCD, 6:261–62, 267, 272.
101. *CSPVen 1640–42*, p. 47.
102. PRO 31/3/72, f. 103; Salvetti I, ff. 62–63, 67. On Goodman, see Newcome, *Memoir*, app. O; he was converted in 1638 by William Claybrooke (alias John Hanmer), who himself was a former Church of England clergyman, recently converted. See Anstruther, 2, s.v. "Claybrooke"; PRO 31/9/130, ff. 164–68.
103. Salvetti I, f. 79; PRO 31/3/72, ff. 177, 188; AAW A.29, no. 101; *CSPVen 1640–42*, p. 73. It may be at this time that the meetings with Rossetti occurred during which Rossetti claimed to have convinced Laud to go over to Rome.
104. Salvetti I, f. 58; *CSPVen 1640–42*, pp. 91–92; Rushworth, 3:1263; Pearl, *London and the Outbreak of the Puritan Revolution*, p. 108; BL 8647, ff. 235–38.
105. Pastor, *History of Popes*, 29:324.
106. PRO 31/3/72, f. 183; *CSPD 1640*, p. 365 (Weckherlin to Conway).
107. "I Puritani dicono pubblicamente che questo sia stato la causa che ha fatto risolvere il Re di rompere il parlamento" (Salvetti I, f. 53; cf. Yonge, f. 77r).
108. PRO 31/3/72, ff. 130, 163, 182; *CSPVen 1640–42*, p. 47.
109. *CSPVen 1640–42*, p. 52.
110. The complex negotiations for a papal loan can be followed through BL 8646–50, until the outbreak of the Irish Rebellion, when they shifted course.
111. *CSPVen 1640–42*, p. 49.
112. The title continues: *By an Infernal spirit, and the next day conveyed into England upon the Pope's command.* . . .
113. *CSPD 1625–40*, pp. 624–25.
114. Bodl., Bankes MS 18/9, and see also 49/12, 57/5; and *CSPD 1640–41*, pp. 12,

32–33, 181. Henrietta Maria had given birth in 1639 to a daughter who died almost immediately.

115. Salvetti I, ff. 86, 91; PRO 31/3/72, ff. 195, 283; *CSPVen 1640–42*, p. 59.

116. *CSPVen 1640–42*, p. 75; Baillie, 1:200.

117. BL 8647, f. 93. A list of popish officers drawn up in December, when parliament had ordered the army purged of them, indicates perhaps twice as many as in the 1639 army in the upper ranks, but still not a very large number (SP 16/473, no. 52). I am grateful to Conrad Russell for this reference.

118. Yonge, f. 77r; PRO 31/3/72, f. 210; *CSPVen 1640–42*, p. 61.

119. "Nella quale la continuazione della nostra religione anche dipende" (Salvetti I, f. 104).

120. Boynton, *Elizabethan Militia*, pp. 21, 76, 241; Dodd, *Stuart Wales*, chap. 1 and pp. 76–86; Dodd, "Pattern of Politics," pp. 31–39.

121. *CSPD 1637–38*, p. 584; *CSPD 1638–39*, pp. 404, 513–14; *CSPD 1639*, pp. 95–103; *HMC Second Report*, p. 73; Dodd, "Pattern of Politics," pp. 30, 42–47.

122. *Letters of Lady Brilliana Harley*, p. 32; Weckherlin Diary, entries of 1 March, 3 April, 16 April, 29 May, and 19 June 1639.

123. "Principalissima e cattolica grandemente" (Add. 15,390, f. 160).

124. *CSPD 1623–25*, p. 288; Dodd, "Pattern of Politics," p. 41; *CSPD 1639–40*, p. 605. For the Somersets and their network of Catholic relations in the peerage and gentry, see Hibbard, "Popish Plot," pp. 547–50; and *DWB*, s.v. "Somerset family."

125. Sir John Winter, the queen's secretary, was Worcester's nephew; for details on him, see *Hist. Reb.*, 2:479–84; on the Welsh Jesuits, see Hibbard, "Popish Plot," pp. 578–80. Cf. Dodd, *Stuart Wales*, chap. 1; and Dodd, "Flintshire Politics," pp. 31–33.

126. *DWB*, s.v. "Devereux"; "Herbert family, earls of Pembroke"; and "Herbert family, earls of Powis"; Dodd, *Stuart Wales*, pp. 42, 56–57, 60–62, 81–83, and chap. 2 passim; Dodd, "Wales in Parliaments," p. 86; Dodd, "Pattern of Politics," p. 41; Dodd, "Wales and Second Bishops' War," p. 94. See also Snow, *Essex the Rebel*, pp. 194–204; Smith, *Herbert Correspondence*, pp. 2–5, 204.

127. PRO 31/9/92, ff. 310–13; *CSPD 1636–37*, p. 177; Dircks, *Marquis of Worcester*, pp. 22–23.

128. *CSPD 1636–37*, p. 177; *CSPD 1638–39*, pp. 456–57; *HMC Twelfth Report*, app. IX, pp. 8–9; Dodd, "Pattern of Politics," p. 41.

129. Dodd, "Wales and Second Bishops' War"; *Wynn Calendar*, pp. 257–58.

130. Bridgewater's letter to the deputy lieutenants of Herefordshire dated 21 July 1640; see Huntington Library, Ellesmere MSS 7433, 7434. The king's letter to Bridgewater, in *CSPD 1640*, p. 483, specified the counties in question as Pembroke, Carmarthen, Radnor, Hereford, Monmouth, Glamorgan, and Brecon. A letter from the deputies of Pembrokeshire to Bridgewater, referring to Worcester's commission, is in *CSPD 1640*, pp. 599–600.

131. AAW B.47, no. 92; AAW A.29, no. 109. Montagu was in Wales in July 1640, at St. Winifred's Well (AAW A.29, no. 103).

132. First mention was made in November 1639; see *HMCD*, 6:204. See also Clarke, "Breakdown of Authority, 1640–41," pp. 271–74.

133. Hopton mentioned Tyrone, Tyrconnell, William Burke, Domenico del Rosario, O.P., the earls of Antrim and Westmeath, and Viscounts Barry and Roche (Clar. MS 17, ff. 155–56, 181–82; *CSP*, 2:69–70, 70–71). See also Stevenson, "Franciscan Mission and Irish Rebellion."

134. Baillie, 1:257; *CSPVen 1640–42*, pp. 4, 21.

135. Salvetti I, ff. 83 ("o in altro che potesse occorrere"), 114–15; PRO 31/3/72, ff. 142 ("Pense se servir de dix mil Irlandais, autant pour tirer raison de ses sujets

d'Angleterre, comme pour la guerre d'Écosse"), 257; *CSPVen 1640–42*, p. 59.

136. *CSPD 1640*, pp. 602–3; Clar. MS 19, ff. 30, 48, 51.

137. Salvetti I, ff. 103, 107, 108, 109, 110, 116, 126, 129; PRO 31/3/72, f. 231.

138. PRO 31/3/72, ff. 230, 231, 239–40; *CSPVen 1640–42*, p. 62.

139. See chap. 5 above.

140. The documents are reproduced in Rushworth, 3:1310–23, and in Prynne's *Rome's Masterpiece* (1644), as reprinted in Laud, *Works*, 4:465–503. I have generally used Prynne's version, which is somewhat more complete and seemingly more accurate in detail. On Habernfeld, see chap. 3 above.

141. Laud, *Works*, 4:466–68, 472–74.

142. Ibid., 475–77; and Clar. MS 19, f. 20.

143. Laud, *Works*, 4:469–72.

144. Ibid., pp. 480–91 for the "Large Particular Discovery."

145. Ibid., pp. 483–84.

146. Ibid., p. 484.

147. It was alleged that Hamilton's chaplain was in communication with Con; the fact that Con and Hamilton were personally corresponding seems not to have been known. Richelieu's "agent" was the Scottish chaplain, Thomas Chambers, a relative of Con who had traveled to Scotland and England several times in the 1630s.

148. Laud, *Works*, 4:485–86.

149. On Captain John Reade's military activities, see chap. 6 above. Reade was a court Catholic with a London residence and was mentioned by Panzani a number of times in the mid-1630s (Panzani Diary, ff. 86, 137, 148, 149, 152).

150. Laud, *Works*, 4:486–88.

151. Ibid., 469–72, 489–91.

152. Clar. MS 19, f. 60; PRO 31/3/72, f. 77; Mathew, *Mathew*, pp. 86–87.

153. Laud, *Works*, 3:418–19; 4:493n; see *HMCD*, 6:332, for Mathew's arrest. I find no indication of the investigation or of Mathew's arrest in the privy council register for this period.

154. Laud, *Works*, 4:472.

155. John Browne is suggested as the informant in Gardiner, *History of England*, 9:229n1. On Browne, see chap. 9 below.

156. The description of Mathew resembles that given by Fontenay in 1634; see Ranke, *History of England*, 5:448.

157. Downing, *A Sermon Preached to the Renowned Company of the Artillery 1 September 1640*, pp. 2–22. See Zagorin, *Court and Country*, pp. 144–45, 197.

158. D'Ewes (N), pp. 35–36, 537; *CJ*, 2:29. The sheriff of London had been given the book by two Londoners, one of whom claimed to have got it from a cobbler with a recusant wife. The book was said to have been sent from Rotterdam; I was unable to locate the title in the Short Title Catalog, Wing catalog, or BM catalogs of printed books.

159. Salvetti I, f. 103.

160. Guthrie thought it an invention of the queen herself; see *General History*, 3:986. A letter from Boswell to Laud, from The Hague, 12 June 1640 (*Harl. Misc.*, 9:200–201), speaks of papists disguised as Puritans in an antiepiscopal conspiracy and of Romish priests supporting the Scottish Covenant; James Murray and John Naper (Napier?) are named. Boswell suspects a popish plot to alienate foreign Protestants from the Church of England and to leave England isolated and vulnerable to a popish coup.

161. "Fort affectionné au bon parti, ennemi du lieutenant" (PRO 31/3/72, f. 244). See ibid., ff. 193, 225; *CSPVen 1640–42*, pp. 63, 66; *CSPD 1640*, p. 464; Salvetti I, ff. 72,

79; Pearl, *London and the Outbreak of the Puritan Revolution*, pp. 99–103; Brown, *Itinerant Ambassador*, p. 232.

162. *CSPD 1640*, pp. 168–69, 208–9, 270.

163. *CSPVen 1640–42*, pp. 45–46; cf. also ibid., p. 50; Salvetti I, ff. 67, 73 ("il migliore et più potente amico che habbino a questa corte," referring to Strafford); and PRO 31/3/72, ff. 141, 151, 167–71, 221.

164. See PRO 31/3/72, ff. 136–37, 202, and 265, for reports that Elizabeth of Bohemia had urged Charles I to call a parliament. For the disengagement of important courtiers, see *CSPVen 1640–42*, p. 46 ("those interested in the public cause"); PRO 31/3/72, f. 232 (those who are "pour le peuple"); and Salvetti I, ff. 67, 71, ("i Puritani"). Weckherlin's closer relations with Leicester can be traced in *HMCD*, 6:158, 171, 178, 332.

165. All these were members of the committee of eight for Scottish affairs. See PRO 31/3/72, f. 141, where Montreuil earlier mentioned Laud and Juxon instead of Cottington (ibid., ff. 129–30; and cf. *CSP*, 2:83). Laud apparently excused himself; and it seems that Hamilton was a controversial nomination, opposed by the Spanish as too pro-French (Elliott, "Three Ambassadors," pp. 165–81).

166. PRO 31/3/72, f. 218; Salvetti I, f. 98; *CSPVen 1640–42*, pp. 43, 53–54.

167. The agreement is outlined in two printed sources: *CSP*, 2:84–86 (which mentions additional money for England from Spain after the loan is repaid) and L&C, 6:510–11 (25 May 1640). Olivares wrote to Strafford about the agreement in June, and it seems that this is the letter that is referred to as arriving in July in *CSPVen 1640–42*, p. 60. Strafford's answer of 18 July is printed in *HMC Thirteenth Report*, app. I, pp. 3–4, and is endorsed by Pym. See also L&C, 6:498, 512–13, 514, 516–17; Jennings, *Wild Geese*, pp. 35, 318–19.

168. Reynald, "Le Baron de Lisola," p. 316, on the king's anxiety; Salvetti I, ff. 83, 92, 95; PRO 31/3/72, ff. 135, 151, for Montreuil's report in May that a huge sum had been brought by the Spanish envoys. See also PRO 31/3/72, ff. 218, 226; and *CSPVen 1640–42*, pp. 48–66 passim.

169. *CSPVen 1640–42*, p. 87; Salvetti I, f. 115.

170. See, for example, the countess of Carlisle's letter to Leicester on 7 May 1640 in *HMCD*, 6:201–3.

171. *CSPVen 1640–42*, pp. 43, 48; see also *HMC Thirteenth Report*, app. I, pp. 11–12. Sir Richard Forster, Montreuil's informant at the queen's court, claimed detailed knowledge of the negotiations; see PRO 31/3/72, f. 199. Velada reported on English suspicions; see Elliott, "Three Ambassadors," pp. 165–81.

172. PRO 31/3/72, ff. 105, 271–72, 285, 306; Avenel, 6:684 and 8:362n1; *CSPVen 1640–42*, p. 41. The marquis of Villa went with the duchess of Chevreuse; see *CSPVen 1640–42*, p. 42.

173. PRO 31/3/72, ff. 311–17. See Reynald, "Le Baron de Lisola," p. 315, for Lisola's comment that the Spanish felt uneasy about dealing with the Protestant Soubise.

174. PRO 31/3/72, ff. 167–71, 174, 176, 182, 204, 223–24, 241, 244, 257, 267–68; *CSPVen 1640–42*, pp. 61, 66; Reynald, "Le Baron de Lisola," p. 317. Strafford used Cottington and Sir Richard Forster in putting out these feelers to Montreuil.

175. *CSPVen 1640–42*, p. 81; cf. pp. 66, 77–78, 92.

176. "Assez fort pour le peuple" (PRO 31/3/72, ff. 232–33); cf. *CSPVen 1640–42*, pp. 62, 71. Northumberland spoke against the dissolution of the Short Parliament and fell into disfavor with the king. Leicester, who was desperately attempting to get his arrears paid, was still working through anyone at court who might help him; see *HMCD*, 6:258, 261–62, 270–71.

177. PRO 31/3/72, ff. 167–71, 202, 232–33.
178. Add. 4,460, f. 74v. Walter Frost was a secret courier between the English opposition leaders and the Scottish Covenanters in 1639–40; see Aylmer, *State's Servants*, p. 254.
179. PRO 31/3/72, ff. 257–58; *CSP*, 2:94. The petition is in *CSPD 1640*, pp. 639–40. The king was unable to detach Bedford and Essex from this group, and Bedford and Hertford indeed tried to get council backing for their stand (Clar. MS 19, f. 29).
180. Salvetti I, f. 109; *CSPVen 1640–42*, pp. 78–79. The London petition for parliament in September 1640, a copy of which is in *CSPD 1640–41*, p. 94, also complains bitterly of papists in London.
181. Manning, "Aristocracy and Downfall of Charles I," pp. 43–45.
182. *CSPVen 1640–42*, p. 79; Salvetti I, ff. 116, 126. "Così piaccia a Dio di avere in protezione gli interessi de' Cattolici, che non siano separati della causa di Sua Maestà" (Add. 15,392, ff. 314–15); also see similar expressions on ff. 326, 339 (September and November 1640).
183. Salvetti I, ff. 103, 108–9; PRO 31/3/72, f. 293, for their refusal to visit the royal camp while Strafford and the Catholic lords were there.
184. Salvetti I, ff. 58–59, 126, 138; PRO 31/3/72, f. 319. See George Gage's long letter of 6 November 1640 (N.S.), giving an account of the search for arms, which involved the invasion of his own house and of Rossetti's residence next door (PRO 31/9/130, ff. 72–75). The search was apparently on the orders of Vane, not Windebank.
185. *CSPVen 1640–42*, pp. 91–92. The queen mother's agent in Rome, Leonardo Fabbroni, boasted that she had indeed met with the king and some of the lords who had persuaded him to call parliament and had given them advice based on her governing experience in France (BL 8657, ff. 91–92).
186. PRO 31/3/72, ff. 288, 319; Clar. MS 19, f. 60; Salvetti I, f. 136; *CSPVen 1640–42*, pp. 91–92.
187. PRO 31/3/72, ff. 260–61, 265, 295.
188. Ibid., ff. 295 ("homme fort elequent, de grand credit parmi le peuple"), 300–301.
189. *CSPVen 1640–42*, p. 93; *CSPD 1640–41*, p. 53.

Chapter 8

1. Salvetti I, f. 150; *CSPVen 1640–42*, pp. 94–95.
2. *CSPVen 1640–42*, pp. 96–97, 111.
3. *Negotium Posterorum*, 1:69, as cited in White, *Coke and the Grievances of the Commonwealth*, p. 188.
4. Russell, "Religious Unity," p. 220n3.
5. On the order for test communion, see *CJ*, 2:24; D'Ewes (N), p. 18; PRO 31/3/72, f. 325. It was held on 29 November at St. Margaret's; see Wilson, *Pulpit in Parliament*, p. 41.
6. D'Ewes (N), p. 9n59; for the speech as a whole, see ibid., pp. 8–11; and Kenyon, *Stuart Constitution*, pp. 204–5. Fletcher, *Outbreak of the English Civil War*, discusses Pym's strategy in chap. 1.
7. D'Ewes (N), p. 8; and Kenyon, *Stuart Constitution*, p. 203.
8. D'Ewes (N), p. 10+n74; Kenyon, *Stuart Constitution*, p. 205.
9. As Kenyon noticed (*Stuart Constitution*, p. 190).
10. *CSPVen 1640–42*, pp. 100, 102, 118, 137.
11. D'Ewes (N), p. 16; *CJ* 2:24; PRO 31/3/72, f. 325.
12. In 1640 Davenport published his *Apologia Episcoporum* after complicated discussions

with Laud; although printed in Cologne, it quickly became known in England (Dockery, *Davenport*, pp. 96–97). Davenport had been introduced to Laud by one of the latter's chaplains, Augustine Lindsell, as someone who could contribute to the literary defense of the episcopacy (ibid., p. 54).

13. *HMC Ninth Report*, app. II, pp. 351–52; I am grateful to Diane Smith for careful translation of this document. See also Domenicus de Gubernatis, *Orbis Seraphicus*, vol. 2, pt. 1, pp. 712–15; and Giblin, "Aegidius Chaissy."

14. D'Ewes (N), p. 57; Powis, ff. 10, 21.

15. Rushworth, 4:396. In Laud's reply to the charges on 26 February 1641, he specifically mentioned his investigation of the Habernfeld Plot (Rochester, f. 39).

16. Rushworth, 4:493.

17. For more detail about the campaign against Strafford, see Hibbard, "Strafford and the Papists."

18. D'Ewes (N), p. 51n6; *CSPVen 1640–42*, p. 96.

19. PRO 31/3/72, f. 352. In February there would be efforts to get the Catholic lords out of parliament, partly because they were thought to favor Strafford (AAW B.47, no. 96); in mid-March a number of them did leave (Rochester, f. 52r).

20. D'Ewes (N), pp. 24–30; see also the account from Rawlinson MS C956 in ibid., app. 8.

21. D'Ewes (N), pp. 25–26, 532. See Keeler, *Long Parliament*, s.v. "Sir John Clotworthy"; Zagorin, *Court and Country*, p. 199; Keeler, "Opposition Committees," pp. 134, 136. The charges against Radcliffe brought by Pym in December alleged that he had "traitorously confederated with the earl (Strafford) to countenance papists, and build monasteries" (Nalson, *Impartial Collection*, 1:702).

22. D'Ewes (N), pp. 27–28, 532. One of Sir Robert Harley's correspondents in the autumn of 1640 was harping on the theme of Welsh and border papists and their suspicious activities (*HMC Ninth Report*, app. II, pp. 67–69). He particularly mentioned Sir Basil Brooke, whose country home was in Shropshire (*DNB*, s.v. "Sir Basil Brooke").

23. D'Ewes (N), pp. 24–25+nn8, 11. The letter from Rossetti is discussed in BL 8649, ff. 147–51. Rigby, a later regicide, was a personal as well as a political foe of some Lancashire royalists such as Stanley. On Rigby, see *DNB*; Keeler, "Opposition Committees," p. 142; Keeler, *Long Parliament*; Sanford, *Great Rebellion*, p. 481; Hexter, *King Pym*, pp. 20n, 29n, 49; Glow, "Pym and Parliament," p. 395.

24. PRO 31/3/72, f. 325. Sometime before the end of February, Dom David Codner was given a position as chaplain and preacher to the queen mother, which was arranged through Luca Fabbroni as a means of protection for Codner (BL 8619, f. 99).

25. D'Ewes (N), pp. 532–33; *CJ*, 2:26–27; Rushworth, *Tryal of Strafford*, p. 3.

26. D'Ewes (N), pp. 60–62+n8; for Pym's speech on the charges, see *Somers Tracts*, 4:216–17; for the charges themselves, see *LJ*, 4:97.

27. PRO 31/3/72, f. 333; Powis, f. 3r; *CSPVen 1640–42*, p. 95.

28. D'Ewes (N), pp. 53, 55, 73, 328; PRO 31/3/72, f. 340; Salvetti I, f. 149; *CSPVen 1640–42*, p. 100.

29. Bristol Archives Office, Smyth Family Papers, no. 136d (letter of 21 November 1640, from Sir Baynam Throckmorton to Thomas Smyth). Cf. Powis, f. 10; *CSPVen 1640–42*, pp. 100, 108.

30. D'Ewes (N), pp. 78–79; *CJ* 2:39. On Glynne, see Keeler, *Long Parliament*; Keeler, "Opposition Committees," p. 142; Dodd, "Welsh Opposition Leaders," pp. 106–7; Dodd, "Caernarvonshire," pp. 1–3.

31. Powis, f. 13.

32. D'Ewes (N), p. 89.

33. D'Ewes (N), p. 90. Montagu, Digby, and Mathew were again complained of and there

was talk of closing the Capuchin chapel (Salvetti I, f. 150; PRO 31/3/72, f. 341).

34. Salvetti I, f. 157; *CSPVen 1640–42*, p. 103; AAW A.29, no. 116, and B.47, no. 94.

35. Cottington also enjoyed an unusual immunity; Montreuil expected an attack on him in December (PRO 31/3/72, f. 361). There were rumors in April that he would be accused of treason (AAW B.47, no. 103), and he resigned in May (PRO 31/3/72, f. 533).

36. Bankes, *Corfe Castle*, p. 73; *CJ*, 2:44. Denzil Holles was apparently intended for his post, but did not get it.

37. Salvetti I, f. 154; *CSPVen 1640–42*, pp. 96, 98, 105; PRO 31/3/72, f. 352.

38. PRO 31/3/72, ff. 350–52; Salvetti I, f. 160; *CSPVen 1640–42*, p. 105.

39. See PRO 31/3/72, ff. 345–46, for Montagu urging the queen to help save Strafford; for Mathew's retreat, see ibid., f. 341. On 7 December D'Ewes reported Mathew as "gone upon the proclamation" (D'Ewes [N], p. 112). His presence at "Mr. Pleydom's" house in December is noted by one of Sir Robert Harley's correspondents, who refers to him as "the Jesuit papist" and fears he sponsors plots (*HMC Fourteenth Report*, app. II, p. 69). The reference is probably to the Plowden family of Shropshire; mention is made also of Sir Basil Brooke's house and Redcastle, the Montgomeryshire home of the Powis family. For his February escape, see AAW B.47, no. 97.

40. PRO 31/3/72, ff. 387, 447; *CSPVen 1640–42*, pp. 112, 131–32.

41. On the negotiations, see PRO 31/3/72, ff. 300, 385, 475, 509, 519; *CSPVen 1640–42*, pp. 126, 129, 132, 134, 137, 143. For Spanish attitudes, see L&C, 6:530.

42. Spain had tried hard to prevent this marriage; see L&C, 6:526, 528; PRO 31/3/72, f. 475; *CSPVen 1640–42*, pp. 116, 120–22.

43. PRO 31/3/72, ff. 364, 370, 396–98, 437; Salvetti I, ff. 157, 160, 165, 187–88, 201.

44. *CSPVen 1640–42*, pp. 130, 136; Charles Lewis stayed with the earl of Essex during this visit. For his activities, see PRO 31/3/72, ff. 330, 464, 475, 482, 486–87; Salvetti I, ff. 198, 201; *CSPVen 1640–42*, pp. 130, 133, 135, 147.

45. PRO 31/3/72, ff. 494–95, 503–4, 539; Salvetti I, ff. 211–12, 214, 231; *CSPVen 1640–42*, pp. 135, 138, 139, 144.

46. Salvetti I, f. 167; PRO 31/3/72, ff. 370, 378–79; *CSPVen 1640–42*, pp. 103, 108, 113, 124; BL 8649, ff. 184–86.

47. *CSPVen 1640–42*, pp. 111–12. Holland said that Montagu was behind the queen's pressure on the king to save Strafford at all costs (PRO 31/3/72, ff. 368–69).

48. Rossetti had suggested French aid in December. The queen hoped to use Mazarin in France as an intermediary to secure a papal loan; see Add. 15,391, f. 114; Albion, *Charles I and Court of Rome*, p. 361; Gardiner, *History of England*, 9:258–59. I hope to pursue the complicated story of this loan negotiation.

49. PRO 31/3/72, ff. 344, 345, 352, 416, 423–24.

50. Ibid., ff. 332, 338–39, 347, 456.

51. Ibid., ff. 331, 337, 365–71, 379, 387, 414, 435–36.

52. Ibid., ff. 416, 423–25, 449, 464–65.

53. Ibid., ff. 379, 385–87. Powis, f. 39, reports "fear of great armies in France and Spain."

54. *CSPVen 1640–42*, pp. 117–18.

55. *HMC Ninth Report*, app. II, pp. 348–51; I am grateful to Diane Smith for careful translation of this document.

56. *CSPVen 1640–42*, pp. 117–18; Gardiner, *History of England*, 9:134–35, 175, 244, 251–52, 310; Albion, *Charles I and Court of Rome*, p. 361; Add. 15,392, ff. 283–86.

57. Pastor, *History of Popes*, 29:333; Gardiner, *History of England*, 9:258–59.

58. Salvetti I, f. 153; for the parliamentary action, see D'Ewes (N), pp. 58–59, 183–84; *CJ*, 2:40. Crawford's horse troops were particularly mentioned.

59. "Il espéroit revenir avec ces mêmes hommes à la conquête de ce pais" (PRO 31/3/72, ff.

434–35); see also ff. 354–55, 373–74, 380–81, 389, 421, 444–45, 446, 481, 507, 540. In January 1641 Nithsdale was harboring the Franciscan David Tyrius in his London residence (PRO 31/9/92, ff. 94–96).

60. *CSP Ven 1640–42*, p. 140.

61. Ibid., pp. 114, 127; see also Gardiner, *History of England*, 9:310. The first reference to help from Ireland seems to be in a letter of Rossetti, 12 February (O.S.), in BL 8649, ff. 184–86. For this part of the background to the Irish Rebellion, see Clarke, *Old English*, chap. 4; Coonan, *Irish Catholic Confederacy*, chap. 7; and Kearney, *Strafford in Ireland*, pp. 188–89, 204–6.

62. "Ritroverà altri del medesimo ordine refugiati qui per i medesimi rispetti, talché l'Inghilterra è hoggi obligata alla Francia nel mandarli così grandi hospiti" (Salvetti I, f. 189). César de Vendôme was the bastard brother of Louis XIII and brother to the duke of Longueville.

63. Leonardo Fabbroni, her agent at Rome, reported that she was interceding with "Puritan leaders" in parliament on Rossetti's behalf (BL 8657, f. 101).

64. PRO 31/3/72, ff. 392–93, 394–95, 404, 405, 431–32; Salvetti I, ff. 147, 169, 178–79; *CSP Ven 1640–42*, pp. 112, 114.

65. Jacques Nompar de Caumont, duke of La Force (1558–1652), Protestant governor of Béarn and participant in the Soubise rebellion of 1621–22; see Bonney, *France under Richelieu and Mazarin*, p. 385, and Tapié, *France in the Age of Louis XIII and Richelieu*, pp. 381, 391. He did not in fact join the conspiracies at the end of the reign.

66. Louis-Charles-Gaston Nogaret de La Vallette, duke of Candale (1627–58), son of the exiled Bernard, duke of La Vallette, and grandson of the governor of Guyenne; see Bonney, *France under Richelieu and Mazarin*, pp. 289–91, 296.

67. PRO 31/3/72, ff. 347–48, 374–75, 376, 378, 392–93, 394–95, 405, 408–10, 433–34, 450–54; Salvetti I, ff. 181, 191–92; *CSP Ven 1640–42*, pp. 120–21, 134.

68. On Goodman, see Anstruther, vol. 2; Pastor, *History of Popes*, 29:230–31; MCR, 3:73; Dodd, "Wales in Parliaments," p. 71. Weckherlin leaves no doubt of his opinion; in his diary for 22 January 1640, he referred to instructions to write a reprieve for Goodman, "the scurvie priest or Jesuit condemned."

69. PRO 31/3/72, ff. 417–18; D'Ewes (N), pp. 277–78; *CSP Ven 1640–42*, p. 119; Baillie, 2:295; for Pennington, see Pearl, *London and the Outbreak of the Puritan Revolution*, pp. 119, 200–201.

70. D'Ewes (N), pp. 279, 285–87, 289–90, 292, 294, for the debate on Goodman; *CJ*, 2:72–73, 74.

71. AAW A.30, no. 1.

72. D'Ewes (N), pp. 300–301, 320–21+n24, 333; *CJ*, 2:75; for Littleton's speech and the king's reply, see Rushworth, 4:158–60, 166. Goodman died in the Gatehouse in 1645.

73. D'Ewes (N), pp. 289–91, 302; *CJ*, 2:74.

74. D'Ewes (N), p. 291; Gardiner, *History of England*, 9:412. The queen's letter to the county collectors, along with other documents from the collection, was printed in Henrietta Maria, *A Coppy of the Letter*.

75. D'Ewes (N), pp. 291–92; *HMC Fourteenth Report*, app. IV, p. 59. See Tupling, "Causes of the Civil War in Lancashire," for religious background to the civil war in Lancashire. On Moore, a member of Lincoln's Inn, and Kirkby, see Keeler, *Long Parliament*; Glow, "Committee Men," pp. 1–10. Moore and Kirkby were related by marriage, but ended on different sides in the civil war—Moore a regicide, Kirkby a royalist.

76. D'Ewes (N), pp. 291–92; Powis, f. 33v. Baillie (1:295) identified Digby and Winter as sons of the "powder plotters." Sir Henry Bedingfield was also mentioned as a chief

collector. In Rushworth, 4:157, and *CJ*, 2:74, another man, Henry Beckett (or Birket, or Becket), is named; he was a collector for London and Middlesex. See Henrietta Maria, *A Coppy of the Letter*, p. 8.

77. There are four sometimes conflicting reports of these investigations: (a) D'Ewes (N), pp. 295–96, for 28 January only; (b) Rushworth, 3:1327–29, for 28–29 January; (c) D'Ewes's notes in Harl. MS 165, for 28–29 January, cited at length in D'Ewes (N), pp. 295n1 and 302n2; and (d) Peyton, for 28 January, cited in D'Ewes (N), p. 295n2.

78. Powis, f. 34.

79. D'Ewes (N), p. 291n8. See above, p. 178, on Richard Forster, the queen's messenger to France in February 1641, who had for several years been providing information to the French agents in England. Forster was a confidant of Con, as he appears to have been of Cottington; this raises very interesting questions about the information Montreuil could have passed on to the parliamentary leaders.

80. For Montagu's reticence, see Powis, f. 34. Cf. D'Ewes (N), p. 295+nn, for Peyton and Rushworth's indications as to whether Montagu implicated Con. The secular priest report is in AAW A.30, no. 1.

81. Falkland and Strode soon returned from the committee to ask for a delay in its meeting so the members might hear Pym's report on the charges against Strafford (D'Ewes [N], pp. 296–97). Members of the "Digby-Montagu committee" are listed in *CJ*, 2:74.

82. There are no significant discrepancies in accounts of this day's interrogation. See D'Ewes (N), pp. 302n6, 545; and Rushworth, 3:1329. Rushworth gives a fuller account of Digby's speech.

83. Montagu added that "by his acquaintance he is confident that he would have acquainted him with his jurisdiction if he had any, but did not"(D'Ewes [N], p. 545).

84. D'Ewes (N), p. 545; Rushworth, 3:1329.

85. AAW A.30, no. 1.

86. D'Ewes (N), pp. 302n6, 545; *CJ*, 2:75. Brooke had by now fled the city; he would be captured at York in January 1642 (*DNB*; Gillow).

87. Salvetti I, ff. 173–74.

88. AAW B.47, no. 94.

89. Ibid., no. 97; PRO 31/3/72, f. 438.

90. D'Ewes (N), pp. 323–25. Once again, in referring to Rossetti, D'Ewes identifies him as Con, indicating the central role the earlier agent occupied in the minds of Protestant observers of court Catholicism. See also *CSPVen 1640–42*, p. 125.

91. D'Ewes (N), pp. 302n6, 545; the matter had first been raised in November. Montagu had been in Wales in the summer of 1640 on a pilgrimage to Saint Winifred's Well.

92. D'Ewes (N), p. 301; Powis, f. 34v. Bodvile was a vigorous antipapist, cousin to the Wynns of Gwydir; he had Catholic relatives and may have had special information about south Welsh Catholic activities (*DWB*, s.v. "R. Bodvile," "Hugh Owen," "John Bodvile"; Keeler, *Long Parliament*, pp. 110–11; *Wynn Calendar*, pp. 272, 273–74). See also Hibbard, "Popish Plot," pp. 578–80, and sources cited there.

93. D'Ewes (N), p. 301: the list of counties over which Worcester had authority is incorrect.

94. Ibid.

95. On Middleton, see *DWB*; *DNB*; Keeler, *Long Parliament*; Dodd, *Stuart Wales*, pp. 179–84; Griffith, "Chirk Castle Election Activities," pp. 33–38. On Price, see Keeler, *Long Parliament*; he had a personal feud with Sir Percy Herbert. On Glynne, see n. 30 above; in February 1642 Glynne would conduct the trial of the petitioning bishops, of whom the Wynn patron Williams was leader (Roberts, *Mitre and Musket*, p. 181).

96. D'Ewes (N), p. 301; *CJ*, 2:75, for a list of those added to the committee. See also Dodd, "Wales in the Parliaments," pp. 71–72.

97. *HMCD*, 6:377–78; Baillie (1:310) said that Worcester refused to appear, but that Lord Herbert was "much at court, the papists in Wales follows [*sic*] him much." See also D'Ewes (N), p. 325+n14; *CJ*, 2:78.

98. D'Ewes (N), pp. 346–47, 348+n12, 349; Dodd, "Wales in the Parliaments," p. 72. On Reynolds, a lawyer of the Middle Temple, see *DNB*; Keeler, *Long Parliament*; and Glow, "Committee Men," p. 2.

99. D'Ewes (N), pp. 297–98; Rushworth, 2:61–75.

100. D'Ewes (N), p. 297.

101. Ibid., p. 11+nn79, 80; p. 14+n25; p. 60+n.

102. Ibid., pp. 213, 229–30.

103. On Mrs. Hussey and Father O'Connor, see ibid., pp. 25+n13, 30–31, 287, 292; *CJ*, 2:73.

104. Powis, f. 40.

105. Rochester, f. 19; D'Ewes (N), pp. 325, 346–48, 350–51.

106. Rochester, ff. 19–20; D'Ewes (N), p. 36+n10.

107. D'Ewes (N), p. 357. In 1641 Montagu's letter to his father on his conversion, together with his father's answer and a reply from Lord Falkland, was printed in pamphlet form.

108. D'Ewes (N), pp. 357, 359–60. Mathew had not previously been named in the investigation; he may have been implicated by a paper found in Windebank's study, a copy of a letter allegedly written to him by Urban VIII in May 1639 (Rushworth, 2:1324–26). Rochester noted in his diary that Mathew was out of London in February (Rochester, f. 25r). For Waller's speech, see ibid., f. 20.

109. D'Ewes (N), pp. 406, 409, 410–11+n7; Baillie, 1:304.

110. The king's appointment of seven opposition peers to the privy council on 19 February made the Commons edgy; see Gardiner, *History of England*, 9:292–94. For the debate, see D'Ewes (N), pp. 392–93, 484+n9, 486–89, 492–94, 498; *CJ*, 2:105; *HMC Twelfth Report*, app. II, p. 275; Powis, f. 50; Rochester, f. 25.

111. D'Ewes (N), pp. 486–89. Two sources suggest that other lords were joined in Holland's effort, either Bedford (PRO 31/3/72, ff. 467–68) or Hertford (AAW B.47, no. 98, letter of George Gage, 15 February 1641).

112. Salvetti I, f. 215, noted that few priests actually left. For their names and Montagu's role, see AAW B.47, no. 100 and A.30, no. 7. On the proclamation, see PRO 31/3/72, ff. 488–89.

113. Rushworth, 8:42, for Stapleton going on 23 March to the Lords to request a conference that Erle and Reynolds were to manage (*LJ*, 4:186–87, 188, 191, 197, 200).

114. For Mathew's escape, see Salvetti I, f. 215; AAW B.47, no. 97; and Matthew and Calthorp, *Life of Matthew*, p. 312. He and Brooke were named in an arrest warrant on 30 April (Harl. MS 478, f. 21). For Brooke, see Powis, f. 116; arrested in York in January, he was still in prison in August, when he was put under house arrest with the brother of Speaker Lenthall. Digby, presented for recusancy in February, had his case dropped by royal warrant, but parliament ordered the case continued (AAW B.47, no. 97). In June 1641 Digby was examined by one of the recusant committees (*DNB*); by September he was in Flanders. On 26 May a committee of the Commons was instructed to administer the oaths of allegiance and supremacy to Sir John Winter (*CJ*, 2:155); by 20 July 1641, he had taken one oath (BL 8622, f. 3).

115. See Rushworth, *Tryal of Strafford*, pp. 489–514, especially pp. 489–90, 497, for Whitelocke's argument. He insisted (p. 509) that the oath of allegiance was available and could have been used, and asked witnesses (pp. 493–94) if any Scottish Catholics had been made to take this oath. See also Schwarz, "Aristocratic Protest," pp. 25–26.

116. Verney, *Proceedings in the Long Parliament*, pp. 20–21.

117. AAW B.47, no. 101 (16 March 1641).

118. Rushworth, 8:654.

119. The Scottish historian Spalding later conflated the Irish army question with the "Spanish Armada," referring to Vane's paper as "bearing a consent of the King's cabinet council . . . for in bringing of the Spanish Armada . . . for help and support of the papists" (Spalding, *History of the Troubles*, 2:300). For Pym's speech, see Rushworth, 8:661–63.

120. Russell, "Theory of Treason," pp. 49–50.

121. *LJ*, 4:207, 216; AAW B.47, no. 105 (20 April 1641); Salvetti I, f. 224–25.

122. See Gardiner, *History of England*, 9:308–17, 324, for the chronology. Was Pym waiting to make most dramatically effective use of these revelations? Was he exploring the possibility of French involvement?

123. *CJ*, 2:132; Harl. MS 478, ff. 30a–31a; Baillie, 1:315. The document is in Gardiner, *Constitutional Documents*, p. 84.

124. Powis, f. 124; a word is omitted that I was unable to read.

125. Rochester, f. 60.

126. Gardiner, *Constitutional Documents*, p. 84.

127. Powis, f. 139; Bristol Archives Office, Smyth Family Papers, no. 56. In *Protestation Protested*, Henry Burton expressed anxiety about the failure of the Protestation to denounce present evils in the church (Hughes, "Henry Burton," pp. 196–97).

128. *LJ*, 4:243. Nalson, *Impartial Collection*, 2:237, mentions Winchester, Rivers, and Audley. I am grateful to Paul Christianson for advice on this point.

129. Salvetti I, f. 230. However, P. R. Newman has recently cast doubt on the usefulness of the lists of nonjurors as a means of identifying Catholics; see "Roman Catholics in Pre-Civil War England: The Problem of Definition," *Recusant History* 15 (1979): 148–52.

130. Rochester, f. 60v; Harl. MS 478, f. 66b; PRO 31/3/72, f. 543.

131. *LJ*, 4:243; Nalson, *Impartial Collection*, 2:237; Foley, 5:1010 (Father Philip to Montagu): "All the popish lords did absent themselves" from the vote on the attainder; corroborated in Rochester, f. 63.

132. Rushworth, 8:740–41.

133. Gawdy 1641, ff. 40, 42, 44, 67–68. See *CSP Ven 1640–42*, pp. 150–51, concerning a supposed treaty with France for ten regiments. See also BL 8655, f. 134, for a discussion of the army plot in terms of Catholic participation and a French landing at Portsmouth. In Harl. MS 4,931, f. 127, there is a list of "the names of such, as ran away, upon the discovery of a plot by the popish side, in the beginning of May 1641"; the list names not only Percy, Jermyn, Suckling, Davenant, Goring, and Slingsby, but also Cottington, Lord Powis, Lord Carnarvon, Digby, "Mr. Crofts," Montagu, and Lady Savage. The countess of Carlisle was identified as Strafford's go-between with the plotters.

134. Powis, ff. 128–29, 140; Salvetti I, f. 231.

135. Harl. MS 478, f. 34.

136. Harl. MS 478, f. 32, mentions the appointment of a committee on 4 May to "examine . . . the swarming of priests and Jesuits about this town and to examine Suckling." Gawdy 1641, f. 40, refers to "a strict order to be taken against all priests." *MCR*, 3:172–73, indicates a number of arrests and presentations made at Middlesex sessions in May 1641 for attendance at mass at Somerset House and the house of the Portuguese ambassador.

137. See Baillie, 1:351; Geyl, *Orange and Stuart*, pp. 1–10; and Gardiner, *History of*

England, 9:257–59, 288–89, 342–43, for aspects of this plan. It is alluded to by Rossetti in a letter of 30 April 1641 (BL 8649, ff. 452–59).

138. PRO 31/3/72, ff. 465, 474, 501–2, 504, 540–42, 545, 546–51.

139. For Spain's desperate need of soldiers in 1640–41, see Elliott, *Revolt of the Catalans*, chap. 17.

140. *CSPVen 1640–42*, pp. 134, 145; PRO 31/3/72, f. 542.

Chapter 9

1. *CSPVen 1640–42*, pp. 150, 152, 154.

2. In late November 1641, Richard Browne reported from Paris that the friends of France in the House of Commons reported all that went on to the French ambassador, who in turn had influence over the activities of that house (Ranke, *Französische Geschichte*, 2:504–5).

3. Powis, f. 139; Rochester, f. 65; Gawdy 1641, ff. 44, 51; Salvetti I, ff. 212–37; *CSPVen 1640–42*, pp. 151–52, 161, 162, 167.

4. On Browne, see chap. 3.

5. Durkan, "Career of John Brown," p. 168; AAW B.47, no. 104; *CSPD 1639–40*, p. 289.

6. AAW B.47, nos. 103, 104. Gawdy 1641, f. 34, names Sir Robert Pye as a member of the committee. On Carpenter, see Anstruther, 2:46–47; BL 8641, ff. 43–44; BL 8643, f. 6. He had apostatized before 1637, and in June 1637 preached at St. Paul's Cathedral.

7. The copy of the confession in AAW (A.30, no. 33) shows that it was the basis for at least two printed pamphlets: *The Confession of John Browne, a Jesuit . . .* and *A Discovery of the Notorious Proceedings of William Laud . . . confessed by John Browne, a Prisoner in the Gatehouse . . . October 15, 1641*. The pamphlets have no material in common. In addition to this printed matter, the confession included a list of priests in England, with special reference to collectors of contributions for clergy groups. Because the printed versions are incomplete and inaccurate, I have used the A.A.W. copy.

8. AAW A.30, no. 33, pp. 101–3. Browne claimed that monopolies arranged through courtiers were a money-raising measure for Catholic clergy; he named Winter, Brooke, and a "Mr. Plowden" in this connection. This must be Francis Plowden, Esq., of Plowden Hall, Salop and Shiplake, Oxon—grandson of the famous Elizabethan lawyer, Edmund Plowden—who was involved in the soap monopoly and whose Jesuit brother Thomas had been active around London in the 1620s and 1630s. See *CSPD 1639–40*, p. 193, and Foley, 4:537–40. Francis Plowden's son, Edmund (1616–66), was a collector in 1639 in Shropshire.

9. Robert Pendryck, Sir William Hamilton's secretary, had been deputed to serve as the queen's agent at Rome until Digby arrived. Pendryck was named as heir to his personal effects in Con's will; his letters to Vane in 1640 are in SP 85/7 (Italian states), ff. 161, 163. For Pendryck's work at Rome, see AAW A.30, no. 7; PRO 31/9/137, f. 28; Birrell, "Catholics Without a Bishop," p. 145. In 1651 he was living at Trinità dei Monti in Rome. William Pendryck (1583–1650), superior of English Carmelites, lived with Father Philip. Another brother, Alexander Pendryck, was principal of the Scots' College, Paris, in the 1620s and 1630s (Hay, *Blairs Papers*, pp. 106–7).

10. See AAW A.30, no. 33, pp. 104–7, for preceding quotations from Browne's confession.

11. Ibid., pp. 108–11. Browne soon repented and his "Palinodia" of June is in PRO 31/9/133, f. 111. He was still in the Gatehouse in November 1641, but had arrived in

Antwerp by April 1642, where he died before the end of 1643.

12. On Thomson, see Thaddeus, *Franciscans in England*, p. 30; and Anderson, "William Thomson of Dundee," pp. 99–103. He was one of the "conciliatory" group at court, one of those who had licensed Davenport's *Deus, Natura, Gratia* in 1634 (Dockery, *Davenport*, p. 83).

13. He was released in mid-August; his own account of his imprisonment and interrogation is in PRO 31/9/92, ff. 113–28. Questions about money raising for Catholic colleges abroad were preoccupying the Commons at this time; see Rushworth, 4:301 (26 June), for directions to the committee on the "popish hierarchy" to study the question of pensions.

14. Harl. MS 478, f. 25.

15. Ibid., f. 40b; for rumors about popish plots in May, see Gawdy 1641, f. 48; Powis, ff. 140, 149.

16. Gawdy 1641, ff. 87, 89; Verney, *Proceedings in the Long Parliament*, p. 89; see Rushworth, 7:257, for a copy of the letter.

17. Gawdy 1641, ff. 87, 88; *CJ*, 2:188–89; Rushworth, 4:300; Nalson, *Impartial Collection*, 2:310, 315, 317.

18. The document is in Gardiner, *Constitutional Documents*, pp. 91–94. See *LJ*, 4:285–87; Gawdy 1641, f. 86.

19. On Newcastle, see Add. 15,392, ff. 43–44; *CSPVen 1640–42*, p. 172. On Duppa, see AAW B.47, no. 101, for attacks on him and Newcastle in the House of Commons in mid-May.

20. When his letters were seized in May, the marquis of La Vieuville helped him out; see BL 8655, f. 121; *CSPVen 1640–42*, pp. 170, 175, 196–97.

21. BL 8653ii, ff. 429, 434; BL 8654, f. 7; BL 8655, f. 151; Gawdy 1641, ff. 87–88; Salvetti I, f. 259.

22. Gardiner, *History of England*, 9:400–404; Rossetti continued to correspond with the queen and to relay English news to Rome (Pastor, *History of Popes*, 29:328–29). His later correspondence is in BL 8650–55.

23. This canon, named Piombino, apparently never actually arrived in England. His letters to Rome from The Hague in June and July 1642 are in BL 8652, ff. 1, 61, 152–56. On Thomson's assistance, see PRO 31/9/137, f. 28; BL 8655, ff. 93, 121, 131, 140–41; by July 1642 he was carrying messages between Henrietta Maria and Rossetti in Cologne on possibilities of papal aid for England (BL 8657, ff. 184, 190).

24. Harl. MS 163, f. 347; Salvetti I, ff. 240, 241, 250, 263, 277, 281, 289, 291, 296; *CSPVen 1640–42*, pp. 161, 167, 184, 199, 203, 211, 227, 230.

25. Rushworth, 2:301–3; 7:752–54. The printed version appeared in November 1641: *The Impeachment and Articles of Complaint against Father Philip*.

26. AAW B.47, no. 97; Anglia A.VII, no. 48.

27. Gawdy 1641, ff. 39–40, 52–53, 57, 69, 92; *CJ*, 2:144, 153; AAW B.47, no. 100; Salvetti I, f. 243; *CSPVen 1640–42*, p. 165.

28. Delays on disarmament can be traced in *LJ*, 4:272–316 passim, and in *CSPD 1641–43*, p. 100. On Saye and Sele, see Anglia A.VII, no. 48, for the wards; Gawdy 1641, f. 83. Cf. Rochester, ff. 86, 93; Bray, *Correspondence of Evelyn*, 4:51–52, 60.

29. There are two quite different printed versions of this petition—one appealing in rather idealistic terms for toleration (*A New Petition of the Papists*, in BM, Thomason E. 169 [7]), the other political in tenor and disavowing resistance theory and the doctrine of equivocation (*To The Honorable, The Knights, Citizens and Burgesses of The Commons House in Parliament Now Assembled. The humble petition of the Lay-Catholics Recusants of England*, in BM, Thomason 669 f. 4 [23]).

30. *LJ*, 4:384–87, contains the order of 30 August to disarm recusants. See Salvetti I, ff. 245, 263, 303; *CSPVen 1640–42*, pp. 179, 180. Reluctance over the blanket disarmament of Catholics may have existed in the counties as well as in the House of Lords. As late as 24 September 1641, Thomas Barrington reported from Essex, "I find a strange tepidity, and full of needless scruples, in the execution of that brave ordinance of both houses, for the disarming of papists" (Beinecke Library, Howard of Escricke MSS). I am grateful to Conrad Russell for drawing my attention to this set of papers.

31. Gawdy 1641, f. 68; see Bodl., Nalson Deposit 12, ff. 268, 269, and Nalson Deposit 13, ff. 11–12, for the examination of Charles Allen and Clifton Thorold (*vere* Francis Thorold: see Anstruther, 2:318–19).

32. Edmund Cannon, an aged secular priest, on 20 April 1641; John Abbot (alias Rivers), on 30 July 1641. See Anstruther, 1:62–63, on Cannon; ibid., 2:1–2, on Abbot; also Foley, 5:207–20.

33. Anstruther, 2:344–45, on Webster. See also *CSPVen 1640–42*, p. 195; Salvetti I, f. 273; an account of his martyrdom in AAW A.30, no. 17, 18. Several pamphlets, quite inaccurate, purported to describe Webster's case: *A New Plot Discovered, practised by an assembly of Papists . . . for William Waller alias Walker, alias Ward, alias Slater, a Jesuit*; *The Papists' Conspiracie, or, A Plot which was first contrived and counselled by a Papist Priest. . . .*

34. AAW A.30, no. 21, gives the names of priests in prison in August 1641: the seculars Muskett, Goodman, and John Southworth, as also the Jesuit Henry Morse. But Caraman has Southworth leaving in January 1641 to become chaplain to Sir Henry Gage in Flemish service, returning with Gage to the royalist army later that year (*Henry Morse*, pp. 145–46, 148–56, 169–73). Southworth was subsequently arrested yet again, in 1654 and then martyred (Anstruther, vol. 2). At least three other priests were condemned in April 1641—the secular John Whitbread (alias Wilmot, Turner, Torman, or Windmore) in Newgate, the Benedictine Peter Wilford (alias Taylor), and the secular Edmund Cannon—and another Benedictine, Andrew Waferer, in August. Wilford, Cannon, and Waferer featured in the "seven priests case" in December, on which see below. Whitbread was reprieved in December, but was still in Newgate in July 1648 (Anstruther, vol. 2, s.v. "John Whitbread" and "Edmund Cannon"; *LJ*, 4:466, 470).

35. Codner, for example, had left England with the queen mother through Arundel's intervention (*CJ*, 2:259, under his alias of Matthew Savage). Christopher Davenport was still living in London in 1642 under the alias of Hunt, protected also by Arundel (Dockery, *Davenport*, p. 115).

36. Giustiniani had closed his chapel to avoid trouble and was much vexed. On Clopton, see Anstruther, vol. 2; AAW A.30, no. 12; Salvetti I, ff. 263–64, 273, 294, 300; Rochester, f. 82; and *CSPVen 1640–42*, pp. 189–93. Clopton was in Rome by August 1642.

37. Harl. MS 478, ff. 26–27; Powis, ff. 138, 143; *CSPVen 1640–42*, pp. 145–46, 148, 154.

38. Rochester, f. 84; *CSPVen 1640–42*, pp. 195n, 198, 203, 219; Hine, "Disturbances Outside the Portuguese Embassy," pp. 72–74. Salvetti I, ff. 263–64, claimed that most of the priests maintained by ambassadors were the king's subjects, so that the ordinance would cause a lot of trouble.

39. Salvetti I, ff. 258–59; Rochester, f. 92; Marsys, *Histoire de la Persécution*, pp. 95–96; *CSPVen 1640–42*, p. 207; Cobbett, *Parliamentary History*, 2:901–2; Bray, *Correspondence of Evelyn*, 4:73.

40. *CSPVen 1640–42*, pp. 154–61, 164.

41. Gawdy 1641, ff. 40, 42, 44, 51; PRO 31/3/72, f. 591; Salvetti I, f. 281; *CSPVen 1640–42*, pp. 148, 150–51, 152, 179.

42. Harl. MS 478, ff. 55, 57–60; Rochester, ff. 66, 74; Gawdy 1641, f. 44; Salvetti I, ff. 233, 236, 246; PRO 31/3/72, ff. 546–48, 558.

43. Gawdy 1641, ff. 68, 87; *CSPVen 1640–42*, p. 214.

44. Cobbett, *Parliamentary History*, 2:903–5; D'Ewes (N), pp. 347–48; Rochester, ff. 83, 85, 87–88, 95; *LJ*, 4:374, 381, 394; Bray, *Correspondence of Evelyn*, 4:53–55, 66–67; Salvetti I, ff. 285–86, 287, 290–91; *CSPVen 1640–42*, pp. 187, 203, 216. The Spanish ambassador was still pressing for four thousand Irish in September, and the king was still attempting to satisfy him (English parliamentary commissioners to Lenthall, 3 September 1641, in Beinecke Library, Howard of Escricke MSS).

45. *CSPVen 1640–42*, pp. 164, 175. He got the Capuchin superior released (ibid., p. 207).

46. Salvetti I, ff. 259, 277–78, 280; *CSPVen 1640–42*, pp. 176–79, 187–88, 216, 230–31.

47. PRO 31/3/72, f. 82; *CSPVen 1640–42*, pp. 155, 162.

48. Cobbett, *Parliamentary History*, 2:856–59. The printed version of the king's speech is *His Majesty's Manifest Touching the Palatine Cause; and the Votes of Both Houses of Parliament concerning the same* (London, 1641).

49. Cobbett, *Parliamentary History*, 2:859–60, 870–76, 877–80; Nalson, *Impartial Collection*, 2:328–29; Rochester, f. 80b; *LJ*, 4:300–301; Salvetti I, ff. 261, 266; PRO 31/3/72, ff. 593–94; *CSPVen 1640–42*, pp. 178–79, 182.

50. John Gauden, *The Love of Peace and Truth* (London, 1641); see Batten, *John Dury*, p. 90; Turnbull, *Hartlib, Dury and Comenius*, pp. 219–20.

51. Batten, *John Dury*, pp. 85–86; in 1640 Dury had already sent a narrative account to Hartlib of his negotiations for ecclesiastical union that was meant to be circulated in parliament. On the petition published in May 1641, see Webster, *Hartlib and Advancement of Learning*, p. 32. Dury's 1641 publications include *Summary Discourse on Peace Ecclesiastical* and *Motives to Induce the Protestant Princes to Mind the Work of Peace Ecclesiastical*.

52. Batten, *John Dury*, p. 91; Webster, *Hartlib and Advancement of Learning*, p. 37. On the authorship of *Macaria*, see Webster, "*Macaria*." *England's Thankfulness* is reprinted in Webster, *Hartlib and Advancement of Learning*, pp. 90–97. Comenius's *The Reformation of Schools* came out in 1642.

53. Hughes, "Henry Burton," pp. 213–14.

54. Downing, *A Discovery of the False Grounds the Bavarian Party Have Laid*. Mede's *Key of the Revelation* would appear in 1643. See Christianson, *Reformers and Babylon*, pp. 124–29.

55. For example, Samuel Fairclough's *The Troublers Troubled, or Achan Condemned and Executed*, an April sermon to the House of Commons that urged adoption of harsh measures against heresy, printed in London in 1641.

56. Salvetti I, f. 272. John Dury had already written to Alexander Henderson; see Batten, p. 87. The Scottish parliament made a declaration in the prince's favor and promised troops (Salvetti I, ff. 293, 301, 303; *CSPVen 1640–42*, p. 223).

57. *CSPVen 1640–42*, pp. 183, 200; Wedgwood, "Elector Palatine," pp. 5–7; Rochester, f. 94a. Unlikely as this story sounds, it is repeated also by Rossetti as early as 7 May: "Hanno minacciato il Re di voler levare la corona, et incoronare il principe di Waglia"; Rossetti adds later on that this was told him secretly "dal Sig^r Visconte," who heard it from the queen herself (BL 8649, ff. 479–82).

58. On the Incident, see below.

59. Reynald, "Le Baron de Lisola," pp. 322–26, 331–36. On 9 December 1641, at the London residence of Soubise, after delicate negotiations carried on through various intermediaries, Lisola obtained from the prince Palatine a signed agreement to abstain

from any alliance for the next two months, by which time he hoped that English soldiers might be available for the Palatine's use under the imperial banner. See also *CSPVen 1640–42*, pp. 226. For Soubise's activities in the mid-1620s, see Russell, *Parliaments and Politics*, p. 71. For the general context, see Polišenský, *War and Society*, p. 238.

60. D'Ewes (C), pp. 381–83.

61. As would Sir Richard Cave, M.P. for Lichfield in the Long Parliament; see Keeler, *Long Parliament*.

62. As late as October 1640, Dury was writing from Hamburg to Laud's secretary Dell, as well as to Hartlib; see Turnbull, *Hartlib, Dury and Comenius*, pp. 216–19; Batten, *John Dury*, p. 95. The preface to *A Motion Tending to the Public Good* is dated 30 December 1641; see Webster, *Hartlib and Advancement of Learning*, pp. 97–110.

63. Lamont, *Prynne*, pp. 124–40.

64. Salvetti I, f. 246; *CSPVen 1640–42*, pp. 163, 166.

65. *CSPVen 1640–42*, pp. 179, 186; Baillie, 1:295; Verney, *Proceedings in the Long Parliament*, pp. 105–9.

66. Salvetti I, f. 266; Pym, *Reasons of the House of Commons to stay the Queen's going into Holland*.

67. Salvetti I, f. 276; Rochester, ff. 82, 84.

68. Pastor, *History of Popes*, 29:333; BL 8650i, ff. 5, 8, 89–94.

69. L&C, 6:541–42.

70. This is a controversial matter that is carefully discussed by Lowe in his 1960 thesis, "Negotiations between Charles I and the Confederation of Kilkenny"; see especially pp. 7–9 on the king's July message to Antrim and Ormonde. New evidence has since come to light that tends to corroborate Lowe's opinion; see Lamont, *Baxter and the Millennium*, pp. 330–32. See also Clarke, *Old English*, chap. 4; and Hill, *MacDonnells*, pp. 448–51, 470–73. According to Rossetti's letters from Cologne after the outbreak of the Irish Rebellion, the king had planned a seizure of power by his Irish allies about the time of the first army plot; the clearest accounts are in letters of 2 February (N.S.) 1642 (BL 8651, ff. 117–19) and 9 February (N.S.) 1642 (BL 8651, ff. 158–59).

71. Coonan, *Irish Catholic Confederacy*, pp. 91–94; *LJ*, 4:374, 381, 394; Warner, *Nicholas Papers*, 1:21; *CSPVen 1640–42*, p. 202.

72. PRO 31/3/72, f. 593; Salvetti I, f. 279; *CSPVen 1640–42*, p. 223; Bray, *Correspondence of Evelyn*, 4:113.

73. Stevenson, *Scottish Revolution*, pp. 238–39.

74. Bray, *Correspondence of Evelyn*, 4:76, 85, refers to the activities of Mandeville, Pym, and others; the king replied that the queen should deal with it. Cf. Rochester, f. 96; *CSPVen 1640–42*, pp. 231–32.

75. Cobbett, *Parliamentary History*, 2:915. On the treatment of the Incident as a popish plot, see the letter from Sir Edward Nicholas in Bray, *Correspondence of Evelyn*, 4:92.

76. DNB, s.v. "Daniel O'Neill"; Coonan, *Irish Catholic Confederacy*, pp. 91–94.

77. D'Ewes (C), pp. 18–21, 58–59, 155–59. The French ambassador may have been in back of the harassment of Monsigot. who was questioned by the lord mayor of London, released ca. 18 November, and then fled the country (D'Ewes [C], p. 176+n).

78. D'Ewes (C), p. 61n3; Bray, *Correspondence of Evelyn*, 4:119; Salvetti I, ff. 319, 322, 326; Gardiner, *History of England*, 10:92–93, 112, 146.

79. D'Ewes (C), p. 180; Salvetti I, ff. 306–7, 312. As both Rossetti and O'Neill were considering ways and means of getting such troops to Ireland, parliament was quite justified in its fears (BL 8651, ff. 90–93).

80. BL 8650, ff. 368, 411; 8651, ff. 1–6, 33–34, 65, 98–99.

81. *CSP Ven 1640–42*, pp. 241, 243–45, 247–49; Salvetti I, f. 316; "Ardiscono di farla principale autore di detta sollevazione, chiamandola la sollevazione della regina" (Salvetti I, f. 338).

82. Lowe, "Charles I and Confederation of Kilkenny," pp. 7–10; Gardiner, *History of England*, 10:50–54, 112–13.

83. Bray, *Correspondence of Evelyn*, 4:97.

84. *HMC Fifth Report*, pp. 349–52. I cannot trace this Progers or discover his relation to the Progers serving as messenger between Nicholas and Charles I in mid-November 1641 (Bray, *Correspondence of Evelyn*, 4:122).

85. Not surprisingly, as Pym and Holles appear to have been its authors.

86. Cobbett, *Parliamentary History*, 2:930–32.

87. D'Ewes (C), pp. 250–54, 349, 351–52, 376; the petition concerning the Remonstrance is in Gardiner, *Constitutional Documents*, pp. 202–5.

88. For the preamble and text of the Grand Remonstrance, see Gardiner, *Constitutional Documents*, pp. 205–8, 208–32.

89. Ibid., pp. 208, 215–16.

90. Ibid., pp. 216–20.

91. Bray, *Correspondence of Evelyn*, 4:130; *LJ*, 4:446. This anxiety was expressed, for example, in the desire of the Commons to remove Jerome Weston, second earl of Portland, from the position of governor of the Isle of Wight. His wife and mother were Catholics, and his Catholic sister Catherine had married Richard White, brother of the soon-to-be-notorious secular priest, Thomas White (alias Blacklo). See D'Ewes (C), pp. 63–64, 67, 161–62, 171–72.

92. Bray, *Correspondence of Evelyn*, 4:98–99; *CSP Ven 1640–42*, pp. 236–37. On Bedingfield, see Nalson, *Impartial Collection*, 2:661–62, 690–91; D'Ewes (C), pp. 179–80.

93. D'Ewes (C), pp. 144–45, 147n2; Bray, *Correspondence of Evelyn*, 4:126–27.

94. D'Ewes (C), pp. 149, 154, 160–64, 176–77; *CSP Ven 1640–42*, p. 251.

95. D'Ewes (C), p. 261; *MCR*, 3:82, 87–88, 90–94 passim.

96. *LJ*, 4:439–40; *CSP Ven 1640–42*, p. 251.

97. D'Ewes (C), p. 71+n32. Clarendon noted that Philip's action made a great impression: "Great liberty was taken to inveigh against the religion of the court, and bold and apparent glances at the person of the queen" (*Hist. Reb.*, vol. 6, app. M, p. 307).

98. D'Ewes (C), pp. 59, 71, 76, 77–78, 79–80, 164n2, 177–78, 181, 191–92, 213, 221, 317n34; *LJ*, 4:418, 462, 466; *CJ*, 2:304; Nalson, *Impartial Collection*, 2:594, 597, 599, 605, 661, 662, 691, 692, 711; Salvetti I, ff. 324, 327–29; *CSP Ven 1640–42*, p. 258. *A True Relation of the French Embassage* publicized Philip's letter.

99. D'Ewes (C), pp. 76–80, 148–49, 154, 160–64, 176–78, 180–81, 190–92, 213, 221–22, 317; *LJ*, 4:466; *CSP Ven 1640–42*, p. 251. Of the two named priests, I am unable to identify Jones; Andrews may be Richard Bartlet (alias Andrews [1577–1645]), S.J., who came from Worcestershire. He may have been the priest identified as Worcester's protégé; see Anstruther, vol. 2; Foley, 6:253–54.

100. D'Ewes (C), pp. 69, 131, 150+n13, 181+n26; *CJ*, 2:302; *HMC Franciscan*, p. 108; Salvetti I, ff. 307, 313; *CSP Ven 1640–42*, p. 251.

101. D'Ewes (C), p. 98n13; Bray, *Correspondence of Evelyn*, 4:109; Nalson, *Impartial Collection*, 2:607; *CSP Ven 1640–42*, p. 246.

102. D'Ewes (C), pp. 162, 375+n5; Nalson, *Impartial Collection*, 2:814; Salvetti I, f. 342; Harl. MS 163, f. 9; Gawdy 1641, f. 53; Peyton, f. 182. On the French ambassador, see Harl. MS 163, f. 13, and D'Ewes (C), p. 375+n5.

103. *CJ*, 2:315; D'Ewes (C), p. 142. They are identified as "Mr. Gifford" and "Walter

Coleman." On Coleman, see below. "Mr. Gifford" may be John Wakeman (alias Green or Gibbons), listed in 1637 in the Gatehouse as a "concealed Jesuit"; see Anstruther, vol. 2.

104. See D'Ewes (C), pp. 261, 270, 273; *CJ*, 2:339, 340, 365.

105. The *seculars* were: (a) John Hackshott (alias Hammond [d. 1663]), who was condemned 8 December 1641; (b) Edmund Cannon, who died between 1643 and 1648; and (c) John Whitbread (alias Wilmot), still in Newgate in July 1648. On all these, see Anstruther, vol. 2; on Cannon and Whitbread, see nn. 32 and 34 above.

The *Benedictines* were: (a) Peter Boniface Wilford (alias John Taylor [1584–1646]); and (b) "Edmond Frier," probably Andrew Waferer (alias William Herne, Andrew Friar, or Mr. Richmond). Waferer was a convert, long on the mission, captured by the pursuivant Wadsworth and condemned in August 1641. Described as a "concealed Benedictine," he died in Newgate by 1648 (Anstruther, vol. 2). On both these, see Birt.

The *Franciscan* was Walter Coleman (d. 1645), on whom see n. 106 below. The *Bridgettine* was John Abbot (alias Rivers), nephew of Archbishop Abbot and a former Jesuit. In and out of jail in the 1630s, he was condemned 30 July 1641 for refusal of the oath; he died in prison in 1650 (Anstruther, vol. 2).

106. John Hackshott, who described himself as the queen's servant (D'Ewes [C], p. 270), and Walter Coleman, who dedicated his book *La danse macabre* to Henrietta Maria (Allison, "Franciscan Books," pp. 53, 64–65).

107. D'Ewes (C), pp. 273–74, 294; *CJ*, 2:339, 365. Those who were to have been spared were Cannon, who was in prison before 11 November 1640 and was said to have taken the oath (Anstruther, vol. 1; *LJ*, 4:466, 470); and Peter Wilford (on whom see Birt, p. 128, and Anstruther, vol. 2, who says he was sentenced again in May 1642).

108. On the case of the seven priests as a group, see D'Ewes (C), pp. 375, 378–79; *LJ*, 4:501, 708, 732; *CJ*, 2:519, 520; Gawdy 1641, f. 39; Salvetti I, ff. 324, 326; *CSP Ven 1640–42*, pp. 264–65.

109. Salvetti I, f. 345; *CSP Ven 1640–42*, p. 285; on Green, see Anstruther, vol. 1; on Roe and Barlow, see Birt.

110. Bray, *Correspondence of Evelyn*, 4:127; *Hist. Reb.*, vol. 6, app. M, p. 307; Cobbett, *Parliamentary History*, 2:936.

111. Nalson, *Impartial Collection*, 2:646–51; D'Ewes (C), pp. 145, 149, 150, 152–54, 160–63.

112. D'Ewes (C), pp. 171, 199–200, 318, 340; Harl. MS 162, ff. 396, 399; Gawdy 1641, ff. 35, 48–49, 71; the list is in *LJ*, 4:449–50. See *The True Relation of a Bloody Conspiracy by the Papists in Cheshire*. Brooke, named a delinquent in the previous spring, was arrested in York in January 1642 and imprisoned in London; his trunks were searched by a parliamentary committee (Harl. MS 162, f. 354; Gawdy 1642, f. 14).

113. Bray, *Correspondence of Evelyn*, 4:119; Salvetti I, f. 312; *LJ*, 4:429, 488.

114. D'Ewes (C), pp. 271–72; Gawdy 1642, ff. 8, 11, 12; Salvetti I, ff. 326–27, 331; *CSP Ven 1640–42*, pp. 269, 272, 289; Cobbett, *Parliamentary History*, 2:1029–30. A number of the petitions were printed early in 1642 (e.g., those from London, Middlesex, Essex, and Hertford); they associated the bishops with the "popish lords," calling for the exclusion of both.

115. D'Ewes (C), pp. 148, 397–98; Dircks, *Marquis of Worcester*, p. 39; see Huntington Library, Ellesmere MS 7352, for Harley's anxiety. The pamphlets implicating the Somerset family, more or less based on the Beale plot, included *A New Plot against Parliament . . . likewise the reason of the Guard placed at the Earl of Worcester's*; *A Great Discovery of a Damnable Plot*; and *A Discovery of a Horrible and Bloody*

Treason . . . with a plot by the earl of Worcester in Wales. All were published in
London in November 1641. See D'Ewes (C), pp. 163, 164, 168.

116. Dircks, *Marquis of Worcester*, pp. 32–33. It is not altogether clear what sum came
from Barberini himself and what from the Somersets in 1642–43; see Albion, *Charles
I and Court of Rome*, pp. 375–78; Pastor, *History of Popes*, 29:332–33.

117. D'Ewes (C), pp. 58–59, 69–70; Bray, *Correspondence of Evelyn*, 4:105–6; Salvetti I,
f. 306; *CSPVen 1640–42*, p. 241.

118. D'Ewes (C), pp. 98n, 115–16, 162; Bray, *Correspondence of Evelyn*, 4:109.

119. Salvetti I, ff. 316, 342, 345; BL 8651, ff. 118–19; Nalson, *Impartial Collection*,
2:780–81; *CSPVen 1640–42*, p. 276.

120. Cobbett, *Parliamentary History*, 2:984–86.

121. Harl. MS 162, f. 322; Nalson, *Impartial Collection*, 2:836–37; *CSPVen 1640–42*, p.
280; *A Great Conspiracy of the Papists against the Worthy Members of Both Houses
of Parliament*; *The Papists' Design against the Parliament and the City of London
Discovered*; *A Plot against the City of London Discovered*.

122. Cobbett, *Parliamentary History*, 2:1033–35; Gawdy 1642, f. 3 mentions a specific
reference to the queen's evil interest.

123. Gawdy 1642, ff. 45, 50, 54–55; Harl. MS 162, f. 325; Cobbett, *Parliamentary
History*, 2:1042.

124. Salvetti I, f. 345; *CSPVen 1640–42*, pp. 262, 277, 283, 292.

125. In his answer to the Grand Remonstrance, he said that parliamentary veto over his
councillors "were to debar us that natural liberty all freemen have; . . . it is the
undoubted right of the crown of England to call such persons to our secret counsels, to
public employment, and our particular service as we shall see fit" (Gardiner, *Constitutional Documents*, p. 235; the complete answer is on pp. 233–36).

126. Cobbett, *Parliamentary History*, 2:1091; *CJ*, 2:433; Harl. MS 162, ff. 343, 386–87;
Gawdy 1642, f. 41; Bray, *Correspondence of Evelyn*, 4:49, 130, 133.

127. Most importantly, perhaps, the queen was still offering advice constantly; see Green,
Letters of Henrietta Maria, pp. 49–154, for her letters to him in 1642.

128. Rushworth, 4:510; MCR, 3:74, 81.

129. Gawdy 1642, ff. 44–45, 59; Harl. MS 163, ff. 15–16.

130. Gardiner, *Constitutional Documents*, pp. 245–47.

131. Cobbett, *Parliamentary History*, 2:1117–18; the entire declaration of both houses
"setting forth the cause of their fears and jealousies" is in ibid., pp. 1114–20.

132. Harl. MS 163, ff. 15, 17.

133. Lindley, "Impact of the 1641 Rebellion," pp. 143, 163–65, 169–70, 176; *Hist. Reb.*,
1:399–400.

134. Baillie, 2:66, 80; Stevenson, *Scottish Revolution*, pp. 270, 273; Lowe, "Antrim and
Irish Aid to Montrose," pp. 191–98 passim. For an account of how this expedition
looked to a Scottish Jesuit who participated in it, see Leith, *Memoirs of Scottish
Catholics*, 1:280–341. Joyce Malcolm argued in two recent articles that the king's
military situation was so desperate before the Irish soldiers were brought over that on
balance the use of the Irish cannot have hurt the king more than it helped him; see
"Charles I in 1642" and "Impact of the Crown's Irish Soldiers."

135. Dircks, *Marquis of Worcester*, p. 43; *DWB*, s.v. "Somerset family"; see Hibbard,
"Popish Plot, Note D: The Irish Rebellion: Rinuccini and Glamorgan," pp. 581–82,
for sources.

136. *Hist. Reb.*, 2:505; Rushworth, 5:78–83; Newman, "Catholic Royalist Activists."

Chapter 10

1. Lake, "Elizabethan Identification of the Pope as Antichrist," especially pp. 166–69.
2. *Hist. Reb.*, 1:215–17, 241–50.
3. Bonney, *France under Richelieu and Mazarin*, p. 284.
4. See appendix below.
5. Parker, *Europe in Crisis*, pp. 118–19.
6. Bonney, *France under Richelieu and Mazarin*, chap. 16, describes how the intendants actually brought more pressure to bear on the Protestants than either Richelieu or Mazarin would have initiated.
7. Russell, "Religious Unity," p. 220; see pp. 219–21 for an exploration of the interplay between religious unity and political obligation.
8. Clifton, "Fear of Catholics," pp. 39, 54.
9. Ascoli, *Grande-Bretagne devant l'opinion française*, 2:167, notes that the restoration of Charles II was seen by the French as the prelude to the restoration of Catholicism in England. Haley, in "'No Popery' in the Reign of Charles II," emphasizes royal favor to Catholics in the background to the "popish-plot" crisis of 1678–81.
10. Hughes, *Rome and Counter-Reformation*, p. 274.

Appendix

1. Lamont, *Prynne*, pp. 103–16.
2. Composed in 1636 but not printed because of Prynne's imprisonment, this contained the alleged testimony of two English Jesuits concerning the Church of England; it was incorporated in the 1643 publication of *Popish Royal Favorite*.
3. Prynne's specific information about priests was mainly from the 1620s and taken from Gee and others; see *Quench-Coal*, pp. 36–41, 67.
4. Prynne, *A New Discovery of the Prelates' Tyranny*, on the Star Chamber trial of Prynne, Burton, and Bastwick. See Lamont, *Prynne*, pp. 107–8.
5. Prynne's reputation for factual accuracy has been defended by a Catholic historian who claims Prynne did not fabricate information, although he did rely uncritically upon his sources; see Anstruther, *Hundred Homeless Years*, p. 140.
6. *Canterburies' Doom* (1646) uses much of the same material but is aimed entirely at Laud; see Lamont, *Prynne*, pp. 119–34.
7. The original was ordered printed by parliament on 1 August 1643; Prynne's references in *Popish Royal Favorite* to *Rome's Masterpiece* indicate that the latter was the first composed. The pamphlet is reprinted in Laud, *Works*, 4:465–503.
8. Laud, *Works*, 4:503.
9. Prynne, *Popish Royal Favorite*, pp. 1–9, 14–18, 30–32, 56–58; Prynne mentions documents borrowed from John Glynne and Robert Reynolds, and material provided by the pursuivant John Pulford. See Magee, *English Recusants*, pp. 94–98, 137.
10. Prynne, *Popish Royal Favorite*, pp. 35–37.
11. Ibid., pp. 35–56, 59–64. Prynne had copies of documents on the episcopal controversy of 1624–33 that demonstrated French involvement.
12. Ibid., pp. 12–24, 30, 57–58.
13. Ibid., pp. 57–59, 71–73. See also the "Epistle to the Reader": "having already fully possessed themselves of his Majesty's royal person, issue, forces, forts, affections, bearing chiefest sway in all his late counsels, proceedings, as we may now discern, to our greatest grief."

14. See Prynne, *Hidden Works of Darkness*, pp. 145–89, on Laud.

15. Ibid., pp. 212–17; see pp. 219–22 for three letters of January 1642 from Rome to the Irish rebels, Lord Maquire and Sir Phelim O'Neill.

16. Ibid., pp. 253–55.

17. Lamont, *Prynne*, pp. 138–41.

18. Ibid., chap. 4. Bulstrode Whitelocke and William Walwyn were openly skeptical, but L'Estrange and Sanderson accepted the essential outline of the plot.

19. Cited in Lamont, *Prynne*, pp. 132–33, 137, 198.

20. Vicars, *Jehovah Jireh*, pp. 7–8, 15–17, 23–24. See *DNB*, s.v. "John Vicars."

21. Wallington, *Historical Notices*, 1:l–li, 117, 118.

22. Even Weldon, whose *Court and Character of . . . Charles I* (1651) is most concerned with court corruption and constitutional issues, refers to Noy as "a great Papist, if not an Atheist," and as a protector of papists, suggesting a link between Catholicism and ship money (p. 195).

23. Baxter, *Reliquiae*, p. 128. This matter has now been fully explored by Lamont, in *Baxter and the Millennium*, chap. 2.

24. Warwick, *Memoirs*, pp. 81–84. George Bate, in a very early royalist work, *A Short Narrative*, (Lat. ed., 1649; Engl. ed., 1652), dwelled on the papist issue; see pp. 1–21 passim.

25. Dugdale, *Short View*, pp. 1–41 and 42–53. MacGillivray points out that there is an inconsistency in Dugdale's views. Dugdale claimed that the Scots used religion as a "cover" for rebellion, but also believed that Protestant fervor was inherently subversive ("Sir William Dugdale," pp. 116, 124).

26. Strafford MS 34, two unnumbered folios on the origin of the Scottish troubles. The piece is attributed to Sir George Radcliffe by Wedgwood (*Wentworth*, p. 221). The manuscript is undated, but may be from the 1650s. I have not found a printed copy; it is not in Knowler or in Whitaker's *Life of Radcliffe*. On Radcliffe and his association with Ormonde in the 1640s, see *DNB*; on his position as adviser to the duke of York in the 1640s and 1650s, during which time he negotiated with French Jansenists, see Whitaker, *Life of Radcliffe*, p. 287.

27. *Hist. Reb.*, 1:123 and 56–136 passim, on the period 1629–37. Of this latter section, pp. 109–29 are devoted to church policy in the 1630s.

28. *Hist. Reb.*, 1:148; see also pp. 194–95 on Con. Clarendon's comments on the court Catholics were so disapproving that they were appended by the editor to the reprint of an anti-Catholic tract, *The Pope's Nuntioes* (see Clarendon's comments in *Somers Tracts*, 4:52).

29. *CSP*, 2:336; *Hist. Reb.*, 1:48–53, 241–50.

30. For supporting indications, see the case of Wren below. As a minister, first of Charles I and then of Charles II, Clarendon had unusually compelling reasons for disavowing the existence of Catholic intrigue and was thus probably motivated as much by self-preservation as by loyalism. I am grateful to Conrad Russell for raising this point.

31. L'Estrange, *Reign of King Charles*, pp. 127–28, 137–38, 146–47, 158–60, 165, 169. See *DNB*, s.v. "Hamon L'Estrange" and "Sir Roger L'Estrange," for the author's connection with Clarendon, who seems obliquely mentioned in the preface to the history as an important source of information.

32. Sanderson, *Compleat History*, pp. 200, 224, 248–49, 287–88. Sanderson was secretary to the earl of Holland; on him, see *DNB*, where Firth describes Sanderson's account as "of little value."

33. Wren, "Origins and Progress of the Revolution," in *Collectanea Curiosa*, 1:228–53. Wren died in 1672, which puts a terminal point to the composition of this account;

there appears to be no other printed version of this pamphlet, and it is little known. See *DNB*, s.v. "Matthew Wren."

34. Wren, "Origins and Progress of the Revolution," 1:238.

35. Ibid., p. 239. He concludes: "And this will appear the more credible to him, who shall consider how favorable to the Presbyterian party, through the whole course of affairs, those resolutions have been which came from the queen's side."

36. Kenyon, *Stuart Constitution*, p. 451.

37. Nalson, *Impartial Collection*. 1:xxxvii–xxxix and xlv–xlviii.

38. Lamont, *Prynne*, pp. 143–48, who argues that the similarities between the two plot stories discredit both of them; the issue seems to me more complex than that. Israel Tonge, who figured in the later plot, was in Hartlib's circle in the 1650s (Webster, *Hartlib and Advancement of Learning*, pp. 62, 70).

Bibliography

Manuscripts

GREAT BRITAIN

Bristol
    Archives Office
        Papers of Smyth Family of Ashton Court (acc. no. 36074).
London
    Archives of the Archbishop of Westminster
        Series A. 26, 27, 28, 29, 30. Correspondence and Papers of English Secular Clergy,
            1632–54.
        Series B. 27. Correspondence and Papers of Richard Smith, Bishop of Chalcedon,
            1624–36.
        Series B. 47. Correspondence and Papers of English Secular Clergy, 1632–41 (formerly
            MS Anglia A. VIII, at Stonyhurst College).
    Archives of the English Province of The Society of Jesus (114 Mount Street)
        Anglia 33 (I). Papers of the English Jesuits, Seventeenth Century, Jesuit Archives,
            Rome (microfilm and notes at Mount Street).
        Epistolae Generalium Anglia I(2). Letters of the Jesuit General to England, 1626–41,
            Jesuit Archives, Rome (photocopy at Mount Street).
        Stonyhurst Anglia A. VI, VII. Papers of English Jesuits, Sixteenth through Eighteenth
            Centuries: "Collectanea" (photocopy at Mount Street).
    British Museum
        Additional MSS 4,168–70. Letterbooks of Sir Thomas Roe, 1638–40.
        Additional MS 4,460. Rev. Henry Sampson, Manuscript Day Book.
        Additional MS 5,754. Documents Relating to Military Affairs.
        Additional MS 6,521. Anonymous Proceedings in the House of Commons, March,
            1641.
        Additional MS 8,657.
        Additional MS 11,043. Scudamore Papers, Vol. 3, Correspondence, 1550–1700.
        Additional MS 11,045. Scudamore Papers, Vol. 5, Rossingham Newsletters, 1638–41.
        Additional MSS 14,827 (1642) and 14,828 (1641). Parliamentary Diary of Fram-
            lingham Gawdy, 1642 and 1641.
        Additional MSS 15,390–15,392. Transcripts of Letters of Papal Agents in England,
            from the Vatican Archives, Rome, 1637–40.
        Additional MSS 17,677P–17,677Q. Transcripts from The Hague, Letters of A. Jo-
            achimi, 1637–39.
        Additional MS 21,203. Diary of Henry Morse, S.J., 1637.
        Additional MSS 27,962H–27,962I. Transcripts of the Newsletters of the Florentine
            Agent Salvetti, 1637–42.
        Additional MS 28,082. Papers Relating to the Army, 1640–1702.
        Additional MS 29,587. Miscellaneous Political Papers, 1559–1705.

Additional MS 35,331. Diary of Walter Yonge, 1627–42.

Additional MS 36,530. Miscellaneous State Papers, 1581–1644.

Additional MS 37,157. Papers of Lord Herbert of Cherbury.

Additional MS 37,343. Bulstrode Whitelocke's Annals of His Own Time, Vol. 3, November 1634 to July 1645.

Additional MS 41,846. Middleton Papers; Kenelm Digby Papers.

Harleian MSS 162–63. Parliamentary Diary of Sir Simonds D'Ewes, 1642.

Harleian MS 478. Parliamentary Diary of John Moore, 1641.

Harleian MS 1,219. Tracts and Papers . . . [from the Time of] Charles I.

Harleian MS 3,888. Nicholas Archbold, O.F.M. Cap., "Evangelicall Fruict of the Seraphicall Franciscan Order" (1623–45).

Harleian MS 4,234. Letters from the Privy Council, 1638–42.

Harleian MS 4,931. Anonymous Proceedings in Both Houses of Parliament, April, 1640.

Harleian MS 6,424. Parliamentary Diary of John Warner, Bishop of Rochester, 1641–42.

Harleian MS 7,001. Original Letters . . . , ca. 1633–1734.

Microfilm Deposit 285. Duke of Northumberland, Alnwick MSS, Vol. 14, Letters and Manuscripts, 1636–39.

Microfilm Deposit 325. Duke of Northumberland, Alnwick MSS, Vol. 725, Letters, 1631–1863.

Sloane MS 650. Relation of Passages in Scotland Touching Church Worship, 1637–39.

Sloane MS 1,467, No. 35. "The Pope's Cabinet Council discabineted by a new Discovery and Authentic History."

Sloane MS 1,470.

Stowe MS 531. Miscellaneous Extracts from Public Records.

Lambeth Palace Library

Lambeth MSS 943. Papers of William Laud.

Public Record Office

C231/5. Crown Office Docquet Book.

E351/2803. Miscellaneous Exchequer Documents: Account of N. Page, Clerk of the Kitchen, for Diet of Duchess of Chevreuse, 1638.

PRO 30/53/7; 12. Powis Papers: Correspondence of Lord Herbert of Cherbury; Accounts of Proceedings in the House of Commons, 1640–41.

PRO 31/3/69–72. Transcripts of Dispatches of Seneterre, Bellièvre, and Montreuil, French Diplomats in England, 1636–41 (Baschet Transcripts).

PRO 31/9. Transcripts from Roman Archives (Vatican Library and Archives et al.) Concerning English Affairs.

PRO 31/9/17B. Transcripts of Gregorio Panzani's Letters from England, 1634–37.

PRO 31/9/18–23. Transcripts of Carlo Rossetti's Letters from England and Cologne, 1639–44.

PRO 31/9/124. Transcripts of George Con's Correspondence with Ferragalli, 1636–39.

PRO 31/9/126–29. Barberini Miscellany from the Time of Charles I: Transcripts of Letters from DuPerron, George Leybourne, Robert Philip, Henrietta Maria, David Chambers, Earl of Angus, and Others Concerning English Affairs.

PRO 31/9/130. Transcripts of Miscellaneous Letters from England to Cardinal Francesco Barberini in Rome.

PRO 31/9/133. Transcripts of Letters and Papers Concerning Scottish Catholics.

PRO 31/9/135. Transcripts of Letters from Cardinal Francesco Barberini to Walter

Montagu, Robert Philip, Marie de Medici, Henrietta Maria, and Others in England.

PRO 31/9/136. Transcripts of Letters from Leonardo Fabbroni, Marie de Medici's Roman Agent.

PRO 31/9/137. Transcripts of Letters from Walter Montagu and Others to the Barberini Family, 1636–76.

PRO 31/9/140. Transcripts of Correspondence between Cardinal Francesco Barberini and Cardinal Richelieu, Marie de Medici, and Fantucci.

PRO 31/10/10. Transcripts of Letters from Cardinal Francesco Barberini to Gregorio Panzani, Leander Jones, Robert Philip, and Others.

PRO 31/10/11. Transcripts of Ferragalli's and Barberini's Letters to George Con, 1636–38.

PRO 31/3/69–72. Transcripts of Dispatches of Seneterre, Bellièvre, and Montreuil, French Diplomats in England, 1636–41 (Baschet Transcripts).

S.O. 3/11, 12. Signet Office Docquet Books, 1634–44.

SP 77/28, 29. State Papers Flanders, 1638–39.

SP 78/105–7. State Papers France, 1638–39.

SP 81/44, 46. State Papers Germany, 1638, 1639.

SP 84/154–55. State Papers Holland, May 1638 to August 1639.

SP 94/40, 41. State Papers Spain, 1638–39.

SP 105/15, 16. Entry Book of Balthazar Gerbier, 1638–39.

Maidstone
  Kent Archives Office
    Sackville of Knole MSS, U. 269. Cranfield Correspondence and Papers, 1635–40.

Manchester
  John Rylands Library
    English MSS 736, 737. Papers of Charles Towneley of Towneley.

Oxford
  Bodleian Library
    Ashmole MS 800.
    Ashmole MS 1153/46–53. "Pigg's Coranto."
    Bankes MSS 6/24; 18/8, 10, 19; 23/17; 37/54; 42/78; 44/46; 49/12. Papers of Attorney General Bankes, 1634–41.
    Carte MS 63/36–37. Wandesford Correspondence, 1638–39.
    Clarendon MSS 6, 8, 11, 15–19. Correspondence and Papers, Chiefly of Secretary of State Windebank, 1633–40.
    Nalson Deposit 12, 13.
    Rawlinson MS C911/467–519. Papers of John Dury.
    Rawlinson MS D720/273–74. Copy of "Advices and Motives."
    Tanner MSS 177, 395.

Reading
  Berkshire Record Office, Downshire Deposit
    Trumbull MSS. Miscellaneous Correspondence.
      Vol. 19. Papers and Letters, 1630–37.
      Vol. 20. Papers and Letters, 1638–44.
      Weckherlin Papers and Letters, 1615–61.
      Weckherlin Diary, 1633–42.
    Trumbull Additional MSS.
      Bundle 4. Miscellaneous Papers, 1620–47, Mainly of G. R. Weckherlin.

Bundle 7. Miscellaneous Documents, Drafts, and Copies of Official Papers, ca. 1560–1750.

Sheffield
Central Library, Wentworth Woodhouse Collection
Strafford MSS 3, 8, 10, 15, 17, 18, 19.

Stratton-on-the-Fosse, Somerset
Downside Abbey, Transcripts and Notes from Roman Archives Relating to English Benedictine Affairs
Downside No. 1332. Gasquet's Notes and Translations from the Archives of Congregation de Propaganda Fide.
Scritture originali riferite nelle Congregazioni Generali ("Lettere antiche"), vols. 11, 15, 43, 100, 105, 106, 132, 134, 135, 137, 138, 139, 347.
Acta 6–8 (1632–34), 11–12 (1637–38).

ITALY

Rome
Vatican Archives
Nunziatura d'Inghilterra 3A. Diary of Gregorio Panzani during his Mission to England (currently being edited by Dr. David M. Lunn, to whom I am indebted for all references).
Vatican Library
Barberini Latini MSS (microfilm provided through Vatican Film Library, Pius XII Memorial Library, St. Louis University, St. Louis, Missouri)
8618. Correspondence of John Cecil to Rome on English and Scottish Affairs, 1610–25.
8619. Correspondence of Bishop Smith and of David Codner, O.S.B., 1620s and 1630s.
8639–8644. Correspondence of George Con, June 1636 to October 1639.
8646–8652. Correspondence of Carlo Rossetti, June 1639 to December 1642.
8653. Correspondence of Rossetti and Others, 1643.
8654. Correspondence of Rossetti, January to July 1644.
8655. Letters of Rossetti to Ferragalli, 1639–43.
8657. Correspondence of Leonardo Fabbroni (resident at Rome for Marie de Medici), 1635–42.
8659. Letters of Walter Montagu to Cardinal Barberini and Others, 1636–76.

UNITED STATES

Madison, Wisconsin
University of Wisconsin Library
Gerould Cat. No. 137. Parliamentary Diary of Sir Thomas Peyton, 1642 (typescript at Yale University Parliamentary Diaries' Center, Sterling Library, New Haven, Ct.)

New Haven, Connecticut
Yale University, Beinecke Library, Osborn Collection
Howard of Escricke MSS (acc. no. 76.12.3).

San Marino, California
Henry E. Huntington Library
Ellesmere MSS 7352, 7433, 7434. Papers of the Earl of Bridgewater (transcripts provided by Dr. Penry Williams of New College, Oxford).

Printed Primary Sources

BIOGRAPHICAL DICTIONARIES

Anstruther, Godfrey. *The Seminary Priests*. Vol. 1, *Elizabethan 1558–1603*, Ware/
　Durham, 1968. Vol. 2, *Early Stuarts 1603–1659*, Great Wakering, Essex, 1975.
Batterel, L. *Mémoires domestiques pour servir à l'histoire de la Congrégation de l'Oratoire*.
　Edited by A.M.P. Ingold and E. Bonnardet. 5 vols. Geneva, 1902–11.
Birt, Dom Henry Norbert. *Obit Book of the English Benedictines, 1600–1912*. Edited by
　David Lunn. London, 1970.
Dictionary of National Biography. Edited by Sir Leslie Stephen and Sir Sidney Lee. 63 vols.
　London, 1885–1900.
Dictionary of Welsh Biography. Edited by John Edward Lloyd and R. T. Jenkins. London,
　1959.
Domenicus de Gubernatis a Sospitello (O.F.M. Cap.). *Orbis Seraphicus*. Edited by Marcel-
　linus a Civetia and Theophilus Domenichelli. Vol. 2, pt. 1. Claras Aquas, 1886.
Douglas, Sir Robert. *Peerage of Scotland*. Edited by Sir J. B. Paul. 9 vols. Edinburgh,
　1904–14.
Foley, Henry, ed. *Records of the English Province of the Society of Jesus . . . in the Sixteenth
　and Seventeenth Centuries*. 7 vols. in 8. London, 1875–1909.
Gillow, Joseph, ed. *A Literary and Biographical History of the English Catholics from . . .
　1534 to the Present Day*. 5 vols. London, 1885–1902.
Keeler, Mary Frear. *The Long Parliament, 1640–1641*. Philadelphia, 1954.
Wood, Anthony à. *Athenae Oxonienses*. 4 vols. London, 1813–20.

PARLIAMENTARY PROCEEDINGS

Coates, Willson H., ed. *Journal of Sir Simonds D'Ewes*. New Haven, 1942.
Cobbett, William, ed. *The Parliamentary History of England from the Earliest Period to the
　Year 1803*. 36 vols. London, 1806–20.
Cope, Esther, ed., with Coates, Willson H. *Proceedings of the Short Parliament of 1640*.
　Camden Society, ser. 4, vol. 19. London, 1977.
Journals of the House of Commons, 1547–1714. 17 vols. London, 1742–.
Journals of the House of Lords, 1578–1714. 19 vols. London, 1767–.
Notestein, Wallace, ed. *Journal of Sir Simonds D'Ewes*. New Haven, 1923.
Rushworth, John. *The Tryal of Thomas, Earl of Strafford (1641)*. London, 1680.
Verney, Sir Ralph. *Notes of Proceedings in the Long Parliament*. Camden Society, ser. 1,
　vol. 31. London, 1845.

OFFICIAL DOCUMENTS

Avenel, Georges d', ed. *Lettres, instructions diplomatiques, et papiers d'État du Cardinal de
　Richelieu*. 8 vols. Paris, 1853–77.
Calendar of Clarendon State Papers. Edited by Octavius Ogle, W. H. Bliss, and W. D.
　Macray. 3 vols. Oxford, 1869–76.
Calendar of State Papers, Domestic. Edited by M. A. E. Green, John Bruce, et al. 27 vols.
　London, 1857–97.
Calendar of State Papers, Venetian. Edited by H. F. Brown and A. B. Hinds. Vols. 10–38
　(1603–75). London, 1900–1940.
Clarendon State Papers. Edited by Richard Scrope and Thomas Monkhouse. 3 vols.
　Oxford, 1767–86.

Elton, Geoffrey, ed. *The Tudor Constitution.* Cambridge, 1962.

Gardiner, S. R., ed. *Constitutional Documents of the Puritan Revolution, 1628–1660.* Oxford, 1899.

Groen van Prinsterer, Guillaume, ed. *Archives ou correspondance inédite de la maison d'Orange-Nassau.* Ser. 2, 5 vols. Leiden/Utrecht, 1857–61.

Hardwicke, Philip, earl of, ed. *Miscellaneous State Papers, 1501–1726.* 2 vols. London, 1778.

Howell, Thomas B., ed. *A Complete Collection of State Trials.* 21 vols. London, 1816–26.

Kenyon, John, ed. *The Stuart Constitution.* Cambridge, 1966.

Lonchay, Henri, and Cuvelier, Joseph, eds. *Correspondance de la cour d'Espagne sur les affaires des Pays-Bas au XVIIe siècle.* 6 vols. Brussels, 1923–27.

Loomie, Albert J., ed. *Spain and the Jacobean Catholics.* Vol. 2, *1613–24.* CRS Records Series, vol. 68. London, 1978.

Nalson, John, ed. *An Impartial Collection of the Great Affairs of State from the Beginning of the Scotch Rebellion in the Year 1639 to the murder of King Charles I.* 2 vols. London, 1682–83.

Privy Council of England. *Register: 1 June 1637–30 June 1645.* 12 vols. London, 1967–68.

Privy Council of Scotland. *Register.* Edited by John H. Burton, David Masson, P. H. Brown, and Henry Paton. Edinburgh, 1877–.

Rushworth, John, ed. *Historical Collections of Private Passages of State, etc.* 8 vols. London, 1680–1701.

Rymer, Thomas, and Sanderson, Robert, eds. *Foedera.* 20 vols. London, 1704–32.

Steele, Robert R., ed. *A Bibliography of Royal Proclamations . . . 1485–1714.* 2 vols. Oxford, 1910.

CORRESPONDENCE, DIARIES, AND WRITINGS

Baillie, Robert. *Letters and Journals.* Edited by David Laing. 3 vols. Edinburgh, Bannatyne Club, 1841–42.

Baker, L. M., ed. *Letters of Elizabeth, Queen of Bohemia.* London, 1953.

Berington, Joseph, ed. *Memoirs of Gregorio Panzani.* Birmingham, England, 1793.

Bray, William, ed. *Diary and Correspondence of John Evelyn.* 3d ed. 4 vols. London, 1854.

Bromley, Sir George. *A Collection of Original Royal Letters.* London, 1787.

Bruce, John, ed. *Letters and Papers of the Verney Family.* Camden Society, ser. 1, vol. 61. London, 1853.

Calendar of Wynn (of Gwydir) Papers, 1515–1690. National Library of Wales, Aberystwyth, 1926.

Collins, Arthur, ed. *Letters and Memorials of State . . . Written and Collected by Sir Henry Sydney . . . [Sydney Papers].* 2 vols. London, 1746.

Dagens, Jean, ed. *Correspondance du Cardinal Pierre de Bérulle.* 3 vols. Paris, 1937–39.

Ferguson, James, ed. *Papers Illustrating the History of the Scots Brigade in the Service of the United Netherlands (1572–1782) from the Archives at the Hague.* 3 vols. Edinburgh, Scottish Historical Society, 1899.

Green, Mary Anne Everett. *Letters of Queen Henrietta Maria.* London, 1857.

Hamilton Papers . . . 1638–50. Edited by S. R. Gardiner. Camden Society, n.s., vol. 28. London, 1880.

Harris, P. R., ed. *Douai College Documents, 1634–1794.* CRS Records Series, vol. 63. London, 1972.

Hay, M. V., ed. *The Blairs Papers, 1603–1660.* Edinburgh, 1929.

Howard, Lord William of Naworth. *Selections from the Household Books . . . 1612–1640.*

Edited by George Ornsby. Surtees Society, vol. 68. London, 1878.

Jeaffreson, John E., ed. *Middlesex County Records*. Ser. 1, 4 vols. Middlesex County Record Society, London, 1886–92.

Knowler, William, ed. *The Earl of Strafford's Letters and Dispatches*. 2 vols. London, 1739.

Laud, William. *Works*. Edited by James Bliss and William Scott. 7 vols. Oxford, 1847–60.

Letters of Lady Brilliana Harley. Edited by T. T. Lewis. Camden Society, ser. 1, vol. 58. London, 1854.

Lismore Papers. Edited by A. B. Grosart. Ser. 2, 5 vols. London, 1886–88.

McIlwain, Charles H., ed. *Political Works of James I*. Cambridge, Mass., 1918.

Rous, John. *Diary*. Edited by M. A. E. Green. Camden Society, ser. 1, vol. 66. London, 1856.

Sainsbury, William Noel, ed. *Original Unpublished Papers Illustrative of the Life of Sir Peter Paul Rubens*. London, 1859.

Smith, W. J., ed. *Herbert Correspondence*. Cardiff, Wales, 1963.

Southcote, John. "The Notebook of John Southcote, D.D., 1623–37." In CRS *Miscellany I*, pp. 97–116. London, 1905.

Spicilegium Benedictinum. 5 nos. Rome, 1896–97.

Thibaudeau, A. W., ed. *Catalogue of Collections of . . . Alfred Morrison*. 6 vols. London, 1883–92.

Warner, Sir G. F., ed. *The Nicholas Papers: Correspondence of Sir Edward Nicholas, Secretary of State*. 4 vols. Camden Society, n.s., vols. 40, 50, 57 and ser. 3, vol. 31. London, 1886–1920.

Warner, Rebecca, ed. *Epistolary Curiosities . . . letters . . . Illustrative of the Herbert Family*. Ser. 1, 2 vols. Bath, 1818.

Whitaker, T. D. *The Life and Original Correspondence of Sir George Radcliffe*. London, 1810.

Young, John. *The Diary of John Young, Dean of Winchester, 1616 to The Commonwealth*. Edited by F. R. Goodman. London, 1928.

HISTORICAL MANUSCRIPT COMMISSION REPORTS

HMC Second Report, Appendix, Biddulph of Chirk Castle MSS.

HMC Third Report, Appendix, Devonshire MSS (Bolton Abbey and Hardwick Hall).

———, Appendix, De la Warr MSS.

HMC Fourth Report, Appendix, House of Lords MSS.

HMC Fifth Report, Appendix, Cholmondeley MSS.

HMC Sixth Report, Appendix I, Denbigh MSS.

HMC Eighth Report, Appendix II, Duke of Manchester MSS.

HMC Ninth Report, Appendix II, Earl of Leicester MSS (Heveningham Papers).

HMC Tenth Report, Appendix I, Skrine MSS (Salvetti Papers, 1625–28).

———, Appendix IV, Powis MSS.

HMC Eleventh Report, Appendix VI, Hamilton MSS, vol. 1.

HMC Twelfth Report, Appendixes I–II, Cowper MSS, vols. 1–2 (Coke Papers).

———, Appendix IV, Rutland MSS, vol. 1.

———, Appendix IX, Beaufort MSS.

HMC Thirteenth Report, Appendix I, Portland, vol. 1, Nalson MSS.

HMC Fourteenth Report, Appendix II, Portland, vol. 3, Harley MSS.

———, Appendix IV, Kenyon of Peel MSS.

HMC Buccleuch MSS (Montagu House), vol. 3.

HMC De L'Isle and Dudley MSS, vol. 6.
HMC Denbigh MSS.
HMC Franciscan MSS.
HMC Hamilton Supplement MSS.
HMC Various Collections, vol. 2, Buxton of Shadwell Court MSS.

CONTEMPORARY HISTORIES

Balfour, Sir James. *Historical Works*. Edited by James Haig. 4 vols. Edinburgh, 1825.
Bate, George. *A Short Narrative*. Edited by Edward Almack. London, 1902.
Baxter, Richard. *Reliquiae Baxterianae*. Edited by Matthew Sylvester. London, 1692.
Birch, Thomas, ed. *The Court and Times of Charles I*. London, 1848.
Burnet, Gilbert. *A History of My Own Time*. Edited by Osmund Airy. 2 vols. Oxford, 1897.
————. *Memoirs of the Lives and Actions of James and William, Dukes of Hamilton*. 2d ed. Oxford, 1852.
Clarendon, Edward, earl of. *History of the Rebellion and Civil Wars in England*. Edited by W. D. Macray. 6 vols. Oxford, 1888.
Dugdale, William. *A Short View of the Late Troubles*. Oxford, 1681.
Gage, Thomas. *Travels in the New World*. Edited by J. Eric S. Thompson. Norman, Okla., 1958.
Gordon, James. *History of Scots Affairs from 1637 to 1641*. Edited by Joseph Robertson and George Grub. 3 vols. Aberdeen, 1841.
Guthrie, William of Brechin. *A General History of England*. 4 vols. London, 1744–51.
L'Estrange, Hamon. *The Reign of King Charles (to 1641)*. London, 1655.
Menteith, Robert. *History of the Troubles of Great Britain*. Translated by James Ogilvie. London, 1735.
Sanderson, Sir William. *A Compleat History of the Life and Raigne of King Charles*. London, 1658.
Spalding, John. *History of the Troubles and Memorable Transactions in Scotland. . . .* Edited by James Skene. 2 vols. Edinburgh, 1828–29.
Wallington, Nehemiah. *Historical Notices of the Reign of Charles I, 1630–46*. Edited by R. Webb. 2 vols. London, 1869.
Warwick, Sir Philip. *Memoirs of the Reign of Charles I*. London, 1701.
Webster, Charles, ed. *Samuel Hartlib and the Advancement of Learning*. Cambridge, 1970.
Weldon, Anthony. *The Court and Character of King James and King Charles*. London, 1651.
Whitelocke, Bulstrode. *Memorials of the English Affairs*. 4 vols. Oxford, 1853.
Wren, Matthew. "Of the Origins and Progress of the Revolution in England." In *Collectanea Curiosa, or Miscellaneous Tracts*, edited by John Gutch, vol. 1. Oxford, 1781.

PAMPHLETS

Abernethie, Thomas. *Abjuration of Popery*. Edinburgh, 1638.
————. *A Worthy Speech by Mr. Thomas Abernethie, wherein is discovered the hellish plots . . . wrought in the Pope's court*. London, 1641.
Alsted, John Henry. *Beloved City*. London, 1643.
————. *The World's Proceeding Woes and Succeeding Joys*. London, 1642.
Baillie, Robert. *Canterburian's Self-Conviction*. Amsterdam, 1640.
[Balcanquhal, Walter.] *A Large Declaration Concerning the Late Tumults in Scotland*. London, 1639.

The Beast is Wounded, or information from Scotland by John Bastwick's Younger Brother. Amsterdam, 1638.

Browne, John. *The Confession of John Browne . . . a Jesuit, in the Gatehouse.* London, 1641.

———. *A Discovery of the Notorious Proceedings of William Laud . . . confessed by John Browne, a Prisoner in the Gatehouse . . . October 15, 1641.* London, 1641.

Burton, Henry. *Israel's Fast.* London, 1628.

———. *A Protestation Protested.* N.p., 1641.

———. *A Reply to a Relation.* N.p., 1641.

———. *Sounding of the Two Last Trumpets.* London, 1641. Reprinted in *A Collection of Thirteen Rare Tracts.* London, 1646.

Charles I. *His Majesties Manifest Touching the Palatine Cause, and Prince. Votes of both Houses of Parliament Concerning the Same; published by His Majesty's Command.* London, 1641.

Chillingworth, William. *The Religion of Protestants.* London, 1632.

Comenius, John Amos. *Historia Persecutione Ecclesiae Bohemicae.* Amsterdam, 1648.

Corbet, John. *Ungirding of the Scottish Armour.* Dublin, 1639.

Davenport, Christopher (Franciscus à Sancta Clara). *Deus, Natura, Gratia, sive Tractatus de Praedestinatione.* Lyons, 1634.

———. *Apologia Episcoporum.* Cologne, 1640.

Dering, Sir Edward. *The Four Cardinal Vertues of a Carmelite Friar.* London, 1641.

Digby, Sir Kenelm. *Letters Between Lord George Digby and Sir Kenelm Digby . . . concerning Religion.* London, 1651.

Downing, Calybute. *A Discovery of the False Grounds the Bavarian Party Have Laid.* London, 1641.

———. *A Sermon Preached to the Renowned Company of the Artillery 1 September 1640. Designed to Compose the Present Troubles, by Discovering the Enemies of the Peace of the Church and State.* London, 1641.

Dugdale, William. *A Short View of the Late Troubles. . . .* Oxford, 1681.

Dury, John. *A Brief Relation of That which hath been lately attempted to procure Ecclesiastical Peace among Protestants.* London, 1642.

———. *Consultatio Theologica super negotio Pacis Ecclesiasticae promovendo.* London, 1641.

———. *John Dury His Petition to The Honourable House of Commons in England.* London, 1641.

———. *A Memorial Concerning Peace Ecclesiastical Amongst Protestants.* London, 1641.

———. *A Motion Tending to the Public Good of This Age, and of Posterity.* London, 1642.

———. *Motives to Induce The Protestant Princes to Mind the Work of Peace Ecclesiastical Amongst Themselves.* London, 1641.

———. *A Summary Discourse Concerning the Work of Peace Ecclesiastical, How it may Concurre with the aim of a Civil Confederation Amongst Protestants.* Cambridge, 1641.

Fairclough, Samuel. *The Troublers Troubled, or Achan Condemned and Executed.* London, 1641.

Frubach, Volradus. *Evaporation of the Apple of Palestine.* London, 1637.

[Gibson, Alexander, et al.] *Information to all good Christians within the Kingdom of England.* Edinburgh, 1639.

The Grand Designs of the Papists. London, 1678.

A Great Conspiracy of the Papists Against the Worthy Members of Both Houses of Parliament. . . . London, 1641.

Habernfeld, Andreas ab. *Bellum Bohemicum*. Leiden, 1645.

————. *Hierosolyma Restituta*. Leiden, 1622.

Henderson, Alexander. *Remonstrance of the Nobility, Barrones, Burgesses, Ministers, and Commons*. Edinburgh, 1639.

Henrietta Maria, queen of England. *A Coppy of the Letter. . . .* London, 1641.

Heyricke, Richard. *Three Sermons Preached at the Collegiate Church in Manchester*. London, 1641.

Heywood, Thomas. *The Rat-Trap: or The Jesuites Taken in Their Own Netes. Discovered in This Year of Jubilee, or Deliverance from The Romish Faction*. London, 1641.

Impeachment and Articles of Complaint Against Father Philip. London, 1641.

[Johnston, Sir Archibald.] *A Short Relation of the State of the Kirk . . . for information to our Brethren in the Kirk of England*. Edinburgh, 1638.

Knott, Edward [*vere* Matthew Wilson]. *A Direction to be Observed by N. N.* N.p., 1636.

Leighton, Alexander. *An Appeal to the Parliament, Or Sion's Plea against the Prelacie*. Amsterdam, 1628.

————. *Speculum Belli Sacri; Or the Looking-Glasse of the Holy War*. Amsterdam, 1624.

Macaria. London, 1641.

Marsys, François de. *Histoire de la Persécution près des Catholiques en Angleterre*. Paris, 1646.

Mede, Joseph. *The Apostacy of the Latter Times*. London, 1641.

————. *Clavis Apocalyptica*. London, 1651.

Morton, Thomas. *A Sermon Preached in the Cathedral Church of Durham 1639, 5 May—Before the King*. London, 1639.

Napier, John. *A Plaine Discovery of the whole Revelation of St. John*. Edinburgh, 1594.

A New Plot Discovered, practiced by an assembly of Papists, upon Sunday being the 25 day of July for William Waller, alias Ward, alias Slater, a Jesuit. London, 1641.

The Papists Conspiracie, or A Plot which was first contrived and counselled by a Papist Priest whose late discovery and imprisonment attends the sentence of the law. . . . London, 1641.

The Papists' Design against the Parliament and the City of London Discovered. London, 1642.

Percy, John [alias Fisher]. *Answer unto the Nine Points of Controversy*. St. Omer, 1626.

Pigges Corantoe, or Newes from the North. London, 1642.

The Pope's Nuntioes. London, 1643. Reprinted in *Somers Tracts*, edited by Sir Walter Scott, vol. 4, pp. 50–56. 2d ed. 13 vols. London, 1809–15.

Preston, Thomas, O.S.B. [alias William Howard]. *A Patterne of Christian Loyaltie*. London, 1634.

"The Prophecy of Bishop Ussher." In *Harleian Miscellany*, edited by Thomas Park, vol. 9, pp. 200–201. 10 vols. London, 1808–13.

Prynne, William. *Antipathy of the English Lordly Prelacy*. London, 1641.

————. *Breviate of the Prelates' Intolerable Usurpations*. Amsterdam, 1637.

————. *Canterburies' Doom*. London, 1646.

————. *Certain Queries Propounded to the Bowers at the Name of Jesus*. Amsterdam, 1636.

————. *Divine Tragedy Lately Enacted*. London, 1636.

————. *Hidden Works of Darkness*. London, 1645.

————. *A New Discovery of the Prelates' Tyranny*. London, 1641.

————. *News from Ipswich*. N.p., 1637.

————. *Popish Royal Favorite* (incorporating *Jesuits' Looking Glass* [1636]). London, 1643.

————. *A Quench-Coal*. Amsterdam, 1637.

————. *Rome's Masterpiece*. London, 1644.

Pym, John. *Reasons of the House of Commons to stay the Queens going into Holland. Delivered to the Lords at a Conference the 14 of July 1641*. London, 1641.

Saint Francis of Sales. *An Introduction to a Devout Life*. Paris, 1637.

The Scottish Scouts' Discoveries by their London Intelligencer. London, 1642.

A Second Discovery by the Northern Scout. London, 1642.

Selden, John. *Mare Clausum*. London, 1635.

Stoughton, Dr. John. *Felicitas Ultimi Saeculi*. London, 1640.

A True Narrative of the Popish Plot against King Charles I and the Protestant Religion. London, 1680.

The True Relation of a Bloody Conspiracy by the Papists in Cheshire. London, 1641. Reprinted in *Tracts relating to the Civil War in Cheshire*, edited by J. A. Atkinson. Chetham Society, ser. 2, vol. 65. Manchester, 1909.

A True Relation of the French Embassage. London, 1641 (?).

Two Famous Sea-Fights lately made betwixt the fleets of the King of Spain and the Hollanders. London, 1639.

Vicars, John. *Jehovah Jireh. God in the mount*. London, 1642.

Watson, William (?). *A Sparing Discovery of Our English Jesuits*. N.p., 1601.

Secondary Sources

Adams, S. L. "Foreign Policy and the Parliaments of 1621 and 1624." In *Faction and Parliament: Essays on Early Stuart History*, edited by Kevin Sharpe, pp. 139–72. Oxford, 1978.

Albion, Gordon. *Charles I and the Court of Rome*. London, 1935.

Albrecht, Dieter. *Die auswärtige politik Maximilians von Bayern, 1618–1635*. Göttingen, 1962.

Alcalá-Zamora y Queipo de Llano, J. A. *España, Flandes y el mar del Norte 1618–1639*. Barcelona, 1975.

Alexander, Michael van Cleave. *Charles I's Lord Treasurer: Sir Richard Weston, Earl of Portland (1577–1635)*. Chapel Hill, 1975.

Allison, A. F. "Richard Smith, Richelieu and the French Marriage." *Recusant History* 7 (1964): 148–211.

————. "Franciscan Books in English, 1559–1640." *Recusant History* 3 (1955): 18–65.

Anson, Peter. *The Catholic Church in Modern Scotland, 1560–1937*. London, 1937.

Anstruther, Godfrey. "Cardinal Howard and the English Court (1658–1694)." *Archivum Fratrum Praedicatorum* 28 (1958): 315–61.

————. *A Hundred Homeless Years: English Dominicans, 1558–1658*. London, 1958.

————. "Lancashire Clergy in 1639: A Recently Discovered List among the Towneley Papers." *Recusant History* 4 (1957): 38–46.

————. "Recusant Burials." *London Recusant* 1 (1971): 103–7.

————. *Vaux of Harrowden*. Newport, Monmouth, 1953.

Ascoli, G. *La Grande-Bretagne devant l'opinion française*. 2 vols. Paris, 1927.

Ashton, Robert. *The City and the Court, 1603–1642*. Cambridge, 1979.

Aveling, Hugh. *The Catholic Recusants of the West Riding of Yorkshire, 1558–1790*. Leeds, 1963.

————. *Northern Catholics: The Catholic Recusants of the North Riding of Yorkshire*. London, 1966.

Aylmer, G. E. *The King's Servants: The Civil Service of Charles I, 1625–1642*. Rev. ed. New York, 1974.

————. *The State's Servants: The Civil Service of the English Republic, 1649–1660.* London, 1973.

Bankes, George. *The Story of Corfe Castle.* London, 1853.

Barnett, Pamela R. *Theodore Haak, FRS, 1605–1690.* The Hague, 1962.

Bassett, Bernard. *The English Jesuits from Campion to Martindale.* New York, 1968.

Batten, Joseph Minton. *John Dury, Advocate of Christian Reunion.* Chicago, 1944.

Beatty, John. *Warwick and Holland.* Denver, 1965.

Beller, Elmer A. "The Diplomatic Relations between England and Germany during the Thirty Years War." D. Phil. dissertation, Oxford University, 1923.

Bellesheim, Alphonse. *History of the Catholic Church of Scotland.* 4 vols. Translated by D. Hunter Blair. Edinburgh, 1887–98.

Biaudet, Henri. *Les Nonciatures apostoliques permanentes jusqu'en 1648.* Helsinki, 1910.

Bigby, Dorothy A. *Anglo-French Relations, 1641–1649.* London, 1933.

Bireley, Robert. "The Peace of Prague (1635) and the Counterreformation in Germany." *Journal of Modern History* 48 (1976): 31–69.

Birrell, T. A. "Dutch and English Catholicism in the 17th Century: Contacts, Contrasts, and Analogies." *Recusant History Newsletter,* 1962.

————. "English Catholics Without a Bishop, 1655–1672." *Recusant History* 4 (1957–58): 142–78.

Blackwood, B. G. *The Lancashire Gentry and the Great Rebellion 1640–60.* Manchester, 1978.

Blekastad, Milada. *Comenius.* Oslo, 1969.

Blet, Pierre. "Richelieu et les débuts de Mazarin." *Revue d'histoire moderne et contemporaine* 6 (1959): 241–68.

————. "La Congrégation des Affaires de France de 1640." In *Mélanges Eugène Tissurant IV,* pp. 59–105. Città del Vaticano, 1964.

Bonney, Richard. *Political Change in France under Richelieu and Mazarin, 1624–1661.* Oxford, 1978.

Bossy, John. "The Character of Elizabethan Catholicism." *Past and Present* 21 (April 1962): 39–59.

————. *The English Catholic Community, 1570–1850.* London, 1975.

————. "The English Catholic Community, 1603–1625." In *The Reign of James VI and I,* edited by Alan G. R. Smith, pp. 91–105. London, 1973.

————. "Henry IV, the Appellants and the Jesuits." *Recusant History* 8 (1965): 80–122.

Bowman, Jacob N. *The Protestant Interest in Cromwell's Foreign Relations.* Heidelberg, 1900.

Boynton, Lindsay. *The Elizabethan Militia: 1558–1638.* London, 1967.

Brady, William Maziere. *Annals of the Catholic Hierarchy in England and Scotland, 1585–1876.* London, 1883.

Brown, Michael F. *Itinerant Ambassador: The Life of Sir Thomas Roe.* Lexington, Ky., 1970.

Burrell, Sidney A. "Apocalyptic Vision of the Early Covenanters." *Scottish Historical Review* 63 (1964): 1–24.

————. "Covenant Idea as a Revolutionary Symbol: Scotland, 1596–1637." *Church History* 27 (1958): 338–50.

————. "Kirk, Crown, and Covenant: A Study of the Scottish Background of the English Civil Wars." Ph.D. dissertation, Columbia University, 1953.

Caraman, Philip. *Henry Morse, Priest of the Plague (1595–1645).* London, 1957.

Cassavetti, Eileen. *The Lion and the Lilies.* London, 1977.

Cheney, Edward P. de G. "Van Dyck, John Hoskins, Jean Petitot and the ex-voto of Queen Henrietta Maria." *Burlington Magazine* 6 (1980): 837–38.

Christianson, Paul. *Reformers and Babylon*. Toronto, 1978.

Clancy, Thomas. "English Catholics and the Papal Deposing Power, 1570–1640, Part III: The Stuarts (cont.)." *Recusant History* 7 (1963–64): 2–10.

———. "The Jesuits and the Independents: 1647." *Archivum Historicum Societatis Iesu* 40 (1971): 67–90.

———. *Papist Pamphleteers*. Chicago, 1964.

Clarke, Aidan. "The Breakdown of Authority, 1640–41." In *Early Modern Ireland, 1534–1691*, pp. 270–88. Oxford, 1976. Vol. 3, *New History of Ireland*, edited by T. W. Moody, F. X. Martin, and F. J. Byrne.

———. "The Earl of Antrim and the First Bishops' War." *Irish Sword* 6 (Winter 1963): 108–14.

———. *The Old English in Ireland, 1625–1642*. Ithaca, 1966.

Clarke, J. A. *Huguenot Warrior: The Life and Times of Henri de Rohan, 1579–1638*. The Hague, 1966.

Clasen, Claus-Peter. *The Palatinate in European History, 1559–1660*. Rev. ed. Oxford, 1966.

Clay, Christopher. "The Misfortunes of William, Fourth Lord Petre (1638–1655)." *Recusant History* 11 (1971): 87–116.

Cliffe, J. T. *The Yorkshire Gentry from the Reformation to the Civil War*. London, 1969.

Clifton, Robin. "The Fear of Catholics in England, 1637–1645." D. Phil. dissertation, Oxford University, 1967.

Clouse, R. G. "Rebirth of Millenarianism." In *Puritans, the Millennium, and the Future of Israel*, edited by Peter Toon, pp. 42–65. London, 1970.

Coonan, T. L. *The Irish Catholic Confederacy and the Puritan Revolution*. New York, 1954.

Dagens, Jean. *Bérulle et les origines de la restoration catholique (1575–1611)*. Bruges, 1952.

Davidson, Alan. "Roman Catholicism in Oxfordshire, 1580–1640." Ph.D. dissertation, Bristol University, 1970.

Dethan, Georges. *The Young Mazarin*. Translated by Stanley Baron. London, 1977.

Dickmann, Franz. *Der Westfälische Frieden*. Münster, 1959.

Dircks, Henry. *The Life, Times and Scientific Labours of the Second Marquis of Worcester*. London, 1865.

Dockery, J. B. *Christopher Davenport*. London, 1960.

Dodd, A. H. "Caernarvonshire in the Civil War." *Caenarvonshire Historical Society Transactions* 14 (1953): 1–34.

———. "Colonel Francis Trafford." *Bulletin of the Board of Celtic Studies* 14 (1952): 300–302.

———. "Flintshire Politics in the Seventeenth Century." *Flintshire Historical Society Publications* 14 (1953–54): 22–46.

———. "The Pattern of Politics in Stuart Wales." *Cymmrodorion Society Transactions, 1948* (1949): 8–91.

———. *Studies in Stuart Wales*. Cardiff, 1952.

———. "Wales and the Second Bishops' War (1640)." *Bulletin of the Board of Celtic Studies* 12 (1948): 92–96.

———. "Wales in the Parliaments of Charles I, II: 1640–42." *Cymmrodorion Society Transactions, 1946–1947* (1948): 59–96.

———. "Welsh Opposition Lawyers in the Short Parliament." *Bulletin of the Board of Celtic Studies* 12 (1948): 106–7.

Dodd, Charles [*vere* Hugh Tootell]. *Church History of England*. Edited by Mark Tierney. 5 vols. London, 1839.

Donaldson, Gordon. *Scotland. James V–James VII*. Edinburgh, 1965.

Durkan, John. "Brown's Confession." *Innes Review* 21 (1970): 169–70.

————. "The Career of John Brown, Minim." *Innes Review* 21 (1970): 164–69.

————. "John Francis Maitland, Minim." *Innes Review* 21 (1970): 163–64.

————. "A Minim's Obituary." *Innes Review* 21 (1970): 161–63.

Edwards, Francis. "Henry More, S. I.: Administrator and Historian 1586–1661." *Archivum Historicum Societatis Iesu* 41 (1972): 233–81.

Elliott, J. H. *Revolt of the Catalans: A Study in the Decline of Spain (1598–1640)*. Cambridge, 1963.

————. "The Statecraft of Olivares." In *The Diversity of History: Essays in Honour of Sir Herbert Butterfield*, edited by J. H. Elliott and H. G. Koenigsberger, pp. 117–48. Ithaca, 1970.

————. "The Year of the Three Ambassadors." In *History and Imagination: Essays in Honour of H. R. Trevor-Roper*, edited by Hugh Lloyd-Jones, Valerie Pearl, and Blair Worden, pp. 165–81. London, 1981.

Elton, Geoffrey. "Tudor Government: The Points of Contact, III. The Court." *Transactions of Royal Historical Society*, ser. 5, vol. 26 (1976): 211–28.

Evans, Robert J. W. *Making of the Habsburg Monarchy, 1500–1700*. Oxford, 1979.

————. *Rudolf II and His World*. Oxford, 1973.

Evennett, H. O. *Spirit of the Counter-Reformation*. Cambridge, 1968.

Everitt, Alan M. *Change in the Provinces: The Seventeenth Century*. Leicester, 1969.

Figgis, John Neville. *Political Thought from Gerson to Grotius, 1415–1625*. Reprint. New York, 1960.

Firth, C. H. *Cromwell's Army*. 4th ed. London, 1962.

Fletcher, Anthony. *Outbreak of the English Civil War*. London, 1981.

Foisil, Madeleine. *La Révolte des Nu-pieds*. Paris, 1970.

Forster, Leonard Wilson. *Georg Rudolf Weckherlin: Zur Kenntnis Seines Lebens in England*. Basel, 1944.

Foster, Michael. "Sir Richard Forster (?1585–1661)." *Recusant History* 14 (1978): 163–74.

Foster, Stephen. *Notes from the Caroline Underground*. Hamden, Conn., 1978.

Fraser, William. *The Book of Carlaverock*. 2 vols. Edinburgh, 1873.

————. *The Douglas Book*. 4 vols. Edinburgh, 1885.

Fullerton, Georgiana. *Life of Elizabeth, Lady Falkland, 1585–1639*. London, 1883.

Gardiner, S. R. "Charles I and the Earl of Glamorgan." *English Historical Review* 2 (1887): 687–708.

————. *History of England, 1603–1642*. 10 vols. London, 1883–84.

Geyl, Pieter. "Frederick Henry and Charles I, 1641–1647." In *History of the Low Countries: Episodes and Problems*, pp. 43–78. London, 1964.

————. *Orange and Stuart*. Antwerp, 1963.

Giblin, Cathaldus. "Aegidius Chaissy, O.F.M., and James Ussher, Protestant Archbishop of Armagh." *Irish Ecclesiastical Record*, ser. 5, no. 85 (1956): 393–405.

————. "John Brown and John Francis Maitland, Scottish Minims." *Innes Review* 6 (1955): 145–49.

Glow, Lotte. "Committee Men in the Long Parliament August 1642–December 1643." *Historical Journal* 8 (1965): 1–15.

————. "Pym and Parliament: The Methods of Moderation." *Journal of Modern History* 36 (1964): 373–97.

Gouhier, P. "Mercenaires Irlandais au service de la France (1635–1664)." *Revue d'histoire moderne et contemporaine* 15 (October–December 1968): 672–90.

Green, Mary Anne Everett. *Elizabeth Electress Palatine and Queen of Bohemia.* Rev. ed. London, 1909.

Griffith, G. M. "Chirk Castle Election Activities: 1600–1750." *National Library of Wales Journal* 10 (1957–58): 33–50.

Grose, Clyde I. "England and Dunkirk." *American Historical Review* 39 (1933): 1–27.

Grun, Ruth E. "A Note on William Howard, Author of 'A Patterne of Christian Loyaltie.' " *Catholic Historical Review* 42 (1956): 330–40.

Guilday, Peter. *English Catholic Refugees on the Continent, 1558–1795.* New York, 1914.

Haley, K. H. D. " 'No Popery' in the Reign of Charles II." In *Britain and the Netherlands,* edited by John S. Bromley and E. H. Kossman, vol. 5, pp. 102–19. The Hague, 1975.

Haller, William. *Foxe's "Book of Martyrs" and the Elect Nation.* London, 1963.

Hammond, Vincent E. "Scottish Propaganda and the Origins of the English Civil War." Unpublished article.

Hanlon, Sister Joseph Damien. "The Effects of the Counter-Reformation upon the English Catholics, 1603–1630." Ph.D. dissertation, Columbia University, 1959.

Hardman, Anne. *English Carmelites in Penal Times.* London, 1936.

Haskell, Patricia. "Sir Francis Windebank: The Personal Rule of Charles I." Ph.D. dissertation, Southampton University, 1978.

Havran, Martin. *Caroline Courtier: The Life of Lord Cottington.* Chapel Hill, 1973.

––––––. *The Catholics in Caroline England.* Stanford, 1962.

––––––. "Informers in England during the Reign of Charles I." *American Ecclesiastical Review* 143 (1960): 289–303.

––––––. "Sources for Recusant History among the Bankes Papers in the Bodleian." *Recusant History* 5 (1960): 246–55.

Hawkes, Arthur J. "Sir Roger Bradshaigh of Haigh, Knight and Baronet, 1628–1684." *Chetham Society Miscellany* 7 (1945).

Hawkins, Michael. "The Government: Its Role and Its Aims." In *The Origins of the English Civil War,* edited by Conrad Russell, pp. 35–65. London, 1973.

Hervey, Mary F. S. *The Life, Correspondence and Collections of Thomas Howard, Earl of Arundel.* Cambridge. 1921.

[Hess], Father Cuthbert, O.F.M. Cap. *The Capuchins.* 2 vols. London, 1928.

Hexter, J. H. *King Pym.* Cambridge, Mass., 1941.

Hibbard, Caroline. "Charles I and the Popish Plot." Ph.D. dissertation, Yale University, 1975.

––––––. "Early Stuart Catholicism: Revisions and Re-Revisions." *Journal of Modern History* 52 (1980): 1–34.

––––––. "Strafford and the Papists." Unpublished article.

Hill, Christopher. *Antichrist in Seventeenth-Century England.* Oxford, 1971.

Hill, George. *MacDonnells of Antrim.* Belfast, 1873.

Hine, Margaret-Clare. "Disturbances Outside the Portuguese Embassy in London in 1641." *London Recusant* 5 (1975): 72–74.

Hodgetts, Michael. "Recusant Liturgical Music." *Clergy Review* 61 (1976): 151–57.

Hughes, Philip. "The Conversion of Charles I." *Clergy Review* 8 (1934): 113–25.

––––––. *Rome and the Counter-Reformation in England.* London, 1942.

Hughes, Richard T. "Henry Burton: A Study in Religion and Politics in Seventeenth Century England." Ph.D. dissertation, University of Iowa, 1972.

Hughes, Thomas. *The History of the Society of Jesus in North America.* 3 vols. in 4. London, 1907, 1917.

Huxley, Gervas. *Endymion Porter: The Life of a Courtier, 1587–1649.* London, 1959.

Jennings, Brendon, ed. *Wild Geese in Spanish Flanders, 1582–1700.* Dublin, 1964.

Kearney, Hugh. "Ecclesiastical Politics and the Counter-Reformation in Ireland, 1618–1648." *Journal of Ecclesiastical History* 11 (1960): 202–12.

———. *Strafford in Ireland*. Manchester, 1957.

Keeler, Mary Frear. "Some Opposition Committees, 1640." In *Conflicts in Stuart England: Essays in Honor of Wallace Notestein*, edited by W. H. Aiken and B. D. Henning, pp. 129–46. New York, 1960.

Kepler, J. S. *The Exchange of Christendom: The International Entrepôt at Dover, 1622–1651*. Leicester, 1976.

Ketton-Cremer, Robert W. *Norfolk in the Civil War*. London, 1969.

Kleinman, Ruth. "Belated Crusaders: Religious Fears in Anglo-French Diplomacy, 1654–1655." *Church History* 44 (1975): 34–46.

Lake, Peter. "The Significance of the Elizabethan Identification of the Pope as Antichrist." *Journal of Ecclesiastical History* 31 (1980): 161–78.

Lambley, Kathleen. *The French Language in England*. Manchester, 1920.

Lamont, William. *Godly Rule: Politics and Religion, 1600–1660*. London, 1969.

———. *Marginal Prynne, 1600–1669*. London, 1963.

———. *Richard Baxter and the Millennium: Protestant Imperialism and the English Revolution*. London, 1979.

Lea, Kathleen. "Sir Anthony Standen and Some Anglo-Italian Letters." *English Historical Review* 47 (1932): 461–77.

Leith, William Forbes, ed. *Memoirs of Scottish Catholics during the Seventeenth and Eighteenth Centuries*. 2 vols. London, 1909.

Leman, Auguste. "Urbain VIII et les origines du Congrès de Cologne de 1636." *Revue d'histoire ecclésiastique* 19 (1923): 370–83.

Lindley, Keith J. "The Impact of the 1641 Rebellion upon England and Wales, 1641–1645." *Irish Historical Studies* 18 (1972): 143–77.

———. "The Lay Catholics of England in the Reign of Charles I." *Journal of Ecclesiastical History* 22 (1971): 199–222.

———. "The Part Played by the Catholics." In *Politics, Religion, and the Civil War*, edited by Brian Manning, pp. 127–78. London, 1973.

Little, Bryan. *Catholic Churches Since 1623: A Study of Roman Catholic Churches in England and Wales from Penal Times to the Present Decade*. London, 1966.

Lomas, Sophia C. "The State Papers of the Early Stuarts." *Transactions of Royal Historical Society*, n.s., vol. 16 (1902): 97–132.

Loomie, Albert J. "Gondomar's Selection of English Officers in 1622." *English Historical Review* 88 (1973): 574–81.

———. "King James I's Catholic Consort." *Huntington Library Quarterly* 34 (1971): 303–16.

———. "Olivares, the English Catholics and the Peace of 1630." *Revue belge de philologie et d'histoire* 47 (1969): 1154–66.

Lowe, John. "The Earl of Antrim and Irish Aid to Montrose in 1644." *Irish Sword* 4 (1960): 191–98.

———. "The Glamorgan Mission to Ireland, 1645–46." *Studia Hibernica* 4 (1964): 155–96.

———. "The Negotiations between Charles I and the Confederation of Kilkenny, 1642–1649." Ph.D. dissertation, London University, 1960.

Lunn, David Maurus. "Benedictine Opposition to Bishop Richard Smith (1625–1629)." *Recusant History* 11 (1971): 1–20.

———. "The English Benedictines and the Oath of Allegiance, 1606–1647." *Recusant History* 10 (1969): 146–64.

_____. *The English Benedictines, 1540–1688*. London, 1980.

Lutz, Georg. "Rom und Europa während des Pontifikats Urbans VIII (1623–1644): Politik und Diplomatic-Wirtschaft und Finanzen-Kultur und Religion." In *Rom in der Neuzeit*, edited by Reinhard Elze, Heinrich Schmidinger, and Hendrik S. Nordholt, pp. 72–167. Wien-Rom, 1976.

Magee, Brian. *The English Recusants*. London, 1938.

Makkai, Lia. "Hungarian Puritans and the English Revolution." *Acta Historica* 5 (1958): 13–45.

Malcolm, Joyce. "A King in Search of Soldiers, Charles I in 1642." *Historical Journal* 21 (1978): 251–73.

_____. "All the King's Men: The Impact of the Crown's Irish Soldiers on the English Civil War." *Irish Historical Studies* 22 (1979): 239–64.

Manning, Brian. "The Aristocracy and the Downfall of Charles I." In *Politics, Religion, and the Civil War*, edited by Brian Manning, pp. 37–82. London, 1973.

Marañón, Gregorio. *El Conde-Duque de Olivares: La pasión de mandar*. Madrid, 1952.

Martz, Louis. *The Poetry of Meditation*. New Haven, 1965.

Mathew, David. *Scotland under Charles I*. London, 1955.

_____. *Sir Tobie Mathew*. London, 1950.

_____. "Wales and England in the Early Seventeenth Century." *Cymmrodorion Society Transactions 1955* (1956): 36–49.

Matthew, A. H., and Calthrop, Annette. *Life of Sir Tobie Matthew*. London, 1907.

MacGillivray, Royce. "Sir William Dugdale as Historian of the English Civil War." *Lakehead University Review* 2 (Fall 1969): 116–34.

McGrath, Patrick. *Papists and Puritans under Elizabeth I*. London, 1967.

Meyer, A. O. "Charles I and Rome." *American Historical Review* 19 (1913): 13–26.

Miller, John. *Popery and Politics in England, 1660–1688*. Cambridge, 1973.

Morrah, Patrick. *Prince Rupert of the Rhine*. London, 1976.

Mout, Nicolette. "The Contacts of Comenius with the Netherlands before 1656." *Acta Comeniana* 1 (1970): 221–29.

Newcome, Richard. *A Memoir of Gabriel Goodman . . . with some account of Ruthin School . . . also, of Godfrey Goodman*. Ruthin, Wales, 1825.

Newman, P. R. "Catholic Royalist Activists in the North, 1642– 46." *Recusant History* 14 (1977): 26–38.

_____. "Roman Catholics in Pre–Civil War England: The Problem of Definition." *Recusant History* 15 (1979): 148–52.

Notestein, Wallace. *Four Worthies*. New Haven, 1957.

Nurse, Bernard. "A Chapter in the Recusant History of Cheam in Surrey: Henry Floyd, S. J. and Bartholomew Fromond Versus the Pursuivants." *London Recusant* 3 (1973): 102–13.

Ogilvie, James D. "Bibliography of the Bishops' Wars, 1639–1640." *Glasgow Bibliographical Society Records* 12 (1923): 1–12.

Oman, Carola. *Henrietta Maria*. London, 1936.

Parker, Geoffrey. *The Army of Flanders and the Spanish Road, 1567–1659*. Cambridge, 1972.

_____. "The Dutch Revolt and the Polarization of International Politics." In *Spain and the Netherlands: 1559–1659*, pp. 65–81. London, 1979.

Pastor, Ludwig von. *History of the Popes*. Translated by Ernest Graf. 40 vols. London, 1899–1953.

Pearl, Valerie. *London and the Outbreak of the Puritan Revolution*. Oxford, 1961.

Percival-Maxwell, Michael. *The Scottish Migration to Ulster in the Reign of James I*.

London, 1973.

Peters, Robert. "Some Catholic Opinions of King James VI and I." *Recusant History* 10 (1970): 292–303.

Petersson, R. T. *Sir Kenelm Digby, the Ornament of England, 1603–1665.* London, 1965.

Polišenský, Josef. *Anglie a Bílá Hora.* Prague, 1949.

———. "Denmark-Norway and the Bohemian Cause in the Early Part of the Thirty Years War." In *Festgabe für L. L. Hammerich*, pp. 215–27. Copenhagen, 1962.

———. *Nizozemska Politike a Bílá Hora.* Prague, 1964.

———. *The Thirty Years' War.* Translated by Robert Evans. London, 1971.

———. *War and Society in Europe, 1618–1648.* Cambridge, 1978.

Prat, Jean-Marie. *La Compagnie de Jésus en France du temps du Père Coton: 1564–1626.* 5 vols. Lyon, 1876, 1878.

Prawdin, Michael. *Marie de Rohan, Duchesse de Chevreuse.* London, 1971.

Pritchard, Arnold. *Catholic Loyalism in Elizabethan England.* Chapel Hill, 1979.

Ranke, Leopold von. *Französische geschichte.* 5 vols. Stuttgart, 1852.

———. *History of England, Principally in the Seventeenth Century.* 6 vols. Oxford, 1875.

Reeves, Marjorie. *Joachim of Fiore and the Prophetic Future.* New York, 1976.

———. *The Influence of Prophecy in the Later Middle Ages: A Study in Joachimism.* Oxford, 1969.

Reid, James S. *History of the Presbyterian Church in Ireland.* 3 vols. 2d ed. Belfast, 1867.

Reinmuth, Howard S. "Lord William Howard (1563–1640) and His Catholic Associations." *Recusant History* 12 (1974): 226–34.

Revill, Philippa and Francis Steer. "George Gage I and George Gage II." *Bulletin of the Institute of Historical Research* 31 (1958): 141–58.

Reynald, Hermile. "Le Baron de Lisola, sa jeunesse et sa prémière ambassade en Angleterre (1613–1645)." *Revue historique* 27 (1885): 300–52.

Roberts, B. D. *Mitre and Musket: John Williams, Lord Keeper, Archbishop of York, 1582–1650.* London, 1936.

Roberts, Michael. *Gustavus Adolphus.* 2 vols. London, 1953–58.

Robinson, W. R. B. "The Earls of Worcester and their Estates, 1526–1642." B. Litt. thesis, Oxford University, 1959.

Rood, Wilhelmus. *Comenius and the Low Countries.* New York, 1970.

Rostenberg, Leona. *The Minority Press and the English Crown: A Study in Repression, 1558–1625.* Nieuwkoop, 1971.

Rubinstein, Hilary L. *Captain Luckless: James, First Duke of Hamilton.* Totowa, N.J., 1976.

Russell, Conrad. "Arguments for Religious Unity in England, 1530–1650." *Journal of Ecclesiastical History* 18 (1967): 201–26.

———. *The Crisis of Parliaments: English History, 1509–1660.* New York, 1971.

———. "Parliament and the King's Finances." In *The Origins of the English Civil War*, pp. 91–118. London, 1973.

———. "The Parliamentary Career of John Pym, 1621–1629." In *The English Commonwealth, 1547–1640*, edited by Peter Clark, A. G. R. Smith, and Nicolas Tyacke, pp. 147–66. New York, 1979.

———. *Parliaments and English Politics, 1621–1629.* Oxford, 1979.

———. "The Theory of Treason in the Trial of Strafford." *English Historical Review* 80 (1965): 30–50.

Ryan, Clarence J. "The Jacobean Oath of Allegiance and English Lay Catholics." *Catholic Historical Review* 28 (1942): 159–83.

Sabine, George H. *A History of Political Theory.* 3d ed. New York, 1961.

Sainty, J. C. *Lieutenants of Counties, 1585–1642*. London, 1970.

Sanford, John L. *Studies and Illustrations of the Great Rebellion*. London, 1958.

Schubert, F. H. *Ludwig Camerarius (1573–1651): Eine Biographie*. Kallmünz, 1955.

_____. "Die Pfälzische Exilregierung im Dreissigjährigen Krieg: Ein Beitrag zur Geschichte des politischen Protestantismus." *Zeitschrift für Geschichte des Oberrheins* 102 (1954): 575–680.

Schwarz, Marc. "Viscount Saye and Sele, Lord Brooke and Aristocratic Protest to the First Bishops' War." *Canadian Journal of History* 7 (1972): 17–36.

Scott, Eva. *Rupert, Prince Palatine*. Westminster, 1899.

Sharpe, Kevin. "The Earl of Arundel, His Circle and the Opposition to the Duke of Buckingham, 1618–1628." In *Faction and Parliament: Essays on Early Stuart History*, edited by Kevin Sharpe, pp. 209–44. Oxford, 1978.

_____, ed. *Faction and Parliament: Essays on Early Stuart History*. Oxford, 1978.

Sitwell, Gerald. "Leander Jones' Mission to England, 1634–1635." *Recusant History* 5 (1960): 132–82.

Smuts, R. Malcolm. "The Puritan Followers of Henrietta Maria in the 1630s." *English Historical Review* 93 (1978): 26–45.

Snow, Vernon. "The Arundel Case, 1626." *The Historian* 26 (1964): 323–49.

_____. *Essex the Rebel: The Life of Robert Devereux, the Third Earl of Essex, 1591–1646*. Lincoln, Nebr., 1970.

Sprunger, Keith L. "Archbishop Laud's Campaign against Puritanism at The Hague." *Church History* 44 (1975): 308–20.

Stevenson, David. "The Irish Franciscan Mission to Scotland and the Irish Rebellion of 1641." *Innes Review* 30 (1979): 54–61.

_____. *The Scottish Revolution, 1637–1644*. Newton Abbot, Devon, 1973.

Stone, Lawrence. *The Crisis of the Aristocracy, 1558–1641*. Oxford, 1965.

Stoye, John W. *English Travellers Abroad, 1604–1667*. London, 1952.

Stradling, Robert. "Catastrophe and Recovery: The Defeat of Spain, 1639–43." *History* 44 (1979): 205–19.

Strickland, Agnes. *Lives of the Queens of England*. 12 vols. London, 1840–48.

Summerson, John. *Inigo Jones*. London, 1966.

Tapié, Victor L. *France in the Age of Louis XIII and Richelieu*. Translated and edited by David McN. Lockie. London, 1974.

Tavard, Georges. "Scripture and Tradition among 17th Century Recusants." *Theological Studies* 25 (1964): 343–84.

Taylor, Harland. "Trade, Neutrality and the 'English Road,' 1630–1648." *Economic History Review*, ser. 2, no. 25 (1972): 236–60.

Taylor, Maurice. *The Scots College in Spain*. Valladolid, 1971.

Thaddeus, Fr., O.F.M. Cap. *Franciscans in England 1600–1850*. London, 1898.

Toon, Peter, ed. *Puritans, the Millennium and the Future of Israel: Puritan Eschatology, 1600 to 1660*. Cambridge, 1970.

Townshend, Dorothea. *Life and Letters of Mr. Endymion Porter*. London, 1897.

Trappes-Lomax, T. B. "Who Was John Taylor the Diplomatist?" *Recusant History* 7 (1963): 43–45.

Trevor-Roper, Hugh. *Archbishop Laud, 1573–1645*. 2d ed. London, 1962.

_____. "Three Foreigners: The Philosophers of the Puritan Revolution." In *Religion, the Reformation and Social Change*, pp. 237–93. 2d ed. London, 1972.

Trimble, William R. "The Embassy Chapel Question, 1625–1660." *Journal of Modern History* 18 (1946): 97–107.

Tupling, G. H. "The Causes of the Civil War in Lancashire." *Lancashire and Cheshire*

Antiquarian Society Transactions 65 (1955): 1–32.

Turnbull, G. H. *Hartlib, Dury and Comenius*. Liverpool, 1947.

———. "The Pansophiae Aratyposis of Comenius and Its Continuation." *Acta Comeniana* 16 (1957): 113–51.

———. "Plans of Comenius for his stay in England." *Acta Comeniana* 18 (1958): 7–28.

Tyacke, Nicolas R. N. "Arminianism in England in Religion and Politics, 1604–1640." D. Phil. dissertation, Oxford University, 1968.

———. "Puritanism, Arminianism and the Counter-Revolution." In *The Origins of the English Civil War*, edited by Conrad Russell, pp. 119–43. London, 1973.

Waller, J. "William Chillingworth: A Study." *Journal of Ecclesiastical History* 6 (1955): 175–89.

Webb, W. K. L. "Thomas Preston, O.S.B., alias Roger Widdrington." *Recusant History* 2 (1954): 216–68.

Webster, Charles. "*Macaria*: Samuel Hartlib and the Great Reformation." *Acta Comeniana* 2 (1971): 147–64.

———, ed. *Samuel Hartlib and The Advancement of Learning*. Cambridge, 1970.

Wedgwood, C. V. "The Elector Palatine and the Civil War." *History Today* 4 (1954): 3–10.

———. *The King's Peace, 1637–1641*. London, 1955.

———. *The King's War, 1641–1647*. London, 1958.

———. *The Thirty Years' War*. London, 1955.

———. *Thomas Wentworth, First Earl of Strafford: A Reevaluation*. London, 1962.

White, Stephen. *Sir Edward Coke and the Grievances of the Commonwealth*. Chapel Hill, 1979.

Whitmore, Patrick J. S. *The Order of Minims in France*. The Hague, 1967.

Wiener, Carol Z. "The Beleaguered Isle, A Study of Elizabethan and Early Jacobean Anti-Catholicism." *Past and Present* 51 (May 1971): 27–62.

Williams, Ethel C. *Anne of Denmark*. London, 1970.

Wilson, John F. *Pulpit in Parliament*. Princeton, 1969.

Wormald, B. H. G. *Clarendon: Politics, History and Religion, 1640–1660*. Cambridge, 1951.

Yates, Francis. *The Rosicrucian Enlightenment*. London, 1972.

Young, Michael. "Sir John Coke (1563–1644)." Ph.D. dissertation, Harvard University, 1971.

Zagorin, Perez. *The Court and the Country: The Beginning of the English Revolution*. London, 1969.

Zimmerman, Benedict. *Carmel in England, 1615–1849*. London, 1899.

Index